Urbanization, Urban Development and Metropolitan Cities in India

About the Editor

Surinder Aggarwal is at present Professor of Geography at Delhi University. He has studied Geography at the universities of Punjab (India), Akron and Kent State (USA). He has taught geography in the US and India and delivered lectures and conducting research on wide ranging topics on Urban Management, Environmental Health and Mega Cities. He was co-editor of the widely received book on Asian City : Processes of Development, Characteristics and Planning published by Kluwer. He has been a Visiting Professor at the University of Bonn, and a Fulbright Scholar at the University of Akron, Ohio. Among several research and teaching assignments within India and abroad, Professor Aggarwal has been honored to be a Full Member of the International Geographical Union (IGU), Commission on Health and Environment and IGU Task Force on Mega Cities. Professor Aggarwal is on Board of Asian Urban Research Association (AURA) located at the University of Akron, USA. He has been associated with WHO-SEARO and Asian Development Bank for conducting research related to Healthy Cities and Resettlement issues and policies in South-East Asia respectively. More recently, Ministry of Education and Research (BMBF), Germany has honored him to be on their panel of experts on selection and evaluation of Research Projects on Emerging Mega Cities in the developing countries.

Urbanization, Urban Development and Metropolitan Cities in India

Dr. V. Nath

Edited by

DR. S.K. AGGARWAL

CONCEPT PUBLISHING COMPANY, NEW DELHI-110059

Cataloging in Publication Data—DK
Courtesy: D.K. Agencies (P) Ltd. <docinfo@dkagencies.com>

Nath, Viswambhar, b. 1923.
Urbanization, urban development and metropolitan cities in India / V. Nath ; edited by S.K. Aggarwal.
p. cm.
Includes bibliographical references.
Includes index.
ISBN 8180694127

1. Cities and towns—India—Growth—History. 2. Urbanization—India—History. 3. City planning—India. 4. Urban policy—India. I. Aggarwal, Surinder K., 1943- II. Title.

DDC 307.760 954 22

ISBN -13: 978-81-8069-412-7
ISBN -10: 81-8069-412-7

First Published 2007

Published and Printed by
Ashok Kumar Mittal
Concept Publishing Company
A/15-16, Commercial Block, Mohan Garden
New Delhi-110059 (INDIA)

Phones : 25351460, 25351794
Fax : 091-11-25357103
Email : publishing@conceptpub.com

Acknowledgements

This acknowledgement is rather different because it comes not from the author who passed away four years ago but from his wife. Soon after my husband's death I took on the task of getting all his writings which had been published in various journals over the fifty years of his academic life and the ones he was working on when he left suddenly. All works are being brought out in five volumes. This is the first in the series.

Dr. V. Nath published his first article, "The Lahore-Amritsar Emerging Industrial Area" in 1946 in Punjab Geographical Journal and the last of his essays was published in 2004. In view of the odd situation where I, who is not a Geographer, undertook the task of compiling the work on subjects ranging from urban geography, urban and regional planning, city and town planning, economic development, urban policy and administration. It took much longer to bring this book to publication stage than it would otherwise. However, it was a learning experience for me to spend four years after his passing away and put together finished and unfinished thoughts and ideas he was trying to expound on the subjects, through his writings. In this task of publishing Dr. Nath's works, I came across two individuals who gave me unstinting support and encouragement. They are, the Editor, Professor Surinder Aggarwal, former Head, Department of Geography, Delhi University and Ashok Kumar Mittal of Concept Publishing Company.

Professor Aggarwal took on himself the entire burden of editing this volume including updating, selection of papers, organizing the material and writing a detailed and comprehensive 'Introduction' to the book. Without his untiring dedication to bring out this book, it would have taken much longer and would not have the sharpness of focus which he was able to contribute as an expert on the subject. I am grateful to Prof. Aggarwal for all that he has done to bring out this book in the shape it is. I am also thankful to Ms Reena Singh and

Ms Shyomali Sen, M.Phil students in the Department of Geography, for proof reading and other suggestions to improve the quality of the book.

Mr. Ashok Mittal, the publisher, who got to know Dr. V. Nath in the course of publishing his first book: 'Development A Saga of Two Worlds' published in June 2002, has stood by me through checking and rechecking various drafts and personally looked into the manuscript to reach its final stage.

I am grateful to my three children, Virendra, Arvind and Jyoti in encouraging me to fulfil the task. Jyoti has also helped in initial proof reading and in writing about the book on its jacket.

July 23, 2006 **Kamla Nath**

Contents

Introduction

The study of urbanization in India by its very nature involves a time dimension covering a period of about 5000 years. The first phase of urbanisation is associated with the Harappan, Aryan and Dravidian civilizations, dating back from around 2350B.C to 600 B.C. During the Second phase India witnessed a mixed and subdued form of urbanisation under the reign of the Hindu and Muslim rulers. However, the roots of the present patterns of urbanisation as well as the urban geometry of many of India's major cities can be traced back to the British Period, which was characterised by selective development of a few port cities and their immediate hinterlands. Cities like Calcutta, Bombay and Madras were developed to facilitate trade of raw material for the imperial power. It is noteworthy that the causative factors behind urbanisation varied from time to time, leading to not one but several urbanisation processes at different points in time. The city of Delhi manifests this fact very well, where, on one hand stands the cramped Mughal town of Shahjahanabad, while on the other stands the British built architectural marvel of modern India, the New Delhi (Ramachandran, 1989). In India, hence, since historic times, urbanisation has been instrumental in structuring the spatial landscape of the country. In a country where cities like Harappa and Mohenjodaro once flourished and are regarded as architectural marvels of any urban system, urbanisation is not a new concept. India is often portrayed as a land of villages; nevertheless, in reality, it is equally a land of towns and cities. It is in fact an old concept with newer connotations in present times. In present context, urbanisation is no longer a conscious process but a natural one. This is perhaps why India is expected to have a large number of urban centres and a high urban growth in the near future.

In the post-Independence period, urbanisation has entered a new and more important phase. In contrast with the British period, which witnessed a period of urban stagnation, the post-Independence period is notable for rapid urbanisation, particularly for one lakh and million cities. There has been an almost five-fold increase in India's urban population during the last five decades. During this period, urban growth and pattern is characterised by uneven distribution with few larger (metropolitan and mega) cities growing at a faster rate and containing un-proportionate large share of urban population while the numerous small and medium size towns exhibiting a slow and sluggish growth with low share in total urban population. Despite planned efforts, the pattern of growth and distribution has not changed much. Urbanization has not extended much in the backward regions of many states like Bihar, Orissa, Rajasthan, Madhya Pradesh, and Andhra Pradesh and many Northeastern states. It has rather confined to chiefly industrially and agriculturally progressive states of Maharashtra, Gujarat, Tamilnadu, Karnataka, Punjab and Haryana. Rural migration of the poor has remained the major source of population growth at least in the metropolitan cities. More recently small and medium entrepreneurs and tertiary sector employees are replacing it. It is realised that unless the redistribution of urban population happens, facilitated by both market and state forces, the skewed urbanization pattern will hamper the urban economy and will remain a major source of social malaise, housing shortages and environmental degradation within the big cities, in particular.

The process of rapid urbanisation is essentially a modern phenomenon. This is because such rapidity is essentially linked to the advent of industrialisation and later sustained through the development of the tertiary sector (Prakash Rao, 1983). However, in India urbanisation is seldom linked to industrialisation although there are instances of an area first getting industrialised and then getting urbanised (classic examples are of the steel cities in India like Jamshedpur, Bokaro etc.). The Indian definition of urban areas and towns thus differs fundamentally from their Western counterparts. Accordingly, urban areas are defined first of all, in terms of their administrative organization, namely in the form of local self-government (municipality, corporation or cantonment board) and secondly, the criteria of population defines an area as urban or rural (Ramachandran, 1989). Urbanization process in India, however, needs to be fuelled by small and medium scale industrialisation process in order to generate more jobs and revenue in a sustained manner. Informal sector growth of course absorbs unemployed migrants, however, these do not generate much revenue for the city to invest into dilapidated or meagre social and economic infrastructure.

Urbanization often brings about variety of spatial, economic, social, demographic and environmental changes. Some of these are positive while others are negative. Urban areas at present contribute more than two-third to the national domestic product, whereas they contain only 30 percent of the national population. Cities offer job opportunities, provide better infrastructure, promote social and economic mobility and their impact is revealed in improved indicators of health such as life expectancy, infant, child and mother mortality rates. On the contrary, Indian cities suffer from acute housing shortages, environmental pollution, water and power shortages and crowded and inefficient transport network. Generally, urbanisation and sub-urbanization leads to decline in area under agricultural, forest and wetlands leading to food insecurity and damage to the rural and urban ecosystems. The big cities are leaving ecological footprints on their hinterlands by vast consumption of both non-renewable and renewable resources like water, forest and land. Ineffecive and inefficient urban management, multiplicity of authorities, inadequate revenue base, lack of coordination between various municipal agencies, non-participatory attitude of stakeholders has lead to the present urban chaos. Despite their tremendous potential to provide quality of living conditions, the above constraints limit their sustainable growth. Unless some serious legal, institutional, governance and economic planning interventions are initiated, the future of Indian cities will remain unproductive, unhealthy and unsustainable.

This book is an endeavour to study this very process of urban growth, urban development constraints, urban policies and strategies to produce an integrated rural-urban model of urban development in India. The author, Dr. V. Nath, a geographer by training and a practicing development economist, policy maker and analyst has written these essays over a period of about 45 years during his varied job and life experiences in India and abroad. The present editor has tried to place these essays in a proper perspective by retaining the prime contents and thrust of the writings. At places, we have tried to update the essays with latest statistics and by including maps and diagrams.On the one hand, the author looks at the different patterns of growth exhibited by a city while on the other he examines the variegated urban problems that urbanisation inherently breeds. In this context, special focus has been lent to the metropolitan cities of India, which serve as the economic, political, administrative and socio-cultural nerve centres of the country and on the contrary they represent poverty, misery and squalor. The essays grouped in the two sections provide the reader a comprehensive understanding of the urban development trends, processes, problems, scenarios and strategies for a balanced rururban growth. Since these essays are written by an expert who has the distinction of being an academician, administrator, policy maker and a practitioner, they provide an added value of giving an incisive and critical account of 50 years of urban development and metropolitan planning in India.

The book is divided into two sections. The first section deals with urbanisation and urban development, where the author has discussed the principle processes of urban development, looked into newer concepts of urban growth and suggested new approaches like an integrated growth concept of rural and urban areas with corridor development approach and integrated urban fringe development to achieve a balanced state of urban development in Indian cities. The second section deals with metropolitan cities. This section takes up specific problem-oriented issues like poverty, housing shortages and infrastructure inadequacies experienced by our few major metropolitan cities like Delhi, Mumbai, Kolkata, and Chennai. The author also highlights on few ideal city models such as that of Bangalore, which needs to be replicated in order to achieve the same level of urban cohesion and efficiency. Regional planning and Master Plan for large metro cities is also suggested for integrated development of rural and urban areas

Urban Development and Urbanization Process in India

Urban places have played an important role in the evolution of India's cultural, political, economic and social life. The evolution and shape of our cities and the resultant urbanization has not been simple rather a product of multiple forces including industrialization, planned development, history, urban planning and our cultural and social ethos. All these processes individually as well as collectively resulted in urban development. In India, however, urban development has remained fairly slow, uneven, segregated, and lop-sided, considering the size and diversity of the country. Furthermore and foremost a lack of clear vision of the role of urbanization in economic development produced this pattern. The author also asserts that urbanization must be looked upon not as an abnormal or undesirable phenomenon, but as an integral part of the process of economic development of the country. The author in this section provides an insight into the different patterns and processes of urban development evolved over the last 100 years and also examines the reasons and forces that have shaped it (Chapters 1, 2, 3 and 4). Chapters 5, 6 and 7 elaborate the strategies and policies that could correct the unplanned and erratic urban growth and reduce some of the problems resulting from such a growth.

Undivided India contained nearly 25 million urban people at the turn of twentieth century and their share in total poulation was close to 11 percent only and annual growth rate was very low at less than 1 percent. At present, after 100 years , the total urban population of independent India has crossed 300 million mark and its share in the total population has reached close to 28 percent. When we compare this growth with other parts of developing and developed world, it ranks very low considering the time frame. However, the sheer number of 300 million is equivalent to the total urban population of most European countries. According to Census of India projections nearly 38 percent of the total population will be living in urban areas and growth rate will staganate close to the present 3 percent. Apparently, according to Nath, Indian urban growth shall remain slow as compared to many industrially developed countries as the growth of urban India is not fuelled by industrial spread across various size settlements. Another outstanding feature of Indian urbanization is the skewed distribution of urban population across various size settlements and the wide range in their growth rates.

The proportion of the urban population living in the cities (urban places with populations of 100,000 or more) had increased progressively from 44% in 1961 to 60% by 1981, and has reached almost 70% by 2001. In the next few years almost 30% of the urban population would be living in the metropolitan cities, and cities with population of 100,000 or more. The number of metropolitan cities has increased from 9 in 1971 to 12 in 1981 and 35 in 2001. Since Independence, there has been a tremendous increase in number of urban areas as well as concentration of population in such urban centres. According to Nath , the causes for such rapid urbanization is attributed to the growth of modern type of industry, commerce and service occupations (including public administration) all of which are concentrated in urban areas, and especially in the cities. Expansion in Government services, commerce and industry, as a result of World War II and migration of displaced persons from Pakistan after the partition of the country in 1947 are also accountable for rapid urban growth during immediate post-independence period. In later years, migration from rural areas contributed bulk of urban growth.

Rapid growth of the cities, and of the metropolitan cities in particular, than that of smaller urban places has in some respect led to a skewed pattern of urbanisation. Economies of scale, wide consumer market, improved economic infrastructure and historical advantage lead to the concentration of economic activities in big cities. In the absence of a clear urban policy for the development of small and medium towns, the population movement and resource flow continued in favour of large cities. This is why many small and medium towns have failed to compete with the big metropolitan cities and over time have lost their potential to grow. Despite the economic importance, the metropolitan cities also face an excessive concentration of urban population that has been instrumental in giving rise to a plethora of urban problems like creation and proliferation of slums (due to lack of proper housing), scarcity of water and electricity and other civic amenities and most importantly leading to the deterioration of the physical environment of our cities. However, the financial resources of municipal corporations to meet the growing demand for essential services is meagre leading to the prevailing chaos and adverse living conditions, at least for the poor. The author therefore has recommended large increases in public and private investment for expansion and improvement of urban housing and infrastructure. On the positive side, however, there is increasing contribution of the urban sector in the national economy. It is important to note that the contribution of urban sector to GDP is currently expected to be in the range of 50-60 percent. In this context, enhancing the productivity of urban areas is now central to the policy pronouncements of the Ministry of Urban Development. Cities hold tremendous potential as engines of economic and social development, creating jobs and generating wealth through economies of scale. They need to be sustained and augmented through the high urban productivity for country's economic growth. National economic growth and poverty reduction efforts will be increasingly determined by the productivity of these cities and towns. For Indian cities to become growth oriented and productive, it is essential to achieve a world class urban system. This in turn depends on attaining efficiency and equity in the delivery and financing of urban infrastructure (Ministry of Urban Affairs, Urban Reforms).

This section also looks at the kind of urban development that has taken place in the plan periods. This is very significant considering the fact that the Five-Year Plans take major initiatives related to development in our country and also the total outlay is determined by the plans as well. In the initial plans, there was stronger emphasis on rural development rather than urban development. According to Nath, the Gandhian thinking with focussed attention on the importance of rural development prevented concentration of investment in urban areas. It was only in the Third Plan that the urban issues began to engage the serious attention of the planners. Increasing attention began to be directed towards urban problems owing to the rapid and haphazard and uncontrolled growth of cities like Delhi, Bangalore and Poona necessitating urgent need for planned development. It was in the Third Five-Year Plan that dispersal of industry and balanced regional development was emphasized. Thus the location of industries gained importance. The author has therefore looked into the individual development of different industrial complexes in the country and has also tried to analyse the subsequent development that they have initiated in nearby as well as the peripheral regions. In this regard, he also describes the 'growth point' concept popularised by Western regional planners.

Developing suitable strategies for management of rapid urban growth constitutes a major challenge for development planners and policymakers, asserts Nath. The strategies must satisfy two essential conditions. First, they must meet the needs for gainful employment, housing, and essential services of the rapidly increasing urban population at acceptable economic and social costs. Secondly, they must ensure that urban growth contributes to national and regional economic growth, particularly through growth-inducing urban-rural interactions. The strategies will require advances in several directions. Above all, they call for a spatial pattern of urbanization that is better adapted to the economic and social conditions of India than the one which has been allowed to develop during the last several decades; low-cost technologies for construction and for delivery of urban services; and suitable political and administrative structures for management of large urban systems. However, in India, it can be admitted that industrial dispersal to underdeveloped regions, have proved to be ineffective, as they have in most other developing countries. The results have been threefold: increasing unemployment and underemployment in the cities and very low productivity in their informal sectors, which have had to absorb most of the in-migrants; acute housing shortages and increasing pressures on urban services, which have led, in turn, to increasing congestion and the proliferation of slums; and progressive deterioration of the physical environment. The author in Chapter 3 of this section entails that over the years the idea of development of dispersed industrialization, which can contribute to dispersed urbanization, has only led into promotion of few small- scale and agro- based industries, failing to promote growth of skills and entrepreneurship in small and medium sized cities. The belief that balanced industrialisation would help to diminish the regional variation in urbanisation, however, failed to bring success.

The author has also laid emphasis on the need to integrate rural and urban development for regional development to take place. Any kinds of competition between rural and urban development plans are irrelevant in today's world. It is true that only about one-fourth of India's total population, 23.3% in 1981 and 27.8.7% in 2001, is urban but more than 60% of the GDP is estimated to be produced in the non-agricultural sectors which are concentrated in urban areas. Nath believes that as bulk of population is in rural areas therefore political parties have to promise rural development so as to win elections. It is noteworthy that with increasing emphasis on integrated urban and rural development, the problem of stagnating villages as well as uncontrolled urbanisation in few large urban centers of importance can be easily tackled. The author has also dealt with the issue of development of peripheral rural regions or suburbs around the big cities, which are zone of very high rural-urban interaction. Since further concentration of industries within city centres is undesirable, or is in some case impossible, there is a growing tendency to locate industry on the urban periphery and this has led to growth of satellite industrial townships in the suburban areas. The development of industrial areas in the Thane-Kalyan region outside Bombay city and of industrial townships like Faridabad, Shahdara and Ghaziabad around Delhi, are examples of such direction. However, such development often leads to uncontrolled urbanisation in the periphery, which proves detrimental to any further useful development in the area. The author also introduces certain new urban concepts such as 'hinterland', 'rurban corridors' in Chapters 6 and 7. The purpose of introducing such concepts is to understand the fact that a city has a functional relationship with its periphery and therefore, for a holistic development of both regional and urban planning should be well integrated for the purpose of development.

Metropolitan India

In principle, metropolitization refers to the emergence, growth and spatial expansion of metropolitan cities (with population exceeding 1 million) to produce urban agglomerations in response to migrating population and the internal demand from the residential, industrial and tertiary sectors. This expansion process generates a pressure for additional peripheral land and commensurate growth in transport, healthcare, civic services and other improved quality of living conditions. Urban form is also changing from compact cities to dispersed cities and making them less energy efficient. Considering the poor financial base and lack of urban governance approach, most metropolitan cities get burdened with acute housing shortages, especially for the poor, degraded environment, inefficient and inadequate public transport, and chaotic urban expansion. Consequently, emergence of slums, poverty, high crime rate, acute scarcity of safe drinking water and prevalence of environmentally related diseases characterize our present metropolitan cities. Furthermore, metropolitan cities have become socially exclusive in recent years. The poor and lower-middle income people are ignored by the decision makers and are not considered as stakeholders. That makes sufficient bases for the present conflict between the poor and other powerful groups. Judiciary and the non-government groups intervene to address the equity issues and are the only negotiators and hope for the oppressed powerless groups. Middle-income groups, ignored in the past, are however gradually asserting themselves in the power structure and decision making process to influence the city contours and shaping the city economy and form with their growing demand for housing and other social and economic infrastructure. The sustainability of the emerging and existing metropolitan and mega cities is, therefore, at risk due to social conflicts, rapid resource depletion, and enormous externalities produced to damage the existing city ecosystems. Mega and other big cities are leaving their huge footprints on their immediate and distant hinterlands. Solutions to such issues are not so simple. Urban governance that includes resource mobilization, participatory or inclusive planning, decentralization of power, and social equity concerns and sustainable development approaches are the present buzz words to save the cities from chaotic development and a development with a human face. In brief, the metropolitan cities of today are the cities of hope and despair simultaneously and the greatest challenge before us is to transform them into cities of joy and opportunities for both rich and the poor.

Growth of metropolitan cities is essentially a post-independence phenomenon in India.The number of metropolitan cities grew from one in 1901 to 23 in 1991 and 35 in 2001.The number of metropolitan cities till 1941 were only 2, however, during the decade 1981-91, the number of such cities rose to 12 in 1981. Along with an increase in the number of metropolitan cities, there has also been a disproportionate rise in the growth of population in such cities. In 1901, percentage of urban population living in metropolitan cities was 5.84 per cent. This share increased to 32.62 per cent in 1991 and 37.8 per cent by 2001. In addition to internal development, development around the metropolitan cities, the physical expansion of built-up area beyond their municipal boundaries has been very conspicuous. Much of this development has occurred in a spontaneous, haphazard and unplanned manner. What were essentially rural villages beyond municipal limits have now been unmistakably transformed by the location of residential, commercial and industrial complexes. All these developments related to spatial sprawl create problems related to provision of civic amenities and hence, it is very often argued that there is a hidden disparity between the inner-city and the outer-city dwellers.

Nath has very aptly addressed such issues in his several essays (Chapters 1 to 4 in particular). According to him cities characterize differently and play several roles. They act as vehicles of growth and modernization; centers of power; provider of quality of life conditions with better environmental and social infrastructure. Metropolitization is a very potent force in shaping the urban geometry and economy of the country. On the contrary they also create spatial and economic disparities; hotbed of crime and insecurity; and sources of environmental pollution. Despite such serious problems, there is lack of action towards urban renewal, implementation of the city plans, de-politicizing of municipal bodies, and inadequate and insufficient investment for expansion in provision of services like water supply, sewerage and roads.

Among all the spatial, social and economic problems, Nath was more concerned about the most visible issue of human poverty and its spatial and social manifestation in slums and lack of environmental infrastructure across all metropolitan cities of India. More recent works on urban India echo similar sentiments. Deprivation, exclusion, filth, squalor and disease in the slums of metropolitan cities represent an ugly face of urban poverty in India (Hust and Mann, 2005). The extremes of metropolitan poverty and human degradation are not represented by the slum dwellers only but by the pavement dwellers, whose numbers are in the tens of thousands in Mumbai, Delhi and Kolkata. Concentration of poverty in such cities is largely attributed to massive migration of the rural poor (underprivileged, landless and artisans) in hope of employment opportunities in the informal and industrial sectors. Unfortunately, he finds that the new poor migrants are not much organized and face tough resistance from the organized guild-like organizations to find employment and have not much option other than to live in squalor and dehumanizing conditions of the slums. In his assessment, programmes of development and welfare, undertaken by the central, state or local governments or by the non-governmental organizations are few, limited in scope and size and have had much less impact in ameliorating their poverty than have programmes for the rural poor. Reducing the incidence of poverty and disparities in income and consumption had been stated as an important objective of the earlier five-year plans. Urban poverty was not clearly stated as an important issue to address. Only the Eighth Five Year Plan addresses urban poverty as an issue not only for present but to continue in future. That reflects a significant change in policies to ameliorate urban poverty. A variety of programmes for poverty relief were introduced under this plan. Nonetheless, the author feels that there is a need to analyse poverty in a deeper sense and also to address the issue of slum and pavement dwellers in more comprehensive manner.

In his view the cities play ambivalent roles. They need more people as economic growth is faster due to economies of scale, ready market, pools of financiers, entrepreneurs, managers and skilled workers. Conversely, rapid rise in population leads to proliferation of slums where in the urban poor live in miserable conditions struggling to have access to water, sanitation and other basic services. In order to deal with such problems, the three *megalopolises* of India – Kolkata, Mumbai and Delhi formulated their perspective plans in the form of Master Plans to deal with the problems of housing and basic services for the in-migrants. However, year after year, such Master Plans have achieved very little to solve such problems of metropolitan cities as pointed out by the author in the first chapter of section 2.

The author has provided a detailed insight on the planning aspect of metropolitan cities in India. In chapters 5, 6 and 7, he has discussed the salient features of urban planning of Delhi, explicates its historical perspectives as well as talked about the need to introduce special measures to cope with growing pressures of an exploding population. For Delhi, redevelopment of both Shahjahanabad and New Delhi are important issues before the planners. In case of Shahjahanabad, the object is to relieve the present congestion, unsanitary conditions, and pollution and provide essential services to restore a healthy environment. In case of New Delhi, the object is to achieve high-density land use and restoration of cultural heritage of the British Raj. However, three principal requirements need to be inculcated for achievement of the planners' objective. These are spatial planning, environmental planning and transport planning. Furthermore, the author has provided a detailed study of a South Delhi residential colony, which has moved from an ideally liveable situation to a virtually non-liveable one due to deterioration in the physical as well as the social environment. The author feels that the metropolitan cities are the melting pots of different cultures and classes of people and therefore should be dealt with in a very sensitive manner.

The author strongly advocates the need for the implementation of better regional plans and master plans for our metropolitan cities. For a city like Delhi, which is functionally interrelated to so many satellite towns, the implementation of a National Capital Region Master Plan is an emergent need so that the whole functional region falls under the purview of a single plan document. Similarly, an industrial city like Bangalore, which has little contiguity with its neighbouring industrial areas, must form a single cohesive industrial region so as to provide benefit to the small industrial players. The author feels that all these regional issues of development hinge on the will power of our politicians, which at the moment is strongly lacking.

REFERENCES

Hust, Evelin and Michael Mann (eds.) (2005), Urbanisation and Governance in India, Centre de Sciences Humaines and South Asia Institute, Manohar, New Delhi.

Prakasharao, V.L.S. (1983), *Urbanisation in India: Spatial Dimension*, Concept Publishing Company, New Delhi.

Ramachandran, R. (1989), *Urbanisation and Urban Systems in India*, Oxford University Press, Delhi.

SECTION I

Urban Development and the Urbanization Process in India

1

Urbanization in India with Special Reference to Growth of Cities (1901–1951)[1]

Although the population of India is still predominantly rural, the progress of urbanization during the last two decades has been fairly rapid. During the first three decades of the century, the rate of urbanization was very slow. Between 1901 and 1921, urban population showed a net increase of only three million and its proportion in the total population of the country, changed only from 9.9 to 10.2 percent. Between 1921 and 1931, the increase in urban population was greater, over 6 million. But it was during the thirties that urbanization began at a rapid rate. During the decade 1931-41, urban population of undivided India (including the areas which now forms Pakistan) increased by more than 12 million, and the proportion of urban population to the total went up from 11 percent to 12.9 percent. During the forties, the rate of urbanization has been even more rapid. The urban population of Indian Union alone (excluding Pakistan) has increased by over 18 million and the proportion of urban population in the total has increased to 17.3 percent (Annex. Table 1.1).[2]

PATTERN OF URBANIZATION

In the absence of separate data on the natural increase of urban and rural population, it is not possible to determine what proportion of the increase in urban population during each decade has been due to natural increase and what proportion is due to migration. However, assuming the rate of natural increase of urban population to be the same as that for the entire population for each decade, certain calculations have been made in Annex. Table 1.1. It will be seen from this table that during the 1941-51 decade, natural increase of urban population would have amounted to about 5.9 million. The balance 12.2 million[3], therefore, represents migration. The net increase on account of influx of displaced persons from Pakistan accounts for some of this (about 2 million) and the balance (about 10 millions) represents migration to towns from rural areas within the Indian Union. As the natural increase of the rural population of the Indian Union during the decade is about 36 millions, it is clear that migration to urban areas has absorbed 28 percent of the natural increase of rural population. The proportion of the increase in working population of rural areas absorbed by urban migration would undoubtedly have been considerably higher than this, because, as is well known, the percentage of workers in the population migrating to towns is generally higher than in the general population. Urbanization is, therefore, already a very significant factor in relieving the pressure of population and in particular in absorbing the increases in working population of rural areas.

GROWTH OF CITIES[4]

A notable feature of urban development in India is the very rapid growth of cities and large metropolitan centers. In 1931, there were 35 cities in Undivided India with a total population of 9.14 million. By 1951, the Indian Union alone had 73 cities and their population totalled 23.55 million. Thus, in 20 years, the population of cities has increased almost three times. In 1951 city population formed 38 percent of the urban population and nearly 7 percent of the total population of the country. During the 1941-51 decade, out of the total increase of 18 million in the urban population, one-half (i.e. 9 million) was accounted for by increase in city population (Table 1.1).

Among the cities also, there is a marked concentration of population in the very large urban centres. Over 12 million people or half of the city population is concentrated in 8 cities with a population of five lakhs and over. Five metropolitan centres – Kolkata, Mumbai, Chennai, Delhi and Hyderabad – each with a population of one million and over have a total of about 10 million people. On the other hand 48 cities with population between 100,000 and 250,000 have only about 6 million inhabitants.

The great majority of Indian cities are commercial centres of agricultural regions. Capitals of States, industrial centers and transportation

Table 1.1 Growth of City Population

Year	*Population (Millions)*	*Percentage Change.*
Undivided India		
1901	6.22	—
1911	6.66	7.2
1921	7.74	16.1
1931	9.14	18.0
1941	16.53	80.8
Indian Union		
1941	14.66	—
1951	23.55	60.6

Source: Census of India 1951 Vol. I India Part II. A IV.

centres have also originated in most cases as regional centres. Specialized single-function cities like those found in new countries like USA or in the industrial areas like the English Midlands or the Ruhr Valley of Germany are few in number. Jamshedpur the steel town; Kolar Gold field, the mining center; and Visakhapatnam, the export port are the most important examples of such specialized cities. A detailed analysis of the growth of cities during the 50 years' period, 1901-51, which was undertaken by the author showed that during this period population of 13 cities increased by more than 300 percent, of 12 between 200 and 300 percent, of 28 between 100 and 200 percent and of 17 by less than 100 percent. The highest percent-age increase was shown by Jamshedpur, which was a village of a few hundred people at the time of the establishment of the Tata Iron and Steel Works but had grown into a city with a population of 218,000 by 1951. The largest increase in absolute numbers was recorded by metropolitan Kolkata, whose population increased from 1.08 million in 1901 to 3.45 million in 1951.

In order to get an idea of the growth of different types of cities, cities were divided into the following 8 classes, depending upon their economic functions: (i) Capital (C) (ii) Not Capital but with important Government offices (G), (iii) Industrial Centers (I), (iv) Port (P), (v) Regional Commercial Centres (R), (vi) Pilgrimage

Center (P1), (vii) Hill Station or other resort town (H), and (viii) Military Station (M). Each city was given one or more symbols depending upon its important functions. This analysis showed that the most rapidly growing cities during this period were mostly industrial centres, capitals and non-capitals with important Government offices. Of the 13 cities with population increases of more than 300 percent, 3 are capitals, 2 non-capitals with important government offices and 3 industrial centres. Of the cities with population increases between 200 and 300 percent, 5 are capitals, and 3 industrial centres.

CAUSES OF URBANIZATION

The principal cause of urbanization in India as in other countries, is the growth of modern type industry, commerce and service occupations (including public administration) all of which are concentrated in urban areas, and especially in the cities. During the last decade, two other factors have accelerated the movement of population to urban areas and especially to the cities:

1. Expansion in Government services, commerce and industry, as a result of Second World War.
2. Migration of displaced persons from Pakistan after the partition of the country in 1947. A large number of displaced persons living in the urban areas of Pakistan, as also those living in rural areas but following non-agricultural occupations (mostly petty trade and money lending) have settled down in the urban areas in India. As against this emigration to Pakistan from the urban areas of India has been considerably less.

However, the influence of these two factors should not be over-rated. The trend towards urbanization, observable since 1931, would itself account for the greater part of the increase in urban population. Projection of the 1931-41 rate of urban increase, for instance, would result in an increase in urban population of 14.5 million in 1941-51 as against the observed increase of 18 million. Also, it must be pointed out that the very fact that displaced persons have settled down in urban areas, and have been absorbed, by and large, in the urban economy is a result of the existence of adequate employment opportunities in urban areas. The increase in urban population due to settlement of displaced persons should therefore be considered only a special phase of the general process of urbanization.

THE COSTS OF URBANIZATION

Urbanization is very costly and this cost itself is likely to stand in the way of rapid urbanization of the country. Take housing for example. In the rural areas, most of the landless labourers and submarginal cultivators, who constitute the great majority of the migrants to towns, live in huts and similar very modest dwellings. These are made from local materials (e.g. mud, straw etc.) by their own labor so that the monetary cost is very little. There is no elaborate provision for sanitation, water supply facilities etc. Such living conditions are possible in the rural areas. But, when these people move into towns, provision has to be made for a minimum standard of housing, say, a one-room tenement for a family, as also for providing basic necessities like water, sanitary facilities, roads, transportation etc. Provision of such facilities is, however expensive, especially in the large cities. The cost of a one-room tenement for an industrial worker family in Mumbai is estimated at between Rs. 3500 to 4000. In other cities, where buildings costs are lower the cost ranges between Rs. 2000 to Rs. 3000. Even if the Government estimates are considered somewhat high (which is doubtful), Rs. 2000 may be taken as minimum average cost of a one-room tenement in urban areas. The number of additional families in urban areas as a result of the growth of urban population during the last decade may be estimated roughly at 3½ million. To provide housing alone for this number at the minimum standard of a one-room tenement would mean a capital outlay of Rs. 700 crores. The expenditure for all the other civic amenities would be in addition. What this expenditure of 700 crores means to the country, will be appreciated by a comparison with the total development expenditure of the country. The total investment in the public sector under the First Five Year Plan is of the order of Rs. 400 crores per year and if the estimated investment in the private sector is added, it would be between six and seven hundred crores per year. Thus, provision of minimum housing for the increase in urban population alone would take approximately 10 percent of the total investment of the country.

As a result partly of high costs and partly on account of other difficulties like shortages of building materials, expansion of housing and other facilities in the urban areas lagged far behind the growth of population in the forties. The result was that acute shortages of housing, and of other facilities like water supply, transport, etc. developed. The situation is now much better, in most cities as a result of the building activity of the last four or five years. But although no figures can be produced to support this statement, one can say on the basis of common observation that expansion in housing and other facilities has still not caught up with the population increase of the 1941-51 decade.

THE PROSPECT FOR URBANIZATION

Although it is extremely difficult to forecast the future trends in urban development, a few observations may be made on the basis of the demographic trends of the past few decades and the foreseeable trends in the economic development of the country:

The First Five Year Plan did not envisage rapid industrialization. Its emphasis was mainly on increase in agricultural production and on development of rural areas. Although these two are likely to continue to receive primary attention in the Second Five Year Plan and in the future development efforts generally, there is also likely to be much greater emphasis on industrial development. But it is more than probable that this industrial development would be of a somewhat different type than industrialization in the West. It would differ in two major ways:

1. It may have a much larger component of small scale industry, and
2. Industry may be widely dispersed in small and medium sized towns instead of being concentrated in a few areas.

The emphasis on small-scale industries is necessary for tackling the enormous problem of providing employment to the large manpower of the country. The industrial dispersal to small and medium towns is a trend in all countries, and is being accelerated by such developments as transmission of electricity over long distances at economic rates, and growth of motor transport. In a country like India the very high cost of development of large urban centres is also likely to be a factor against increasing concentration of population in large cities.

Accordingly, one may not expect a period of very rapid urbanization, with emphasis on growth of large cities as characterized in the USA and other western countries and has more recently characterized the economic development of USSR. One can, however, expect, a fairly moderate growth of urban areas, with increasing accent on development of small and medium sized towns. During the present (1951-61) decade, maintenance of the growth rate of the last decade, is the minimum that can be expected in view of the fact that economic activity is being maintained at a high level, and is likely to be further accelerated due to the working of the Five Year Plans. Projection of the 1941-51 trend of growth would give an additional urban population of about 25 million by 1961; the actual increase may be higher.

GROWTH TRENDS[5]

As regards growth trends for individual types of towns, we may say the following:

- Capitals will continue to grow as the sphere of governmental activity will continue to expand, especially in the social welfare and economic fields.
- Many small and medium sized towns will grow rapidly as agricultural production increases and the rural areas develop, and especially as electricity and communications are further extended. Towns with special advantages like cheap electric power, availability of raw materials or good communications will grow most rapidly.
- Some of the medium-sized and smaller cities, whose advantages have not been sufficiently realized, may grow rapidly. Examples of such rapid growth during the last decade have been Bangalore, Poona and Dehradun. But the number of such cities is likely to be small.
- Large cities are extremely congested, especially in their central areas. They are not likely to maintain the phenomenal growth rates of the last one or two decades; their growth will be slower and will be mostly at the periphery. The process of growth of suburbs and satellite towns, which has already started, is expected to be accelerated. Close proximity to large cities is still a great advantage for business, and for many

types of industries. Transport, skilled labor, power, water supply and numerous other facilities can still be had much more cheaply in cities than elsewhere. A crucial advantage is the remarkable concentration of capital, enterprise and educated manpower in the cities.

UNDERSTANDING URBANIZATION

Urbanization is a process of great economic and social significance. Although in the case of India, there are difficulties and the character of the process may differ from that in the West due to particular social and economic conditions, there can be no question that urbanization is likely to be an important feature of the demographic situation in India during the next few decades. It must be looked upon not as an abnormal or undesirable phenomenon; but as an integral part of the process of economic development of the country. The character of the movement, the forces that impel it at the rural and urban ends, the fluctuations in it from year to year should be carefully analyzed and properly understood. Such understanding is very important for formulation of economic and social policies and for the proper direction of the movement itself. I am glad to say that during the last two years, attention has been directed towards this problem. The National Sample Survey, which undertakes collection of comprehensive economic data for the whole country has been extended to urban areas. Under the auspices of the Research Programme Committee of the Planning Commission, a large number of universities are undertaking detailed studies of urbanization in most of the important cities of the country. These studies and surveys will collect detailed information on various aspects of urbanization – the magnitude and character of migration, the social and economic conditions of the migrant, to mention only one, which will make possible much better understanding of the urban problems than is possible with the data available at present.

ANNEXURE

Table 1.1: Rural-Urban Population and Net Migration from Rural to Urban Areas 1901-51

Census Years	*Total Pop. (000's)*	*Change (%)*	*Rural Pop. (000's)*	*Urban Pop. (000's)*	*(%) Rural*	*(%) Urban*	*Increase in Urban Pop. (000's)**	*(%)**	*Natural Increase Urban Pop. (000's)**	*Net Migration**
				Undivided India (Excluding Burma)						
1901	283,810	–	255,713	28,097	90.1	9.9	–	–	–	–
1911	303,041	6.7	274,421	28,620	90.6	9.4	523	1.9	1882	-1359
1921	305,730	0.9	274,546	31,184	89.8	10.2	2,546	8.9	257	2288
1931	338,171	11.6	300,705	37,465	89.8	11.0	6,281	20.1	3617	2664
1941	388,998	15.0	339,302	49,696	87.1	12.9	12,231	32.6	5620	6611
				Indian Union (excluding Jammu & Kashmir State)						
1941	314,766	–	271,036	43,730	86.1	13.9	–	–	–	–
1951	356,829	13.4	295,004	61,825	82.7	17.3	18,095	41.4	5860	12,235

*Calculated by applying the rates of natural increase of the total population to the urban population in each decade.

Source: Census of India, 1951 Volume I India Part II–A IV.

NOTES

1. *Source*: Paper Presented at UN Population Conference, Rome 1954
2. (post script: in 2001 this proportion was 33.4 percent of the total population)
3. The actual figure would be somewhat higher than this, because natural increase of the urban population is less than that of the general population, but the difference is not likely to be large.
4. The term 'city' is used in the Indian Census for a town with population of 1,00,000 and over
5. Recently, Times of India August 7,2003 in 'Cities of Despair' Sidharth Aggarwal says, 'the big cities will grow bigger. The relatively smaller will burst. Slum dwellers already form 40-50 percent of the population in the metros. In the coming decades this will be the fate of all 10 lakh-plus cities . . . . Also while rural population is growing at 1.7 percent and urban at 2.75 percent, although rural birth rate is higher. So we are looking for a massive migration into cities."

2

Urbanization in India: Retrospect and Prospect[1]

While significant progress has been made in the post-Independence period in devising a strategy of rural economic development, leading to brisk economic growth over several parts of rural India, no suitable strategy has evolved for the management of urban growth. The Green Revolution of the 1960s has resulted in growth rates averaging 5 or 6 percent a year for almost two decades in Punjab and Haryana and in some districts of Uttar Pradesh and Rajasthan where wheat output has increased rapidly. Increasing agricultural output has been accompanied, particularly in Punjab and Haryana, by growth of small-scale industries and by extensive urbanization along the principal arteries of communication. Similar developments are taking place, although much less advanced, in several other areas.

In urban areas, however, the record of the past thirty to thirty-five years has been one of neglect and inadequate allocation of the resources of public finance and good management required for efficient urban administration and for the expansion of housing and essential services for the rapidly growing urban population. Half-hearted attempts to slow down growth of the large cities, based on such strategies as industrial dispersal to underdeveloped regions, have proved to be ineffective in India, as they have in most other developing countries. The results have been threefold: (i) increasing unemployment and underemployment in the cities and very low productivity in their informal sectors, which have had to absorb most of the in-migrants; (ii) acute housing shortages and increasing pressures on urban services, which have led, in turn, to increasing congestion and the proliferation of slums; and (iii) progressive deterioration of the physical environment.

Developing suitable strategies for management of rapid urban growth constitutes a major challenge for development planners and policymakers. The strategies must satisfy two essential conditions. First, they must meet the needs for gainful employment, housing, and essential services of the rapidly increasing urban population at acceptable economic and social costs. Second, they must ensure that urban growth contributes to national and regional economic growth, particularly through growth-inducing urban-rural interactions. The strategies will require advances in several directions. Above all, they call for a spatial pattern of urbanization that is better adapted to the economic and social conditions of India than the one which has been allowed to develop during the last several decades; low-cost technologies for construction and for delivery of urban services; and suitable political and administrative structures for management of large urban systems.

GROWTH OF THE URBAN POPULATION

Three projections of growth of total population and urban population for the period 1981-2001, contained respectively in the *World Development Report* 1984, the seventh Five Year Plan (1986-1990), and in a recent article by R. Mohan, are presented in Table 2.1.

They are close enough to indicate convergence of views on two major points: progressive reduction in the growth rate of the total population because of declining fertility and continued rapid increase in the urban population, due both to natural increase of the resident urban population and rural-to-urban migration.

The *World Development Report* 1984 (WDR) has, on the assumption of a high rate of rural-to-urban migration, projected a growth rate of the urban population averaging 4.2 percent a year during the 1980-2000 period. The migration would be rapid enough to bring down the rate of growth of the rural population by as much as 0.8 percent below the rate of natural increase of the total population. The rates of growth of the urban population in the other two projections are significantly lower. The seventh Five-Year Plan's projection assumes a rate similar to the average rate of 3.5 percent experienced during the 1961-1981 period. Mohan, however, projects a sharp slowdown of the urban growth rate during the 1990s with a similar decline in the growth rate of the total population.

Table 2.1: Projection of Total Population of India (in millions)

	World development report		*Seventy Five Year Plan*			*Mohan*		
	1980	2000	1981	1991	2001	1981	1991	2001
Total Population	685	994	685	837	986	697	850-856	993-1,018
Average growth rate (%)	1.9			2.0		1.65	2.2[a]	
Urban population	160	353	160	230	326	164	234-236	315-320
Average growth rate (%)	4.2			3.7	3.5	3.8	3.1	
Urban pupulation/total population (%)	23.3	35.5	23.3	27.5	33.1	23.5	27.3-27.5	31.0-31.5
Growth rate of GDP per capita								
Hight-case Scenario		3.2[b]	3.2[c]	3.35	—	n.a.	—	
Low-case Scenario		2.5[b]						

Sources: (a) *World Development Report 1984*, app. Table 19, pp. 254-255, and Text table 4.3 p. 67;

– Seventh Fiver Year Plan 1986-1990, Table 2.1, pp.11-12

– R. Mohan "urbanization in India's Future," *Population and Development Review* 2(4) (December 1985), Table 7, p. 630, and Table 8, p. 631.

Total population is projected under three variables of decline in fertility while urban population is projected under two variants; methodology of the projection is explained on pp. 642-643.

[a] 2.2 percent during 1981-1986 falling to 1.47-1.68 percent during 1996-2001.

[b] 1985-1995

[c] 1986-1991

Under all three projections, the total urban population by the end of the century would be twice (or more) the 1981 figure of 160 million and would constitute around one-third of the total population. The WDR's figures of a total urban population of 353 million and an urban/total population ratio of 3.5 percent by the year 2000 are the highest.

Both the WDR and the Seventh Plan also assume rapid growth of gross domestic product (GDP) per capita. The WDR projections are based on the World Bank's global model under which growth of the economies of less-developed countries (LDCs) during the decade 1985-1995 is projected under two scenarios: a high-case scenario, based on the assumption of relatively favourable conditions for growth of the industrial economies and world trade, and a low-case scenario based on the assumption of relatively unfavorable conditions. The economics of the LDCs would grow significantly faster under the high-case scenario than under the low-case scenario. For India, however, the WDR's projection of growth rate of GDP per capita even under the low case scenario — 2.5 percent a year is almost twice as high as the average rate of 1.3 percent a year experienced during the 1960-1992 period (Table 2.2).

Table 2.2: Growth Rates of GDP Per Capita in India and Low-Income Developing Countries: 1960-1995

Average Annual Growth Rates of GDP Per Capita (%)					
				1985-95 (Projected)	
Countries	*1960-73*	*1973-79*	*1980-85*	*Low case scenario*	*High case scenario*
Low income developing countries	3.0	2.9	3.2	2.7	3.4
		Low-incomes			
Asian[a]	3.4	3.3	3.7	3.0	3.7
Africa	1.0	-1.0	-1.6	2.5	3.2[c]
India		1.3[b]			

Source: World Development Report, 1984. Text Table 3.2 p. 36 and App. Table 1, pp. 218-19.

a Includes China, Indonesia, and all countries of South Asia (Afghanistan, Bangladesh, Bhutan, Burma, India, Nepal, Pakistan, and Sri Lanka).

b 1960-82.

c Assuming India's annual growth rate to be 0.5 percent lower than that for low-income Asia, as under the low-case scenario.

The projection of the Seventh Plan approximates the WDR's high-case scenario rate of 3.2 percent a year. The Seventh Plan projects an average growth rate of 5.0 percent a year for total GDP during the 1986-2000 period about 50 percent higher than the rate, averaging 3.5 percent, experienced during 1960-1982. The projections of both the WDR and the Seventh Plan thus assume a radical change in the performance of the Indian economy during the 1985-1995 period from that during 1960-1982. The growth rate projected under the low-case scenario is almost double the rate actually achieved during the 1960-1982 period.

The performance of the Indian economy during the past five years has been relatively good. Average economic growth for 1980-1985 is estimated at around 5.4 percent a year, which translates into a growth rate of GDP per capita of well over 3 percent a year (Ninan, 1985). But the experience of five years is simply too short to provide an adequate basis for projection because the Indian economy is still influenced greatly by the monsoons and other factors. The second critical factor will be experience with the economic liberalization policies which have been followed since the late 1970s but which have been given much greater emphasis by the new government.

By 1981, more than 60 percent of the urban population was living in cities with populations of 100,000 or more-a proportion that has gone up progressively from 38 percent in 1951 (Fig. 2.3).

Table 2.3: Distribution of India's Urban Population by Size of Urban Places, 1951-1981

Population	*Percentage of Urban Population in Urban Places*			
	1951	*1961*	*1971*	*1981*
1 Million & above	n.a.	22.5	25.1	26.3
500,000 – 1 million	n.a.	3.1	6.2	13.4
100,000 – 500,000	n.a.	18.1	17.6	20.7
50,000 – 100,000	12.2	12.1	13.5	11.6
20,000 – 50,000	17.8	20.0	18.3	14.4
Below 20,000	31.9	23.4	19.5	13.6

Sources: Population Census of India: 1951-1981.

Table 2.4: Growth Rates of Urban Places of Different Size Classes, 1961-81

Urban places	*1961 Population (millions)*	*Annual Growth Rate (%)*	*1971 Population (millions)*	*Annual Growth Rate (%)*	*1981 Population (millions)*
Four metropolitan cities (Bombay, Calcutta, Madras, Delhi)	14.2	3.3	19.8	3.3	27.5
Other cities with population of					
1 million or more	3.5	8.1	7.6	6.0	13.6
500,000 – 1,000,000	3.9	5.6	6.8	12.0	20.9
100,000 – 500,000	14.3	2.9	19.6	5.3	32.3
All cities	35.1	4.3	53.4	5.9	94.3
Towns with population of					
50,000 – 100,000	9.5	4.5	14.7	2.2	18.2
20,000 – 50,000	15.7	2.4	19.9	1.2	22.4
Below 20,000	18.5	1.3	21.1	0.1	21.3
Total urban population	78.9	3.7	109.1	3.7	156.2
Cities with population of 500,000 or more	20.8 (11)*	5.1	34.2 (19)*	6.1	61.0 (42)*
Population of the 11 cities with populations of 500,000 or more in 1961	20.8	3.1	28.3	3.8	41.1

* Number of cities.

Source: Population Censuses of India: 1951-1981.

On the other hand, the proportion of urban population living in the smallest urban places (population below 20,000) dropped progressively from 32 percent in 1951 to 13.6 percent in 1981. Of the urban population, by 1981 as much as two-thirds were living in the larger cities with population 500,000 or more. The number of such cities went up rapidly from eleven in 1961 to forty-two in 1981.

Data on growth of population during 1961-1981 in urban places of different size classes (Table 2.4) indicate more rapid growth rates for the cities, particularly the larger cities, than for the smaller urban places. The fastest growth rates were recorded by the cities with populations of 500,000 or more, excluding, however, the four metropolitan cities of Kolkata, Mumbai, Chennai, and Delhi. These cities registered average growth rates of 3.3 percent a year during both decades, lower than the growth rates recorded by most other cities. The lowest growth rates were recorded by the small urban places with populations below 50,000 and especially those with populations below 20,000. The slow growth of the smallest urban places appears to have been due in part to a definitional change adoption in the 1961 Census of more restrictive criteria for designating a place as urban (Mitra, 1978).

Three factors contributed to rapid growth of the larger urban places: natural increase of the urban population; in-migration from villages or smaller urban places; and expansion of urban boundaries to include adjacent villages and small towns. The third factor appears to have been particularly important in cities with populations of 500,000 or more. The increase in the number of such cities contributed half of the population increase recorded during this period: 20.8 million out of 41.2 million.

Rapid increase in the population of cities, especially the larger cities with populations of 500,000 or more, may be expected to continue. Extrapolation to the year 2000 of the average growth rate of 5.5 percent recorded by the cities during 1961-1981 would take their total population to 178 million more than half the projected total urban population of 353 million.

THE SPATIAL PATTERN OF URBANIZATION

During the early 1960s, much discussion took place about the most appropriate spatial pattern of urbanization for India. The impetus for the discussion came from industrial planners and economists who were concerned with location of industries and from urban planners who were preparing urban development plans. Industrialization was seen as the key element in urbanization despite mounting evidence that the needs of modern industry for labour were relatively limited-far less than they had been in the nineteenth century when Europe and North America were undergoing industrialization and that the rate of postwar urbanization in India and most other developing countries was far greater than that required to meet the demands of modern industry.

The consensus was in favour of dispersed development of industries, which would contribute to disperse urbanization. Several strands of thought converged to form this consensus. First was the realization that urbanization, with a focus on rapid growth of the large metropolitan cities, would involve high costs of expansion.

These costs would be much lower, however, in small urban places and on the outskirts of large cities, and there would also be greater scope for use of simple technology and cheap local materials. Self-help by the beneficiaries could reduce the costs further. The data then available indicated that the unit costs of providing housing in the central areas of Mumbai and Kolkata were two to three times higher than in small towns (Wurster, 1962). Transportation costs were also much lower with dispersed urbanization because mass transport facilities could be avoided; workers could travel the short distance to their workplace by bicycle or on foot.

The second strand of thought was promotion of small-scale and agro-based industries. The employment potential of such industries was much larger than that of large, capital-intensive industries. Furthermore, growth of small and agro-based industries in medium-sized or small towns would promote growth of entrepreneurship and diffusion of industrial skills. While the relationship between dispersed development of small-scale and agro-based industries and expansion of employment and development of agriculture was clearly seen, the perception of a wider relationship between dispersed urbanization and rural development was not common. Few could envision small towns, such as market centers, serving as foci of economic growth in micro regions through their various functions-marketing and processing agricultural produce, distributing consumer goods and agricultural inputs, servicing and repairing implements, and manufacturing a limited range of consumer goods for the micro regional market. One reason for lack of interest in the latter relationship was dominance, especially in the states of rural-based, tradition-oriented political leaders who did not see the links between rural and urban development. They viewed towns and villages primarily as competitors for scarce resources of finance and manpower and were concerned with obtaining the maximum resources for the villages, which they believed had long been neglected.

A third consideration was the need to accelerate development of backward regions. The political leaders of these regions first concentrated their efforts on securing large, centrally financed resource development or industrial projects: irrigation and hydroelectric projects in the early 1950s and public-sector industrial projects in the late 1950s and early 1960s. The projects were seen as the nuclei of regional growth which would through their multiple backward and forward linkages set in motion a process of rapid economic growth in the regions (Planning Commission, Third Five Year Plan, pp. 149). The location of industries supplying the regional market or the location of "footloose" industries which, though supplying much larger markets, could be sited within the regions – was regarded as an important component of the programmes in the late 1960s.

Official intervention for promoting dispersed industrial development included both incentives and sanctions. From the outset the emphasis was on the former. The principal incentives were providing land and various infrastructure facilities needed by the industrial units (electricity, water, road and railway connections, drainage) quickly and at low cost, providing concessional loans and other fiscal incentives for the entrepreneurs, and providing technical assistance for project appraisal and selection of equipment, for example, or in certain areas of management. These facilities were provided typically for industries locating in the industrial estates or industrial areas which began to be built by the state governments from the mid-1950s under a programme sponsored by the central government. While promoting development of small industries and industrial dispersal remained the professed objectives for industrial estates, their actual locations indicated that the state governments attached at least equal importance to promoting the industrial development of the state. Thus while many industrial estates and areas were built in backward regions or near medium sized or small towns, some of the largest and most successful ones were located in the vicinity of large cities, including the state capitals and metropolitan cities like Delhi, Chennai, and Mumbai. In their eagerness to promote development of industry, the state governments were ready to provide these facilities wherever the prospective industrialists wanted them.

Official interest in the strategies of industrial location and urbanization had waned, however, by the late 1960s because the attention of policymakers and planners had shifted to the urgent task of overcoming serious imbalances in the economy, particularly an acute food shortage and large external payments deficits. Growth of agricultural and cereal output, which had been well ahead of the growth of population in the 1950s, had slowed down in the 1960s – partly because agricultural development had not received under the second and third Five-Year Plans (1956-1966) the attention and the resources it had received under the First Plan (1951-1956). The development strategy of the Second and Third Plans had focused on industrialization, particularly development of basic, heavy industries in the public sector. Widespread and severe drought, during both 1965-1966 and 1966-1967, led to a steep fall in agricultural output, and famines were avoided only by massive imports of cereals, (about 10 million tons in each year). The balance of payments deficits were due partly to the large investment needs of the new industrial units. Furthermore, the returns in terms of increased output from these heavy investments and related infrastructures were being delayed because of the nature of the investments and the serious gestation problems that some of the largest units were facing.

Despite this lack of interest, one element of the strategy of industrial location has remained: encouraging location at the outskirts of cities (including satellite towns of the large metropolitan cities) and in backward regions. Such locations have continued to be encouraged through substantial capital investment by the state governments in developing industrial areas and estates and by the other measures mentioned above. Particularly generous fiscal incentives continue to be given, and the powers of the central and state governments for licensing industries have been used to promote location of industries in the backward regions.

On the other hand, there has been little action to check rapid growth of the large cities despite evidence of increasing deterioration in urban conditions. The inevitability of rapid growth of the cities, including the largest like Mumbai and Delhi, has been accepted. Indeed, not only has the growth not been discouraged, but it has at times been encouraged by official actions. Thus, in Mumbai, the proposals to concentrate further development on the mainland across the bay from the present city (including the progressive shift of offices of the Maharashtra government to this area) in order to relieve the congestion in the central business district, and to connect the two parts by a number of bridges, have not been implemented. On the contrary, further concentration of population and economic activities in the central area of the city was allowed and even encouraged by permitting construction of high-rise residential and commercial buildings and by the Maharashtra government itself selling land reclaimed from the sea in the Nariman Point area for high-rise construction.

The current policy of economic liberalization gives the private sector much greater latitude in industrial decisions, including location of industries. Licensing of industries is now restricted to large industrial units with projected investments of Rs. 250 million or more. This latitude should favour siting industries near the large cities because such location continues to be the most attractive for all entrepreneurs except those wishing to establish huge industrial units. The reasons for the attractiveness of near-city location range from ease of supervision of the unit by the owners or managers from their homes in the cities to access to capital, skilled labour, and the output of ancillary industries. The wider range and higher quality of infrastructure and social services (from telecommunications to education and health) in or near the cities is itself very attractive, because the range of such services is limited away from the cities and their functional efficiency is low. States like Maharashtra may continue their policy of diverting industries away from the over urbanized Mumbai-Poona region to the less developed regions of the state, but the dominant trend among the state governments will be toward further back-pedaling on the industrial location issue and encouraging prospective investors to locate industries almost anywhere they want. Indeed, the state governments' efforts to attract industrial investment in their states are expected to become aggressive in the future, culminating at times in intense competition to attract large industrial units.

RESOURCES FOR URBAN DEVELOPMENT

At the heart of India's urban problem are grossly inadequate inputs of finance and management needed for efficient functioning of urban government and for expansion of housing and services to keep pace with the rapidly growing urban population. Provision of adequate finance will not be easy because of the great demand. But steady progress toward reducing the present inadequacy can be made if there is greater perception of the interdependence between urban and rural development. The present shortages of urban housing and the inefficiency of urban services not only cause great hardship to the urban population but also result in enormous losses of output. They act as a major disincentive on productive investment. The latter effect is most apparent in the case of services such as electric power, for prolonged cuts and erratic supplies have become a daily occurrence in most cities.

Despite the consensus among planners in favour of promoting dispersed urbanization, the high-cost alternative of increasing concentration of the urban population in the large cities has been allowed to develop. Little progress has been made with respect to the other policy measures also. Thus the Sixth Plan report mentioned:

A ceiling on urban land, prescribed under the Urban Land [Ceiling and Regulation] Act 1976, was meant to prevent speculation in land and to ensure the optimal allocation of land to different users. The implementation of the Act has experienced great difficulties and the State Governments have not been able to implement it effectively. In the meantime, there is a general feeling that costs of land have increased substantially, and fears are expressed that urban housing might become too expensive for a large number of people (Planning Commission, Sixth Five Year Plan 1980-85, pp. 346-347).

Most of the funds needed to finance expansion or improvement of urban housing and essential services will have to be provided, as at present, by grants and loans by the central government and channeled through the state governments or by loans from financial institutions which are controlled by the central or state governments. It would be unrealistic to expect the municipal bodies, even of the largest cities, to raise more than a small proportion of the funds needed for these purposes. The municipal bodies' powers of taxation are limited; taxes on property and *octroi*, an indirect tax on goods coming into the city, are their principal sources of revenue.

Table 2.5: Percentage of Revenue and Capital Expenditure of the State Government Financed through transfers from the Central Government: 1951-1984

	Five-Year Plans					
	I	*II*	*III*	*IV*	*V*	*VI*
Revenue transfer as percentage of revenue expenditures of states	22.4	28.2	33.4	35.1	39.5	41.1
Loan transfer as percentage of capital expenditure of states	71.9	58.7	64.5	63.2	83.1	74.6
Aggregate transfers as percentage of aggregate expenditures of states	37.8	39.8	45.7	47.4	42.1	41.6

Source: K.K. George and I.S. Gulati, "Center-State Resource Transfers, 1951-84: An Appraisal," Economic and Political Weekly, 22(7) (16 February 1985), p. 290.

Urban Planning

Formulation of plans for all cities with populations of 500,000 or more will mean coverage of the largest and most dynamic part of the urban sector which moreover is most in need of them. As mentioned earlier, these cities already had about 40 percent of the total urban population by 1980 and the proportion is expected to increase to more than 50 percent by the end of the century. Furthermore, the needs for expansion of housing and urban services are higher than in the smaller urban places because of their more rapid growth, and projects involving large expenditures and often requiring solution of complex technical problems have to be undertaken in the big cities.

The plans for individual cities and towns should form part of the five-year and annual plans of the states in which they are located, so that they can be financed as part of the state plans. Preparation of urban plans and their integration with the plans of the states will also give the municipal bodies a strong incentive for greater mobilization of local resources. The practice of matching grants, under which the cost of implementing a project is shared between the state government and local communities, has been successfully used for rural development programmes. It can be used even more effectively for urban development programmes because the potential for local resource mobilization is greater in the urban areas.

Management

The principal need is for providing high-quality managers and technical officers to run large cities (populations of 500,000 or more) and for implementing development projects and programs. A number of related developments lead us to expect progressive improvement in the availability of high-quality managers and technical officers for urban administration and urban development projects.

Better Political Executives

In the period immediately after Independence, most political talent was drawn into national or state-level politics, which offered the most challenging opportunities for exercise of political power. Municipal bodies were deprived of high-quality political executives, who had been available during the pre-Independence period. Indeed, up to the mid-1930s, before the advent of popular governments in the British-administered provinces, municipal bodies offered some of the few opportunities available to Indians for exercise of political power. Nehru, Sardar Patel, and several other leaders of the Independence movement, who rose to top-level positions in central and state governments after Independence, won their political spurs in municipal administrations. This position of municipal administration as the nursery of national and state-level leaders could be restored in the late 1980s or the 1990s because of the limited opportunities now available in the national and state governments and the increasing importance of urban affairs.

Better Managers and Technical Officers

Similar developments—limited opportunities in the state or national governments and increasingly attractive opportunities in municipal administrations—should attract a growing number of well-trained administrators and professional officers to the latter. Gone is the heady expansion of the public sector, including both the civil service and the public enterprises, which absorbed most of the available managerial and technical personnel in the 1950s and the 1960s and provided exciting opportunities for participating in the formulation of national economic and social policies and the establishment of large public enterprises. Such opportunities will, in future, be available only to a very few members of the higher administrative services, the highly talented or exceptionally lucky. For the great majority, particularly the newcomers to the services, the prospect is merely one of doing routine administrative jobs in various ministries and departments of the state or national governments. Major expansion of public-sector enterprises is not envisaged under the new economic liberalisation policies. On the contrary, the trend will be towards divestment by turning over certain units to private or joint-sector companies. The principal remaining challenge in the public sector is that of increasing productivity or reducing the losses of the public enterprises. This challenge will be met, however, by attracting competent executives from both the administrative services and the corporate private sector.

Significant numbers of talented and experienced members of the higher administrative or technical services are already available for secondment to the municipal bodies of the large cities. Most of those who have filled top management or technical positions in these cities find that these posts offer opportunities for achievement which are as good as any available in the state or national governments. The commissioner and the senior technical officers of the municipal corporation of a large city can immediately see the results of their decisions—in expansion of housing, in clearance or improvement of slums, and in improvement of essential services, which translate, in turn, into increases in economic activity or in the welfare of hundreds of thousands of people. Most of their counterparts in the state or national bureaucracies, on the other hand, see themselves as merely cogs in a giant machine who have only a minor role in its functioning.

Increasing Participation of Business Leaders in Urban Affairs

The prospects of expansion—and the consequent growth of opportunities for management and technical personnel—are greater in the private sector (corporate or other) than in the public sector. But the challenges and opportunities in municipal administration will, in the near future, begin to attract a significant number of managers and technocrats from the private sector. One reason for this trend will be the increasing participation of leaders of business and private industry in urban affairs. Such participation had been inhibited earlier – by the antibusiness intellectual climate of the 1950s to the mid-1970s and by "anti-non-Bengali" sentiment such as that expressed in Kolkata, where Bengalis regarded the leaders of business and industry, most of whom are non-Bengalis, as "alien exploiters".

Resentment of "outsiders" will remain an important political force, especially in less developed states such as Assam, where the educated youth (particularly those in low-paid positions or unemployed) keenly resent the dominance of the public services, business, and industry by non-natives. Nevertheless, even though political agitation such as that in Assam during 1979-83 may be repeated, the dominant trend in the states will be toward encouraging investment in business and industry by both natives and non-natives. The courting of business leaders by the present Marxist government of West Bengal is not an aberration; it is part of a nationwide trend. After coming to power, the Marxists realized the vital need for stopping the capital flight from West Bengal and attracting new investments in order to expand employment and income in the state. Consequently, their leaders muted their antibusiness rhetoric and joined governments of other states in actively seeking private investment.

THE PROBLEM OF THE FOUR GIANT CITIES

Despite the improved prospects of acquiring the funds and top-level personnel for urban administration and undertaking projects to meet the needs of urban growth, the prospects of the four giant cities, Mumbai, Kolkata, Chennai, and Delhi, are much less sanguine. Indeed, in the case of Mumbai and Kolkata, where the urban systems already show inability to cope with the present populations, it is not at all clear how the pressures created by the projected doubling of the population during the twenty years 1980-2000 will be met.

The *World Bank Report 1984* projected the population growth of the four cities by the year 2000 (Table 2.6). All four cities are included in the twenty-five megalopolises which will have a population of more than 10 million by the year 2000. Except for Delhi, the projected growth rates of the cities are higher than those experienced during 1961-1981. If one assumes that the natural increase of the population already resident would not be significantly different from the national average of 1.9 percent projected in the *World Bank Report* for 1980-2000, less than half the projected increase in their populations would, except in the case of Chennai, be due to in-migration.

Table 2.6: Projected Population Growth and Growth Rates of Mumbai, Kolkata, Chennai, and Delhi

City	*Population (millions)*		*Annual Growth Rate (%)*	
	Actual	*Projected*	*Actual*	*Projected*
	1980	*2000*	*1961-1981*	*1980-2000*
Mumbai	8.2	17.1	3.5	3.7
Kolkata	9.2	16.7	2.3	3.0
Chennai	4.3	12.9	4.0	5.7
Delhi	5.7	11.7	4.5	3.7

Source: World Bank Report 1984.

The potential for and constraints on growth of individual cities appear to have been given some consideration in projecting their growth. The rate projected for Kolkata is significantly lower than the rates projected for the other three cities, but it is still considerably higher than the actual rate for 1961-1981. The problems of managing the urban system and providing essential services are most acute in Kolkata; it suffered capital flight following the industrial and political unrest of the late 1960s, and investor confidence has been slow to return. Keeping these constraints in view, its projected rate for 1980-2000 can well be considered too high.

Projection of rapid growth for Chennai can be justified on several grounds. First is a favourable environment for industrial growth, relative freedom from industrial unrest, a disciplined labour force with willingness and aptitude for learning new skills, and moderated wage levels—all leading to lower labour costs per unit of output than in Mumbai or Delhi. Second, Chennai has a large hinterland with diverse agricultural and mineral resources which has, moreover, been experiencing vigorous growth. And third, except in the case of water, Chennai has less difficult problems of expanding the infrastructure than the other three cities. Even so, the projected rate, which will result in trebling of the population in twenty years, appears to be too high.

The growth potential of Delhi, however, may have been underestimated. Growth of employment in the central government will continue to be an important factor for the city. Furthermore, Delhi is the principal city serving a large region, a large part of which, located in Punjab, Haryana, and western Uttar Pradesh, has experienced rapid growth of agricultural production income in the last two decades to reach significantly higher levels than the national average. Furthermore, the region has the potential for maintaining higher rates of growth than the national average.

Growth projections for Mumbai are high because of the rapid development of the economies of both the city of Mumbai and the state of Maharashtra. Mumbai is also the principal city of western India, giving it national importance in the Indian economy. This importance together with the city's developing industrial and services economic base make high population growth rates inevitable.

Without knowing the assumptions and the methodology of the projections, it is impossible to comment on them in detail. The principal questions about the prospects of these cities do not relate, however, to the details of the growth projections; they relate primarily to whether continued rapid growth of their populations to two or three times their present sizes in twenty years can be sustained in the face of existing pressures on housing and essential services. Could such increases not lead to the virtual collapse of the urban administration in one or more of these cities? Alternatively, given the serious resource constraints of the Indian economy and the limitations of the political and administrative systems, is there enough time to undertake the needed reforms of urban administrations and implement the development programmes required for the expansion of housing and urban services in these cities?

The questions cannot be answered. The requirements of the cities for both finance and high-quality management for the purposes mentioned above will be very high indeed. Furthermore, in areas of expanding water supply and urban transport where there are major environmental constraints and high cost, technically complex solutions will have to be devised. Procedural delays could also be long especially in the case of housing, for the intervention of the courts could seriously delay acquisition of land. Finally, the record of the recent past is not reassuring. Problems have been ignored for long periods, and even after major projects have been finally approved, their implementation has often been slow and in many cases fitful.

The answers to the questions will relate, finally, to political judgment and the will to provide the needed resources and ensure that institutional and administrative reforms are undertaken and that projects and programmes are implemented with speed and efficiency. Some of the tasks that will need special attention in these cities include housing, food supply, water and electricity, transport, maintenance of peace and security, and restriction of in-migration.

Housing

Expansion and improvement of housing will remain the most difficult problem. The present deficiency is so acute and growing so rapidly, and the costs of expansion of housing are so high in comparison with the incomes of the great majority of urban residents, that the best that can be hoped, even with the most intensive effort, is avoidance of a serious aggravation of the present situation. In Delhi, for instance, the current estimate is of a shortage of 300,000 dwelling units and a requirement of 1.62 million units over the next two decades (HT, 18th May, 1985).

In Mumbai, "the shelter problem is theoretically very neatly defined. The demand for shelter works out to 60,000 units each year in the Mumbai metropolitan region (45,000 units in Greater Mumbai and 15,000 in the metropolitan region). The supply in the formal sector, private and public, is now around 20,000 units each year and the difference between demand and supply has resulted in an accrual to the slum settlements in the metropolis. Not only was 40 percent of the total population in 1976 living in slums but the slum population is growing faster than the overall population" (Abraham, 1985).

Acquisition of land for public housing for the poor is itself a most difficult problem. Reference was made earlier to the fact that acquisition of land for such housing was delayed and the area of land available for this purpose was progressively reduced by private interests who obtained political support and used a series of court injunctions against acquisition (Dutt and Venugopal, 1983).

Food Supply

Ensuring both adequate supplies of cereal to the cities and their availability at prices fixed by the government, never easy, should not be unmanageable if the growth rate of cereal output achieved in India during the last twenty years can be maintained. The spread of the wheat revolution from its core area in Punjab, Haryana, and western Utter Pradesh into eastern Uttar Pradesh, Bihar, and West Bengal and the improvement in the last few years in the rate of growth of rice output give hope of this prospect. But increasing, or even maintaining, the present low levels of consumption of foods rich in proteins, minerals, and vitamins (such as milk, meat, poultry products, and fruits and vegetables) or even such essentials as oils and fats will be very difficult unless there are major improvements in the technologies of producing, processing, and transporting these staples and their prices get more in line with the incomes of the great majority of urban residents.

Water and Electricity

The problem of providing adequate water and electricity could grow even worse unless there are sustained efforts to increase supplies. Large investments in expansion of the systems of supply, transmission, and distribution, as well as progressive improvements in their management, will be needed. Expanding the water supply may present a more complex problem than that of electricity. The customary difficulty and high cost of providing adequate and safe water to cities are multiplied in the four largest cities. The acute shortage of water experienced in Chennai in 1984 is an indication of these difficulties. Large and expensive works, involving the transport of water over long distances, will be needed for all four cities. In Kolkata and Delhi, the urgent need for reducing dangerously high pollution levels is expected to be met, however, by the Ganga Cleanup Project.

Transport

Expansion of the transport system to cope with the needs of growth will present special problems in all the cities except Chennai. The worst case again is Kolkata, where the transport system is a nightmare. Because the planners for Delhi have never gotten around to conceptualizing an efficient transport system, the existing system is approaching conditions of near chaos. In Mumbai, too, the transport system is greatly over-loaded and the cost of its expansion will be immense. If a large part of the projected growth takes place on the mainland across the bay from the present city, large investments will be required for construction of bridges and other works linking the transport systems of the two parts of the city. Only in case of Chennai, where the transport system is much less overloaded, would expansion be manageable.

Maintaining Peace and Security

This task will require political and administrative management of a very high order. Above all, the cities must ensure access to the basic needs for food and water, access to other essential services and housing, and opportunities for gainful employment. The tensions ever present below the surface in the Indian cities, (Dutt, 1983) tensions which find their outlet in periodic outbreaks of violence, can be kept within manageable limits, and the growth of underworld activities curtailed, only when these fundamental conditions are met.

Restricting In-Migration to the Cities

From time to time there is demand for curbing in-migration to these four cities, and to smaller cities such as Bangalore, which have experienced very rapid growth during the last two or three decades.

The motives for the demand may be political, or they may be techno-administrative. Thus the Siva Sena, a militant Pro-Maharashtrian organization, threatened in May 1985 to launch an Assam-like agitation to ban migration into Mumbai and reduce the number of "outsiders" (Hindustan Times, 1985). Its motive was purely political; its main support is among the majority Maharashtrian population of Mumbai which has long resented the domination of commerce, industry, and increasingly also the white-collar services by Non-Maharashtrians. They also fear they will lose their majority status if rapid in-migration to the city continues.

But such a measure has never been seriously considered. Indeed, the prime minister has ruled out any curb on in-migration, which in any event would be unconstitutional. Even if the constitutional difficulties were to be overcome at some future date, the immense task of enforcing the restrictions would remain. The only solution to the problem of in-migration to the giant cities is to increase the attraction of alternatives, including satellite towns.

India's cities and urban regions face a difficult future. Urban infrastructure and housing are inadequate and cannot absorb the massive numbers of newcomers. Urban economic and social conditions are deteriorating, which results in higher levels of unemployment and social unrest. Migration from the countryside continues unabated and in some cases is accelerating. In these adverse circumstances India's urban areas must become the focus for new policy initiatives emphasizing population control, rural development, and urban growth containment.

NOTE

1. Published in *Urbanization in Asia – Spatial Dimensions and Policy Issues*: Eds: Frank J. Costa & Dutt A.K. *et al.*, 1989.

REFERENCES

Abraham, A. (1985) "*Housing for the Poor*", *Economic and Political Weekly,* 20 (6) pp. 226.

Dutt, A.K. and Venugopal, G. (1983) *Spatial Patterns of Crime among Indian Cities, GeoForum,* London.

George K.K and Gulati, I.S. (1985) *"Center-State Resource Transfers, 1951-84: An Appraisal,"* Economic and Political Weekly, 22(7), p. 290.

Government of India,(1985) *Seventh Five-Year Plan* (1985-1990), vols. 1 and Planning Commission, Government of India Press, New Delhi.

Government of India, Population censuses of India: 1951-1981.

Hindustan Times, (18 May, 1985), *Delhi in 2001*, New Delhi), p. 3.

Hindustan Times, (25 May, 1985*), "P.M rules out curbs on migration"*, New Delhi, p. 3.

Mitra, A. (1978) *"Micro Planning of Space"*, in Allen G. Noble and Ashok K. Dutt (eds.), *Indian Urbanization and Planning: Vehicles of Modernization*, (1978), Tata-McGraw-Hill, New Delhi.

Mohan, R. (1985) "*Urbanization in India's Future*", *Population and Development Review* 2(4) pp. 630.

Ninan, T.N. (1985) *The Economy – Buoyant Mood, India Today*, New Delhi.

Government of India, Planning Commission, *Third Five-Year Plan*, p. 149.

Government of India, Planning Commission, *Sixth Five-Year Plan 1980-85*, pp. 346-347.

World Bank, (1984) *World Development Report 1984,* World Bank, Washington, D.C.

Wurster, C.B. (1962) *"Urban Living Conditions, Overhead Costs and the Development Patterns"*, in Roy Turner (ed.), *India's Urban Future,* University of California Press, California.

3

Urbanization and Urban Development in India: Some Policy Issues[1]

INTRODUCTION

This paper forms part of an on-going programme of studies on urbanization and urban development in India. It discusses trends in growth of the urban population during the 20 years, 1961–81, and projections of the growth to the end of the century. Trends in distribution of the urban population by cities and smaller urban places, inter-state variations in urbanization and changes in the contribution of the urban population to the national GDP are reviewed, and the implications of the trends and projections for national policies on urban and regional development are referred to briefly.

The policies and programmes relating to expansion/improvement of urban housing and of physical and social infrastructures in the cities, outlined in the Sixth and Seventh Five Year Plans, are examined in relation to the demands for expansion/improvement of these created by rapid urban growth and economic development. Reference is made to the prospect of progressive aggravation of the shortages which are already acute in the large cities, and to the adverse effects of the shortages on the urban environment, the levels of living of the urban population, the productivity of the urban workers and national economic growth. Proliferation of slums and rapidly increasing pollution of air and water are the more visible symptoms of the urban malaise.

Reversal of these trends will require radical changes in perception of urban problems by policy makers at national, regional and local levels and among the general public, changes in policies and programmes and institutional and legislative reforms. In particular, there will be need for much larger provisions of finance and manpower for formulating and implementing development projects. Unfortunately, however, these changes are not likely to come before the mid-1990's, and could come only after one or more urban crises. The four giant cities of Kolkata, Mumbai, Delhi and Chennai are most vulnerable to such crises.

The need for policy-related studies on urbanization and urban development is emphasized. The most urgent need is for studies on social benefit-cost analysis of projects for expansion/improvement of urban housing and infrastructures and the policies and programmes aimed at industrial dispersal and regional development. The studies will contribute to making needed changes in the policies on urbanization and urban development, and improving formulation and implementation of urban development projects.

URBANIZATION: TRENDS AND PROJECTIONS, 1961–2001

Growth of the Urban Population

With the publication of the *Seventh five-year plan 1985–90* (Government of India Planning Commission, 1985), the earlier large differences between the available projections of the growth rate of the urban population during 1981–2001 have been greatly reduced and there appears to be emerging a convergence of views in favour of continuation of rapid growth of the urban population during this period, at rates similar to or higher than those experienced during 1961–81 (Government of India, 1980; World Bank, 1984: 67).

Three projections of growth of the total population, of the urban population and of gross domestic product *per capita* up to the end of the century (contained in World Bank, 1984; Government of India Planning Commission, 1985; and Mohan, 1985 respectively are presented in Table 3.1). They are close enough to indicate agreement on the following:

1. progressive reduction in the growth rate of the total population with decline in fertility; but
2. continuing rapid growth of the urban population due both to natural increase of the resident urban population and rural-to-urban migration.

Table 3.1: Projections of Total and Urban Population and of GDP *Per Capita*

	World Development Report, 1984			*Seventh five-year Plan, 1986–90*					*Mohan*				
	1980		*2000*	*1981*		*1991*		*2001*	*1981*		*1991*		*2001*
Total population*	685		994	685		837		986	697		850–856		993-1018
Average growth rate**		1.9			2.0		1.65			(2.2 during 1981–86, falling to 1.47–1.68 during 1996–2001)			
Urban population*	160		353	160		230		326	164		234–236		315–320
Average growth rate**		4.2			3.7		3.5			3.8		3.1	
Urban population/ total population (%)	23.3		35.5	23.3		27.5		33.1	23.5		27.3–27.5		31.0-31.5
Growth rate of GDP per capital:													
High-case scenario		3.2***			3.2****		3.35				n.a.		
Low-case scenario		2.5***											

1. Growth rate of GDP *per capita* for India is projected at 2.5 percent under the low-case scenario. The rate for the high-case scenario is not projected in the WDR, but is inferred as being lower than the rate for 'low-income Asia' by 0.5 percent per annum, as under the low-case scenario.

Total population is projected under three variants of decline in fertility, while growth of the urban population is projected under two variants.

Sources: (a) World Bank, 1984. (b) Government of India Planning Commission, 1985. (c) Mohan, 1985.

* Figures for population are in millions., ** Figures for growth rates are in percent *per annum*, *** 1985–95, **** 1986–91

The *World development report* (WDR) (World Bank, 1984) projected, on assumptions of relatively high rates of growth in both GDP *per capita* and rural-to-urban migration, a growth rate of the urban population averaging 4.2 percent per annum, during 1980–2000. More than half of the growth would be due to rural-to-urban migration, which would be so rapid as to bring down the average rate of growth of the rural population to 1.1 percent per annum, less than two-thirds of the rate of natural increase of the total population (Table 3.1). The rates of growth of the urban population in the other two projections were significantly lower. The *seventh plan* projected an average growth rate of about 3.6 percent per annum for the two decades 1981–2001, very similar to the average rate for the previous two decades. Since the growth rate of the total population was projected to decrease progressively, from 2.3 percent per annum during 1961–81 to 2.0 percent per annum during 1981–91 and to 1.65 percent per annum during 1991–2001, the projection implied progressive increase in rural-to-urban migration. Mohan's projection of growth of the urban population had two variants, but the figures for 1991 and 2001 under both were close enough to give almost the same rates of growth of the urban population: 3.8 percent per annum during 1981–1991 and 3.1 percent per annum during 1991–2001. The deceleration of the growth rate during the 1990s projected by him was thus much greater than the marginal deceleration projected in the *seventh plan* (Table 3.1).

Under all three projections, the total urban population by the end of the century would be double (or more) the 1981 figure of about 160 million, and would constitute about one-third of the total population of the country. The *WDR*'s figures of total urban population of 353 million and an urban/total population ratio of 35.5 percent by the year 2000 were the highest.

Both the *WDR* and the *seventh plan* had also projected rapid growth of gross domestic product (GDP) *per capita*. The projection of the WDR was based on the World Bank's global model under which growth of the economies of the LDCs during the decade 1985–95 was projected under two scenarios: (a) a 'high case' scenario, based on the assumption of relatively favourable conditions for economic growth in the LDCs – rapid economic growth in the industrial economies and expansion of world trade, resulting from good macroeconomic management by the governments of these countries within a framework of economic policies aimed at achieving growth with monetary and price stability; and (b) a 'low case' scenario, based on the assumption of significantly slower growth in the industrial countries and in world trade, because of inappropriate or inadequate policy responses by the governments of the industrial countries for correcting the imbalance and distortions in their economies. Economic growth in the industrial countries and expansion of world trade are considered by the Bank to be the critical factors affecting economic growth in the LDCs, because the latter is considered to be closely related to the export performance of the LDCs. The growth rates projected for the LDCs were 3.4 percent per annum under the 'high case' scenario and 2.7 percent per annum under the 'low case' scenario. The projections for India under the two scenarios were 3.2 percent per annum and 2.5 percent per annum respectively (Table 3.1). It should be noted that the growth rate projected for India, even under the 'low case' scenario, was almost twice as high as the average rate of 1.3 percent per annum estimated for 1960–82.

The projection of the *seventh plan* of growth rate of GDP *per capita* during 1981–2001 approximated the *WDR*'s 'high case' scenario rate of 3.2 percent per annum; the plan projected an average growth rate for total GDP of 5 percent per annum during the two decades, almost 50 percent higher than the rate averaging 3.5 percent per annum, estimated for 1960–82.

Increasing Concentration of the Urban Population in the Cities

The proportion of the urban population living in the cities (urban places with populations of 100,000 or more) which had increased progressively from 44 percent in 1961 to 60 percent by 1981, is projected by Mohan to reach almost 70 percent by 2001 (Tables 3.2 and 3.3). Almost 30 percent of the urban population would be living by the latter year in the metropolitan cities, i.e., cities with population of 100,000 or more. The projection, although in conformity with the trend for 1971–81, could prove to be an underestimate, however. The number of metropolitan cities, which had increased from nine in 1971 to 12 in 1981, was projected by Mohan to nearly double to 22 by 1991 (Mohan, 1985: 633), and would undoubtedly increase further by 2001. Since increase in the number of metropolitan cities was identified by him as the principal reason for progressive increase in the proportion of the urban population living in them (Table. 3.2), an

Table 3.2: Distribution of Urban Population by Size of Urban place, 1961–1981

Percentage of Urban Population in Urban Places with Population of:	*1961*	*1971*	*1981*
1 million and above	22.5	25.1	26.3
500,000 – 1 miillion	3.1	6.2	13.4
100,000 – 500,000	18.1	17.6	20.7
50,000 – 100,000	12.1	13.5	11.6
20,000 – 50,000	20.0	18.3	14.4
Below 20,000	23.4	19.5	13.6

Source: Population Censuses of India – 1961–1981

Table 3.3: Actual and projected distribution of the urban population in India over various size classes of urban places: 1971–2001

Year		*Metro-politan*	*Class size*					*Total*	*Projected*	*Projected*
			I	*II*	*III*	*IV*	*V*	*Urban*	*Urban*	*Rural*
			(Per cent of total urban population)						*(millions)*	
1971	(i)	25.4	30.2	11.3	15.6	11.3	4.7	108.3		423
	(ii)	25.5	28.6	11.6	18.1	12.5	4.1	100.4		429
	(A)	25.7	30.6	11.3	16.4	11.3	4.7	106.6		422
1981	(i)	27.6	29.7	11.2	14.6	12.9	4.1	152.3		506
	(ii)	28.2	33.1	11.2	14.9	9.5	3.2	145.9		506
	(A)	26.9	33.5	11.6	14.3	9.5	4.1	156.1		502
1991 (Projected)	(i)	28.1	36.3	12.0	12.4	7.9	3.3	235.7	236	604
	(ii)	28.3	36.5	11.7	12.4	7.9	3.4	235.6	236	605
2001	(i)	29.1	39.6	11.8	10.3	6.4	2.8	333.6	315	704
	(ii)	29.2	40.1	11.4	10.3	6.4	2.8	333.4	315	703

Notes: Percentages calculated from figures given in Mohan (1985: 633). The size classes are: Metropolitan: 1 million and above; class I: 100,000–1 million; Class II: 50,000–100,000; Class III: 20,000–50,000; Class IV: 10,000–20,000; Class V: below 10,000.

A is the actual population according to the Census of India; (i) and (ii) are calculated from Mohan's two projections, which are explained in the Appendix on (pp. 642–643).

increase of more than 100 percent in the number of metropolitan cities during 1981 to 2001, could push the proportion of the urban population living in them to well beyond 30 percent.

More rapid growth of the cities than that of smaller urban places, leading to increasing concentration of the urban population in the cities, has been noted by many analysts of Indian urbanization. Bose has commented also on stagnation of small and medium-sized towns (Bose 1973: 87–94). These conclusions rest primarily on the data on distribution of the urban population by urban places of different size classes, provided by the decennial censuses of population.

The observed more rapid growth of the cities and of the metropolitan cities in particular, than that of smaller urban places could be due to one on more of the following reasons.

1. More rapid growth of population of larger urban places than that of smaller places;
2. Increase in the number of the cities, with continual addition to their ranks of smaller towns and cities after they crossed the population thresholds – of 100,000 for the cities and 1,000,000 for the metropolitan cities. Thus, the number of cities increased from 145 to 216 during 1971–81 with the number of the 'metropolitan cities' increasing, as mentioned earlier, from 9 to 12; and
3. Incorporation or extension of the administrative boundaries of the cities to include villages and small towns which were outside the boundaries earlier. This factor has been important in the cases of several rapidly growing cities in certain periods, such as the 1940s in the case of Mumbai and the 1950s for Delhi, during which major extensions of their boundaries took place. But its importance has diminished after adoption by the Census of the 'urban agglomeration' as the unit for indicating the population of the cities.

Analyzing the data for 1971 and 1981, Mohan concluded that when the number of urban places in the different size classes was held constant, the average growth rate, 3.62 percent per annum during 1971–81, for the cities was not significantly higher than the rates for the smaller urban places and that the fastest rate of growth was recorded by the towns of the smallest size class, with populations of 5000–9999 (Table 3.4). He added that his finding was in line with that of M.K. Jain for 1951–61 and 1961–71 (Mohan, 1985: 622).

Table 3.4: Annual Growth Rate of the Urban Population in India by Size of Town: 1971–81

	1971		*1981*	
Size Class In 1971	*Number Of Towns*	*Urban Population (Millions)*	*Urban Population (Millions)*	*Population Growth Rate, 1971–81 (% Per Year)*
Metropolitan And class I*	145	60.1	85.8	3.62
Class II (50,000-99,999	178	12.0	16.9	3.44
Class III (20,000–49,999)	560	17.2	23.7	3.28
Class IV (10,000–19,999)	818	11.7	16.1	3.29
Class V (5,000–9,999)	596	4.3	6.3	3.83
Total	2297	105.3	148.8	3.52

* Million and Above

Note: Many towns were excluded from classes III, IV and V in 1981 because they could not be traced in the 1981 census. These missing towns were either declassified or had been amalgamated into larger towns or cities

Source: Mohan (1985: 622, Table 2).

Thus the observed more rapid growth of population of the urban places of larger size classes appears to be due principally to continuous addition to their numbers. Analysis of the data for the 1991 census will be of interest because it will either confirm the conclusion further or lead to appropriate modification of it.

Regional Variation in Urbanization

Analyzing state data on growth rates of the urban population during the three decades 1951–81, Mohan realized that more rapid rates of urban growth, of 4–5 percent per annum, were recorded during 1971–81 in the less urbanized, less developed (lower *per capita* income) states, such as Bihar, Orissa, Rajasthan and Madhya Pradesh than in the more developed, more urbanized states like West Bengal, Gujarat, Maharashtra and Tamil Nadu, in which the rates ranged between 2.5 percent and 3.5 percent per annum. The rates for 1971–81 in several of the former were higher than those for the earlier decades, while those in the latter states were lower (Mohan, 1985: 623). He referred also to more active town formation (i.e., more rapid increase in the number of towns by conversion of larger villages into towns) in the relatively backward states than in the more developed ones.

Contribution of the Urban Population to the GDP

Official estimates of the contribution of the urban and rural populations to GDP are not available, presumably because of the difficulties in making the estimates and the limitations of the estimates that are made. However, using urban/rural distribution of the labour force in the three principal economic sectors — primary, secondary and tertiary – the sectoral distribution of GDP at factor cost, and the value added per urban and rural worker, Mohan estimated that the urban population contributed 47 percent of the total GDP in 1980–81. Projecting the distributions to 1994–95 he estimated that the proportion would increase to 58 percent by that year. It is interesting to note that the contribution of the urban population to GDP in both 1980–81 and 1994–95 was estimated at twice its proportion in the total population, the respective figures being 46.9 percent and 23.6 percent for 1980–81, and 57.7 percent and 29.0 percent for 1994–95. The urban-to-rural ratio of value added per urban worker, which was estimated to have increased from 2.7 in 1970–71 to 2.87 by 1980–81, was projected to go up further to 3.34 by 1994–95.

Increasing contribution of the urban population to the GDP and increasing urban-rural disparities in net domestic product per worker and *per capita* income are due to concentration in the cities and towns of the manufacturing and service sector activities in which productivity per worker is higher than in agriculture, and which experience moreover faster growth than agriculture in the development process (Sundaram, 1986; Government of India Planning Commission, 1985: 14). Too much importance should not be attached, however, to the increasing disparity in average urban and rural *per capita* incomes because it does not mean increasing disparity in levels of living of the great majority of the urban and the rural populations. There are two reasons for the latter. First, intra-urban disparities in incomes are higher than those in the rural areas. Secondly, the cost of living is significantly higher in the urban than in the rural areas partly because urban residents have to incur expenditures, such as on house rent and for travel to work, which are either not incurred by the villagers or are much lower. A more realistic comparison of the welfare of the urban and rural populations is provided by data on the incidence of poverty. Figures on the proportions of urban and rural population below the 'poverty line', available continuously for 14 years, 1960–61 to 1973–74 and for two later years 1977–78 and 1983, indicate that 40–50 percent of the urban population was below the 'poverty line' during the period 1960–61 to 1973–74. The corresponding figures for the rural population were higher by 2 to 10 percentage points in most of these years, but were lower in two years. The preliminary estimates for 1983 also indicated a higher percentage of population below the poverty line for the urban population (34.8%) than for the rural population (32.2%) (Sundaram, 1986: 10-14, 36).

Considering the limitations of the primary data – the estimates of consumer expenditure made by the National Sample Survey – and of the concept of the 'poverty line', on which these figures are based, the safest conclusion is that the incidence of poverty is probably similar in both the urban and the rural areas.

Policy Implications

This analysis of the trends in urbanization during the past two to three decades and of the projections to the end of the century has important implications for the national development strategy and policies relating to urban and regional development. The assumptions on which the strategy and the policies are based must be reexamined and appropriate adjustments made in them, in order to reduce the disparity between their objectives and the observed trends. The specific policy measures and the development programmes/projects included in the plans must also be changed appropriately. The adjustment process will involve major changes in resource allocations. It will be greatly assisted by policy-related studies, some of which are discussed below.

The national development strategy and policies on urban development are based on the assumption of relatively slow urbanization, and have as an important objective discouraging concentration of the urban population in the large metropolitan cities, primarily by building medium-sized and small towns as counter magnets to the large cities to which a large proportion of the rural migrants could be attracted. The strategy and policies must be modified, however, to provide for the prospects of continuing rapid urbanization up to the end of the century (and beyond), and increasing concentration of the urban population in the cities, including the large metropolitan cities. This will involve putting in place appropriate policy measures and development programmes/projects of adequate size to ensure expansion/improvement of urban housing, and the physical, economic and social infrastructures of the cities to keep pace with the growth of demands on account of population increase and economic development, and to alleviate the most acute shortages of urban housing and infrastructures.

Furthermore, institutional development measures and legislative reforms will need to be undertaken to

(a) attract larger private investment in housing for middle income groups, and for expansion and improvement of facilities for supplying services such as power and telecommunications, which can be sold at economic prices,
(b) ensure efficient management of the infrastructures and services; and
(c) improve urban administration in general.

At the same time the policy of building medium-sized and small towns as counter magnets to the large cities and as 'growth centres' must be modified to take account of its limitations. The development programmes and fiscal concessions, which are particularly generous in the case of growth centres located in backward regions, must be adjusted accordingly. The adjustment should aim particularly at improving the benefit/cost ratios of the development programmes and concessions by reducing their present high financial and social costs and increasing their benefits. The process will involve significant changes in resource allocations and will, as discussed in a latter at section, be assisted by studies on the social benefit-cost analysis of the development programmes and the concessions.

There are two principal objectives in the national strategy of regional development: (i) to reduce interregional disparities in economic growth and development by promoting economic growth in the slow growing and backward states; and (ii) to build small towns and large villages as micro regional service centres from which modern production techniques, essential inputs and services – administrative, economic, social and recreational – are provided to groups of villages. The service centres are seen as foci of modernization and economic development at the micro regional level. Because urbanization is an essential ingredient of economic development, the observed trend of more rapid urbanization during 1971–81 in the less developed states than in the more urbanized and more developed states, holds the promise of acceleration of economic growth in the former and reduction over time of interregional disparities. Active town formation in the less urbanized and less developed states, similarly, is promising for development of small towns and large villages as micro regional service centres and for economic development at the micro regional level.

PROBLEMS RELATING TO THE URBAN ENVIRONMENT

Shortages of Urban Housing and Infrastructures

The most serious problems are related directly or indirectly to the extreme shortage of housing, and to inadequacy of physical and social infrastructures to meet the needs of the urban low-and middle-income groups. Expansion and improvement of housing during the past 35 years has been far less than the needs arising from: (a) preexisting shortages which were acute in the large cities – Kolkata, Mumbai and Delhi and (b) increase in demand created by rapid growth of the urban population, some rise in *per capita* income and changes in lifestyles even of the urban poor. The shortages are the principal cause of the progressive deterioration of the urban environment during the past 20–25 years. Proliferation of slums is the most visible symptom of the environmental deterioration. The other major symptom is rapid increase in the levels of air and water pollution in or near the cities, far above the internationally accepted levels for maintaining human health and safety. The levels of air or water pollution in the largest Indian cities, notably Mumbai and Kolkata, are among the highest in the world. Apart from the factors mentioned above, the increase in pollution is due to the failure of the municipalities and the other concerned authorities either to take adequate pollution control measures themselves or to enforce pollution control regulations effectively.

The prospects for expansion and improvement of urban housing and infrastructures are assessed, keeping in view the following:

1. Growing demands created by rapid growth of the urban population and its increasing concentration in the cities;
2. The existing acute shortage of urban housing and pressures on the infrastructures and service facilities; and
3. Policy statements on expansion and improvement of urban housing and infrastructures and resource allocations for them in the Sixth and the Seventh Five Year Plans. Institutional development and legislative reforms, which also have an important influence on the expansion/improvement are referred to very briefly.

Before discussing the prospects, however, it is necessary to make a distinction between total investment in the urban areas and that undertaken specifically to meet the needs for housing and services of the urban population. Since manufacturing industries and the service sector activities – public administration, trade and finance, transport and storage, and others – in which large investments are made in the development process to sustain their rapid growth, are all concentrated in the urban areas, total investment in the latter is quite large, and it constitutes a large proportion of the total investment in the economy. But most of the investment is made either directly in these sectors or in infrastructures, buildings etc., required for them. The concentration of the investment in the urban areas leads, however, to the erroneous impression of an 'urban' bias in development planning' (Lipton, 1980). Secondly, it tends to mask the fact of quite inadequate investment for meeting the needs of the urban population.

Separation of the two types of urban investment, although essential, often presents serious difficulties. This is because expansion of infrastructures and service facilities is accomplished typically through projects designed to meet both non domestic and domestic needs. In case of buildings, while the distinction between nonresidential and residential buildings is easily made, difficulties arise when the same building is put to both nonresidential and residential uses.

The shortages of housing and the pressures on the infrastructures and service facilities, which are quite incapable of coping with the rapidly increasing demands on them, are most serious in the large cities. Furthermore, overcoming the shortages through expansion and improvement projects requires much larger investments, and also presents more difficult problems of organization and management in the large cities than in the smaller urban places, although there is some disagreement on the unit costs of expansion and improvement of the infrastructures and service facilities also being higher in the cities (Linn, 1982). Urban administration and maintenance and operation of the infrastructures and the social services are also more difficult and complex in the large cities than in smaller urban places. Urban administration is more difficult partly because of the large size and ethnic diversity of the populations of the large cities and existence of large disparities of income and consumption within it. The latter two are a major source of social tension in the Indian cities, which has been erupting into violent conflict with increasing frequency in recent years. The large size of the infrastructures and of social service systems requires efficient maintenance and operation by high-quality managers and technicians; however, they are in short supply and are not attracted by the pay scales and other conditions of service offered by the cities.

The large inputs of finance, technical and professional manpower and high-quality management needed for the expansion and improvement of urban housing and infrastructures and social services must be provided, *at present and in the foreseeable future*, primarily by the public sector, although with appropriate changes in policies, progressively larger contributions could be made also by the private sector. Programmes, such as slum improvement and provision of site-and-service housing, for the urban poor, can be undertaken only with large subsidies from the government. Similar subsidies are required for expansion and improvements of water supplies and sanitation services, if these have to be provided to the urban poor, free or at nominal rates. Private investment in housing is concentrated at present on meeting the needs of the affluent and middle-income groups, or in commercial buildings. With the present high prices of urban land and the high construction costs, financial returns from construction of housing for even lower middle-income groups are not high enough to attract large private investment.

However, the necessary public sector resources of finance and technical manpower have not been available during the past 35 years, and judging from the policy statements and financial allocations in the Sixth and the Seventh Five Year Plans, they are unlikely to become available in the foreseeable future. Public investment in urban housing remains extremely small. In both plans, outlays proposed for 'housing and urban development' constituted only about 2.5 percent the total public sector outlays, and related only to small programmes of providing housing for selected groups, such as industrial labour and the 'economically weaker sections' of the community, slum improvement and urban planning and development. As regards expansion and improvement of urban infrastructures and service facilities, special provisions were made only for water supply and sanitation; expansion and improvement of all the others, had to be financed mainly from the allocations for them under the national plans.

During the last few years, the shortages of power and telecommunications in the large cities, and of inter city transport and other services, revenues from which can cover most of the costs of their expansion and operation, have been reduced significantly. Besides large public investments, improvements in management and increasing application of technological advances, have contributed to the improvement. There is the prospect also of further reduction or even elimination of the shortages, particularly if user charges are raised to reflect the true costs of providing the services and private investment is attracted for the expansion and improvement projects.

But as the following discussion indicates, similar improvement is not expected in housing for the urban low-and middle-income groups, or in water supply, waste disposal, or mass transit facilities which cater to their basic needs. The token provisions for housing and related development programmes in both plans, despite clear recognition of the progressive aggravation of the urban housing shortage – from 5.1 million dwelling units at the beginning of the *Sixth plan* to 5.9 million dwelling units at its end – indicate the planners' reluctance to give higher priority to these programmes and commit large funds for them. Both plans stated that the responsibility for providing urban housing is primarily of the private sector. The *Sixth plan* had stated also that 'the public sector has only a marginal though promotional role in the provision of urban housing (Planning Commission, 1980: 392).

The *Seventh plan* stated, 'The time has now come for the Government to set before itself a clear goal in the field of housing and launch a major housing effort; not so much to build but to promote housing activity through the supply of fiscal and financial infrastructure such that every family will be provided with adequate shelter within a definite time horizon (Government of India Planning Commission, 1985: 293). It recommended strengthening of the two existing institutions, the Housing and Urban Development

Corporation (HUDCO), which undertakes construction of housing for the groups mentioned above, and the Housing Development Finance Corporation (HDFC), which caters for fairly well-to-do groups, and establishment of a new institution, the National Housing Bank to increase the flow of private investment in housing. The Bank is expected to obtain funds from the capital market and through deposits from prospective house owners; the small provision of Rs 500 million for it in the plan is intended only for establishing it and providing it with initial working capital.

But the plan did not recommend provision by the government of any incentives, fiscal or otherwise, to assist the Bank in attracting sufficient funds and thus contributing to reducing significantly the shortfall of private investment in housing for the urban low and middle income groups. However, the 1987-88 budget did begin to introduce fiscal incentives to increase such investment.

Such incentives are essential if the Bank is to attract large enough funds to assist construction of housing on a large scale. Even in an affluent country, such as the USA, private investment in housing for the middle income groups is assisted through financial incentives, such as provision (until recently) of loans at low rates of interest by the Federal Housing Administration, and exemption from income tax of house owners' interest payment on mortgages for their houses. Housing for low income groups is constructed primarily by the city administrations and is heavily subsidized by the federal, state and city governments. Mass transit projects are similarly heavily subsidized.

The planners and other policy makers could not but be aware that with the present high prices of urban land, and high construction costs, most of the private investment in housing will remain concentrated on meeting the demands of the rich and the upper middle-income groups, and that the housing needs of the urban poor will continue to be ignored. Referring to the scarcity and high cost of urban land, the *Sixth plan* stated that, 'there is a general feeling that costs of land have increased substantially... fears are expressed that urban housing might become too expensive for a large number of people. It would be useful, therefore, to initiate systematic investigations into the functioning of urban land markets and to identify the causes of the increase in the value of land. Measures can then be recommended to promote a more efficient and equitable functioning of the urban land market so that these enormous and unwarranted increases in land values are checked' (Government of India Planning Commission, 1980: 393). But the *Seventh plan* makes no reference to any such investigations or to measures to reduce the prices of urban land, which have continued to increase rapidly.

The planners and other policy makers in the central and state governments must be aware also of the growing dichotomy in the large cities between provision of services, such as health care and education, for the affluent on the one hand and the low-and middle-income groups on the other. Private hospitals and nursing homes, having the latest equipment and other facilities, staffed by specialists trained in the USA, UK or Europe, and charging prices which only the affluent can afford to pay, are coming up in increasing numbers. A similar trend is developing in education, with a rapid increase in the number of 'public' schools, and privately run professional colleges, which charge high fees and generally require, in addition, substantial 'donations' for admission to them. But the public services catering to the needs of the middle-and low-income groups – the white and blue collar workers in manufacturing and service industries, the large numbers employed in the urban informal sector, the unemployed and others – continue to deteriorate because they are starved of funds, not only for the expansion needed to meet growing demands, but also for efficient maintenance and operation.

Token provisions for low-income group housing and slum improvement and absence of provisions for major expansion and improvement of essential public services, such as health care and education, indicate that the *planners and other policy-makers are quite reconciled to progressive aggravation of the present shortages of urban housing and deterioration of the public services.* This attitude of theirs is due mainly to the thinking that investment in expansion and improvement of urban housing, infrastructures and services is consumption-oriented. The contribution of the investment to the welfare of the urban population, increasing the productivity of the urban workers and thereby accelerating national economic growth, is not appreciated. The latter two will result principally from the following:

1. Increase in the quantum of productive work with reduction in losses of the workers' man days on account of sickness, and of man hours during the working day because of savings of the time now spent by the workers in commuting to work,

or in obtaining essential services, such as medical care for themselves or their families in public hospitals;

2. Higher and better-quality output by healthier, less tired and more satisfied workers; and
3. Similar saving of time of the workers' wives or other members of their families, spent at present in waiting at public taps for obtaining the daily needs of water, traveling to work, obtaining medical treatment, etc. The time saved could be spent in work yielding supplementary income for the family, or in better homemaking and child care.

The effect of the increase in productivity on national economic growth would be quite large. The urban skilled workers, professionals and entrepreneurs are the most productive and dynamic element in our population. Furthermore, as mentioned in Section I, almost 50 percent of the GDP is already being generated in the urban areas and the proportion is expected to increase to almost 60 percent by the year 2000. Studies on social benefit-cost analysis of programmes for expansion/improvement of urban housing and infrastructures, discussed in Section III below, will, by quantifying their costs and benefits, contribute to reducing the neglect of such programmes by the policy-makers.

A second reason for opposing larger investment in the programmes aimed at improving living conditions in the large cities is the view, not stated often but widely held nevertheless, that the improvement will only increase the attraction of the cities for potential migrants and accelerate migration into them. The validity of the view needs to be tested, however, through studies on motives for migration to the large cities. In this context, the relative importance of the 'pull' and 'push' factors on which there has been much discussion in India, needs to be evaluated under the conditions of the 1980s.

There is a similar hiatus between perception of problems and action to overcome them in the areas of institutional and legislative reform. The *Seventh plan* stated, 'Apart from the fact that many of the municipal bodies are moribund or have been superceded, they are being administered badly, have undeveloped and/or eroded tax systems and suffer from lack of capital funds for development. The services they provide have deteriorated over the years and there seems no sign of reversal. Over-crowded and under-serviced, an increasing proportion of areas of urban conglomerations are being turned into slums' (Planning Commission, 1985: 297). The plan recommended revitalization of these bodies and major reform of urban tax administration, but no specific recommendations were made in this regard.

Legislative reform is a similar case. Thus the planners and other policy-makers are well aware of the need for reform of the present rent control laws, because of which virtually no repair or renovation of the older housing stock of the cities has been undertaken for more than four decades, with the result that most of the stock is in an advanced stage of deterioration. Furthermore, the laws reduce the incentives for both construction of housing for renting to the middle and low income groups, and the availability of the houses that are constructed. A proportion of the new houses are not rented by their owners for fear of their rents being controlled, and because of the difficulty of evicting the tenants when they want the houses for themselves. But the silence of both plans on reform of the rent control laws, and the scarcity of official statements on it, indicate that neither the central government nor any of the state governments are ready to undertake the reform.

The gloomy prospect outlined above would change if there was a radical change in policies followed by effective action in the areas of formulation and implementation of development programmes, and institutional and legislative reforms. Such change is unlikely, however, except under threat of a crisis such as the total breakdown of civic administration in a large metropolitan city. The crisis will bring home to the central and state governments the magnitude and severity of the urban problem, and the need for urgent and effective action to meet it. The parallel here is with the change in policies and programmes relating to environmental protection and pollution control, following the Bhopal tragedy of December 1984, but such radical change can be mentioned at present as no more than a possibility.

Proliferation of Slums

Proliferation of slums, unavoidable in the present and foreseeable future situation of extreme shortage of housing for the urban poor presents, however, very difficult problems; political, legal, economic, social and moral. The official policies (or rather non-policies) towards the slums reflect an ambivalence which is partly inherent in the situation but derives also from the ambivalent attitude of the urban affluent and middle income groups towards the slum dwellers. The policies have four major components:

1. to prevent establishment of slums in the central areas of the cities and on public (or private) lands which are designated for other essential uses;
2. to clear these areas of slums, generally by moving their residents to housing colonies located in the peripheral regions of the cities. The removal generally requires use of force by the police or other authorities, although it is often accompanied by providing house sites and financial assistance for resettlement in these colonies to a proportion of the residents;
3. to tolerate existence and expansion of existing slums in other locations; and
4. sporadically to undertake slum improvement programmes, such as improvement of approach roads, extension of bus routes and electricity and water lines, improvement of sanitation within the slums particularly by construction of drains and improvement of arrangements for disposal of solid waste, providing public water taps and street lights, and opening of schools, training centres, health centres, community centres, etc.

These programmes are undertaken most frequently before elections to the municipal bodies or to the state legislatures, and have the political motive of winning the support of the slum dwellers for the party in power. Besides improving the environmental conditions of the slums and reducing the hardships of their residents, the programmes mean recognition by the authorities, first *de facto* but later also *de jure*, of the rights of the slum dwellers to continue to live in them undisturbed.

Slum clearance is a traumatic process which causes great hardship and generally also enormous financial loss to its victims. They are left shelterless and the demolition of their homes means that their savings of many years are wiped out. As a result, it encounters fierce resistance from the slum dwellers and leads frequently to litigation which may be bitter and prolonged. The trauma and the bitterness are mitigated only partially by the provision of alternative house sites in the peripheral regions and financial assistance for rehabilitation and resettlement in them. Delays in providing the sites or the financial assistance, or in extending the basic services to the new locations due to bureaucratic inefficiency, indifference or corruption, represent one set of causes of the resentment and opposition. A second set relates to the hardship, loss of income and increase in expenditure suffered by the slum dwellers, on account of separation by long distances between their places of living and of working. The long journeys to work in the city centres are time-consuming and expensive; frequently public transport needed for the journeys is just not available. Many workers, especially those working in the informal sector, lose their jobs and become destitute. Further loss is caused by the womenfolk and other members of the households losing their jobs as domestics, etc., in the households of affluent and middle-income groups.

Recognizing these difficulties and problems of eviction and relocation of slum dwellers, the *Sixth five-year plan* placed emphasis on environmental improvement of slums, mainly through improvement of drainage, sewerage and sanitation, which were considered to be the principal causes of an area becoming a slum. The plan proposed an investment of Rs 1500 million to benefit 10 million out of the estimated 33.1 million slum dwellers by 1985. Nearly one-fifth of the total urban population was estimated to be living in slums.

The *Seventh plan* continued the emphasis on environmental improvement, and increased the total allocation for it to Rs 2696 million, to benefit about 9 million slum dwellers; just over half of the 17.5 million estimated not to have been covered by the *Sixth plan* programme by 1985. Allocation *per capita* was raised to Rs 300 from Rs 100 in the *Sixth plan*. The plan also recommended providing security of tenure to the slum dwellers so that, 'they may develop a stake in maintaining and improving their habitat' (Planning Commission, 1985: 290, 299).

It is evident from the above that the programmes of slum improvement included in the plans are neither comprehensive nor adequate in coverage. Environmental improvement is undoubtedly important, but so are expansion and improvement of other essential services, notably medical care, education (including education for citizenship and in improved hygiene) and training to equip for productive employment the large numbers of unemployed, most of whom turn to crime to survive. It is noteworthy that the need for providing security of tenure was recognized only in the *Seventh plan*. Furthermore, allotment of alternative house sites in colonies located at long distances from the city centres, is made only to small proportions of the slum dwellers. The planning of the new colonies is poor, and there are long delays in providing essential services to them. Often the colonies are virtually forgotten after the evicted slum dwellers are moved to them.

These deficiencies reflect an ambivalence among the planners and other policy-makers towards the slum dwellers, which is, in our view, a reflection of the attitude of the urban affluent and middle-income groups towards them. The services of the slum dwellers, who constitute the great majority of workers in almost all sectors of the urban economy, are needed and wanted. But the affluent and the middle-income groups do not care where and how they live, except that they should not live in the central areas of the cities, where most of them work. This attitude is similar in many ways to that of the South African whites towards the blacks: the whites also want the blacks to work in the cities, but not to live in them. The ambivalence must end and give place to clear policies, backed by appropriate programmes which are comprehensive and adequate in coverage.

Pollution of Water and Air

The other major symptom of deterioration of the urban environment is rapid increase in the levels of water and air pollution. The increase is due to a complex of reasons, of which the most important are related to the failure of the municipal bodies or other concerned authorities to:

(a) expand systems of disposal of solid and liquid waste, put in place adequate systems of sewage treatment,
(b) enforce pollution control regulations to reduce or eliminate discharges of polluting affluents into the rivers and other water bodies by industrial units, power stations etc., and of particulate matter in the atmosphere, and
(c) take measures, such as requiring proper maintenance of motor vehicles to reduce pollution from their exhausts. The rapid increase in the number of motor vehicles is a principal cause of increasing air pollution over or near the large cities. The two-

or three-wheeler vehicles, powered by two-stroke engines, are the principal source of noise pollution in the cities.

Following the Bhopal tragedy, there is greater awareness among the policy makers, the news media and the urban population of the dangers of location of hazardous and highly polluting industries near large cities or other areas of high population density. There is also greater awareness of the need to strengthen the laws relating to pollution control and to enforce them more strictly. The personal interest taken by the Prime Minister in environmental issues and in the project for cleaning the river Ganga has also contributed to the increased awareness. However, it will be some time before the awareness results in more effective pollution control measures. The Ganga Clean-up Project, of which the principal component is improvement and expansion of sewerage treatment facilities in cities or towns located along the river, through repair, renovation or expansion of existing facilities or construction of new ones, is the first major project to reduce pollution levels. It will have to be followed by several others, stricter enforcement of pollution control laws, and avoiding the location of hazardous and polluting industries before a significant reduction in pollution levels can be expected.

The greatly increased awareness of environmental problems and the need for effective action to meet them is reflected in the chapters in the *Sixth* and *Seventh Plans* and particularly in the increase of more than 10 times in the outlays for environmental programmes in the *Seventh Plan*. The outlay in the *Seventh Plan* was Rs 4279 million including Rs 2400 million for the Ganga Action Plan, compared with Rs 400 million in the *Sixth Plan*. The *Seventh Plan* also stated that 'water borne pollution from both community and industrial sources is probably the most important health hazard in India' (Planning Commission, 1985: 388).

NEED FOR POLICY-RELATED STUDIES

The city surveys conducted in the 1950s by the leading Indian Universities for the Research Programmes Committee of the Planning Commission were the first set of urban studies done in the post independence period. The surveys concentrated on collection of data on the economies and the demographic and other social characteristics of the cities. Some of the data proved useful later for preparation of 'master plans' of the cities, but most of it remained unutilized.

Beginning with Delhi in the late 1950s, long-term 'master plans' were prepared during the 1960s for several cities, including Kolkata, Mumbai and Bangalore among the largest cities. The studies conducted for preparation of the plans concentrate on meeting their data needs, e.g. estimating the needs for expansion and improvement of housing, water supply, transport and other infrastructures and preparation of projects and programmes for meeting the needs, but they also provided much useful data on their economies and demographic and social characteristics. Projections of growth of population, and of employment in manufacturing and service sectors were of particular interest. Some data was collected also on the relationships of the cities with the regions of which they formed part and of which they were the industrial, commercial and other services centres. Since then, most studies by official agencies, have been undertaken to meet the data needs of individual projects and programmes, while studies by individual scholars or nonofficial agencies, have related primarily to subjects of interest to them.

Reference has been made earlier to the need for studies which could assist formulation of policies and programmes for urban and regional development. The studies should include evaluation of existing policies and programmes and should provide data for refinement or modification of these and initiating new ones. Three such studies are discussed below to illustrate their range and potential contribution to policy formulation:

1. Comparative social benefit-cost analysis of investment in urban housing and infrastructures, and in the directly productive sectors such as agriculture and manufacturing (and in infrastructures to meet the needs of these sectors) which are given high priority in the plans;
2. Social benefit-cost analysis of programmes and incentives for industrial dispersal and regional development; and
3. Working of the urban development and planning institutions – the development authorities of the large cities and agencies

having responsibility for preparation of plans for urban regions, such as the National Capital Region.

The emphasis on social benefit-cost studies arises from the urgent need to improve efficiency of allocation and utilization of resources for urban and regional development.

Comparative Social Benefit-cost Analysis of Investment for Improvement of Urban Housing and Infrastructures and in the Directly Productive Sectors

The studies, which are needed urgently, will contribute to ending the present anomalies and distortions, which are a major reason for public and private investment in urban housing and infrastructures, and funds for maintenance of the existing stock of housing in good condition and efficient operation of essential services, remaining much below the needs.

The principal anomaly is that manufacturing industries and service sector activities, located in the cities or in their peripheral regions, appropriate the economies of agglomeration provided by the cities without having to contribute adequately to the costs of providing housing for their workers, or of expansion, improvement and efficient operation of the infrastructures and service facilities, the needs for which are created by their presence. Taxes on buildings levied by the municipalities, meet only a small proportion of the costs of providing the services; official buildings, such as the offices of the central and state governments and of many public sector enterprises, are generally exempt from payment of these taxes. User charges on services, such as water supply, waste disposal and mass transit, which are provided by the municipal bodies or other agencies, are kept low, much lower than the costs of providing the services, while welfare services such as education and medical care, are provided free or on payment of nominal charges. Provision of low-priced or free services contributes to keeping wages in manufacturing and service sector enterprises lower than they would be otherwise. The deficits of the city governments in maintaining and operating the infrastructures and services are met by subsidies from the central and/or state governments, which also provide most of the funds for their expansion and/or improvement. The situation contributes to confusion of fiscal responsibilities, inefficiency and waste. Furthermore, since the allocations by the central or the state governments for these purposes are much smaller than the needs, there is an acute housing shortage and the services, provided by the cities, progressively deteriorate.

The benefits and costs of investment in housing for workers and other low or middle-income groups, and in urban infrastructures and services facilities must be measured following social accounting principles. The costs should be calculated using shadow prices (e.g. for interest on capital) wherever necessary. Appropriate adjustments should be made for externalities, such as the hardships, ill health and loss of efficiency, suffered by the urban residents as a result of the shortages of housing, infrastructures and service facilities.

The benefits should include both direct benefits of meeting the basic needs for shelter, water, education, medical care, etc., and indirect benefits, mentioned earlier, such as increases in productivity and income of the urban residents resulting from improvement in their health or from the savings of their time and energy.

It could be argued that the benefits from improvement in productivity of the workers are illusory in a situation of over manning in most manufacturing and service enterprises and that those from the savings of time and energy of the other members of their families are also spurious because they already have much leisure. However, such arguments suffer from the same flaw as the earlier argument, based on the now discarded concept of zero marginal productivity of agricultural labour in the situation of large unemployment or rural underemployment, in India and other densely populated low income developing countries.

The comparative social benefit-cost analysis will have several benefits. First, it will assist in more rational perception of priorities in public investment. Investment in housing and urban services will no longer be treated as 'consumption oriented' and given much lower priority than investment in the directly productive (and associated infrastructure) sectors. The analysis could demonstrate, for instance, that the benefit-cost ratios in projects of slum improvement, or of providing site-and-service or other housing for the low-and middle-income groups, or of improvement of water supplies, sanitation, urban transport, etc., were similar to or higher than those in many projects in the directly productive sectors, such as agriculture and manufacturing.

Secondly, the costs can, after measurement, be passed on to the users of the services and those responsible for creating the externalities through appropriate fiscal or other means, in much greater measure than is possible in the absence of such analysis. Thus, manufacturing, commercial and other establishments can be made to contribute much more than they do at present to the costs of providing housing to their workers (even in improved slums) and to the expansion, maintenance and operation of the infrastructures and service facilities. The polluting industries can be made to pay for the clean-up of water or air, required as a result of their activities.

There will undoubtedly be stiff resistance to such transfer of the costs, on the ground that it will increase costs in manufacturing, commercial and other sectors, but the transfer will also provide a powerful incentive to the enterprises for reducing costs by increasing efficiency, and for reducing discharges of polluting liquid or other wastes. These would be achieved through better management, reducing over manning, conservation of energy and water, switch-over to lower waste producing processes, finding economic uses for waste products and, finally, by installing equipment for reducing discharges of polluting effluents. There would also be a strong incentive for shifting of industries to the peri-urban areas of the metropolitan cities, to industrial suburbs, satellite towns, and to 'growth centres' located in rural regions, in order to escape the high social costs of agglomeration in the cities.

Social Benefit-cost Analysis of Programmes and Incentives for Industrial Dispersal, Development of 'Growth Centres' and of Micro Regional Service Centres

Reference has been made in the beginning to the principal objectives of the national policies on urban and regional development, which are:

1. dispersal of industries away from the large cities, particularly their central areas, to relieve congestion in them and slow down their growth, and to promote the growth of smaller cities and towns;
2. acceleration of economic growth in the backward regions,

including location of industries in the 'growth centres' within those regions;

3. building up small towns or large villages as micro regional service centres.
4. the first two objectives are sought to be achieved through a number of measures of which the following are the most important:
   (a) development in the peripheral regions and satellite towns of the large cities, in small cities and towns and in the 'growth centres', industrial estates or areas, provided with all the physical and economic infrastructures needed by the industries;
   (b) giving financial assistance – low interest loans from official financial institutions, and subsidies – and technical assistance. The latter is of particular value to small enterprises;
   (c) giving priority in allocation of scarce resources such as foreign exchange for imports of equipment, spares and raw materials and of construction materials in periods of shortage of these; and
   (d) grant of fiscal concessions including exemption from payment of specified taxes for limited periods. The financial and other incentives are particularly generous for industries locating in regions designated as 'backward'.

The development programmes and concessions have high financial and social costs, which are borne primarily by the central and/or state governments, and to a lesser extent by the private sector. Building of industrial estates or areas requires large investments; the financial and technical assistance involves considerable expenditures; and the fiscal concessions involve foregoing of revenues by the governments. The costs, both financial and social, of location of industries in the backward regions are often very high. Industrial units locating in them may incur losses or go through extended periods of low returns to capital because of deficiencies in infrastructures and difficulties in attracting and retaining high quality managers, technical personnel and skilled workers. National economic growth may be slowed, if large investments have been made in the industrial units.

Development of small towns or large villages as micro-regional service centres is promoted by locating in them a complex of facilities which provide economic, administrative, social and recreational services to the villages located in the micro regions. The economic services include *inter alia*, agricultural extension; distribution of agricultural inputs, such as chemical fertilizers, improved seed and pesticides, and intermediates like cement and steel, and consumer goods; institutional credit, and marketing and processing of agricultural products. The 'service centres' are seen as focal points for providing essential services to the villages and for radiation of modernizing ideas and production techniques. They are also considered to be the most suitable locations for industries serving the micro-regional (or larger) markets, processing agricultural produce, or manufacturing simple consumer goods. The industries, construction works and the service facilities located in them are important sources of off-farm employment and additional income in villages located near them.

Reference has been made earlier to more rapid urbanization and more active town formation in the less urbanized and less-developed states than in the more urbanized and developed ones and the promise that this development holds for success of the policies relating to regional development and development of micro-regional service centres.

Such analysis needs to be supplemented, however, by carefully designed case studies of selected growth centres, industries and micro-regional service centres. Studies, on the one hand of 'growth centres' and industries, which have experienced rapid growth and have also contributed to vigorous growth in the regions served by them, and on the other, of centres and industries which have failed to achieve these, will assist in refinement of the policies of development of 'growth centres' and industrial dispersal to the backward regions. By identifying the factors which contribute to success or failure of these policies, they will make possible concentration of resources in growth centres and industries with greater chances of success. The financial and technical assistance and the fiscal or other concessions, provided by the governments, could also be modified to improve their benefit-cost ratios. Similarly, studies of both successful and unsuccessful micro-regional service centres will assist selection of small towns or large villages as such centres, and of the service facilities to be located in them.

Working of Development Authorities and Regional Planning Agencies

Within the last two decades or more, development authorities have been established for several metropolitan cities including Delhi and Kolkata. The concept of planning for sufficiently large regions which include, besides the metropolitan cities, their satellite towns and large rural areas, has been accepted and planning authorities have been established for them. Thus the National Capital Region, comprising besides the Delhi State, large areas of the adjoining states of Haryana and Uttar Pradesh, and a small area in Rajasthan, has been adopted as the planning region for providing the framework for preparation of the long-term 'master plan' for the Delhi metropolitan area, and for expansion of the physical and social infrastructures in it. But there is urgent need for defining more clearly than is the case at present, the functions of these bodies and their relationships with the municipal corporations, the ministries and departments of the central and state governments and the semiautonomous agencies, such as electricity boards, which have a responsibility for providing electricity, water and sewerage, transport and other services. Thus the DDA, originally established for updating of the 'master plan' of Delhi and overseeing its implementation, has over the years assumed a variety of functions, including construction of low-and middle-income group housing and some purely municipal functions, such as approval of building plans. The latter create conflicts of jurisdiction and problems of coordination of activities with the other agencies. The planning authority for the NCR is facing serious problems of coordination and of acceptance of its recommendations by the central or state governments, and the other concerned agencies.

Studies on the working of these bodies, with focus on the problems that they face, will assist in clearer definition of their functions, and their relationships with the other agencies concerned. They will provide the bases for recommendations to make them more efficient and effective.

CONCLUSION

This survey has emphasized the urgent need for reappraisal with a view to making needed changes in the national policy on urbanization and in programmes of urban development. The reappraisal has to be based on acceptance of the prospects of: (a) continuance of rapid urbanization at least to the end of the century at rates comparable to or higher than the average rate for 1961–81; and (b) increasing concentration of the urban population in the cities. The current rapid deterioration of the environment, particularly of the large cities, caused by an acute shortage of housing, pressures on infrastructures and service facilities, proliferation of slums and growing pollution of water and air, has to be checked and reversed.

The needed changes in policies and programmes will require large increases in public and private investment for expansion and improvement of urban housing and infrastructures, and major institutional and legislative reforms. They would be greatly assisted by policy oriented studies relating particularly to social benefit-cost analysis of investment in urban housing and infrastructures, and the working of urban development and planning institutions. However, the change process can only start with appreciation within the central and the state governments of the magnitude and severity of the urban problem and the urgency of alleviating it in the interests of both welfare and economic growth.

NOTES

1. Published in *International Journal of Urban Regional Research*, Edward Arnold, ISSW 0309-1310. This paper was presented at the meeting of Committee 21, 'Urban and regional development', of the International Sociological Congress, New Delhi, August 1986. This revised draft takes into account the changes in policies and other developments up to March 1987.
2. Growth rate of GDP *per capita* for India is projected at 2.5 percent under the low-case scenario. The rate for the high-case scenario is not projected in the WDR, but is inferred as being lower than the rate for 'low-income Asia' by 0.5 percent per annum, as under the low-case scenario.the Appendix on (pp. 642–643).

REFERENCES

Bose, A. (1973) *Studies in India's urbanization 1901–71,* Tata-McGraw Hill, Mumbai and New Delhi.

Government of India Population Censuses of India: 1961–1981.

Government of India, Planning Commission, (1980) *Sixth five-year plan 1980–85,* Government of India, New Delhi.

Government of India, Planning Commission, (1985) *Seventh five-year plan 1985–90,* Government of India, New Delhi.

Linn, J.F. (1982) *The costs of urbanization in the developing countries*, Economic Development and Cultural Change 30 (3) pp. 625–48.

Lipton, M. (1980) *Why poor people stay poor: a study of urban bias in world development*, Heritage Publishers, New Delhi.

Mohan, R. (1985) *Urbanization in India's future*, Population and Development Review 11 (4).

Sundaram, K. (1986) *Growth, inequality and poverty: the Indian experience.* Centre for Policy Research, New Delhi.

World Bank (1984) *The World Development Report*, The World Bank, Washington DC.

4

Integrated Rural and Urban Development: A Strategy for Spatial Development in India[1]

INTRODUCTION

The principal argument of this paper is that integrated rural and urban development should be the centerpiece of the national spatial development strategy and that the strategy should be supported by appropriate policies, programs and resource allocations under the five year plans. It is explained that the perception of competition between rural and urban development, which has dominated national planning since its inception in the 1950's, however relevant it may have been in the past, is no longer relevant. Persistence of this perception and its consequent policies and resource allocations in successive five year plans have resulted in giving high priority to rural development and relative negligence of urban development.

THE POLICY BACKGROUND

The high priority for rural development is reflected in policy statements and resource allocations in previous five year plans, manifestos of political parties and pronouncements of political leaders. Its latest manifestation was in the paper "Approach to the Eighth Five Year Plan," prepared by the Planning Commission in May 1990, under the aegis of Janata Party Government, headed by Shri V.P. Singh. It was stated in the paper;

The new mandate rightly stresses the need to correct these distortions and to reorient development policy in such a way that it gives primacy to the immediate and urgent needs of the poor-reserving at least half the public outlays for the benefit of rural areas, and emphasis on village and small scale industries to produce goods and services for mass consumption using labor-intensive techniques, reflect these concerns (Planning Commission 1989: 5).

It is true that only about 1/4th of India's total population, 23.3 percent in 1981 and 25.7 percent in 1991, is urban and that proportion would still be less than 30 percent even by the end of the century (Table 4.1).

Table 4.1: Trends in Total Urban Population and Population of Cities-India (1951-2001)

	1951	*1961*	*1971*	*1981*	*1991**	*2001**
Total population (millions)	361.0	439.2	548.2	683.3	844.3	1029.0++
Urban population (millions)	62.4	78.9	109.1	159.5	217.2	294.0++
Urban/total population (%)	17.3	18.0	19.9	23.3	25.7	28.6
Annual exponential growth rate of urban population(%)	3.47	2.34	3.21	3.83	3.09	3.09
Population of cities (millions)	27.5	39.9	61.2	94.5	138.8	N.A.
Urban population living in cities (per cent)	44.0	50.6	56.1	59.2	63.9	N.A.
Number of million-plus cities	5	6	9	12	23	39++
Population of million-plus cities (millions)	11.7	17.9	27.4	42.1	70.6	N.A.
Proportion of population of million-plus cities to:						
(a) Urban population	17.8	22.6	25.1	26.4	32.5	N.A.
(b) Total population	3.2	4.1	5.0	6.2	8.4	N.A.

Sources: Registrar General and Census Commissioner, India: 1991. (Percentages have been calculated.)
— Projections for 2001: Nath, V. 1991—2938., * Provisional

++ As per 2001 Census, total population is 1027 m, Urban population 285 m (23.8% of the total population is Urban and the number of million and cities is 45.

However, more than 70 percent of the GDP is estimated to be produced in the non-agricultural sectors which are concentrated in urban areas (Planning Commission 1992 Vol. 1: 54). Mohan has estimated that in 1980–81 the urban population contributed 46.9 percent of total output to the economy and the rural-urban ratio of value added per worker has increased progressively from 1:2.7 in 1970–71 to 1:3.34 by 1994–95 (Mohan 1985: 637–39). Furthermore, the poor are not confined to the rural areas as Dandekar and Rath concluded in their pioneering and seminal study. "Poverty in India" (1971). They found that 30 percent of the rural population was below the poverty line in 1961–62 but almost half of the urban population was also so.

It may be expected that the election manifestos of political parties would emphasize the need for high priority to rural development. The rural areas, with 75 percent of the population, have the votes which the parties need for being successful in the elections. The emphasis was justified also in the early 1950s when a large proportion of the villages did not have basic services such as approach roads, primary schools, access to health centers, and even adequate water supply facilities. Agriculture was traditional and productivity per worker and per hectare was low. The villagers felt isolated and neglected. However, it is not justified in the 1990s when the basic services mentioned above, are available to most of the villages. As a result of various agricultural development programs implemented during the previous 4 decades, agricultural production has increased by more than 3 times its level in the early 1950s, with most of the increase coming from increase in productivity. Progress in rural development may be expected to continue in the foreseeable future and could accelerate faster with more efficient implementation of rural development programmes. The emphasis should now be shifted to urban development, neglect of which has two major effects. First, it reduces productivity per urban worker which could be one of the reasons depressing national economic growth. Second, it deprives the rural areas of further progress provided by interaction with the urban areas.

India had a comparatively low rate of increase in GNP per capita (1.9% p.a.) during 1965-90, less than 1/3rd of the rate in China (5.8% p.a.), lower than rates in Pakistan (2.5%) and Sri Lanka (2.9%) and much lower than the rates in the ASEAN countries. Despite India's potential for rapid economic growth because of its wide variety of natural and human resources, the lower rate of GNP could be due, *in part*, to low productivity of urban workers (Table 4.2).

Table 4.2: Growth Rates of GDP and GNP Per Capita in India, China and Selected Countries of South and Southeast Asia, 1965-90 (Percent per Annum).

Country	*GDP*		*GNP per capita (U.S. $)*	
	1965-80	*1980-90*	*1990*	*1965-90*
India	3.6	5.3	350	1.9
China	6.8	9.5	370	5.8
Pakistan	5.2	6.3	380	2.5
Sri Lanka	4.0	4.0	470	2.9
Philippines	5.7	0.9	710	1.3
Thailand	7.3	7.6	1,420	4.4
Indonesia	7.0	5.5	570	4.5
Malaysia	7.4	5.2	2,320	4.0
Singapore	10.0	6.4	11,160	6.5

Source: World Bank 1992, 218.

Note:

Type of Economy	*GNP per capita in 1990*
Low income	Less than $ 610
Middle income	$ 611 – $ 7619
High income	$7620 or more

Large cities with a population of a million or more suffer most from relative neglect of urban development because shortages of housing and of physical and social infrastructures are acute in them. Furthermore, large proportions of their populations are poor and endure conditions of extreme hardship while living in slums and are using grossly inadequate services, ranging from water supply and sanitation to education and health care. There were 23 million-plus cities in 1991: they made up almost 1/3rd of the urban population and more than 8.0 percent of the total population of the country (Table 4.1). Their number is projected to increase to 39 in 2001 by the National Commission on Urbanization (NCU 1988: Vol. II, 40-41) and their share of the urban and total population of the country would also increase.

The perception of competition between rural and urban development should change such that rural and urban areas should be viewed as inter-related parts of a settlement system, which should be developed in an integrated manner. This point will be clearer from the discussion in the next section in which the principal types of rural-urban interaction are described along with their positive and negative effects. It should be added that among the 15 major states of the country, the interactions are greater in the states of Punjab, Haryana, Maharashtra, Gujarat, Karnataka, Tamil Nadu and Kerala and the western region of U.P. in which there is a spatially dispersed pattern of urbanization i.e. there is a large number of small and medium-sized towns and cities along with one or more metropolitan cities. The effects are much less in the States of Eastern and Central India, notably Bihar, Orissa, West Bengal and Assam and the eastern and central regions of U.P. and Madhya Pradesh. These states/regions have a concentrated pattern of urbanization i.e., their urban population is concentrated in a few large cities and the number of small and medium-sized towns/cities is relatively small.

It will be seen that in the states with dispersed urbanization the percentage of urban to total population, is higher than the national average in the majority of districts. On the other hand in states with concentrated urbanization the percentage is lower than the national average in the majority of districts. The best example of concentrated urbanization is West Bengal; almost all its urban population is concentrated in the districts of Kolkata, Howrah, and Hooghly which form part of the Kolkata Metropolitan District and those adjoining CMD while the rest of the state is largely rural.

It can be seen that states with dispersed urbanization are generally at a higher level of economic development than those with concentrated urbanization. The level of economic development of a region is dependent on a complex of factors. It would be useful to investigate if the type of settlement pattern is one of these factors.

PRINCIPAL RURAL-URBAN SOCIO-ECONOMIC INTERACTIONS

The principal types of interaction are listed below and are discussed at some length in subsequent paragraphs:

1. Use by villagers of commercial, industrial, social service and recreational facilities located in cities and towns;
2. Work in cities and towns by villagers living within commuting distance of them and use of such villages as dormitories by workers in the cities. Travel between rural homes and urban work places could be on foot, by bicycle, motorcycle, bus or train;

3. Production by villagers of food including high value perishable foods – milk, vegetables, meat, poultry products, fruit etc. – for urban markets;
4. Diversion of agricultural and other rural lands, located on fringes of cities for residential, industrial, commercial or other urban uses. The diversion is greatest on the periphery of large, rapidly growing cities where hundreds of hectares have been diverted to non-agricultural use and other large areas, which have been bought by developers or others for speculative gains, are lying idle;
5. Rural to urban migration.

Use by Villagers of Commercial, Industrial, Social Service and Recreational Facilities Located in Cities and Towns

The villagers go to urban places in order to sell their produce, to buy consumer, intermediate or producer goods, to obtain short or medium term loans from cooperative or commercial banks or to obtain the other services mentioned above. With progressive modernization of the rural economy as a result of improvement in transport and communications, almost universal electrification, spread of modern production techniques there is the rise of a rural middle class, which wants a high standard of living. The consumer goods include increasing numbers of motor bicycles, television sets, VCRs, gas cookers, refrigerators, air coolers and other durables. The intermediate goods include agricultural inputs, such as improved seeds, chemicals fertilizers, pesticides, fuel and spare parts for power driven equipment, cement, steel bars or corrugated iron sheets, needed for construction, repair or renovation of houses and other structures. The producer goods include both traditional, manually operated agricultural implements, such as ploughs as well as power driven equipment, such as tractors, threshers, and diesel or electricity driven pumps for irrigation.

One would expect that villagers would use the commercial and other service facilities located in small or medium-sized towns which are nearest to them. Based on this assumption, Johnson advocated in 1965 building some 10,000 to 12,000 new, small, market towns particularly in states or regions such as Bihar, Orissa, eastern Uttar Pradesh, and eastern Madhya Pradesh, in which the number of such towns was inadequate, as the most important component of the spatial development strategy for India (Johnson 1965). It is fortunate that no action was taken on the recommendation because its implementation would have meant a colossal waste of scarce public and private resources of finance, manpower and management.

The principal reasons for this reflection in retrospect are the following:

1. Most of the artificially built towns would have failed to grow as service centers. Growth of a town is a natural process, which is determined by a large number of variables, several of which cannot be foreseen;
2. With improvement in transport and communications, spread of information about prices and concentration of the marketable surplus with larger, more affluent farmers, there is a strong trend among them towards using the marketing and agro-processing facilities of larger market towns, most of which are located at district or divisional headquarters. As regards use of social service facilities, particularly facilities for medical or surgical treatment, villagers with even medium income use the facilities of hospitals, located in state capitals and in mega-cities like Delhi, Mumbai, Chennai and Kolkata.

This author does not differ, however, with Johnson's emphasis on the need for intermediate urbanization in order to relieve the growth pressure on cities (Johnson 1965). The strategy is also favoured by the Planning Commission in the Eighth Five Year Plan (Planning Commission 1992 Vol. II: 345 and 354-55) and other experts and policy makers (Lewis, 1972; National Capital Region Planning Board, 1988: 18). His main difference is with Johnson's advocacy of building small market towns with populations of 5,000-20,000. He feels, along with several others, that the towns or cities, which would serve as effective counter magnets to large metropolitan cities, need to be much larger. Using the data of the 1961 Census, Lewis had indicated a population range of 100,000-300,000 (Lewis, 1962). The Regional Plan NCR 2001 (NCRPB, 1988) implies increasing the population to almost 1 million. Meerut, which has been selected in the Plan as one of the 8 priority towns for deflecting population from Delhi had a population of almost 850,000 in 1991 and would have a population exceeding 1 million by 2001. This author would therefore emphasize:

1. Assisting growth of existing towns or cities rather than building new towns, and
2. Flexibility in selection of population range of the small and medium sized towns/cities, having in view the regional diversity in topography, climate, soil, population density and other conditions and the sizes of the existing towns/cities.

Work by Villagers in Cities and Towns Living Within Commuting Distance from Them

Such work increases employment and income thus providing relief from rural unemployment or under-employment and poverty, diversifies consumption among rural households and is also a strong influence for social change. Both, workers from poor landless and artisan families, belonging mainly to the scheduled castes, the scheduled tribes and other disadvantaged sections of rural community, including young men from farmers' families who are not needed for agricultural work or are disinclined towards it, are benefited (Tyagi, 1982). There is less pressure for rural-to-urban migration because rural living and urban work can be combined and there is less need for expanding housing and infrastructure facilities in the cities. The social change effects are produced by spread of urban consumption patterns and weakening of traditional ties of caste and community: they include reduction in disabilities suffered by the scheduled castes and the scheduled tribes.

Basu and Kashyap have noted a progressive increase in rural non-agricultural employment, based on the data of the Census of India 1981 and of the National Sample Survey. They mention that the share of non-agricultural workers in the rural work force increased from 14.3 percent in 1961 to 18.6 percent in 1983. Furthermore, based on their own micro-level studies in 24 regions of India with different agricultural typologies they give details about rural workers in small and medium sized towns (Basu and Kashyap, 1992).

The beneficial economic effects of non-agricultural work by farmers were observed also in a sample survey of farm households located near a small town in Kenya, about 100 kilometres north-east of Nairobi (Evans and Ngua, 1991). Another important finding of the study was that higher and more diversified income, resulting from non-agricultural employment, assisted the farmers in increasing agricultural productivity (per hectare and per worker) by adopting new, improved production practices. With such income, they could take the risks involved in the adoption of improved techniques, which farmers dependent on agricultural income alone were unwilling or unable to take.

Increasing Production of Perishable Foods Benefits both Farmers and Other Groups in Villages

It leads also to the establishment of backward or forward-linked industries in major production centers. Production and sale of milk by small, marginal farmers or the landless who keep one or two milk animals, has been an important component of dairy development in Khera district of Gujarat where the well known AMUL dairy is located. It is being actively encouraged now by the central government as well as by several state governments under the "Operation Flood" program. It may be mentioned that the majority of milk producers in Khera district are women. Payment by the dairy for the milk sold by them, adds to their income, which they can spend on meeting their own needs and those of their children. Furthermore, the payments raise their own status within the household. Production of poultry products, traditionally an activity of scheduled castes and scheduled tribes, has developed during the last four decades into a highly specialized and efficient small industry. Modern poultry farms have been established both near and within metropolitan areas of large cities and at various specialized centers. Production of fruit, which had been an industry with traditional well established centers of production has increased in most of them and has also spread to new centers. The forward linkage industries, such as canning of fruit and vegetables or manufacture of crates and cartons for sending them to markets, and production of butter cheese and powdered milk in the major milk producing regions, generate considerable employment, which is an important spin-off from the production.

There is a great potential for further increase in production of perishable foods for both domestic and international markets. The "Operation Flood" programme, under which pasteurized milk with specified fat contents is being supplied to the majority of residents of large cities, is an example of the potential for increasing production in the domestic market. Production in the highly competitive international markets is increasing, concentrating on products like mangoes or tropical vegetables in which India has an advantage.

Diversion of Rural Land Located on the Outskirts of Cities for Urban Uses has both Positive and Negative Effects

If the land is acquired from small, marginal farmers at low prices and payment of compensation to them is delayed, they become landless and have to work as laborers on construction projects or as domestic servants in the homes of skilled workers, professionals and managers in the new industrial, commercial enterprises. These effects have been noticed in the New Mumbai Area (Banerjee-Guha, 1991) and on a much larger scale in the vicinity of the industrial townships located next to the steel and heavy industry plants in the central and eastern states of India—Madhya Pradesh, Bihar, Orissa, West Bengal and Andhra Pradesh. Furthermore, the dispossessed former land-owners, who belong mainly to the scheduled tribes, suffer loss of social status and self esteem. These effects are the principal cause of discontent among the tribal populations of these states and tensions, which frequently erupted in violent conflict, between them and the new comers.

If payment of compensation is timely and adequate (or generous) and is used by the recipients in buying farmland elsewhere, starting non-agricultural enterprises, such as running of buses or trucks, small industries or retail or wholesale shops, education of children, their income increases and level of living improves. These beneficial effects are lost, however, if the funds are squandered in idleness, ostentatious consumption such as large expenditures on marriages, funerals, or other ceremonies, fighting elections or court cases, buying of expensive consumer goods, or in drinking and use of drugs (Tyagi, 1982, Bose, 1972). Furthermore, the lands are often kept out of cultivation for long periods, awaiting development of new residential colonies, establishment of factories, markets or training institutions, or for speculative gains by unscrupulous buyers. Finally, the habitation areas of the villages are often reduced to *ghettos* within the expanding cities, although most of the houses in them are converted from *kutcha* (built of mud and thatch) to *pucca* (built of kiln-baked bricks and mortar) and have electricity, running water and other services (Tyagi, 1982).

Rural to Urban Migration Reduces Under-Employment or Unemployment in the Villages and Increases Income Through Remittances.

On the other hand, the villagers are deprived of their most productive and dynamic manpower because most of the migrants are young men and women who aspire for more secure and higher income and a better life in the cities than in the villages. Although these aspirations are fulfilled only for a minority and the majority of the migrants find uncertain, low paid employment in the informal sector of the cities and have to live in squalor and misery in their slums, the possible advantages of migration is enough to induce a steady stream of migrants to the cities. Furthermore, most of them are not seasonal migrants, they go to live in the cities through most of their working life and return to their villages only at the end.

Variations in the number of migrants from year to year depends both on variations in employment opportunities in the cities and economic conditions in the villages. Thus, there would be large migration to a city during the period of its rapid growth due to industrial or other developments. Alternatively, scarcity or famine caused by crop failure, due to drought, floods or other reasons, in a rural region, is generally followed by a large emigration from it (Rao, 1990 pp. 24–28).

Migration to large cities at present is and that of the tea gardens of Assam or overseas in the last century, was predominantly from poor and backward districts of eastern U.P., Bihar, Orissa, coastal Andhra Pradesh and Tamil Nadu. The economies of some districts in these regions are often called remittance economies because remittance from migrants is the largest source of income there. However, the fact that the regions have remained backward and poor, despite more than a century of emigration, would indicate that the negative effects of migration has been dominant in these areas.

Migration to the Gulf countries from Kerala, Goa and neighboring districts of Karnataka from the late 1960s to the 1980s, or of Punjab Sikhs to the UK and the USA in the post-war period, are in a different category altogether. In these cases, the migrant and the areas of emigration and in-migration have all benefited. A study of migration of Punjab Sikhs to Britain brought out the following:

1. The migrants were mostly industrial workers, who lived in extremely congested houses in British cities and suffered

considerable hardship. But their children quickly moved, after education, to well paid white collar, skilled or professional jobs or started their own small retail stores or other business.

2. The hard work of the migrants at low wages, contributed to Britain's rapid economic growth during the 1950s and the 1960s.
3. Remittances from the migrants to their families in Punjab had a major share in investment in the improvement of agriculture that sparked the green revolution in the state (Helweg, 1986, 376–386).

How the migrants make out in the areas of in-migration depends on their background, skills and aspirations. The great majority of Punjab Sikhs who migrated to Britain were peasant proprietors eking out a subsistence living in their home districts. They migrated to Britain in search of prosperity and had, therefore, a strong motivation to educate their children and equip them for white collar jobs so that they would not have to endure the hardship of doing heavy manual labor for long hours in factories and living in crowded rooms that they themselves had to endure. It is not surprising, therefore, that their children moved quickly after education to white collar jobs.

Another example is provided by migrants to Delhi in the period before 1961 and the two decades, 1961-71 and 1971-81 for which data are available from the Regional Plan 2001 National Capital Region.

The proportion from Punjab declined during the period from 16.8 to 6.4 percent and in Haryana from 22.1 to 12.9 percent. The proportion of migrants from U.P., on the other hand, increased from 41.7 to 50.1 percent (Table 4.3). The present migrants from Punjab and Haryana are well equipped for finding remunerative jobs in the city and adapting themselves to urban values and patterns of living. Most of them work as carpenters, masons, electricians, repairmen for electric or electronic appliances, drivers of motor vehicles or as skilled workers in factories. They live in well built brick and mortar houses which have facilities with running water, electricity and surface drainage, although they are located in unauthorized colonies. Most of the migrants from U.P., on the other hand, lack such skills. They come from backward and poor districts of central and eastern U.P. and work in low wage jobs as domestic servants, gardeners, watchmen, messengers etc. Most of them live in slums, which lack the facilities mentioned above. Furthermore, their poorly built dwellings are subject to burning up in Delhi's hot summer or to suffer severe damage in its frequent dust or thunderstorms.

Table 4.3: Migrants to Delhi by States of their Origin (%)

State	*Before 1961*	*1961-71*	*1971-81*	*Total*
Haryana	22.1	16.4	12.9	15.5
Madhya Pradesh	1.2	1.7	3.1	2.4
Punjab	16.8	11.3	6.4	9.8
Rajasthan	7.5	7.6	7.6	7.6
Uttar Pradesh	41.7	49.6	50.1	48.2
Others Including Outside India	10.7	13.4	19.9	16.5
Total	100.0	100.0	100.0	100.0

Source: Regional Plan 2001, National Capital Region, 1988, 138.

AREAS OF HIGH RURAL-URBAN INTERACTION

The areas can be divided into two categories:

1. Villages located within daily commuting distance of cities, particularly large cities,
2. Rural Corridors where a number of towns and cities are located within a short distance of one another and the intervening villages are being progressively urbanized. The corridors can be delineated roughly on the map showing districts with higher percentages or urban/total population than the national average in 1991. A more precise delineation will become possible when similar figures are published by the Registrar General and Census Commissioner of India for sub-divisions of districts. The following four corridors are well developed already; others are developing and could be called 'incipient'.

Well Developed Corridors

1. Coastal Gujarat-Maharashtra: from Ahmedabad through Vadodra and Surat in Gujarat to Mumbai and from Mumbai to Pune;

2. Coastal Kerala-Karnataka: from Trivandrum in Kerala to Mangalore in Karnataka, along the west coast of India;
3. Punjab-Haryana-Western Uttar Pradesh: from Amritsar in Punjab through Haryana to Delhi with spurs going from Delhi, south of Faridabad, west to Gurgaon in Haryana and east-north-east through Ghaziabad and Meerut to Dehra Dun and Bareilly in U.P.; and
4. Bihar-West Bengal: from Dhanbad in Bihar through Asansol, Bardhaman and Bandel to the Kolkata Urban Agglomeration in West Bengal.

Incipient Corridors

The more important incipient corridors are the following:

a. from Mumbai eastward to Nagpur and Chandrapur in Maharashtra;
b. from Bangalore in Karnataka to Chennai in Tamil Nadu;
c. from Chennai west to Coimbatore and south-west to Tiruchhirapalli and Madurai in Tamil Nadu;
d. from Mangalore on the coast of Karnataka east to Vijayawada in Andhra Pradesh; and
e. from Kanpur to Lucknow in central Uttar Pradesh.

The corridors have developed mainly during the four decades from 1951-91; the principal factors in their development have been the following:

(i) improvement in transport and communications, particularly expansion of highways and feeder roads;
(ii) establishment of new large and small industrial enterprises; and
(iii) modernisation of agriculture, near universal rural electrification and subsequent expansion of irrigation by electric pumps which has been a major factor in the modernisation.

There is a trend toward the extension of most of the corridors and development of new ones. Thus the coastal Gujarat-Maharashtra corridor is extending at its northern end to include most of former Saurashtra region of Gujarat and at its southern end from Pune to Kohlapur in Maharashtra, Tamil Nadu and Kerala, and could extend in the not distant future to south central Karnataka. The Gujarat-Maharashtra corridor could extend, similarly, to include a large part of Western Maharashtra. The hilly or dry districts within these two sub-regions would then appear as less urbanized, less developed pockets.

PRINCIPAL FACTORS CONTRIBUTING TO INCREASE IN RURAL-URBAN INTERACTION

The most important factors some of which are inter-related, are the following:

1. Rapid urbanization.
2. Growth of modern manufacturing industries and service activities and their concentration in and around large cities.
3. Improvement in transport and communication leading to increasing travel and transport of goods between villages and urban places by villagers on the one hand and by workers in the urban-based industries and service activities on the other.
4. Technological advance in agriculture, leading to increase in agricultural output including output of perishable foods for urban markets. The increase had been aided by the agricultural extension and related programs and extension of irrigation through rapid increase in number of electrified wells and tube-wells as well as by extension of canals.
5. Spread of information through the news and entertainment media – newspapers, magazines, radio and television.

THE PROSPECT: PROBABLE EFFECTS OF ECONOMIC LIBERALIZATION POLICIES

The prospect for the foreseeable future is for a progressive increase in the range and magnitude of rural-urban interactions. The more important factors contributing to it were listed earlier. The increase would be faster than otherwise, if with successful implementation of the economic liberalization policies, initiated in July 1991, the rate of economic growth increased significantly from the average of 5.3 percent per annum achieved during 1980-90 (Table 4.2). There would be rapid expansion of modern manufacturing industries and service sector activities. They would be located, as at present, principally in and around large cities and *rurban* corridors. Their concentration in these locations could be reduced if small or medium sized factories manufacturing components for electrical or electrical appliances, bicycles, motor vehicles etc., were located in other regions also.

An increasing proportion of the work force, for industry, could be drawn from the neighbouring villages, with the spread of the needed skills among the villagers. This will reduce the pressure of migration from villages to large cities. The pressure would be reduced further, if with improvement of transport and communications, the satellite towns and villages at the periphery of large cities were used as dormitories by workers in the cities much more than at present.

Rapid economic growth would result also in significant reduction in rural and urban poverty, if it is accompanied by an enlightened policy on distribution of its benefits. Two other results would be: (i) increase in size of the middle class, estimated currently at almost 200 million and (ii) rapid increase in consumption of manufactured consumer goods including consumer durables and perishable foods by both the rural and urban populations. Expansion/improvement of physical and social infrastructures would be more rapid and their operation would be more efficient as private sector resources of finance and management become available to supplement those of the public sector. Generation and distribution of electricity, telecommunications, construction of highways and operation of passenger road transport are examples of services which are suitable for private sector participation because their output can be priced at levels which would attract participation.

RECOMMENDATIONS

Program for progress towards integrated rural and urban development. The most important programs are listed and discussed briefly below:

1. Expansion and improvement of transport infrastructures, particularly highways and feeder roads. Particular attention should be given to building and maintaining efficient all-weather motorable roads in the central and eastern states where the current network of roads is inadequate and large numbers of villages and small towns remain cut off from the

outside world for short or long periods during the rainy season.

2. Improvement of telecommunications by exploiting aggressively the rapid advances in technology that have occurred during the last two decades and still continuing. The objectives should be, to provide a telephone within 1 kilometre of every village and to extend progressively to all cities facilities like subscriber trunk dialing (STD), telex and telefax that are available at present only in large cities.
3. Implementing a massive education program with the following objectives:
   (i) achievement of functional literacy among all adults by the end of the century (2000);
   (ii) rapid diffusion of marketable skills – technical/ vocational; and managerial – among both rural and urban youth; and
   (iii) multi-faceted social education, which would maximize the positive and minimize the negative effects of rural-urban interaction. Particular emphasis should be given in the program to women with suitable changes in its content to meet their particular needs. The program for them should have an adequate content of education in home-making, nutrition and child care and prevention of endemic and epidemic diseases. It should also aim at reducing the ignorance of and prejudice against members of other castes and communities.
4. Policies and programmes aimed at achieving decentralized industrial development. They should be concentrated in the first few years in relatively developed regions, particularly peripheral regions of large cities and rurban corridors. Their extension to other regions, slow at first, should gather momentum progressively in step with improvement in transport and telecommunications and diffusion of marketable skill among their people. This strategy of step-by-step development would contribute greatly to the success of the programs and minimize their cost to the economy.
5. Increasing production of high value perishable foods and of industries processing them for both the domestic and inter-

national markets. This should be an important activity of the Ministries of Food and Agriculture of the central and state governments. Near universal rural electrification is a major advantage in such expansion. It aids decentralized industrial development also. However, a concerted effort needs to be made to improve supply of electricity by ending the present frequent and prolonged outages of supply and large fluctuations of voltage. The reasons for these deficiencies and the remedial steps needed to correct them have been detailed in reports of the World Bank and other consultants. Significant reduction in the deficiencies would be of great benefit to farmers and small industrial entrepreneurs, because it would save them the high costs of generation of electricity by diesel-operated motors.

6. *Institutional Cooperation*: The legislation for establishment of the institutions for rural development and administration on the one hand and urban local bodies on the other should specify the pattern of interaction between them. In particular, it is necessary to insure that:
   (i) there is no conflict of jurisdiction between the two sets of institutions at the urban fringe relating particularly to diversion of rural lands for residential, industrial, or other non-agricultural uses, and
   (ii) there is adequate and effective cross-representation between the two sets of institutions. Thus the *Zila Parishads* and *Panchayat Samitis* – elected institutions for rural development and administration at the levels of the district and community development blocks respectively – should have representatives of municipalities located within their areas and the municipalities, should, in their turn, have representatives of the above institutions, as also of market committees, cooperatives and rural banks. The cross-representation will assist greatly in achieving integrated rural and urban development.

Micro-regional plans: Preparation of micro-regional plans can be a useful tool for progress towards integrated rural and urban development. Through them the common problems of rural and urban areas such as unemployment, poverty and deficiency of physical and social infrastructures can be identified and steps taken to alleviate them. Furthermore, policies and programs can be formulated and implemented for development and conservation of natural resources such as water. The most suitable areal units for preparation of micro-regional plans are districts and metropolitan areas of large cities.

The Constitutional (Seventy Fourth Amendment) Act 1992 on Municipal Bodies (See Annexture) which was passed by the Parliament in that year but became effective in April 1993, marks a significant advance in this direction by including provisions for preparation of plans for both districts and metropolitan areas. An extract from the Act is given in the Annexture. Through it, the state governments are directed to constitute Planning Committees for every district and metropolitan area of the country and to prepare development plans for them, it specifies also the constitution of the committees and the content of the plans. The common interests of rural and urban areas have to be taken into consideration in constituting the committees and the content of the development plans. Both the district and metropolitan planning committees would have as their members, representatives of *panchayats* and the municipal bodies. The common interests include spatial planning, sharing of water and other physical and natural resources, the integrated development of infrastructure, environmental conservation and availability of financial and other resources.

District Development Plans. There were about 450 districts in the country according to the Population Census of 1991. Despite the provisions of the Act, simultaneous preparation of development plans for all of them would not be feasible in our view: the funds, and professional personnel, needed for preparation of high quality plans, which keep in view the particular natural and human resources, economic conditions, needs and problems of every district would not be available. Such plans should, therefore, be prepared initially for a limited number of districts and the process should be extended to in a phased manner so as to achieve complete coverage of all districts over a period of years. The phasing would ensure that preparation of district plans does not become a routine activity of district level officials and people's representatives, as some earlier attempts at district planning became.

Metropolitan Plans: This limitation does not apply, however, to preparation of metropolitan plans. From the definition of a metropolitan area given in the Act, it is clear that the metropolitan areas of the 23 million-plus cities would be covered. In fact, metropolitan plans have already been prepared for all these cities by Development Authorities (DA's) established by the state governments. The areal units for preparation of most of the plans are rather large and include the core cities, their satellite towns/cities besides rural areas. In case of Delhi, a much larger region – The National Capital Region – was designated in 1985 and a planning board was established to prepare a regional plan for it. The plan was prepared by the Board in 1988 and became effective in January 1989. This plan provides the global envelope for preparation of plans of the towns/cities included within the region. Thus, the Second Master Plan of Delhi which covers only the Territory of Delhi and had been prepared by the Delhi Development Authority (DDA) in 1985 was not accepted by the Central government, which directed the DDA to revise plan to conform to the objectives, strategy, policies, and programs of the Regional Plan. The revised plan was prepared in 1990 and was immediately accepted and enforced.

As a result of the Act, the states would need to replace the DA's by Metropolitan Planning Committees (MPC's) constituted, as specified in the Act. The principal difference between the two bodies would be that while the DA's are nonstatutory bodies, and consist entirely (or mainly) of officials, the MPC's would be statutory bodies consisting largely of elected representatives of municipalities and panchayats within a metropolitan area. Secondly, the existing metropolitan plans would need to be revised so as to reflect the views of the MPC's. In addition to the functions specified in the Act for the district and metropolitan development plans, they should give special attention to reducing unemployment and poverty, particularly in the rural areas. This will reduce pressure of migration from villages to towns and cities, and from small towns to metropolitan cities.

Need for a national policy on settlements: There is an urgent need for a national policy on settlements. It should be evolved keeping in view the following:

(i) demographic, economic and politico-administrative changes of the past four decades and the prospect for further changes during the foreseeable future;

(ii) present and emerging relationships among settlements of different sizes. They include relationships between small or medium-sized service center towns and the villages served by them, as also among cities and towns of different sizes.

(iii) realistic acceptance and likelihood of continued concentration of modern manufacturing industries and service activities in large and medium-sized cities, despite the policies of the central and state governments, pursued since the mid-1950's, which discourage such concentration and strongly favour decentralized industrial and economic development.

ANNEXTURE

The Constitution Seventy Fourth Amendment Act 1992 on Municipalities "Committee for District Planning"

243ZD. (1) There shall be constituted in every State at the district level a District Planning Committee to consolidate the plans prepared by the Panchayats and the Municipalities in the district and to prepare a draft development plan for the district as a whole.

(2) The Legislature of a State may, by law, make provision with respect to:

(a) the composition of the District Planning Committees;

(b) the manner in which the seats in such Committees shall be filled:

provided that not less than four-fifths of the total number of members of such committee shall be elected by, and from amongst, the elected members of the Panchayat at the district in proportion to the ratio between the population of the rural areas and of the urban areas in the district;

(c) the functions relating to district planning which may be assigned to such Committees;

(d) the manner in which the Chairperson of such Committee shall be chosen.

(3) Every District Planning Committee shall, in preparing the draft development plan:

(a) Have regard to:

(i) matters of common interest between the Panchayats and the Municipalities including spatial planning, sharing of water and other physical and natural resources, the integrated development of infrastructures and environmental conservation;

(ii) the extent and type of available resources whether financial or otherwise;

(b) Consult such institutions and organizations as the Governor may, by order, specify.

(4) The Chairperson of every District Planning Committee shall forward the development plan, as recommended by such Committee, to the Government of the State." (pp. 7-8)

"Committee for Metropolitan Planning"

243ZE. (1) There shall be constituted in every Metropolitan area a Metropolitan Planning Committee to prepare a draft development plan for the Metropolitan area as a whole.

(2) The Legislature of a State may, by law, make provision with respect to:

(a) the composition of the Metropolitan Planning Committee;

(b) the manner in which the seats in such Committee shall be filled:

Provided that not less than two-thirds of the members of such Committees shall be elected by, and from amongst, the elected members of the Municipalities and Chairpersons of the Panchayats in the Metropolitan area in proportion to the ratio between the population of the Municipalities and of the Panchayats in that area;

(c) the representation in such Committee of the Government of India and the Government of the State and of such organizations and institutions as may be deemed necessary for carrying out the functions assigned to such committees:...."

(3) Every Metropolitan Planning Committee shall, in preparing the draft plan:

(a) Have regard to

(i) the plans prepared by the Municipalities and the Panchayats, in the Metropolitan area;

(ii) matters of common interest between the Municipalities and the Panchayats, including coordinated spatial planning of the area, sharing of water and other physical and natural resources, the integrated development of infrastructure and environmental conservation;

(iii) the overall objectives and priorities set by the Government of India and the Government of the State;

(iv) the extent and nature of investment likely to be made in the metropolitan area by agencies of the Government of India and of the Government of the State and other available resources whether financial or otherwise.." (pp. 8-9)

NOTE

1. Proceeding of Fourth Asian Urbanization Conference, Taiwan, January 1994. Eds. Lan Hung, Nora Chiang, Jack F. Williams and Heather L. Bedinarch.

REFERENCES

Bannerjee-Guha, S. (1991), "*Mumbai Urban Development Project – A Solution for the Shelter Problem of the Urban Poor*" Paper presented at the Third International Conference on Asian Urbanization, New Delhi. (mimeo)

Basu, D.N. and Kashyap, S.P. (1992), "*Rural Non-Agricultural Employment in India – Role of Development Process and Rural – urban Employment Linkages", Economic and Political Weekly*, Vol. XXVII. Nos. 51 and 52.

Bose, A (1973), *Studies in India's Urbanization 1901-71*, Tata McGraw Hill Publishing Co. Ltd. New Delhi.

Dandekar, V.M. and Rath, N. (1971), *Poverty in India*, Indian School of Political Economy, Mumbai.

Evans, H.E. and Ngau, P. "*Rural-Urban Relations, Household Income Diversification and Agricultural Productivity". Development and Change*, London. Vol. 22.

Helweg, E.W. (1980), "*Indians in Britain: A Study of the International Relationships of Sending, Receiving and Migrant Societies"*, in Rao, M.A.S.(ed), *Studies in Migration*, Manohar Publications, New Delhi.

Johnson, E.A.J. (1965), *Market Towns and Spatial Development in India*, National Council of Applied Economic Research, New Delhi.

Lewis, J.P (1962), *Quiet Crisis in India*, The Brookings Institution, Washington D.C.

Mohan, R. (1985), "*Urbanization in India's Future*", *Population and Development Review*, New York, Vol. 11. No. 4.

Nath V., "Projections for 2001: 1991 Population Census—Some Facts and Policy Issues-II", *Economic and Political Weekly*, Mumbai, December 21, 1991, Table 2, p. 2938.

National Capital Region Planning Board (1988), Regional Plan 2001 National Capital Region. New Delhi.

Government of India, Planning Commission (1990), *Approach Paper to the Eighth Five Year Plan*, Government of India, New Delhi.

Government of India, Planning Commission, Eighth Five Year Plan, 1992-97, Government of India, New Delhi.

Rao, Ratna, N. (1990) *Social Organization in an Indian Slum*, Mittal Publications, New Delhi.

Registrar General and Census Commissioner, (1991), Census of India, New Delhi.

Report of the National Commission on Urbanization (1988), New Delhi.

Tyagi, V.K. (1982) *Urban Growth and Urban Villages: A Case Study of Delhi*, Kalyan Publications, New Delhi.

5

Cities, Suburbs, the Region and Hinterland[1]

Our cities are growing very fast; but does this reflect the economic growth of the region to which they belong is the question seeking attention. Cities all over the world are expanding rapidly. As their population keeps on increasing, their territorial limits are also expanding, encroaching on areas of the countryside. This expansion of cities, which began in Europe after the Industrial Revolution, was greatly accelerated with the advent of the automobile that made suburban living possible, and has been further accelerated by economic growth in the two decades since Second World War. In parts of Western Europe, eastern USA and Japan, the process has gone so far that large numbers of adjoining cities and towns are coalescing to form gigantic urban complexes and the distinction between urban and rural areas is being obliterated. All the earlier terms used for distinguishing a city from its surrounding rural area – city, metropolitan area, and conurbation have become obsolete and the new concept of 'megalopolis' has been formulated to describe this new phenomenon. Urban growth in India has not gone that far, though the population of Indian cities is also increasing rapidly and their expansion into surrounding rural areas has gathered great momentum in the years following Second World War. Indeed, if present trends continue, it is not unlikely that 'megalopolis' may emerge in some areas like coastal Gujarat (between Ahmedabad and Surat) or in north-east India between Dhanbad and Kolkata, where a number of adjoining cities and towns are experiencing rapid growth.

A major factor which contributes to the rapid growth of cities is the location of industries. Cities with their large markets and reservoirs of capital, entrepreneurial and technical skills, act as powerful magnets attracting industries, especially market-oriented consumer goods industries and those using the latest technology and materials (e.g. electronics, plastics), which have been growing very rapidly in recent years. This locational pull is especially strong in countries like India, in which cities have had a disproportionately large share in the growth of modern industry. However, since further concentration of industries within city centers is undesirable, or is in some case impossible, there is a growing tendency to locate industry on the urban periphery. This development is sought to be directed by those concerned with urban planning, by developing industrial areas outside the cities or by encouraging growth of satellite industrial townships. The development of industrial areas in the Thane-Kalyan region outside Mumbai city and of Industrial Township like Faridabad, Shahdara and Ghaziabad around Delhi, are examples of such direction.

One result of demographic and physical growth of cities is that city planning is increasingly becoming regional planning, with its chief concern changing from policies of location of particular institutions or facilities within a city to a clearer definition of the pattern of land use and functional relationships within a metropolitan region. Secondly, as cities are getting more closely linked with the regions in which they are situated – through transport and communications and diverse economic relations – much greater attention has begun to be given in city planning to analyzing developments within the regions. These trends are reflected in plan policies for the large Indian cities. In the master plan for Delhi, for instance, the unit of planning was the entire area of Delhi State, consisting of the cities of Delhi and New Delhi, the town of Shahdara, and a large rural area. Further, the plan gave considerable attention to the relation between growth of the city and its surrounding (peripheral) region in Punjab and Uttar Pradesh. It took into account the development that were taking place in this region (e.g. ribbon development along the main roads) and made a number of recommendations for directing this development. Its most important recommendation related to development of the satellite towns mentioned above. The relation of Delhi with its hinterland in the north-western parts of India, was also examined in the plan.

PLANS FOR CITY AND SUBURBAN AREAS

In the proposed plan for Kolkata now being worked out, the unit of planning is not the city of Kolkata, but the Kolkata Metropolitan District – an area of about 450 square miles comprising the area of the corporations of Kolkata and Howrah, about 35 municipalities and a large number of villages. The Mumbai Corporation has recently drawn up a plan for the Greater Mumbai Area including Mumbai city proper and a large suburban and semi-urban area, totaling about 170 sq miles. In addition, the Maharashra Government has initiated action on formulating a regional plan for a much larger area of about 1,250 square miles, which includes large parts of Thane district besides the Greater Mumbai area.

THE METROPOLITAN REGION

The 'region' adopted as the unit of physical planning in these cases may be called the 'metropolitan region'. It consists of the city proper and surrounding suburbs and rural areas. The city is already expanding into its suburbs and will expand more in the future because of the compulsive demands of growth, requiring land for housing industries, various social service, transport, and communications and recreational facilities. Demarcation of the 'metropolitan region' is the first step in drawing up the physical plan for a city. A major object of the plan is control of land use i.e. allocation of land for various urban uses. The plan decides the pattern of location of economic activity within the metropolitan region and influences its functioning as an economic and social unit mainly through control of land use.

THE ROLE OF PERIPHERAL REGION IN URBAN DEVELOPMENT

In addition to the metropolitan region, it is useful to distinguish for purpose of city planning two other regions – the peripheral region and the hinterland. The peripheral is the area beyond the metropolitan region. It is essentially rural or semi-urban in character but is strongly affected by the economic and social influences emanating from the city. Its economic life is closely connected with that of the city because employment of industries or service institutions, located within the metropolitan region, is a major source of economic activities for its people. Agriculture and allied vocations in the region are directed towards supplying milk, vegetables, meat, poultry, and other perishable farm products needed by the city. The attitude and values of the people of the region are also affected more by urban influences then those of rural people farther away from the city. The boundaries of the peripheral region are not well defined. At the inner margin, they are subject to change through periodic invasion by industries and service facilities – roads, rail or air terminals. In time, this inner part of region may be absorbed by the expanding metropolis. Where a number of rapidly expanding cities and towns are located close to one another, their peripheral regions may eventually join to form part of a 'megalopolis'.

But a clearly defined concept of the peripheral region is essential for city planning, because it distinguishes an area outside the metropolitan region but, all the same, deeply affected by urban influences. Trends in land use within its peripheral region are of considerable importance for the future growth of a city. These should be closely watched and directed to the extent necessary. The need for location of industries in the peripheral region, in order to prevent concentration within the city area, is one region which may make such direction necessary. For instance, the regional planning work for the area outside Greater Mumbai, recently initiated by the Maharashtra Government, is a reflection primarily of this need. Demands for land for various other non-agricultural uses also increase with the peripheral region as the city grows and the metropolitan region gets filled up. Ribbon development along the main roads and railway lines, haphazard growth of industry or location of noxious industries which it will be difficult to shift later, destruction of large areas of productive land by brick kilns, lands being bought up for speculative purposes, are some of the dangers of unplanned land use in the peripheral region.

Planning of land use in the region is beneficial for another reason also. Parts of the region afford exceptionally good opportunities for intensive agricultural development directed towards producing perishables of high value for the city market. This development will lead to higher rural incomes and levels of living and will make these products available to the people of the city at lower costs. It is therefore essential that large areas of land are not unnecessarily taken out of agricultural use.

THE CONCEPT OF HINTERLAND

The '*hinterland*' is the region for which the city acts as a service center rendering various commercial, administrative and other services. Mumbai, for instance, is the major port and commercial center for Western India, including the whole of Maharashtra and Gujarat and parts of Mysore, Madhya Pradesh and Rajasthan. Similarly, Delhi is the commercial and service center of North-West India. An analysis of trends in economic development within hinterlands should form part of planning for every city, because this analysis would indicate the demands likely to be placed on the city in future. Large increases in agricultural, industrial or mineral production in the hinterland of a city like Mumbai will increase the demands on its port, and on the roads and railways leading to it. They will also mean larger demands on its banking, insurance and other services. These demands will be greater if industrial expansion depends upon use of imported fuels like petroleum or visualizes large exports.

SMALL TOWNS ARE 'TRIBUTARIES' OF METROPOLITAN CITIES

A large metropolitan city is linked with its hinterland through a number of smaller cities and towns. The link between the large cities and those smaller urban centers are similar to those of a river with its tributaries and smaller rivulets. Most towns in Western India have this kind of relationship with Mumbai. Each, in turn, has its own tributary and sub-tributary towns reaching down to small towns which serve a group of villages. The economic and social influences of the large city percolate to the hinterland through these smaller cities and towns, and on that account its role as a base of services for the hinterland becomes real and meaningful. Industrial development undertaken in towns which are found suitable for it will help reduce pressure for industrial location in or near the metropolitan city. Expansion of educational, cultural and other service facilities in the hinterland would similarly reduce pressure on the facilities available in the city. Both these developments are being currently advocated by some to relieve the pressure on large cities like Kolkata and Mumbai.

CITIES AND TOWNS AS SERVICE CENTERS

The 'service' role of an urban center for its surrounding area become most obvious in the case of small towns. The growth of these towns is intimately linked with economic growth in the rural areas served by them. Further, they are themselves major instruments of rural growth because they are the foci of modernization. People from the villages go to them for commercial, administrative, educational or health services. New ideas, processes and techniques radiate from them into the villages. Such towns may well be called 'rural service centers'. They have a growing importance in the economic and social life in the countryside. The latter are using the service facilities located in them far more than they did 10 or 20 years ago and they will use them even more in future, as education spreads among them, modern health services are accepted more widely and agriculture becomes more commercialized. Technological change in agriculture will also be a powerful factor in making the service roles of these towns more important, because the various facilities needed for accomplishing such change – distribution points for chemical fertilizers, pesticides, cement and diesel oil, workshops and facilities for servicing of agricultural implements etc., cannot be located in every village and must be confined to small towns or large villages. Agricultural processing industries and other industries specifically related to agriculture (e.g. manufacture of agricultural implements) have similarly to be located in such towns because of advantages of transport, availability of skilled workers, etc. The more specialized services rendered by the large towns like district and divisional headquarters and large *mandis* will also be used more and more by the people in the villages as their economic and social levels rise. An increasing number among them would wish to go to colleges or universities, for instance, and to use the specialized facilities provided by a large hospital.

It is important that this service role of small and medium-sized towns is adequately appreciated and provided for in their development plans. It will also be an advantage to establish suitable relationships between municipal bodies which are concerned with planning for these towns, and the Panchayati Raj institution which have the responsibility for planning in rural areas. This relationship can be best established at the district level. The provision for association of municipalities with the Zila Parishads, which has already been made in some States, is recognition of this need. But there is need for further progress in this direction.

The regional approach will have to be given an increasingly important place in urban planning in future. The unit of long-term physical planning for a city or town should not be the area included within its municipal limits but the larger, metropolitan region. The relation of the city with its peripheral and hinterland regions should be adequately visualized and provided for in its plan.

This is essential for direction of economic growth in the peripheral region and achieving a better balance between growth within the city and its hinterland. In areas where large, expanding cities and towns are located close to one another, it will be an advantage to draw up a plan for the entire region in addition to plans for individual cities. This regional plan may be less detailed and more flexible than the plans for individual cities; but it should visualize the general direction of development of the area and the interaction of the different cities within it. The service role of the small and medium sized towns for their surrounding rural area should be adequately recognized. This recognition is important for both urban and rural progress because these towns are the foci of modernization in rural India.

NOTE

1. Yojana, January 26, 1965, p. 35.

6

Rurban Corridors and Industrial Development in India[1]

The urban population of India was 217.2 million in 1991 and formed 25.7 percent of the total population of the country. Sixty-four percent of the urban population lived in cities in 1991 (Fig. 6.1).

The proportion has increased progressively from 44 percent in 1951 and 59.2 percent in 1981. Also in 1991, almost a third of the urban population lived in million-plus cities. The corresponding figures for 1951 and 1981 were 17.8 percent and 26.4 percent respectively (Table 6.1).

These figures bring out two principal facts:

1. Increasing urbanization; and
2. Increasing concentration of the urban population in cities and the million-plus cities within them.

These developments have given rise to a multitude of problems–managerial, financial, social and others, because of the difficulties of managing these cities and providing their residents with suitable housing and essential services, especially adequate supplies of electricity and drinking water, intra-urban transport, facilities for disposal of solid and liquid wastes and security of life and property. A question that naturally arises is: Would the trend of increasing concentration of the urban population in cities and million-plus cities within them continue or would alternative patterns of settlement under which these problems are reduced significantly emerge in the foreseeable future?

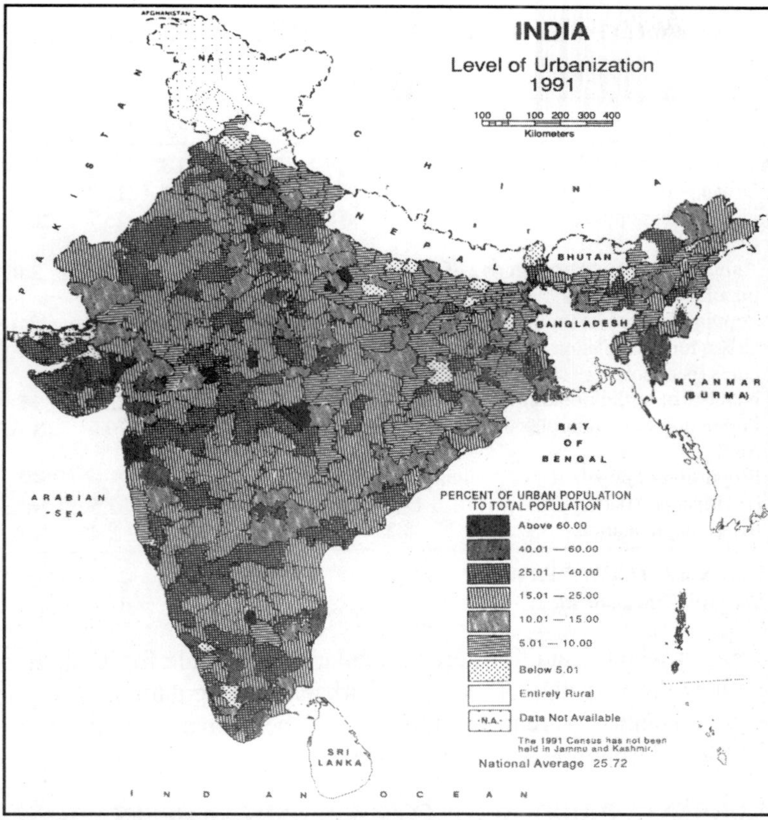

Fig. 6.1: Level of Urbanization, 1991: Districts

Source: Urban India Vol. XIX No. 1 (1999).

This paper is an attempt to examine the above question, though it does not take any view on the subject. However, it explains that the most important alternative pattern would be 'rurban corridors.' The paper first gives the definition of a corridor following which the principal 'Developed corridors,' are described. This is followed by a description of 'Mini and Incipient corridors.' The economic and social conditions which have favoured or would favour the emergence of corridors are also discussed. Next, the advantages of rurban corridors have been listed. The conclusion expresses the view that corridor development will remain limited in the foreseeable future to certain

Table 6.1: Growth of Total and Urban Population and Population of Cities in India: 1951-2001.

	1951	*1961*	*1971*	*1981*	*1991*	*2001*
Total population (million)	361.0	439.2	548.2	683.3	844.3	1029.0
Urban population (million)	62.4	78.9	109.1	159.5	217.2	294.0
Urban/total population (per cent)	17.3	18.0	19.9	23.3	25.7	28.6
Annual exponential growth rate of population (per cent)	3.47	2.34	3.21	3.83	3.09	3.09
Population of cities (million)	27.5	39.9	61.2	94.5	138.8	N.A.
Urban/total population living in cities (per cent)	44.0	50.6	56.1	59.2	63.9	N.A.
Number of million-plus cities	5	9	9	12	23	39*
Population of million-plus cities (million)	11.7	17.9	27.4	42.1	70.6	N.A.
Proportion of population of million-plus cities/total:						
(i) Urban population	17.8	22.6	25.1	26.4	32.5	N.A.
(ii) Total population	3.2	4.1	5.0	6.2	8.4	N.A.

NA: Not Available * Projected
Source: Census of India.

areas in which conditions are particularly favourable for it: districts with a relatively high proportion of urban/total population. Thus, the development of rurban corridors would be primarily within these districts during the next two decades.

RURBAN CORRIDORS: THE CONCEPT AND EXAMPLES

These are linear or curvilinear areas in which a number of cities and towns are located within short distance of one another and the intervening villages are also being progressively urbanized. Most, but not all corridors have a million-plus city at one or both ends. The map shows districts with a higher percentage of urban to total population than the national average in 1991.

ADVANTAGES OF RURBAN CORRIDORS

The principal advantages of development of rurban corridors are the following:

1. Dispersal of industries from the large metropolitan cities thus reducing pressures on electricity and water supply and

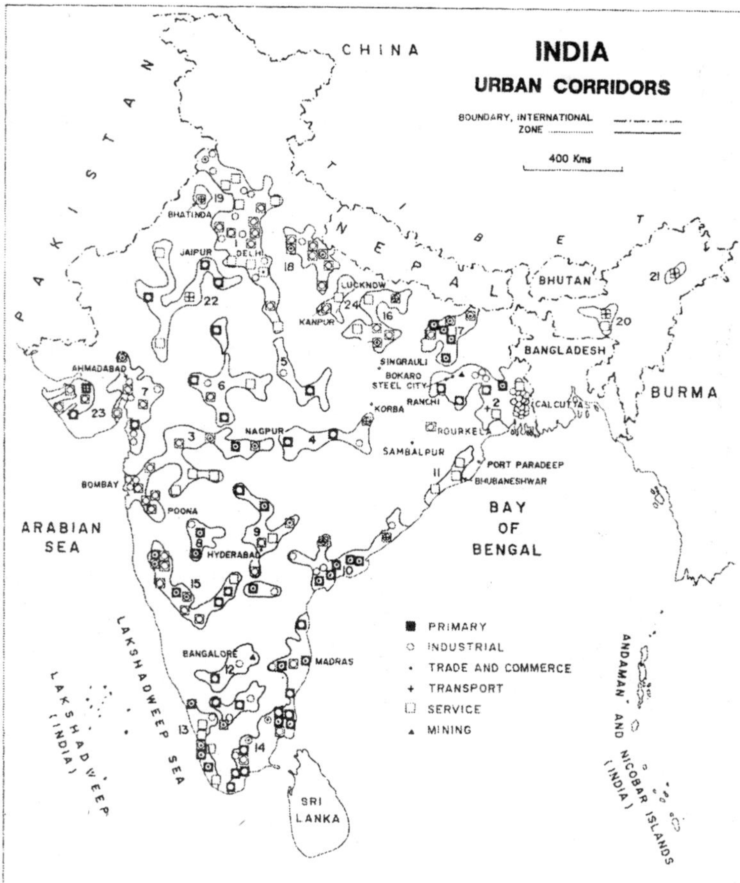

Fig. 6.2: Urban Corridors

facilities for disposal of solid and liquid waste in them. Dispersal of the hazardous and highly polluting industries now located in the large cities to their environs will reduce pollution of air and water in them.

2. Spread of industrial skills and the discipline required for industrial work among the rural and small town populations will increase employment and earnings in them. It will act as a stimulus for diversification of agriculture to meet the demand

for food—including milk, fruits and vegetables, by the industrial workers, thus increasing the income of farmers.

3. Lower cost of land that could also be a significant advantage if the state governments create facilities for training of rural youth in industrial skills within and around the cities and towns in the corridors, and if the emergence of militant trade unions is prevented.

CONDITIONS FOR DEVELOPMENT OF RURBAN CORRIDORS

Essential conditions for the development of rurban corridors are the following:

1. Existence of two or more large cities within a short distance from one another.
2. Adequate supplies of electricity and water.
3. Good road and rail communications.
4. A state government determined to pursue policies for industrial dispersal and expansion of the infrastructure needed for it. The government must also ensure provision of security of life and property for the entrepreneurs and workers in the industrial units. This is a *sine que non* of industrial dispersal because ensuring security of life and property for their residents is becoming a serious problem in some large cities, notably Mumbai and Delhi.

DEVELOPED CORRIDORS

The principal developed rurban corridors are:

1. **The Coastal Gujarat-Western Maharashtra corridor,** which extends from Ahmedabad through Vadodra and Surat in Gujarat to Mumbai and from it to Pune and the sugar mill towns of Western Maharashtra.
2. **The Punjab-Haryana-Delhi-Western Uttar Pradesh corridor,** which extends from Amritsar in the north-west, through central Punjab to Delhi; with extensions to Gurgaon and Faridabad in Haryana, and Ghaziabad and Gautam Buddh

Nagar (NOIDA) in Uttar Pradesh. It goes further to include Modinagar, Meerut and the sugar mill towns between Delhi and Saharanpur in Uttar Pradesh.

3. **The Bihar-West Bengal corridor,** which extends from the coal mining city of Dhanbad in Bihar through Durgapur (Asansol) to the Kolkata Metropolitan District in West Bengal. A short northward extension includes the jute mill towns located up to 60 kilometres north of Kolkata along the Hooghly river.

1. THE COASTAL GUJARAT-MAHARASHTRA CORRIDOR

The first industrial development in this corridor was the establishment of cotton textile mills in Mumbai and Ahmedabad from about 1870, soon after the American Civil War. Cotton textile mills were also established later in smaller cities of Navsari and Bulsar in Coastal Gujarat and cities like Sholapur in Western Maharashtra to take advantage of lower costs of land and labor. The extension of the corridor to Pune and the sugar mill towns of Western Maharashtra is a post-Independence development.

There were four million-plus cities in the corridor in 1991—Ahmedabad and Vadodra in Gujarat, and Mumbai and Pune in Maharashtra. Three cities: Surat in Gujarat, and New Mumbai and Thane in Maharashtra could become million-plus cities by 2001.

Principal Industries

The principal industries located in the corridor are:

- Textiles, originally only cotton, but in the post-Independence period textiles made of blends of cotton or wool with synthetic fibers. The integrated textile mills have been replaced increasingly by powerloom clusters in recent years.
- Clothing for domestic consumption and export.
- Pharmaceuticals and fine chemicals.
- Petroleum refining, manufacture of petrochemicals and products such as plastics for which the petrochemicals industry provides the raw material; manufacture of consumer goods by fabrication of plastics.

- Consumer durables such as cars, refrigerators, air conditioners, washing machines, electrically operated kitchen gadgets and electronic goods such as television receivers.
- A wide variety of machine tools.
- Cutting and polishing of diamonds and zari-works in Surat.
- Sugar and industrial alcohol.
- Electrical equipment such as generators and pumps for lifting water from irrigation wells.
- Dairy products.
- Office and hospital furniture.
- Production of films and television serials.

Coastal Gujarat is literally an industrial workshop today. According to some scholars after the discovery of petroleum off its coast and the growth of the petroleum refining and petrochemicals industries in it, it is over-industrialized and suffers from serious problems of pollution of air and water.

Principal Factors in Development

The principal factors in the development of this corridor are the following:

- Gujarati and Parsee entrepreneurship. This factor has received two large additions in the decades after Independence: (a) the return home of a large number of Gujarati traders from East African countries—Uganda, Kenya and Tanzania—during and after the 1960s. Although traders in these countries, they have established a large number of industries in their home state and Maharashtra; (b) infusion of Sindhi entrepreneurs after the migration of Hindu Sindhis from their homes in Sindh to Mumbai and other towns of Gujarat and Maharashtra.
- Coastal Gujarat is a fertile area in which cotton, coarse cereals (sorghum) and tobacco were the principal crops. Production of liquid milk for Mumbai and other cities in Gujarat and manufacture of dairy products with its centre at Anand is a development of the late 1950s and the early 1960s.

- Discovery of petroleum off the coast of Gujarat (and off-Mumbai) leading to the development of petroleum refining and petrochemicals industries in and around Mumbai and a part of Coastal Gujarat.
- *Zari* work is a traditional handicraft industry in Surat. The availability of a large pool of low cost labour which adapted itself well to cutting and polishing of diamonds has led to the development of this industry whose turnover runs into hundreds of millions. The production is for both export and domestic consumption.
- Production of sugarcane with very high yield per hectare and high sucrose content has led to the establishment of a number of sugar mills and a variety of industries ancillary to the mills in the sugar mill towns like Dahanu in Maharashtra.
- The flowering of Maharashtra entrepreneurship in the post-Independence period. These entrepreneurs have established a large number of industries in the sugar mill towns and taken progressively to manufacture of electric generators and pumps for lifting water from wells for irrigation. The largest Maharashtra entrepreneurial group—the House of Kirloskars with its headquarters at Pune is planning to add motor vehicles to the list of products manufactured by it. Mumbai already has a factory manufacturing passenger cars.

Future Prospects

The prospects for the foreseeable future for this corridor are:

- Extension of the corridor into a part of Saurashtra, when irrigation water becomes available in parts of it after completion of the Sardar Sarovar dam on the Narmada river. With irrigation there will be a large increase in production of groundnut and cotton, the principal crops of the area and expansion of industries such as manufacture of *vanaspati* and refined groundnut oil for cooking and growth of powerloom clusters. A variety of industrial units could locate in towns closest to Ahmedabad in order to escape problems of pollution of air and water of Ahmedabad. Another prospect is for expansion of dairying in the region. The duty free export zone at Kandla port could provide the nucleus for further industrial development in the area.

- Further development of industries in the towns between Mumbai and Pune and Pune and Kolhapur. Many Mumbai based industrialists have been locating their factories in small towns located along the railway and the highway between Mumbai and Pune to take advantage of the lower cost of land and labour in them. Extension of the corridor south to Kolhapur would come later.
- Rapid expansion of the pharmaceutical and office and hospital furniture industries with increasing urbanization and growth of health services for the increasing number of aged people of the middle and high-income groups.
- Rapid expansion of the TV serials producing industry, as the number of television viewers increases in both urban and rural areas. The unfulfilled need of India's rural and urban population for news and entertainment is much greater than has been assumed so far. Mumbai will remain the principal centre for production of TV serials, despite the spread of the industry to regional centres, notably Kolkata and Chennai (formerly Madras) in future.

2. THE PUNJAB-HARYANA-WESTERN UTTAR PRADESH CORRIDOR

Principal Industries

The principal industries in this corridor are:

- Manufacture of carpets and woollen textiles in Amritsar in Punjab.
- Manufacture of consumer durables such as bicycles, motor cycles and sewing machines in Ludhiana. The city had a large woollen hosiery industry in the pre-Independence period. This industry has continued to expand with an increase in domestic demand and growth of exports to countries of Western Europe and Russia. Furthermore, after the return home of Ramgarhia Sikhs, originally artisans such

as carpenters and smiths who became wealthy in Malaysia and Thailand, Ludhiana has become an industrial workshop.

- Manufacture of electric motors and of agricultural equipment such as mechanical threshers was started in the city after the expansion of its irrigated area and availability of large supplies of electricity in Punjab and Haryana after completion of the Bhakra-Nangal dam in Punjab.
- Manufacture of coaches for the railways in the government owned factory in Kapurthala.
- Manufacture of consumer goods ranging from processed foods, textiles and garments to toiletries and drugs in Delhi and its satellite towns of Ghaziabad and Noida, (Gautam Buddh Nagar) in Uttar Pradesh.
- Manufacture of consumer durables — automobiles, components and spare parts for cars, refrigerators, air conditioners and kitchen gadgets in Gurgaon and Faridabad in Haryana.
- A wide variety of machine tools, principally in Delhi.
- Sugar mills and ancillary industries along the road strip between Delhi and Saharanpur. A large multi-industry complex has developed in the post-Independence period in Modi Nagar in Uttar Pradesh.

Besides the Ramgarhia Sikhs, the principal entrepreneurial groups in the region are the Jains and Aggarwals who have been the original residents of the region and Punjabi Khatris and Aroras. The later, originally traders and money lenders in the towns and villages of West Punjab have taken increasingly to establishing small and medium sized industrial units after migration from Pakistan to India.

Factors Limiting Development

1. Dependence on imports of coal, steel, cement, petroleum products and other raw materials.
2. Increasing shortages of electricity and water. Delhi and most of the other cities in the region suffer from these shortages partly because investment in expansion of capacities is seriously hampered by the populist policies of the governments of both Punjab and Haryana to supply electricity and water for irrigation virtually free to farmers. These

policies must be reversed before large public or private investment can be made to remove these deficiencies.

3. Increasing congestion on the roads. Private investment in roads through construction of toll highways which will have the capacity to move traffic at high speed will ameliorate the shortage. The road users, mainly operators of trucks, should be prepared to pay the toll because of the saving in time and expenditure on the repair of trucks that good toll roads will provide.

Industrial development in both the corridors as well as in Chennai in South India received a big boost after the flight of capital from Kolkata and Howrah in the late 1960s, because of militancy of trade unions. The Gujarati, Marwari and Punjabi owners or managers of industrial units relocated their factories in Gujarat, around Mumbai and in the Punjab-Haryana-Delhi-Western Uttar Pradesh corridor and around Chennai after they were manhandled by militant members of the trade unions. There has been no significant movement of industrial capital back into Kolkata and Howrah despite the strenuous efforts of the Communist government of West Bengal to attract such capital.

Future Prospects

The prospects for the foreseeable future are:

- Areal extension of the corridor to include Chandigarh and Patiala in Punjab and possibly Moradabad in Uttar Pradesh.
- The highly polluting and hazardous industries now located in Delhi must move out to towns such as Dharuheda in Haryana and Bhiwadi in extreme north-west Rajasthan where large industrial estates have been developed by the government of the two states. Road communications facilities are adequate and developed land is available at reasonable prices. The movement of these industries to Ghaziabad, Gautam Buddh Nagar or the towns along the road between Saharanpur and Delhi is not so feasible because the area already suffers from serious problems of pollution of air and water and the roads are already over-crowded.

- Expansion of consumer goods and consumer durable industries to meet the large demand of the rural and urban consumers of north-western India. The levels of income and living and the consequent demand for manufactured consumer goods and consumer durables of the urban and rural population of the region is much higher than that of the population of any other region. The green revolution in wheat which greatly increased the income and level of living of farmers, which began in the 1970s, was confined to Punjab, Haryana and Western Uttar Pradesh. Production of cereals has been increasing steadily since then. Furthermore, remittances from soldiers of Punjab, Haryana and Western Uttar Pradesh and of the Sikhs settled in UK and USA make further large contribution to rural incomes.
- Growth of the computer software and information technology industries in and around Delhi and between Delhi and Gurgaon because of the availability of a large pool of educated young men and women in Delhi and the facilities for growth of these industries being offered by the government of Haryana.
- Manufacture of automobiles and components. Maruti Udyog, which produces India's most popular passenger car is located in a suburb of Gurgaon in Haryana. A large automobile assembling plant has been established in Greater Noida (Gautam Buddh Nagar) in Uttar Pradesh. These factories have spawned the growth of a large number of units manufacturing components for cars.
- Modernization of the traditional handicraft industries such as manufacture of brass utensils in Jagadhari in Punjab and Rewari in Haryana; manufacture of decorative brassware in Moradabad in Uttar Pradesh and handloom weaving and manufacture of sports goods in Jalandhar in Punjab and Meerut in Uttar Pradesh, and manufacture of scissors, knives and surgical instruments in Meerut. Modernization will not only improve the quality and assist in the expansion of the industries, primarily for the domestic market, but also for export.

3. THE BIHAR-WEST BENGAL CORRIDOR

The corridor extends from the coal mining city of Dhanbad in Bihar, through Asansol–Durgapur in West Bengal to the Kolkata Metropolitan District and the jute mill towns located up to 60 kilometres north of Kolkata along the Hooghly river. The steel mill and motor vehicles manufacturing town of Jamshedpur and Ranchi where there is a large heavy machine tool factory are not part of the corridor at present, although they could become in future.

In contrast to the other two corridors, which are based on the existence of indigenous entrepreneurs and which concentrate on the manufacture of consumer goods, consumer durables and machine tools, development of this corridor is based on availability of coal, iron ore, limestone and other minerals.

Principal Industries

The principal industries in the corridor are:

- Coal mines, steel mills, and industries based on fabrication of steel such as manufacture of locomotives near Durgapur, commercial motor vehicles in Jameshedpur, and the large steel fabrication industry in Kolkata and Howrah.
- The Government of India owns some of the largest industrial units, notably the coal mines and the steel mills in Bokaro and Durgapur-Asansol and the locomotive manufacturing unit in Chittaranjan in West Bengal. Similarly, the largest steel fabricating units in Kolkata, owned before Independence by the Scots are also owned by the Government of India. The jute mills, also owned by the Scots before Independence are now owned mainly by the Marwaris, originally residents of western Rajasthan who began moving to Kolkata to become traders more than a century ago. The more successful among them, who became multi millionaires or billionaires, have become owners of the jute mills and the tea gardens of Assam, also formerly owned by the Scots. Kolkata is the principal export point for both jute goods and tea. A Bengali entrepreneur, Sir Biren Mukherjee, established the India Iron and Steel Company, now called the Steel Corporation of

Bengal. It was taken over by the Government of India during the 1950s because it was incurring huge losses. Bengali entrepreneurs also established two large companies manufacturing pharmaceuticals in Kolkata. A large number of small and medium sized steel fabrication units and those manufacturing machine tools and components for the large steel fabricating units in Kolkata and Howrah as well as units manufacturing consumer goods, pharmaceuticals, cosmetics and *sarees* are also owned by Bengali entrepreneurs. However, until Independence, the most talented Bengali young men coming from affluent families preferred to become professionals—lawyers, physicians, scientists, teachers and senior officers (*box-wallas*) in Scottish companies to becoming industrial entrepreneurs. Although most of the workers in industries in the corridor are from Bihar, Bihari entrepreneurship has been conspicuously absent. Transport by road of coal, steel and the goods manufactured in Kolkata and Howrah to the markets of north-western and western India is in the hands of the Punjabis, who also form the majority of forest contractors. The Biharis have developed a mafia which thrives on providing protection at a price to the contractors.

Future Prospects

Despite the handicap of shortage of indigenous entrepreneurs, the prospects for the corridor are for some area extension but primarily for deepening of industrial development. The rich mineral resources and replacement of an acute power shortage by a surplus of power are factors favoring such development. However, rail and road transport facilities must be increased for rapid expansion of industries in this corridor. In contrast to the other two corridors, coal and steel based industries such as machinery for mining, heavy machine tools, manufacture of locomotives and commercial vehicles and heavy chemicals including chemical fertilizers will remain the principal industries in this corridor.

Mining of coal and manufacture of steel, heavy machine tools, and heavy chemicals must increase rapidly if India enters a phase of rapid industrial growth. The capital for expansion of these industries must be provided mainly by domestic and foreign private investors. Accordingly, there should be adequate incentives to attract such capital. The expansion of road transport and power would also involve infusion of large domestic and foreign private investment.

MINI CORRIDORS

The only noteworthy mini-corridor at present is the road-cum-rail strip between Bangalore and Mysore city in central Karnataka. Bangalore, once a city of gardens, has become a large industrial city in the five decades after Independence. Two large industrial units–Hindustan Aeronautics, which services aeroplanes for the defense forces and manufactures telephone receivers and other telecommunications equipment and Hindustan Machine Tools which manufactures light machine tools and watches located around Bangalore-are owned by the Government of India. Hundreds of small and medium-sized industrial units are located in and around the city which manufacture components for these units, besides machine tools, telephone receivers and telecommunications equipment and consumer goods. The city has become the software export capital of India and is the centre of a rapidly developing information technology industry because of the availability of a large pool of young men and women trained in the sciences due to the existence of several institutes of science in the city. These industries continue to expand because of the advantage of an early start. There are good prospects for diversification into manufacture of computer hardware with both domestic and foreign investment. The city could remain the principal centre of information technology industries, although some other state governments, notably Andhra Pradesh, are trying hard to establish Hyderabad as a software export centre. Other state governments could also develop these industries in their capital cities because of the rapidly increasing domestic demand for the services provided by them.

The principal industry in the strip between Bangalore and Mysore is manufacture of sugar. Sugar mills were established in the 1940s after the extension of irrigation from a canal on the Cauvery river. Production of raw silk and manufacture of silk textiles is another well-established industry. The short distance (180 kilometres) between the two cities, good road and rail transport facilities, hard working farmers whose sons and daughters can be trained to become industrial workers are factors favouring the development of a mini-corridor.

The principal handicaps of the region are absence of an international airport through which the products of the information technology industries can be exported or sent to other cities in India, good roads and shortage of water and power in Bangalore.

INCIPIENT CORRIDORS

1. Lucknow-Kanpur in Central U.P.

Factors favoring corridor development along the nearly 75 kilometres road between the two cities are: existence of two million — plus cities located at a short distance from each other. A British company established Kanpur as an industrial centre about a century ago with cotton and woollen textiles and manufacture of shoes and other leather goods as its principal industries. Indian entrepreneurs now own these industries. Lucknow, although not an industrial centre, is a growing million-plus city. Industrial development in the strip could benefit if adequate road and rail transport facilities are developed for obtaining coal, steel and other raw materials from the coal mines and steel mills of Bihar and West Bengal. With the existence of a university in Lucknow and an Institute of Technology in Kanpur there is adequate supply of educated young men and women which could lead to the development of information technology related industries, especially in Lucknow.

The principal factors impeding industrial development in the region are the following:

- Lack of attention by successive governments of the state to promoting industrial development.
- Low income and level of living of the urban and rural population of the state.
- A serious problem of pollution of water and air in Kanpur to overcome which no serious effort has been made so far. However, all these handicaps could be remedied in a few years by a government, which is determined to promote industrial development in the state. With such a government which is also determined to improve law and order, the inadequacy of indigenous entrepreneurship would also disappear because the Jains and Aggarwals, two of the most important entrepreneurial groups in India, are residents of Western and Central Uttar Pradesh.

2. Kerala

An industrial corridor should develop in Kerala in the not-so-distant future. Factors favouring its development are the following:

- Existence of a large port at Ernakulam near Kochi.
- Existence of a good airport in Thiruvananthapuram the capital of the state. Improvements to bring the airport to international standards will greatly facilitate export of products of the industries in the region to other regions of India and abroad.
- Existence of a large educated manpower which could be easily trained for work in industries in which education and industrial skills are the principal requirements. The information technology industry and manufacture of precision machine tools are examples.
- Existence of a large petroleum refinery in Kochi could provide the basis for the development of a petrochemicals industry.
- Existence of a number of medium sized towns between Kochi and Thiruvananthapuram, which could become centres of small and medium sized industrial units.
- An entrepreneurial tradition among the Syrian Christians of the state.
- A high potential for development of winter tourism because of existence of a large number of excellent beaches. Local entrepreneurship and work force should not be wanting because millions of Keralites have experience of stay abroad.

The principal limitation is the long distance from the coal and steel mines of Bihar and West Bengal. However, this should not be a serious handicap because most of the industries in the region would be based on skills. Furthermore, adequate supply of hydro-electric power and availability of natural gas from the refineries at Cochin and Mangalore in Karnataka should provide ample fuels.

3. Hyderabad and Andhra Pradesh

Hyderabad, the capital of Andhra Pradesh, has become a very large industrial city in the post-Independence period. The Government of India owns some of the largest industrial units in and around the city.

Indigenous (Andhra) entrepreneurs have concentrated on manufacture of components for these units, besides manufacture of a large number of consumer goods for the markets of Hyderabad and the urban and rural population of the state. The city suffers, however, from serious problems of shortage of water and facilities for disposal of solid and liquid waste. Furthermore, there is no large or even medium sized city or town located at a short distance from Hyderabad that could favour development of an industrial corridor.

There are a large number of sugar and rice mills based on production of rice and sugar in the towns located in the area irrigated by the canals on Krishna and Godavari rivers. The rice and sugar mills are ancillary industries manufacturing components for the rice and sugar mills in cities like Vijayawada. However, industrial development in this area has been limited in comparison with the development in Western Maharashtra.

The present government is trying hard to develop Hyderabad as a rival to Bangalore as a software export centre. Educated manpower is available from the Osmania University in Hyderabad and Vijayawada University in Vijayawada. However, the serious problems of pollution of air and water must be solved and the airport and roads in and around Hyderabad must be improved before this objective can be achieved.

4. Chennai

Chennai has become a large industrial city in the post-Independence period. It benefited from the flight of capital from Kolkata during the late 1960s and the early 1970s. The environs of the city have been and continue to be favoured for manufacture of motor vehicles. Its principal advantage has been the existence of a large pool of skilled labour among which militancy of trade unions has been conspicuous by its absence. However, the problems of shortage of water and electricity in the city must be constantly combated for continued industrial development in and around it. It is noteworthy that an urban-industrial corridor has failed to develop between Bangalore and Chennai which are located at a distance of 250 kilometers from each other. Nor has there been any corridor development between Chennai and any other industrial town in Tamil Nadu. The principal reason for this appears to be long distances between Chennai and other industrial centres of the state—Coimbatore and Salem to the west and Madurai in the south.

CONCLUDING REMARKS

It will be clear from the above description of developed, mini and incipient corridors that development of rurban corridors will remain limited to regions in which conditions are particularly favorable for it. Elsewhere, as the example of Chennai and Hyderabad show, industrial development will continue to be confined to the environs of large cities. Accordingly, despite their advantages, rurban corridors do not provide a basis for industrial dispersal on a large scale. The large cities have the infrastructure, pools of entrepreneurs, managers, technical personnel and skilled workers required for industrial development. Furthermore, investment for infrastructure expansion will also be confined to large cities or their environs because of the presence of the industrialists and businessman located in these cities.

In the more backward states, such as Uttar Pradesh, Bihar, Orissa and Madhya Pradesh, industrial development will be greatly assisted by policies of the government aimed at it. However, it will be concentrated primarily in their capitals or other large cities in the foreseeable future.

Thus, rurban corridors provide an alternative to concentration of industries in large cities, which is essential for reducing pollution of air and water and shortages of electricity and water. However, large scale dispersal of industries to rurban corridors will become possible only at a later stage of economic development in India. The foreseeable near future prospects are for further growth of industries in the existing corridors, besides some areal expansion of these and development of a few mini-corridors in areas in which conditions are favourable for it.

NOTE

1. Published in *Urban India*, Vol. XIX No. 1 (1999).

7

Planning for Urban Growth: A Review of the First Three Plans with A 2001 Post Script for Urban Growth[1]

URBANIZATION IN INDIA

The rapid urbanization of the human population movement of large numbers of people from rural to urban areas and growth of cities and towns that we are witnessing today, began with the industrial revolution. Beginning with England in the latter half of the eighteenth century, industrial development transformed the settlement pattern in every country, be it USA, countries of Western Europe, Japan or Soviet Union. In England, less than 30 percent of the population was urban in 1800; in 1900, after a century of industrial growth, the proportion was over 75 percent and by 1930 it had reached 80 percent. In U.S.A. the increase was from 6 percent in 1800 to 40 percent in 1900 and further to nearly 70 percent in 1960. In Japan and the Soviet Union where industrialization began later, the transformation has been even more rapid. In Japan only 15 percent of the population was urban in 1900, but by 1960 the figure exceeded 65 percent. In U.S.S.R. the change has been from 20 percent in 1930 to about 50 percent in 1960.

This relation between industrial development and urbanization has been the subject of much discussion among economists. Basically, urbanization results from the concentration characteristic of modern industry. The economies of scale that characterises the manufacturing process have their counterpart in concentration of large numbers of people in urban centres. The factories, offices and commercial establishments are located in these centres and the workers live in them. The growth of factory towns called 'coke towns' by Mumford was the first result of the industrial revolution in England. The commercial towns, especially the ports, also grew rapidly because industrial development in England and other European countries was dependent upon foreign trade.

The relationship between industrialization and urban growth is not so clearly established in India so far. Industrialization is still in its early stages. In 1961, less than 5 percent of the workers were engaged in manufacturing industries, as few of the Indian cities and towns are industrial centres, the majority being commercial or administrative centres[2]. But from recent trends it appears that industrialization is on the way to become a major factor in urban growth. According to a recent estimate, 41.3 percent of all the jobs created in the urban areas during the decade 1951-61 were industrial jobs, and with the addition of the commercial and other service jobs, which follow creation of industrial jobs, the proportion of urban jobs owing their origin directly or indirectly to industrial activity was between 65 percent 70 percent.

Rapid urban growth started in India in the 1930s. Earlier, though some cities, such as, Kolkata and Mumbai had been growing rapidly, the proportion of urban population in the total population of the two cities remained between 10 percent and 12 percent respectively. After 1931, however, the urban population has increased rapidly and in 1961, it formed 18 percent of the total population.

The rate of growth of the urban population appears to have slowed down somewhat during 1951-61 (Table 7.1). But this is more apparent than real; because it is accounted almost entirely by the change in definition of urban area introduced in the census of 1961.

As a result of this change, a large number of places, which would have been classified as urban according to the earlier definition, were classified as rural in 1961, and the rate of growth of the urban population during 1951-61 was lower than it would have been otherwise. Using the earlier definition, Bose (1963) estimates the increase in the urban population during this decade at about 38 percent which is only slightly less than the rate of increase in the previous decade. However, the large migration of the 1941-51 decade, caused by Second World War and Partition of the country has not been maintained in the succeeding decade, and migration accounts for a much smaller proportion of the increase in urban population during

Table 7.1: Urbanisation in India, 1901-1961

Year	*Population of India (in millions)*	*Per cent Variation Per decade*	*Urban population (in millions)*	*Per cent Variation Per decade*	*Per cent urban of total population*	*Per cent relative growth of urban population*
	(1)	*(2)*	*(3)*	*(4)*	*(5)*	*(6)*
1901	236.3	—	25.7	—	10.91	—
1911	252.1	+55.73	26.6	+2.4	10.57	–3.12
1921	257.4	–0.31	28.6	+7.3	11.38	+7.66
1931	279.0	+11.01	33.8	+18.4	12.13	+6.59
1941	318.7	+14.22	44.3	+31.1	13.91	+14.67
1951	361.1	+13.31	62.6	+41.2	17.34	+24.66
1961	439.2	+21.50	78.8	+25.9	18.00	+ 3.80

Source: Bose 1963.

this decade than was the case earlier. Whereas during 1941-51, about half of the increase in urban population was due to migration, in 1951-61 less than one fourth has been due to this factor (Bogue and Zachariah, 1962). But as the 1951-61 decade has been free from natural or social disturbances such as famine, epidemic, war or large-scale internal unrest, and as planned development has been the dominant theme in it, its experience is relevant in projecting the future growth of urban population.

PROJECTIONS OF GROWTH

Projections of growth of urban population, which had been made before the data of the 1961 Census became available and had been influenced by the rapid urban growth during 1941-51, had forecast totals of 180 to 200 million by 1981[3]. A more recent estimate made by the Town and Country Planning Organisation, which takes into account the data of the 1961 Census has forecast a total of 165 million by 1981 (TCPO Unpublished). In other words, even according to this lower estimate, the urban population of India will double between 1961 and 1981. This estimate is not likely to be on the high side; it may well prove to be too low—because the natural increase of the population now living in the urban areas will itself grow, at 20 percent per decade and result in an increase of about 45 percent. Some increase will result also from extension of boundaries of the existing cities and towns, and from upgrading of large villages to towns. Therefore, it would be realistic to assume that the urban population of India will at least double between 1961 and 1981.

A large proportion of the urban population is concentrated in the cities. About a quarter (24.5%) lives in the metropolitan areas of the seven 'million + cities'—Kolkata, Mumbai, Delhi, Chennai, Hyderabad, Bangalore and Ahmedabad and nearly half lives in the cities—towns with population of 1,00,000 and over. The large cities are also the fastest growing urban settlements (Table 2A and 2B).

Table 7.2A: Growth of Towns of Different Size-Classes 1931-61 (%)

	Towns with population				
	100,000 and above	*50,000 to 99,999*	*20,000 to 49,999*	*below 20,000*	*All towns*
1931-41	64.5	32.3	23.4	11.5	31.1
1941-51	63.9	33.8	40.8	22.5	41.2
1951-61	48.0	27.6	40.5	7.2	37.7

Source: Bose, A. no 2. p.23

Table 7.2B: Growth of the 'Million + Cities' 1931-61

(In lakhs)

City	*1931*	*1941*	*1951*	*1961*	*Variation 1931-61 per cent*
Kolkata Metropolitan Distt.	24.85	40.54	52.53	65.75	165.0
Greater Mumbai	13.3	16.95	28.39	41.52	218.6
Chennai	6.47	7.77	14.60	17.29	167.2
Delhi	4.47	6.69	14.37	23.44	424.3
Bangalore	3.11	4.11	7.86	12.07	288.1
Ahmedabad	3.14	6.07	8.28	12.06	284.0
Hyderabad	6.67	7.39	10.86	12.51	168.0

Source: Jakobson, L. *Regional Planning for Urbanisation in Eastern India*, (C.M.P.O., Kolkata, p. 34, 1965). (Unpublished) pp. 15-16.

The large cities are also the most truly urban and modern places among the Indian urban settlements. Dominance of industry, commerce, professions and administrative services in the occupational structure, and development of modern facilities of transport and communications and education and medical care have been reached only in them. At the other extreme, the small towns with a population of 20,000 or less are only quasi-urban. Large numbers of people living in them are engaged in agriculture or other primary occupations; modern services are not well developed and they preserve to a considerable extent the characteristic features of the traditional social structure. Most of these small towns are local service centres linked closely with the local economy and culture.

Indian cities and towns have been classified by different experts in different ways. For my purpose here I find classification into pre-industrial and post-industrial towns, based on Sjoberg's concept of the pre-industrial city, most useful. The three metropolitan cities Mumbai, Kolkata and Chennai which were established by the British and which owe their growth primarily to expansion of modern industrial, commercial and administrative activities are post-industrial cities. In the same category are specialised industrial or transport towns such as Jamshedpur and Kharagpur and the new steel towns. On the other hand, the great majority of the small and medium-sized towns—local market centres, district towns, many State capitals—are pre-industrial. In some cases large, post-industrial segments have been added to the older towns. Ahmedabad is an example. More frequently, the older towns, which became the seats of provincial or district administration, cantonments or railway junctions, had a modern section, the civil station, added to them.

The pre-industrial and post-industrial towns differ in significant ways. First, modern services and facilities-transport and communications, electricity, protected water supply, modern education and medical care, banking and insurance are all concentrated in the post-industrial towns or in the post-industrial segments of the older towns. Second, the social structure of the two classes of towns differs considerably. In the older towns the social structure has remained largely traditional, so much so that in the small towns, the patterns of settlement, social interaction and economic activity are chiefly dominated by caste and family. Most of the people of these towns live in localities traditionally inhabited by their caste and engage either in their traditional caste occupations or minor variants of these. Social life continues to be organised on the basis of family and caste. The situation is quite different in post-industrial towns (or the post-industrial segments of the older towns). The typical resident of these the lawyer, the doctor, the distributor of manufactured goods or even the unskilled labourer is engaged in economic activities not as a member of a traditional caste group, but as an individual. Typically, he is a migrant, who has moved away from his village or district. He may not have repudiated traditional values and mores and he may seek residence and group life in the town with people of his region or his caste,[4] but he functions as an individual. The process has gone farthest in the metropolitan cities of Mumbai and Kolkata in which there is at the upper economic and social levels the fullest development of western-style economic activities professions, administrative services, commerce, banking and finance and at the other levels agglomeration of vast masses of people working in factories and offices, who have been torn from their traditional homes and communities, but who have not yet established themselves in the new social matrix. Large numbers of them are unable to live even with their nuclear families, because of their low income and difficulties of finding suitable housing.

These features have had two interesting results. Modern industrial and other economic activities have tended to concentrate in the post-industrial towns (or in the post-industrial segments of the older towns), which have grown much faster than the older towns. But this growth is accompanied by considerable human misery, caused not merely by poverty, extreme over-crowding and shortages of water, transport and other essential services, but also by the fact that the great majority of the people of the cities, torn from their families and traditional communities, are not able to build new, suitable and satisfying patterns of individual and group life.

Attention began to be focused on the extremely unsatisfactory living conditions in the Indian cities in the 1930s. The surveys conducted by the Tata School of Social Work in the industrial labor areas of Mumbai had not a little to do with this. Since then a number of surveys have been conducted, the most recent being the city surveys conducted under the auspices of the Research Programmes Committee of the Planning Commission[5]. These surveys not only reaffirm the findings of the earlier surveys, but also point to the fact that in many cities, conditions of urban living have deteriorated during the last 30 years because expansion of housing and essential services has not kept pace with the increase in population. A visible symbol of this failure is the growth of vast *bustees*—colonies of *kutcha* structures, built of mud and of thatch or of wooden planks and corrugated iron sheets and lacking essential services, such as protected water supply, sewerage or even satisfactory conservancy arrangements. It is estimated by the Kolkata Metropolitan Planning Organisation that nearly a quarter of the population of Kolkata city (about 7,00,000 people) lives in *bustees*, and the number is growing because the rate of new house construction is much less than the rate of increase of population. Even in Mumbai, where *bustees* were relatively few before Second World War, there are now vast sprawling *bustees*. It has been estimated that as against an average annual requirement of 1.7 million new dwellings only about 2,00,000 new dwellings, are being built annually in the urban areas of India. The present shortage of houses in the urban areas has been estimated at 12 million dwelling units which will increase progressively to 25 million units by 1976 if the disparity between growth of demand and the rate of house construction persists (Government of India 1965). In case of Mumbai, the current shortage is estimated by the Municipal Corporation at 1,31,000 dwelling units and the plan provides for construction of 5,82,000 dwelling units by 1981 in order to wipe out the shortage of units and to meet the demand created by population growth during the period (Municipal Corporation of Greater Mumbai). Water supply, sewerage and drainage are equally serious problems. In metropolitan Kolkata, protected water supply is sufficient only for about half of the population. The sewerage system serves only about half of the area of the Kolkata Corporation; the remaining half of the Corporation area, the city of Howrah and most of the suburbs are entirely without sewerage facilities. Drainage is so inadequate that even a light shower results in flooding of large areas of the city. Conditions in Mumbai are somewhat better, though even here the general situation is of acute shortage of water supply and absence of sewerage facilities over large areas. As against the estimated demand of 350 million gallons per day (mgd), available water supply averages 210 mgd. To meet this deficit (and the anticipated increase in demand) the city will have to double its water supply during the next 10 years and to raise it further to nearly three times the present supply by 1981. Sewerage facilities which are largely absent in the suburbs, will have to be extended to them. Water supply and sewerage programmes figure prominently in the Development Plan of Greater Mumbai; nearly 30 percent of the total outlay of Rs. 700 crores is earmarked for them as per the plan (Municipal Corporation of Mumbai).

Even the most elementary facility of primary education which has to be provided to every child in the country by the end of the Fourth Plan or somewhat later is not available for large numbers of children in some cities. In Kolkata metropolitan district, for instance, primary education facilities are adequate only for about 60 percent of the children of school going age (Kolkata Metropolitan Planning Organisation). An enlightened and well financed municipal body as the Mumbai Corporation, is not able to provide satisfactory school accommodation for more than a fraction of the children in primary schools. Out of nearly 700 schools in Greater Mumbai, only one third operate one session per day; the remaining have to run two or three sessions because of shortage of accommodation (Municipal Corporation of Mumbai).

The failure of Indian cities to provide the minimum levels of housing and other services is, to an extent, part of a worldwide phenomenon. Expansion of housing and other services has not kept pace with urban growth in most countries, especially in the early stages of economic development. This is clear as much from the writings of historians, economists and others on conditions in the industrial countries in the last century, as by the existence of vast slums in the older sections of the large British and American cities[6]. Cities in all developing countries today are being flooded with immigrants who cannot obtain proper housing and other services and are living in sprawling shantytowns. These shantytowns, which are mushrooming everywhere, have become the symbol of urbanisation in the twentieth century as the factory slum was the symbol in the nineteenth century.

The principal reason why urban housing and other services do not expand in proportion to the increase in urban population, is the very high cost of creating these. The cost of building an urban dwelling unit was estimated by the Union Ministry of Works Housing & Supply some years ago at between Rs. 2,500 and Rs. 7,500; the variations are due to differences in the value of land and the different kinds of structures that are built in different cities[7]. The cost of providing water and other essential services in cities of different sizes has been estimated at between Rs. 96 and Rs. 307 per capita (Table 3). This for a five-member family dwelling unit works out to be between Rs. 480 and Rs. 1535 (Wurster 1962).

Table 7.3: Cost of Provision of Urban Services by Class of Cities

Major Heads of Development	*Cost Per capita*					
	Class A (Spl.)	*Class A*	*Class B*	*Class C*	*Class D*	*Class E*
1	*2*	*3*	*4*	*5*	*6*	*7*
Water supply (including head works, Treatment plants etc.)	65.00	47.00	39.00	30.00	22.00	18.00
Sewerage (including sewage disposal)	75.00	65.00	55.00	45.00	34.00	28.00
Construction of road and paths	81.00	70.00	41.00	29.00	21.00	16.00
Construction of storm water drains	41.00	29.00	26.00	22.00	20.00	17.00
Provision of street lighting	30.00	25.00	22.00	20.00	19.00	14.00
Horticultural operations	15.00	13.00	10.00	7.00	5.00	2.00
Total	**307.00**	**249.00**	**193.00**	**153.00**	**121.00**	**96.00**

Source: Augmentation of Financial Resources of Urban Local Bodies. *Report of the Committee of Ministers constituted by the Central Council of Local Self Government,* 1963. p. 116.

These estimates will need to be revised upwards now, in order to provide for increase in costs. The present day cost per dwelling unit in case of metropolitan cities, such as Mumbai and Kolkata, would not be less than Rs. 10,000; it may be higher. An idea of the magnitude of investment required to meet the needs of urban growth may be had from an estimate made by Pant in 1961. Turner R (1962 pp 184-189) Working with an average figure of Rs. 1,600 per capita (or Rs. 8,000 per dwelling unit), he calculated the cost of providing housing and municipal services to the new urban population for the period 1961-81 at Rs. 150 billion and adding the cost of education, medical care and other services, the total investment needed for this population at Rs. 195 billion.

Pant's estimate will need to be revised to provide for (i) a lower urban population, (ii) cost differentials in cities of different sizes and (iii) rise in costs since 1961. But if the pattern of urban growth with emphasis on expansion of the big cities remains unchanged, the totals will not be very different from his figures, even now.

The very high cost of urbanization has led some economists to the view that the under-developed countries of Asia cannot afford large-scale urbanization. I quote below the view of an eminent Japanese economist:

"Of course, a certain degree of urbanization inevitably accompanies the development of civilization, but the point is that the under-developed countries in Asia today are in no position to afford the luxuries of urbanization, beset as they are with problems of overpopulation, unemployment, poverty, etc. However, there is a possibility that with the recent developments in the means of transportation (buses, cars, railroads, motorcycles, bicycles) and of mass communications (television, telephone, radio, magazines, newspapers) and the trend toward suburban living in the West, there will be no need for the extensive development of large cities, as was the case in the past in the West, and much of the present investment in urban infra-structure may turn out to be wasteful, as far as the future is concerned" (Oshima,1962).

Whether we agree with this view and the further view that there may be no need for development of large cities in future, we cannot ignore the fact that the costs of providing housing and other essential services are much lower in the small towns than in the large cities. Moreover, in the industries and other establishments located in small towns, a large proportion of the workers can be commuters from neighboring villages. Housing and other services do not have to be provided for them by the employers; they can themselves improve their old homes or build new ones with their new incomes. Community facilities in the villages can be improved by the village communities, of course with assistance from the State. In other words, concentrated investment by the employer, or the State is substituted by investment over a period of time by the individuals and the village communities. Moreover, the investment is much less because much greater use of locally available materials and labor is possible. The very high cost of big-city-urbanization, the failure to incur the cost and the prospect of major savings in cost through dispersal of growth to small towns, lends urgency to the task of evolving a suitable policy on urbanization. In my view this is among the most important issues of economic and social policy in India today.

Evolving a policy on urbanization is equally urgent for balanced regional development. Industries, commerce and other non-agricultural activities, which lead to urbanization, are the growth influences in an economy. Their concentration in a few cities result in growing disparities between the cities and the rest of the country; their dispersal to different regions is essential for initiating economic growth in all parts.

It should be the objective of this policy to evolve a settlement pattern, which is suited to the requirements of a modern agro-industrial economy but which does not impose crushing economic burdens or cause serious social disturbance. Such a pattern can now be evolved by developing countries including India by full and imaginative exploitation of the latest technological advances, which are changing rapidly the patterns of industrial location and urban settlement.

URBAN DEVELOPMENT IN THE PLANS

In the intellectual climate of India of the 1930s and the 1940s there was a strong anti-urban element. Migration of large numbers of people from villages to the cities was deplored on the ground that it denuded the villages of their most dynamic and progressive elements and created in the cities difficult problems of over-crowding, unemployment and inter-group tensions. The thinking was that traditional India lived in villages; cities were aberrations and the central objective of social endeavour should be to revitalise rural life. This thinking, which was in essence the Gandhian thinking, has had a major influence on economic policies in the post-Independence years. It has focussed attention on the importance of rural development and prevented concentration of investment in urban areas (to the neglect of rural areas) which might well have been the case considering that most planners, administrators and businessmen came from the cities. But this thinking under-rates the dynamic role of cities and towns in economic development and social change.

This thinking, together with adherence to the idea that urban development can be financed largely from resources of urban local bodies, account probably for the fact that urban development did not receive adequate attention in the first two Five Year Plans. These Plans are full of the job to be done in the villages. One gets from them a vivid realisation of the rural problem and a detailed exposition of the steps needed to meet it; but a similar treatment of the urban problem is lacking. Even the Second Plan which placed so much emphasis on industrial development, does not give much attention to urban development. In fact, it is not until the Third Plan that the urban problem began to engage the serious attention of the planners. Attention began to be directed to it because rapid and haphazard growth of cities like Delhi, Bangalore and Poona pointed to the urgent need for planned development.

The Third Plan contains a provision for preparing master plans for 50 cities and towns including all the large cities and the principal industrial centres. In this Plan, much larger funds were provided for housing and water supply and sanitation programmes, than had been the case earlier; but urban development programmes were not integrated with national and State Plans. Secondly, while the need for augmenting the resources of municipal bodies was recognised, and the importance of an appropriate policy on urban land was emphasized, no major steps were outlined for improving municipal finances. Indeed the principle that urban development programmes should be integrated with the national and State Plans and should not be left to be financed largely out of municipal resources, has been accepted only in the Fourth Plan.

The Government's policies in the industrial field—encouragement to village and handicraft industries, development of small scale industries, dispersal of industries from the large cities—can be seen as flowing logically from the thinking described above. These policies which were explained in the First Five Year Plan were reiterated in the Second Industrial Policy Resolution of 1956, and also in the Second Five Year Plan (Government of India). Dispersal of industry and balanced regional development were again emphasized in the Third Five Year Plan which contains in its Chapter on 'Balanced Regional Development', a detailed discussion of the various issues involved in industrial location and urban and regional growth (Government of India).

Government can influence location of industries by its powers of control over location of private sector industrial units, by providing fiscal and other incentives for location in particular areas and not in others and by its own decisions on location of industrial units in the public sector. Under the industrial licensing powers conferred on it by the Industries (Development & Regulation) Act, 1951, the Government can refuse location of units in particular areas. Among the measures for influencing location, the most important is the establishment of industrial estates and industrial areas in which developed land with facilities of electric power and water supply (industrial sheds also in industrial estates) is made available to industrialists on attractive terms. Considering the very high cost of land and the long time taken in obtaining it, and the shortages of electric power and water supply, this is a powerful instrument for influencing location. The decisions relating to location of public sector industrial units are, of course, entirely subject to Government policies.

ANALYSIS OF LOCATION OF NEW INDUSTRIAL UNITS

Private Sector Units

An analysis of distribution of new units as well as of units manufacturing new articles, licensed under the Industries (Development and Regulation) Act during the period 1952-64, by size of towns has been made recently by the Town & Country Planning Organisation (TCPO), New Delhi. The results of this analysis are summarised in the annexture, and Table 7.4 below.

It can be seen from the Table that 64.4 percent of the units have been located in and around the cities and as many as 41.4 percent in towns with population of a million or more. On the other hand, only 17.8 percent of the units have been located in the rural areas or in small towns with population of 20,000 or less. Nearly two-thirds of all the units are in the four groups of industries—metals and metal products, machinery and equipment, transport equipment and chemical and allied products. These are considered to be the fastest growing industries and it is note-worthy that the preference for location in large cities is particularly marked in their case. As data of Table 7.4 show, 75 percent of the units in these industries are located in the cities and 53 percent are located in the 'million & cities'. A more detailed analysis reveals that 39.1 percent of the units of the machinery and equipment group and, 40.6 percent of the units in the chemical and allied products group have been located in metropolitan Kolkata and Greater Mumbai alone.

A similar picture emerges from analysis of distribution of employment in factories located in industrial estates given in Table 7.5A. Nearly 70 percent of the total employment in factories in industrial estates is in factories located in the cities. This concentration in the cities is interesting, because industrial estates have been established for encouraging development of small scale industries, dispersal of industries and rural industrialisation as specific objectives of establishing them, and a number of estates are located in the rural areas.

Table 7.4: Distribution of New Units and Units Licensed for the Manufacture of New Articles in Four Selected Categories of Industries (1952-64)

Categories	*No. of Units*	*Size of Towns of with Population*				
	Total	*10 Lakh & Above*	*5 to 10 Lakh*	*2 to 5 Lakh*	*1 to 2 Lakh*	*1 Lakh and Above*
1. Metal & metal Products	535	244(45.5%)	42(7.9%)	47(88%)	45(8.4%)	378(70.7%)
2. Machinery & equipment (excluding transport, but including electrical)	1018	577(54.7%)	82(8.1%)	91(8.9%)	48(4.7%)	798(76.4%)
3. Transport equipment	259	145(56.0%)	11(4.2%)	23(8.9%)	14(5.4%)	193(74.5%)
4. Chemical and allied products	530	270(50.9%)	21(4.0%)	48(9.1%)	49(9.2%)	388(73.2%)
Total of all classes	2342	1236(52.8%)	156(6.7%)	209(8.9%)	156(6.7%)	1757(75.1%)
Total all industries	3618	1497(41.4%)	207(5.7%)	363(10.9%)	264(7.3%)	2331(64.4%)

Source: TCPO, New Delhi (i) and (iv).

Table 7.5A: Distribution of Employment in Functioning Industrial Estates Located in Different Classes of Cities and Towns (1963)

	Class of City/Town With Population	*Total Number of Functioning Industrial Estates*	*Employment*	
			Total No.	*Percent*
	(1)	*(2)*	*(3)*	*(4)*
1.	(above 100,000)	47	19,252	68.85
2.	(50,000–100,000)	20	4,358	15.58
3.	(20,000–50,000)	168	1,128	4.03
4.	(10,000–20,000)	7	1,225	4.38
5.	(5,000–10,000)	4	405	1.45
6.	(below–5,000)	12	1,502	5.37
7.	(village)	1	94	0.24
	Total	107	27,964	100.00

Source: TCPO (i) and (iv).

Public Sector Units

The distribution of public sector industrial units (excepting defence establishments), established in the first three Plans is given State-wise and by classes of towns in Table 7.5B. It will be seen that the largest investment (72.6%) is in industrial units having a small town or green field location. This group is dominated by the steel plants and petroleum-based industries. The next largest investment is in the units located in the medium-sized cities. Among the large metropolitan cities, Hyderabad, Bangalore and Chennai have each attracted more than one industrial unit, but the units are, in most cases small or medium-sized. Industrial units having green field location are all large, proving the point made by many economists that it is the large unit, which can create its own infrastructure that can choose a green field location.

EXPANSION OF SERVICES

The other major influence in urban growth is expansion of services, especially the administrative services. An idea of this expansion may be had from the fact that the number of civilian, non-industrial employees of the Central Government (excluding Railways) has gone

Table 7.5B: Location of Public Sector Industrial Units Started during the First Three Plans, By Size of Towns

Name of the State	*Metropolitan Cities (Population 1 Million and Above)*		*Other Cities*		*Medium Size Towns (Population Between 50,000 and 100,000)*		*Small Towns or Green Field Location*	
	No.	*Investment in Crores*	*No.*	*Investment in Crores*	*No.*	*Investment in Crores*	*No.*	*Investment in Crores*
(1)	*(2)*	*(3)*	*(4)*	*(5)*	*(6)*	*(7)*	*(8)*	*(9)*
Andhra Pradesh	4	44.66	3	12.32	—	—	—	—
Assam	—	—	1	13.00	—	—	1	14.50
Bihar	—	—	4	159.75	—	—	1	41.00
Gujarat	—	—	—	—	—	—	1	32.00
Kerala	—	—	6	26.09	—	—	1	0.15
Maharashtra	1	37.28	1	5.20	—	—	—	—
Madhya Pradesh	—	—	2	66.88	—	—	5	375.73
Mumbai	3	14.11	1	22.30	1	8.30	1	38.00
Mysore	3	18.69	—	—	1	6.00	—	—
Orissa	—	—	—	—	—	—	3	403.84
Punjab	—	—	—	—	—	—	3	40.60
Rajasthan	—	—	1	3.00	—	—	1	3.00
Uttar Pradesh	—	—	2	29.80	1	17.00	2	16.10
West Bengal	1	1.38	—	—	—	—	7	319.84
Total	**12**	**116.12**	**21**	**338.34**	**3**	**31.3**	**26**	**1284.76**

Source: Planning Commission (1964).

up from 5,91,000 in 1951 to 7,54,000 in 1960 (Central Statistical Organisation, 1961). The total number of persons in public services has increased from 2,153,000 in 1951 to 3,311,000 in 1961 (Census of India, 1961). The majority of these employees work in offices located in the urban areas. The number of workers in service activities will increase rapidly in future. In the Perspective of Development, 1960-61—1975-76, the Perspective Planning Division of the Planning Commission has estimated an increase of 23.8 million workers in the services sector—one-third of the total increase in employment during the period (Planning Commission, 1964). Employment in Government service will increase by 82 percent and in all services by 78 percent and the proportion of workers in services will go up from 17.4 percent to 22.0 percent. A large proportion of this increase will be in the urban areas because Government offices, commercial establishments, and all but the most elementary social service facilities are located predominantly in the urban areas.

TRENDS IN URBANISATION: A SUMMARY

The trends in urbanisation in India during the period of the first three Plans may be summed up as follows:

1. The largest metropolitan cities, Mumbai and Kolkata have continued to grow adding new industrial, commercial and service activities. The new, rapidly growing industries—metals, machinery and chemicals—have a marked preference for location in or near the towns and growth of the national and regional economies has resulted in a steady increase in their commercial administrative and service functions. The problems of over-crowding and pressure on essential services, already acute in the 1930s and 1940s, have now reached crisis proportions in these cities. Slums are proliferating and even the best sections of the cities are experiencing the pressures of growth.
2. The other large cities—Delhi, Chennai, Hyderabad, Bangalore, Poona—have also experienced rapid growth. Earlier they were essentially administrative and educational centres and were pleasant medium-sized cities, but now they have become large industrial—commercial—administrative centres with population of a million or more and have begun to experience typical metropolitan problems.
3. A number of smaller cities have experienced rapid growth due to expansion of industries or location of government offices. Ludhiana, Baroda (Vadodara), Coimbatore are examples of cities which have grown rapidly as a result of expansion of private sector industries; Bhopal and Ranchi are cities which have grown because of location of public sector industrial units. In case of the latter, new townships, distinct from the older cities have been established round

the industrial units. A few cities, such as Jaipur and Dehradun have grown on account of location of government offices. But a large number of smaller influences in them being expansion of administrative and other service activities. However, from preliminary indications of location of public sector industrial units during the Fourth Plan, it appears that a few more cities in this group may be selected for location of such units and may experience rapid growth.

4. The largest public sector industrial units, such as the steel plants have been located in backward regions and new townships have grown round them. Location of these units has great significance for economic growth in these regions. Expansion of the units and locations of various engineering and chemical industries near them is already leading to rapid expansion of the townships, each of which has become a major industrial centre. Moreover, the infrastructure facilities created for these units have greatly mitigated the disadvantage of these backward regions for location of industries. It has made them particularly attractive for location of industries which exploit their rich natural resources or are related to the steel industry. However, these developments, while of considerable local importance, have only a limited significance in the total picture of urban growth in the country.
5. The great majority of the smaller urban centres (those with population below 1,00,000) have not experienced significant industrial development. Their growth has been slow, being sustained only by expansion of various service activities. A few towns located in areas which have received canal irrigation and in which agricultural production has increased rapidly e.g., Hanumangarh in Rajasthan and Sirsa in Punjab have grown rapidly, but there are large numbers of stagnant towns in this group.

Metropolitan cities have grown rapidly and a number of not so large cities have grown to metropolitan size. In fact, rapid urban growth appears to be proceeding from the top downwards, bringing within its influence successively smaller cities and towns. It is necessary to understand this phenomenon, if only to ensure that our policies to alter it in future and to achieve a better balance in growth of cities of different sizes and located in different regions, are more effective in future. To an extent this phenomenon is only another aspect of the inter-connected nature of economic activities which results in concentration. Industries find it advantageous to locate in or near established centres because of various advantages which the centres offer. Availability of capital and skilled labour; facilities of marketing, insurance and advertising, and ease of obtaining supplies of machinery, spare parts and semi-finished or complementary products (from other manufacturers) are some of these advantages. They are particularly important for industrial location in the developing countries because they are available in only a few big cities. Secondly, in these countries financiers, entrepreneurs and the decision makers in Government are concentrated in the cities. And as means of transports and communication are not very well developed, the entrepreneurs like to locate their factories within easy commuting distance. This need is imperative in case of new industries in which many problems require personal attention of the entrepreneur. The attraction of Mumbai and Kolkata for the new, rapidly growing industries, in spite of very high costs of labor and land and various other difficulties, demonstrates the strength of these factors.

Location near Mumbai and Kolkata is favoured for another reason also. Much of the recent private sector industrial development is connected with the distribution function. Factories have been set up by importers (including Indian subsidiaries of foreign firms), foreign suppliers or by the two in partnership to pack, assemble, or manufacture well-known products, because the size of the market justified establishment of the factory or because import controls and other restrictions made large imports impossible. Since Mumbai and Kolkata are the principal distributing centres for imported goods, and channels of distribution have been built from them, there is a marked preference for location near them. An analysis of factories located in the Mumbai region during the post-Independence years, will, I am sure, reveal the very high proportion of those manufacturing products which were imported earlier or manufacturing new products sold by large established firms of distributors.

Industrial growth in the next largest cities—Delhi, Chennai, Bangalore, Poona—brings out the importance of the existence of modern infrastructure facilities. In each of these former administrative-service cities, water supply, electricity, transport and facilities for education and medical care were much better developed and a much larger pool of modern housing was available than was the case in the smaller cities. The physical layout of these cities offered scope for more intensive utilisation and could be expanded faster and at lower cost than creation of similar facilities elsewhere. These advantages have proved decisive in attracting new administrative offices and service institutions, as also public sector industrial units. The policy in location of public sector units is now clearly in favour of the smaller cities and towns, but the fact that even now new units are being located near Hyderabad, another city with a good physical layout plan, shows that the attraction of modern infrastructure facilities is too strong to be ignored by decision makers.

I am convinced of the urgent need for dispersal of industries and other economic activities from the large cities and have outlined later in this paper an approach which may prove to be more effective in achieving this objective than some of the other approaches which are advocated currently. But I consider it necessary to mention here that most of the cities of India including the largest cities—Mumbai, Kolkata, Chennai and Delhi—will continue to grow in the foreseeable future. Apart from the attraction of new industries for them, the specialised service functions which these cities perform for the country or for their hinterland regions, will increase in volume with economic growth. These functions are largely non-transferable; they can be performed only by cities having leadership roles in the national or regional economies. Projections of the growth of population of the Kolkata metropolitan district by 1981, made by the C.M.P.O., range from 11.5 million to 14.0 million. The figures for Mumbai are 7.0 million for the municipal area and more than 12 million for the Mumbai region (TCPO, 1965). The Master Plan for Delhi forecasts a population of over 5 million by 1981 (DDA, Master Plan for Delhi); but this figure will undoubtedly be exceeded, because the rate of growth in the years since the Plan was formulated has been higher than that envisaged in the Plan. The figures for Kolkata and Mumbai may be reduced somewhat by appropriate policies; but a substantial growth of these two cities is unavoidable. This fact should be clearly recognized.

TRENDS IN INDUSTRIAL LOCATION AND URBAN GROWTH IN THE ADVANCED INDUSTRIAL COUNTRIES

Before considering the future policies on urban growth in India, I should like to refer briefly to some recent trends in industrial location and urban growth in the advanced industrial countries. This will enable us to see recent developments in India against the background of world-wide trends and to see the directions of future policies more clearly. The most notable recent developments in the industrially advanced countries are two; (i) changes in the factors leading to industrial concentration, and (ii) a marked change in the pattern of urban settlement.

In the nineteenth century, when coal was the principal industrial fuel and most overland transport was by railways, industries concentrated in the coalfields, along railway lines or at the seaports where coal could be imported cheaply. The coalfields of Great Britain, Western Europe and Eastern United States where cheap coal and cheap transport were found together, became major industrial regions. Rail transport in these regions was developed to meet industrial needs; but outside the regions, it itself became a major determinant of industrial and urban growth, and even of settlement of new areas. Western United States, Canada and several Latin American countries were opened up by the railways and towns grew in them at focal points of rail transport. However, recent changes in use of industrial fuels and advances in power generation and transmission techniques have greatly reduced the attraction of industrial location near the coalfields. Coal is no longer the principal source of industrial power in most countries; oil or hydro-electricity has become very important and nuclear energy is rapidly gaining importance. Secondly, generation of power in large central stations, transmission over long distances at extra high voltages and inter-connection of power stations into regional, national or international grids have had the effect of equalising power rates over large areas. Widespread use of motor transport, with its door-to-door delivery, has reduced significantly, if not eliminated entirely for many industries, the advantage of location along railway lines. The results of these changes are seen in the changing patterns of industrial location. Several older industrial areas located near the coalfields, such as the industrial areas of Northern England and Wales are chronically depressed while industries are growing in new areas. Secondly, many industries find location anywhere within a large area equally advantageous. They are not tied to any particular location, and have begun to be called 'foot-loose industries'. Location of units in these industries is frequently decided on such considerations as availability of cheap land, cheap or trouble-free skilled labour, low taxes, or even congenial living conditions for workers and executives.

But along with these decentralising influences, there are certain centralising influences which increase the attraction of industries for location near the big cities. Progressive reduction in case of most industries of the share of raw material and power costs in the value of the finished product, has greatly increased the importance of location near the markets. The new rapidly growing industries—electronics, petro-chemicals, research—in which success depends upon use of the latest techniques, and fashion industries such as women's clothes, which cater for fast changing consumer tastes, find location near big cities a great advantage. Changes in techniques and in consumer preferences are best known in the cities and towns, the cities have the concentration of financiers and decision-makers in business and government, on whom these industries depend. The increasing administrative activities of governments and of large business houses, is a major factor in the growth of big cities. The concentrating tendency of administrative offices is stronger than that of any industry. Consequently, cities everywhere are constantly growing bigger. The population totals of the large metropolitan cities of the world—New York, Tokyo, London, Paris, Moscow—are unprecedented in human history. Kingsley Davis gives the following figures for the metropolitan areas of the world's twelve largest cities.

Table 7.8: Population of Metropolitan Cities (1965)

City	*Population Metropolitan region*
New York	14,114,927
Tokyo	10,117,000
London	8,176,810
Paris	7,369,387
Buenons Aires	7,000,000
Shanghai	6,900,000
Los Angeles	6,488,791
Moscow	6,354,000
Chicago	5,959,213
Kolkata	4,518,655
Mumbai	4,422,165
Beiging	4,010,000

Source: Davis, K. (1965) "*The Urbanisation of the Human Population,*" *Scientific American*, Vol. 213, No. 3, p. 43.

But the new growth is not within the cities, it is in suburbs and satellite towns located in their peripheral regions. The central areas of most cities have in fact lost population in recent decades because of movement of large numbers of people to the suburbs and satellite towns. This brings me to the second major development of recent decades, 'the dispersal of urban settlement.' This dispersal, which began in the 1920s and 1930s, has increased tremendously in the period after Second World War, as a result of mass ownership of automobiles. Living in the suburbs and commuting long distances to work in the central areas of cities, has become the accepted pattern of life in the developed industrial countries. Together, these two developments, tendency of big cities to grow bigger and dispersal of urban settlement have changed the shape and character of cities and led to a tremendous increase in their physical size. From small compact clusters, distinct from the surrounding country-side (which most cities were until recently), they have become vast sprawling masses, which merge imperceptibly at the fringes with the rural areas. The distinctive features of individual cities—layout, design, landmarks—are being over-shadowed by this sprawling growth. Moreover, there have arisen in the major urban-industrial regions of the world — the Atlantic Seaboard of the United States, South Eastern England, Central Japan, parts of Western Europe, gigantic conurbations which extend over thousands of square miles. In the U.S.A., the coastal strip between Boston and Washington D.C. is being covered by an almost continuous conurbation. The major cities-Boston, New York, Philadelphia, Baltimore, Washington D.C. are the principal urban centres in this zone, but there are innumerable smaller cities, towns and suburbs. The New York Metropolitan area alone has 235 urban communities within it. As one travels through this zone, one passes cities, towns and almost unending suburbs with the result that the distinction between town and country is lost and one gets the impression of passing through one unending city megalopolis. Similar developments have occurred or are occurring in the other areas mentioned above.

These developments involve gigantic movements of population and create altogether new problems. Planners, administrators, social scientists, intellectuals everywhere are concerned about them. Their concern arises from different considerations – aesthetic, socio cultural, economic, and strategic. Many of them consider these developments un-aesthetic and are disturbed over destruction of the natural landscape over large areas and creation in its place of an unending suburban monotony. They recognize the advantages of living in suburbs – freedom from congestion, dirt and noise of the big cities, living close to nature and forming part of a small community – but they are concerned with the time and inconvenience involved in the daily movement to work, and with the monotony of suburban life resulting from limited cultural and recreational facilities. Administrators and city fathers are disturbed over the movement to the suburbs of all but the poorest residents of the cities. This movement deprives the municipal bodies of the most enlightened, progressive and dynamic leadership increases their financial difficulties and accelerates degeneration of the older central areas of cities into slums. The aimless, formless, suburban growth is regarded by many planners, social scientists and intellectuals as a threat to the very existence of the city. They feel that it will destroy the city's role as the repository of culture and the centre of human creativity. Concentration of such vast numbers in limited geographical areas is considered, by the strategists to be extremely vulnerable in the nuclear age. The almost insuperable problem of traffic which moves to and from the cities is another cause of concern.

These trends are sought to be countered in various ways. The tendency of industries to concentrate in the conurbations is being discouraged by many governments by giving incentives for location away from these or even by banning location in these. In the United Kingdom, the incentives began to be given immediately after Second World War, with the twin objectives of reducing industrial growth in the South-east and of stimulating growth in the depressed industrial areas of the North and the West which had experienced severe unemployment during the 1930s. In Japan and the Netherlands, where these incentives have begun to be given more recently, the principal object is dispersal of industries from the highly concentrated central areas—the Tokyo Bay area in Japan and Randstad Holland in the Netherlands. The physical sprawl is sought to be countered by urban renewal, development of counter-magnets and satellite towns (new towns in U.K.). Urban renewal aims at rebuilding the central areas of cities, with a view partly to bringing back to them some of the people who have migrated to the suburbs. Counter-magnets and new towns are intended to check haphazard urban sprawl and to impart functional order and aesthetic beauty to urban growth.

These trends in the industrially advanced countries have great interest for the developing countries, not only because the new technological advances affect their urban pattern, but even more because the developing countries can take full advantage of them to evolve new distinctive patterns of industrial location and urban growth. The developed countries have to rebuild and change their cities in order to take advantage of the new technological advances, but the developing countries can also build their cities in accordance with the requirements of these. I believe that these advances can offer to India new patterns of urban settlement which will avoid the crushing economic burden of conventional urbanisation and disruption of community and family life. They can, in fact, enable India to accomplish its transformation from a traditional, predominantly agricultural society to a modern, agro-industrial, society without movement of large masses of people from the villages to the cities.

EFFECTS IN INDIA: GROWTH OF PERIPHERAL REGIONS AND EMERGENCE OF AGRO-INDUSTRIAL REGIONS

The urban growth in India in recent years has been greatly influenced by the emergent global trends. A large part of the growth of our metropolitan cities has been in the suburbs or in industrial townships located in the peripheral regions. In case of Mumbai, development in the immediate post-war years was mainly along the roads going north from the city, but has now spread to the mainland area opposite Mumbai Island. The entire mainland area up to the Western Ghats is affected by this development. From the other side, Poona is expanding rapidly and had it not been for the Ghats, the entire Mumbai-Poona area would have become a continuous urban-suburban belt by now. Urban development in Delhi already covers most of the area of Delhi State and has extended into Punjab and U.P.—to Faridabad and beyond in the South, to Gurgaon in the West and to Ghaziabad in the East. The Master Plan of Delhi was formulated with the Delhi Metropolitan Area of about 800 sq. miles as the unit, but it is now felt that in order to regulate the new developments, a plan should be drawn up for a much larger area of about 4000 sq. miles, this being called the National Capital Region.

Dispersal of industries and urban settlements has been encouraged both by economic factors and by policies of government. The Industrial townships located in the peripheral regions of cities combine the advantages of access to the facilities of the city (which can be reached without too much difficulty) and of cheap land and labour available in the rural areas. Government policies—discouraging location of new industrial units within cities, development in the peripheral regions of industrial estates and industrial areas in which developed land is provided for industries on attractive terms—have also been a major contributing factor. In case of several cities, such as Bangalore, Chennai and Hyderabad, location of public sector industrial units has led to establishment of new industrial townships in the peripheral regions.

A variant of these developments, which is of particular interest for future policies, is industrial and urban growth in the coastal Gujarat area between Ahmedabad and Surat and in the Central Punjab area between Amritsar and Ludhiana. In both these areas, industrial growth has spilled over from the cities to the small towns and even to villages located along the highway, with the result that entire regions are being steadily industrialised and urbanised. There are undoubtedly significant differences between the developments in the two areas. In Gujarat, the typical factory is a large or medium sized unit established by an industrialist having sufficient capital. In Punjab, on the other hand, most factories are very small units run by artisans, whose main assets are their own skill and determination to succeed. These Factories are poorly capitalised, they do not have modern equipment and often face many problems. But in both areas, a dispersed industrial development has become a reality because of certain common features. Transport and communications are good; electric power and water supply are easily available, educational and medical services are well developed; literacy and health standards are quite high; villages and towns are modern, and workers with the necessary skills, awareness of the requirements of modern industry and willingness to do industrial work are readily available. Finally, as the workers can continue to live in the small towns, or villages and come to work on bicycles or by public transport, the employers are not burdened with the need to provide housing and other facilities for them. These advantages compensate more than the disadvantage of locating factories away from the big cities.

Urban and industrial development in these two areas has considerable significance for all those interested in planning for urban growth. Industrial dispersal, development of industry contributing to regional economic growth, integration of urban and rural development which have been important objectives of Government policies, have been achieved in these areas. Moreover, as the majority of workers continue to live in their old homes, the change to industrial employment does not involve the crushing economic burden and social disruption of urbanisation. On the contrary, the new incomes and ideas and new demands for farm products generated by industrial development, contribute to making agriculture more progressive and remunerative. Agriculture in both areas has attained a high level of development, though the cause and effect sequence—the role of industry in improving agriculture or of developed agriculture in attracting industry—can only be ascertained through a field investigation. This is, in fact, a fruitful field of enquiry for students of economic development.

There are perhaps a dozen areas in different parts of the country in which similar developments can be seen in the initial stages or can be initiated by suitable action. The areas between Dehra Dun and Agra in Western U.P. and between Kanpur and Lucknow in Central U.P., the Bangalore-Mysore belt, and parts of Kerala and Maharashtra are examples of such areas. Dispersed industrial and urban growth can be stimulated in these areas by supplying the critical factors, which may be lacking. Similar integration of urban and rural and industrial and agricultural development can be secured through careful planning in the peripheral regions of metropolitan cities, and, on a smaller scale, in a number of medium-sized or small towns which can be developed as local or sub-regional growth nuclei. Development in the peripheral regions of the cities can be concentrated in well planned townships having easy access to the surrounding rural area, so that commuting of workers from villages becomes possible. Moreover, it can be ensured that these townships are self-contained in the matter of services and facilities, so that their residents do not have to travel frequently to the cities. The Third Five Year Plan recommends that large industrial and other projects should be regarded as nuclei of regional growth, round which a number of connected developments take place and a growth process is started (Planning Commission, Third Five Year Plan). Other well selected small or medium-sized towns can be similarly developed as focal points of local or sub-regional growth.

PLANNING FOR URBAN GROWTH: THE REGIONAL APPROACH

Indeed the regional approach appears to be the most fruitful for planning of urban growth in India. The principal ingredients of this approach are: (i) relating growth of individual cities and towns to economic growth in their regions; (ii) selecting in each region (and smaller area) one or more growth points and (iii) considering large macro-regions as spatial systems, different cities and towns of which are inter-connected in a functional hierarchy, and growth of which can be planned as units. I shall illustrate this approach with Western India—Maharashtra and Gujarat, as examples. Mumbai is the principal commercial, financial and transport center in the region. Its apex central place,[8] Ahmedabad, Poona, Nagpur are sub-regional centres. Below these cities, there is a hierarchy of smaller towns—district towns, *mandi* towns block or *taluk*, headquarters towns and finally the very small towns (or large villages) which function as service centres for groups of villages. The total quantum of urban growth in Western India can be calculated within the perspective of growth in the national economy, such as projected in the Perspective of Development, 1960-61 to 1975-76 published by the Planning Commission (1964). Growth of agricultural and industrial production, and of transport commerce, administration and other services can be calculated in the light of national targets, the natural and human resources of the region, the locational advantages of various places within it and the policies relating to location of large industrial enterprises and various resource development projects. But pending such calculation and for the sake of simplicity, let us assume that the urban population of Western India will double, along with that of the rest of the country between 1961-1981 and that the proportion of workers in the urban population will remain unchanged during the period. This will mean an addition of nearly 16.5 million urban people and nearly 5.6 million urban workers. How would these be distributed among the cities and towns of the region? For this purpose, it is necessary first to identify for each city and town the specific service functions which it performs for its service area and calculate the growth needed for efficient performance of the increased volume of services consequent on growth in the service area. For the large industrial cities—Mumbai, Poona, Ahmedabad—the minimum unavoidable growth of industries and other economic activities not directly related to their essential service roles should then be calculated. The balance of industrial and other economic activities can then be distributed among different urban centres in the region in accordance with accepted policies of industrial dispersal and balanced regional development; the bulk of it will have to be concentrated in a few growth nodes which may be built as counter-magnets to the large cities or as focal points for growth of particular areas.

Let us explain this approach starting with Mumbai (Mumbai). The essential service functions of the city are as a port and as a center of business and finance. Its port function is of regional and extra-regional character, because, besides Western India, a large area of North Western India is served. Its function as a center of business and finance is national. The city performs many other important functions at present: it is the capital of Maharashtra and is a major industrial center. But these functions are not essential to its role as a regional or national central place; however, important they may be at present. Economic growth will lead to an increase in all the activities of city. Of these, the function of business and finance center is the least transferable, because it has to be performed in a city having a leadership position in the region and the country. Certain administrative or directional activities of the Central government or the State governments which are connected with business and finance—collection of taxes, import control, export promotion, regulation of the stock exchanges—have also to be located in the city. The expansion of the city needed to meet the increased volume of such activities, consequent on growth in Western India and in the country, will have to be fully provided for. The port function is largely transferable because the bulk of the increase in traffic can be diverted to other ports. Increase in the administrative and industrial function is entirely transferable. It is true that transfer of existing offices and industries will involve much cost and disturbance; but future growth can be diverted to other places without difficulty. Expansion of administrative offices of the Maharashtra Government can be entirely outside the city. It would be an advantage to divert most of it to Poona and Nagpur, which already have many offices of the Government. Diversion of industrial growth to other parts of the region is the most important from the economic stand-point and after some time, the bulk of industrial growth in Western India should be located outside Mumbai city. The inevitable minimum growth near Mumbai should be concentrated in the peripheral region.

Similarly, in case of sub-regional centers like Ahmedabad, Poona, Nagpur, the growth connected with their specific service functions can be calculated and provided for, and the quantum of growth resulting from expansion of industries and other non-essential economic activities can be decided keeping in view social and economic objectives. Nagpur, which has grown rather slowly during the last two decades, could take a much larger industrial growth than either Poona or Ahmedabad. It could, in fact, be built as a principal growth node for the Vidarbha area.

The growth of the smaller towns—district centres, *mandi* towns and other small towns has to be related primarily to growth in the economies of the rural areas which they serve. Modernisation of agriculture, increase in agricultural production, rise in rural levels of living and of social welfare, will add greatly to the commercial, administrative and social service functions of these towns and this addition will be the major influence in their growth. Each of these towns can be visualised as the focal point of modernisation of its service area from which new goods, processes, techniques, ideas and attitudes travel to the villages. The more suitable among these towns can attract various industries, especially industries connected with processing of agricultural produce, fabrication of agricultural implements and manufacture of various consumer goods. They can, in fact, be developed as small commercial-industrial centres.

As explained above, a large part of the industrial growth in the region will need to be concentrated in a number of growth nodes which are built up as counter-magnets to the large cities or as focal points for regional or local growth. One or more such nodes should be developed in each of the backward or stagnant areas of the region—Saurashtra, Khandesh, Marathwada, Vidarbha. As one city or growth area reaches a saturation point, another can be developed. Indeed, the different cities and growth areas in the region can be considered as inter-connected units in a spatial system and urban planning for the region can be viewed as being analogues to planning of power in a region in which a number of generating stations, large and small, are connected to a regional grid.

Such macro-regional planning of urban growth should become an essential part of the exercise in perspective economic planning. It should be the spatial expression of the plans. The urban and regional planners have been saying for some time that our five-year plans lack a spatial dimension and have been urging that a spatial plan should accompany each five-year plan. There is undoubtedly need for drawing up such plans; but the exercise is even more necessary and useful in case of perspective plans. The longer period gives greater flexibility and freedom in location of activities and enables the growth potential of each region and smaller area to be seen more clearly.

Structure, Organisation and Finances of Urban Local Bodies

Micro-regional planning has certain implications for planning and financing of urban development programmes and for the organisation of urban local bodies. It follows from it that urban development programmes cannot remain the responsibility of the municipalities alone; they have to be the joint responsibility of municipal, state and national governments. The fact that it is decided to develop a particular town as a local or a sub-regional growth node and a number of industries are located in it does not mean that the entire responsibility for managing and financing the growth of the town should rest upon its municipality. This body would neither be interested in undertaking the task nor would it be able to do it. The majority of the local people, who would in the initial stages feel more the economic and social strains of rapid growth than its gains, would not be enthusiastic in undertaking large development programmes. The resources of the municipality, derived mainly from property taxes and octroi, would be barely adequate for maintaining elementary services, such as conservancy, street lighting and a rudimentary kind of water supply. Our present municipal system is suitable only for managing medium-sized or small towns which are growing slowly: many will maintain that it has not proved itself to be suitable even for this limited task, but it is certainly not designed for planning and financing of rapid urban growth. The only institution in it which is at all oriented towards expansion and growth is the Improvement Trust. But even the Trust, as the very name suggests, can undertake activities which are in the nature of improvements; it cannot undertake the development programmes required to meet the needs created by doubling or trebling of the population of a town within a few years. Yet it is the development of this order that is already required in a number of towns and will be required in many more in future.

Secondly, the sharp distinction between urban and rural areas which the present structure or municipal bodies implies is being obliterated by suburban and peripheral region growth. One result of such growth is that the municipal area of a city has ceased to be a suitable unit for planning or execution of urban development programmes. The Master Plans of all our major cities (except Mumbai) have been drawn up with the metropolitan area as the planning unit, which includes, besides the municipal area, the suburbs and the semi-urban and even rural areas surrounding the city which is already affected by its growth or are likely to be affected during the period to which the plan relates. The Delhi metropolitan area extends over 800 sq. miles. In Chennai, Kolkata and even in a comparatively small city like Coimbatore the metropolitan areas cover 400 to 450 sq. miles. The plan of Greater Mumbai is the only plan of a major city prepared with the municipal area as the unit; this was possible because the municipal area of the city includes most of the suburbs and is quite *large*—over 150 sq. miles. However, the limitations of planning with the municipal area as the unit, were immediately apparent when the plan began to be scrutinized by the Maharashtra Government. The Government came to the conclusion that the plan for the municipal area should form part of the plan for a much larger area, the Mumbai Region and appointed the Gadgil Committee to demarcate the Region and suggest the outlines of a plan for it. The concept of the metropolitan area as the unit of planning is now generally accepted and legislation is now being introduced in most States to enable the State Governments to establish planning authorities for metropolitan areas and even larger regions.

The various urban development programmes—water supply and sanitation, roads and city transport, services, electric supply—have also to be planned with metropolitan areas or larger region as units. In planning of water supply, for instance, the entire Mumbai region has to be looked at as a unit. The total supplies available within the Region have to be allocated between the city and other towns and among different users keeping in view the likely growth trends in the region. A phased programme of development of different sources and of supply to different areas has to be drawn up. The Mumbai Corporation and other municipalities in the region do have responsibility for running the water supply services within their areas, but overall planning and operation of the system has to be done on a regional basis. This work is being done at present in an *ad hoc* manner in the Maharashtra Secretariat, but it will have to be entrusted before long to a regional water and sanitation authority. Similarly, metropolitan transport and electric supply have to be organised with the Mumbai Region as the unit. Mumbai is fortunate indeed that the area of this Corporation is so large and that transport and electric supply are already organised on a regional basis. However, most other large cities of India are not equally fortunate and are now taking steps to create appropriate institutions for planning and execution of development programmes. The Kolkata Metropolitan District, for instance, comprises 2 municipal corporations, 33 municipalities and 37 non-municipal urban areas. The State Legislature has recently passed a Bill constituting a Metropolitan Water and Sanitation Authority which will be responsible for operation and development of water supply and sanitation services in the entire Metropolitan District. Establishment of the Authority was considered by all concerned with the Kolkata Metropolitan Plan as the essential first step in improving water supply and sanitation facilities in the areas. Similar metropolitan agencies may be created for the other services in the Kolkata Metropolitan District.

Another change needed in the municipal structure is creation below the level of the municipal area of one or more units for decentralised administration of municipal services and for effective citizen participation. Municipal bodies are considered to be local government institutions, but local government in the sense of effective citizen participation becomes a myth when the unit is as large as a metropolitan city with a population of several millions. The ordinary citizen cannot even hope to have his genuine complaints removed; much less can he have any feeling of participation in the government of the city. Perhaps the largest unit at which effective citizen participation can be secured in operation of municipal services is a unit with a population of about 10,000. For participation in community activities, the unit has to be considerably smaller-a neighbourhood of 100 to 200 households. In a city of the size of Mumbai it is necessary to establish several units below that of the municipal area for decentralised operation of municipal services and for citizen participation. The need for such units is not so great in the smaller urban centres; but even in a town with a population between 50,000 and 1,00,000, 2 or 3 units have to be distinguished below the municipal area. An illustrative list of the units needed in case of a large metropolitan city, such as Mumbai and a medium-sized town are summarized in Table 7.9.

Such a hierarchy of units exists already in case of the rural development programme, in which the village, the community development block and the district are distinct units of planning and execution of development programmes and of participation of the people, and have the necessary institutional and administrative structures. A similar development has to take place in the urban areas.

Table 7.9: Units Needed for Large Metropolitan City

Metropolitan City with Population of a Million or More	*Medium-Sized Town with Population between 50,000 and 1,00,000*
1. Metropolitan area Municipal area Zone	Municipal area
(Population 200,000-500,000)	—
2. Township/Suburb/Ward (Population 25,000-50,000)	—
3. Locality (Population 5,000-10,000)	Locality (Pop. 5,000-10,000)
4. Neighbourhood (Population 500-1,000)	Neighbourhood (Pop. 500-1,000)

Concentration of urban population in limited areas should not obscure its large size and the magnitude of the problem of organisation of services and of citizen participation. In most cities there are wards, but these are primarily electoral units. Some large cities have zones, but they are *ad hoc* units constituted for operation of particular programmes. What are visualised here are well-developed units similar to the village, the block and the district at which both administrative and institutional structures exist. The nature of these structures, their composition and their powers need to be considered in far greater detail than is possible within the limits of this paper. But I would urge consideration of this important subject in the interest of efficient operation of municipal services and effective citizen participation in civic affairs.

Organisation

Municipal administration will need to be reorganised to meet the needs of urban growth; its focus must change from maintenance of elementary services in small, slow growing towns to planning and execution of large development programmes. The practice of each municipality recruiting its own technical and administrative staff, which prevails in many States, is obviously an anachronism. It is not attracting persons of the requisite qualifications or capacity to the municipal bodies, because they do not have either the necessary financial incentives or the opportunities to advance in their professional careers. In some States, such as Chennai and Andhra Pradesh, the administrative and technical branches of municipal services have been constituted into State cadres. This step, which enables municipalities to draw their staff from large professional cadres, will have to be taken in the other states also. However, it is only a first step, and will have to be followed by several others to ensure that municipal services are staffed by men having the qualifications, the capacity and the drive needed to carry out development programmes of increasing magnitude and complexity. These steps will be taken and men with the required qualities will be forthcoming *only* when it is recognized that municipal services are important, that municipal administrators, engineers, doctors and other technicians handle large sums of money (and will handle vastly larger sums in future) and that the welfare of the millions depends on them. Secondly, consider whether a proportion of the men of the superior All India Services — administrative, engineering, medical should not spend a part of their professional life on deputation with corporations of large cities. The jobs which they do in the cities will be as important as any that they may be called upon to do. The practice of deputing officers of the Indian Administrative Services, the State Administrative Services and the superior medical services to municipalities and corporations exists already. But such deputations are *ad hoc;* they need to be institutionalised and made part of a policy.

Because urban services have not been attracting suitable men for a long time, there is an acute shortage in India of the men who can handle the enormously complex and difficult tasks connected with urban development and expansion of urban services, and who can apply to those tasks the tremendous technological advances made in the advanced industrial countries in recent years. The nature and extent of this deficiency will become clear when we compare the quality and number of irrigation engineers available in India with the public health engineers. The deficiency of technical men in the various fields of urban development will have to be made up in the first few years after the organisational reforms suggested above have been made. Fellowships and study tours abroad and perhaps short-term deputation of outstanding foreign specialists may be helpful.

Finance

The failure to undertake development programmes on the requisite scale and to attract men of the required quality is connected to an extent with the poor finances of urban local bodies. The problem of finances of urban local bodies was studied recently by a committee appointed by the Central Council of Local Self Government; its Report contains a number of proposals for augmenting the resources of these bodies (Central Council of Local Self Government, 1963).

Implementation of these recommendations and more energetic and aggressive tapping of locally available resources will go a considerable way in improving the finances of those bodies. But it is necessary to recognize that the problem cannot be solved by action at the local level alone—and that co-operative action by the local bodies, the State governments and even the Central government is required to meet it. The financial difficulties of urban local bodies arise primarily from their very inadequate and inelastic tax base. Yields from the property tax and octroi, the principal sources of revenue for urban local bodies, do not increase rapidly; they do not increase fast enough even to keep pace with increase in prices and wages. All the expanding revenue sources—income tax, excises, sales tax are with the Central or State governments and these governments alone can have the funds for financing large urban development programmes. The thinking that urban development is somehow different from other parts of the national and State plans, and can be financed from resources of local bodies alone is untenable in the present situation. The limitations of this thinking have been increasingly evident during the last 15 years, and the planners have tacitly admitted them by providing increasing sums for certain urban development programmes, notably housing and water supply and sewerage. With the Fourth Plan, it has been accepted that urban development programmes should form part of the State and national plans. This is a significant advance which will need to be followed by a series of reforms aimed at enabling local bodies to increase their resources and to take advantage of the various schemes of assistance from the Central and State governments for execution of various development programmes.

Among the local resources which have great promise for the future, urban land deserves particular mention. Development and sale of land has long been the principal source of revenue for improvement of Trusts and Municipal Bodies. Its potential has increased greatly, because of the sharp increases in urban land values in recent years, and because very large areas of land have to be developed. Increase in urban land values, a product of the urban growth process, must make a major contribution to financing of urban growth. The Committee on Urban Land Policy has in its recent report made a number of valuable suggestions for development of urban lands and utilizing the increases in land values for urban development (Ministry of Health, 1965). But perhaps the proposal outlined in the White Paper on urban land issued recently by the British government is unrivalled for its simplicity and effectiveness. The British government propose to take 40 percent to 60 percent of the increment in land values, taking place on conversion of land from a less remunerative to a more remunerative use—from agricultural use to urban land use, for instance—and a similar proportion of the increment resulting from subsequent transactions. In India, we have in the conversion fees levied in many States and in the capital gains tax, the fiscal and local framework for instituting such a development levy. The levy will bring in large revenues and will also simplify and rationalise existing procedures. Yields from it can be so large that several of the low-yielding and vexatious local taxes can be abolished. The levy could be collected by the local bodies or on their behalf by the State government. The latter arrangement will have the advantage of uniformity and efficiency in collection, and also of bringing within the scope of the levy areas undergoing rapid development which are not under the jurisdiction of any urban local body.

A 2001 POST SCRIPT: FURTHER THOUGHTS ON URBAN GROWTH

India will experience rapid urban growth during the next 30 years if the rate of economic growth is 5-6 percent (or higher) as projected by the Planning Commission for the 1970's. 9 percent urban population growth was maintained by the 4 percent economic growth rate of 1941-61 but the rate will be higher especially if adequate investment is made in urban housing and infrastructure. The urban population has actually grown to 159.5 million by 1981 and 217.6 million in 1991. It will exceed 275 millions by 2001 (Statistical Outline of India 2001-2002). Urban population constituted 18 percent of the total population in 1961, its proportion increased to 22.3 percent in 1981; 25.7 percent in 1991 and 27.8 percent in 2001.

There may be marked regional differences in rates of urban growth; regions experiencing rapid industrial and agricultural growth may have significantly faster urban growth than the slower growing regions. Projection of most trends indicates that urban growth will be more rapid in the west, south and the coastal belt than in the rest of the country.

The green revolution will give a fillip to urban growth by stimulating demands for urban located services – marketing and processing of produce, distribution of consumer goods and producers good, credit, transport and communication, social services and (ii) growth of agro-industries. Agricultural growths have already been more rapid in states having a high number of towns/rural population ratio.

The Growth Center Strategy

The growth center strategy aims at expansion of the above mentioned services needed by agricultural growth with the Green Revolution, as well as to provide productive investment outlet for farmers' savings in agro-industries, housing, etc. There is a distinct and important place for growth centers in the urban and settlement pattern of economic growth. But the growth centers alone will neither provide all the urban located needs of the community resulting from economic growth, nor contain the urbanizing forces.

The growth center concept has two fold origin (i) provision of urban located services to modernizing rural agriculture sector; (ii) siphoning off the pressures on large urban centers through location of industries especially agro-industries and others in which there is flexibility in location or dispersed small town location is feasible.

The first derives from Christaller's central place concept; the second follows from the industrial dispersal policy. An essential part of the central place concept is the hierarchy of central places going up to apex metropolitan cities, which serve the whole country. Economic development among the last 20 years has greatly reduced the isolation of villages and increased the range and quantum of rural-urban relationships. Continuation of these with economic growth and rural modernization in future will provide a strong strength to development of growth centers, the primary micro-level growth centers each serving the needs of 25 – 100 villages. But equally, it will impart growth standards to higher level services centers by increasing the range and quantum of intra-center and higher-center regional relationships. The increases in marketing, distribution, credit, demands for higher level education and medical services, etc. will lead to growth of the district, state and macro-region level central places. Rapid growth of state capitals, macro-regional places like Delhi and Chennai and of many districts, high growth towns in Tamil Nadu provide evidence. The large metropolitan cities have a particularly high growth potential because they alone have the modern infrastructure and modern oriented trained man-power needed by the sophisticated rapid growth modern industries (air travel, tourism, research). These cities have and will continue to have the disproportionately large share of the national-international economic relationship.

The two cities of Delhi and Mumbai will experience rapid growth until their populations may be 10 million + by 2000. The Kolkata Metropolitan Development area has a similar or higher growth potential, if its urban malaise could be remedied. In the southern region the primacy of Chennai is less marked, but it can also look towards for a population of 6-7 million. The critical limitations will be essential services such as intra-urban transport and water and investment in housing.

Housing is by and large a cottage industry with each individual trying to build a house, at rapidly increasing costs. It will need to be organized as a modern large sector industry. Very significant economies have been achieved in Europe and elsewhere in this sector and the field is ripe in India.

ANNEXTURE

Distribution of New Units as Well as Units Licensed for Manufacture of New Articles under the Industries (Development and Regulation) Act, 1951, By Size of Towns during 1952-64

Industry Group	*No. of Units Licensed*	*Distribution of Units by size of towns*									*No. of Units licensed for rural area*
		Pop. Above 10 lakhs	*5 to 10 lakhs*	*2 to 5 lakhs*	*1 to 2 lakhs*	*50,000 to 1 lakh*	*20,000 to 50,000*	*10,000 to 20,000*	*5,000 to 10,000*	*Below 5,000*	
(1)	*(2)*	*(3)*	*(4)*	*(5)*	*(6)*	*(7)*	*(8)*	*(9)*	*(10)*	*(11)*	*(12)*
Metal and Metal Products	535	244 45.6%	42 7.9%	47 8.8%	45 8.4%	31 5.8%	68 12.7%	19 3.5%	9 1.7%	2 0.4%	28 5.2%
Machinery and Equipment (excluding transport but including Electrical)	1018	577 54.7%	82 8.1%	91 8.9%	48 1.7%	45 4.4%	79 7.8%	35 3.4%	12 1.2%	7 0.7%	62 6.1%
Transport Equipment	259	145 56.0%	11 4.2%	23 8.9%	14 5.4%	12 4.6%	28 10.8%	11 4.3%	2 0.8%	– –	13 5.0%
Chemical and Allied Products	530	270 50.9%	21 4.0%	48 9.1%	49 9.2%	27 5.1%	41 7.7%	21 4.0%	6 1.1%	2 0.4%	45 8.5%
Textiles	516	92 17.8%	19 3.6%	93 18.0%	37 7.2%	73 14.2%	77 14.9%	33 6.4%	14 2.7%	12 2.4%	66 12.8%
Paper and Paper Products	117	25 21.4%	6 5.1%	8 6.8%	14 12.1%	15 12.8%	21 17.9%	8 6.8%	6 5.1%	2 1.7%	12 10.3%

(*Contd.*)

(Contd.)

Industry Group	No. of Units Licensed	Distribution of Units by size of towns									No. of Units licensed for rural area
		Pop. Above 10 lakhs	5 to 10 lakhs	2 to 5 lakhs	1 to 2 lakhs	50,000 to 1 lakh	20,000 to 50,000	10,000 to 20,000	5,000 to 10,000	Below 5,000	
(1)	(2)	(3)	(4)	(5)	(6)	(7)	(8)	(9)	(10)	(11)	(12)
Food Products	253	48	5	18	30	29	42	17	10	5	49
		19.0%	2.0%	7.1%	11.9%	11.5%	16.6%	6.7%	3.9%	2.0%	19.3%
Petroleum, Coke &Rubber Products	117	19	7	5	6	6	8	4	1	1	60
		16.2%	6.0%	4.3%	5.1%	5.1%	6.8%	3.4%	0.9%	0.9%	51.3%
Stone, Glass Clay & Ceramics Products	175	49	7	15	16	8	28	15	7	1	29
		28.0%	4.0%	8.6%	9.1%	4.5%	16.0%	8.6%	4.0%	0.6%	16.6%
Wood and Wood Products	17	3	–	4	2	1	–	–	2	1	4
		17.6%		23.5%	11.7%	6.0%	–	–	11.7%	6.0%	23.5%
Leather and Leather Products	9	4	3	1	–	–	–	1	–	–	–
		44.4%	33.4%	11.1%	–	–	11.1%	–	–	–	–
Miscellaneous	72	41	4	10	3	3	2	5	–	1	3
		56.9%	5.6%	13.8%	4.2%	4.2%	2.7%	7.0%	–	1.4%	4.2%
Total Per cent-age	3618	1497	207	363	264	250	394	169	69	34	371
Distribution.	100.0%	41.4%	5.7%	10.0%	7.3%	6.9%	10.9%	4.7%	1.9%	0.9%	10.3%

Sources: (a) List of Industrial Undertaking licensed by Central Government under the Industries (development & Regulation) Act, 1951, as on 31st December, 1957. (b) Journal of Industry and Trade, 1958. and (c) Indian Trade Journal, 1959-1964.

NOTES

1. The article is based on three lectures delivered by the author at the Tata Institute of Social Sciences, Mumbai, on February 5 and 7, 1966.
   Source: The Indian journal of social work, Vol. XXVII. No 2 (July 1966)
2. Ashish Bose has classified only 26 out of 107 Indian cities as industrial cities.
3. Pitambar Pant estimated the urban population of 1981 as 200 million; Britton Harris's estimate was 'at least 180 million'.
4. In a recent article on Kolkata, N. K. Bose has described the tendency among immigrants from different parts of the country to congregate in different localities in the city and establish little enclaves of their own.
5. The findings of the Surveys are summarised in, Bulsara, J. F. (1964) *Problems of Rapid Urbanisation in India*: Popular Prakashan, *Mumbai.*
6. For a vivid description of conditions in the industrial towns of ninetieth century England, see Mumford, L.: (1938) Ch.3.
7. Cost per dwelling unit:
   In a four-storey tenement on an expensive site at maximum density (primarily in Mumbai and Kolkata)-Rs. 6,000 to 7,500;
   in a two or three-storey structure on moderate-priced land-Rs. 4,000 to 5,000;
   in a one-storey structure on cheap land, in smaller towns or in the outlying fringe of larger cities-Rs. 2,500 to 3,500
8. For a discussion of the hierarchical order of central places, see Isard W: Methods of Regional Analysis. (Cambridge. Mass, M.T.T. Press, 1960). pp. 222-7.
9. In the smaller city (population 1,00,000 to 3,00,000) it is necessary to interpose another unit, the ward, between the municipal area and the locality. Further work on this aspect of urbanization has been explored in chapter on Rurban Corridors.

REFERENCES

Bogue, D. and Zachariah, K.C. (1962) "*Urbanisation and Migration in India*", in Turner, Roy (ed.) *India's Urban Future,* University of California Press, Berkeley and Los Angeles. p. 31.

Bose, A. (1963) "*Urbanisation in the face of rapid population growth and surplus labour–The case of India*" Paper submitted to the Asian Population Conference, New Delhi, p. 28. (Unpublished).

Bose, N.K. (1965) "*Kolkata, A Premature Metropolis*". *Scientific American,* Vol. 213, No. 3, pp. 90-102.

Britton, H. (1965) "*Urban Centralisation and Planned Development*", in Turner (1962) *no 5.* p.264

Bulsara, J.F. (1964) Problems *of Rapid Urbanisation in India.* Popular Prakashan, Mumbai.

Kolkata Metropolitan Planning Organisation, *A Note on Application of National Goals and Standards to the Kolkata Metropolitan District*, (Unpublished).

Census of India, 1961, Vol. I. Part II B(I). General Economic Tables. p. 701.

Central Council of Local Self Government (1963) *Augmentation of Financial Central Statistical Organisation of the Indian Union. p. 512. Government of India. Resources of Urban Local Bodies*. Report of the Committee of Ministers.

Central Statistical Organisation Government of India, (1961) *Statistical Abstract of the Indian Union*. p. 512.

Davis, K. (1965) *"The Urbanisation of the Human Population", Scientific American*, Vol. 213, No. 3, p. 43.

Delhi Development Authority: Master Plan for Delhi.

Jakobson, L. (1965) Regional *Planning for Urbanisation in Eastern India*, C.M.P.O., Kolkata, p. 34. (Unpublished)

Ministry of Works & Housing Government of India, (1965) *Report on India's Urban Housing, Part II—Facts and Findings*, New Delhi, pp. 21-2.

Mumford, I. (1938), *The Culture of Cities*, London, p. 144.

Municipal Corporation of Greater Mumbai; *Synopsis of the Development Plan for Greater Mumbai*, p. 22

Municipal Corporation of Mumbai: no. 12, p. 1.

Municipal Corporation of Mumbai, no. 12. p. 5.

Municipal Corporation of Mumbai: no 2. p. 28.

Oshima, Harry T. (1962) *A Strategy for Asian Development: Economic Development and Cultural Change*, Chicago, U.S.A. Vol. 10, No. 3, pp. 307-08.

Pant P. "*Urbanisation and Long Range Strategy of Economic Development*" in Turner (1962) (ed.) *no 5*.

Planning Commission, Government of India, *First Five Year Plan*, Chapters XXIV and XXV. pp. 315-33;

Planning Commission, Government of India, *Second Five Year Plan*, pp. 43-50 and pp. 430-33.

Planning Commission, Government of India, *Third Five Year Plan*, Chapter IX. pp. 142-53.

Planning Commission, (1964) *Notes on Perspective of Development India 1960-61 to 1975-76*, Perspective Planning Division, p. 22.

Sjoberg, G. (1960) *The Pre-industrial City*, The Free Press of Glencoe, Illinois.

Town and Country Planning Organisation (TCPO).

(i) Background paper on "*Consideration of Industrial Development and Location with Urban and Regional Planning and Development*", New Delhi, p. 22 (Unpublished).

(ii) *Note on" Projections of Urban Population of India for 1971 and 1981*, New Delhi (Unpublished).

(iii) *Interim Report of the TCPO Panel on Greater Mumbai Development Plan*, New Delhi. p. 28, (Unpublished). (1965).

(iv) Background paper on *Coordination of Industrial Development and Location with Urban and Regional Planning and Development*, New Delhi. p. 19. (Unpublished).

Wurster, C.B, "*Overhead Costs and Development*" in Roy, T. (ed. 1962) no. 5, p. 284.

SECTION II

Metropolitan India

8

Metropolitan Cities: Vehicles of Modernization and Shelter for the Rural Poor

Although more than 70 percent of India's population is still rural, there has been a steady increase in the proportion of the urban population. Secondly an increasing proportion of the urban population is resident in cities (towns with populations of 100,000 and above) and within them in metropolitan cities i.e. cities with a population of 1 million or more. As the figures in Annexture Table 8.1 indicate the number of such cities has increased progressively from 5 in 1951 to 23 in 1991, and is projected to increase to between 36 and 40 by 2001. Almost 30 percent of the urban population and 8 percent of the total population of the country lived in the metropolitan cities in 1991; the corresponding proportion in 1951 was 17.8 percent and 3.2 percent respectively showing progressive increase in the concentration of the urban population into metropolitan cities (Annex Table 8.1). The percent-ages of the total and urban population resident in metropolitan cities are expected to go up progressively.

This paper is concerned with the role of metropolitan cities in national and political economies of the regions in which they are located. Metropolitan cities are the capitals of 10 of the 16 large states. The metropolitan cities lead and reflect economic and social changes in national and regional economies. Improvement of living conditions in them through adequate investment in housing and expansion of basic infrastructures will promote both national economic growth and national integration.

CITIES AS POLITICAL AND COMMERCIAL CENTRES

The metropolitan cities are the political, commercial, industrial and cultural capitals (centres) of the states and regions in which they are located.

Political Centers: Besides Delhi, the national capital, the capitals of 10 of the 16 large states of India are metropolitan cities. The capitals of the remaining 6 states are cities with population between 500,000 and 1 million. Smaller cities are capitals of small states such as Goa and Himachal Pradesh.

The capitals are the seats of political decision making, as also decisions relating to policies for rural and urban development and expansion/improvement of facilities for education, health care and welfare of the people. Located in the capitals are the universities and training centres for professionals – physicians, lawyers, engineers, teachers and computer programmers. The largest university, the principal medical college and teaching hospital, as well as the high court (if the state has one) are located in its capital. The economic decisions made by the government of the states relate to expansion of industries, location of new industrial units, revival or closure of sick units, revival of traditional handicrafts as also development of agriculture in the state. The executives of the largest industrial companies congregate in its capital for obtaining loans for expansion/ modernisation of their existing industrial units and obtaining credit and other facilities for opening new units and incentives for export of products and various other facilities.

Commercial Centers: Most of the capital cities are also large commercial and financial centres. Located in them are the principal markets of the state for a variety of goods – textiles, other consumer goods and consumer durables. Located in them are also the banks and finance companies that provide loans or seed capital for starting new industrial units or expansion/improvement of existing units.

Cities as Industrial Growth Poles

The capitals of most of the large states are also large industrial centres. The proportion of the labour force engaged in industries (including both modern manufacturing industries and traditional handicrafts) ranges typically between 15 and 20 percent, although it is much higher in many cities. It is nearly 30 percent in Delhi. Mumbai, Kolkata and Ahmedabad have been the largest industrial cities in India since the last quarter of the 19th century. Chennai, Bangalore, Hyderabad, Pune and two other cities in Gujarat (Vadodra and Surat) have become major industrial centres during the past three decades.

Nurseries of Small Industries

In every metropolitan city, there are thousands of small industrial units. They may be engaged in traditional industries such as *zari* work in Surat, or new industries such as cutting and polishing of diamonds in Surat and in Mumbai for domestic consumption and export for which the work force of these cities has shown a particular propensity. However, more relevant to economic growth are small enterprises in new industries – such as manufacture of garments and leather goods for export in the 1970s and 1980s. While in Mumbai, the manufacturing was done in factories making brand name garments or leather goods, in Delhi most of the production came initially from householders who employed a few tailors or leather workers and it was only later that medium-sized manufacturing and exporting units came up.

The metropolitan cities are nurseries of small enterprises because in them are located the entrepreneurs and the skilled workers needed for starting such units. Furthermore, located in them are the mechanics who can remedy defects in working of the machines and the banks, which provide loans for running or expanding the enterprises. An entrepreneur starting a new industry would move to an industrial estate located at a distance from his home in a city to avail of lower costs of land, assured supplies of electricity and water and opportunities for expansion of output only when the size of the enterprise is large enough to bear the costs of commuting from home to work and there is an assured market for his or her products. The large market of the metropolitan city itself attracts location of typically urban industries such as food processing – from flour milling to manufacture of pickles and jams – manufacture of furniture, furnishing for homes and offices, clothing and simple consumer durables such as air coolers, other consumer durables – refrigerators, air conditioners and electrically operated kitchen gadgets.

Location of Public Sector Industrial Units

The environs of the metropolitan cities have been found to be most suitable for location of many public sector industrial units. Bangalore, capital of Karnataka, had acquired by the 1960s a large factory manufacturing telephone receivers and other telecommunications equipment besides a factory of Hindustan Machine Tools. Hindustan Aircraft, which was established during World War II for service and repair of planes and located about 30 km. outside the city, has diversified into manufacture of small trainer planes.

Hyderabad has in its environs several large public sector industrial units – Bharat Heavy Electricals, Hindustan Machine Tools, Hindustan Aeronautics, Indian Drugs and Pharmaceuticals, Allwyn Metal Works and several defence-related laboratories. Furthermore, rapidly expanding pharmaceutical drugs and information technology industries are located in its environs. The problems of pollution of air and water, caused by the location of these units, were completely ignored while selecting this location. The first three petroleum refineries established in the early 1950s by the oil companies which had been distributing petroleum products in India for decades were established in a suburb of Mumbai, in complete disregard of the pollution of air that their presence would create for the residents of the city. Their capacities have been increased to meet increasing demand for petroleum products. Several refineries established later have also been located near large cities including Chennai, Kochi and Mangalore in the south.

The first atomic power generation unit was established in the environs of Mumbai in the early 1950s. Another, established a few years later, was also located about 200 kms. south of Chennai.

Public sector steel mills, a heavy machinery plant, mills for refining bauxite to produce aluminum and metallic aluminum, plants for manufacturing locomotive, rails and rolling stock for the railways, plants for manufacture of chemical fertilizers, etc. are located near the sources of raw materials such as coal, iron ore, manganese and limestone in the coal-steel belt of West Bengal, Chhotanagpur region of Bihar, inland Orissa and a large part of Madhya Pradesh. However, all public sector units located in this area have large offices in Kolkata for export of a part of the production and import of raw materials not found in India. They have large offices also in Delhi for approval of their plans for expansion or modernisation or obtaining finance to modernize to reduce their loss by the concerned Ministry of the Government of India.

Proximity to a metropolitan city with its pool of skilled workers and professionals, facilities for obtaining electricity and water supply, proximity to suppliers of components not manufactured by the producer of motor vehicles itself and the large market of the city and the region – north western India in case of Delhi, southern India in case of Chennai and Bangalore, and western India in case of Mumbai and Pune-are the principal factors in choice of these cities for location of motor vehicles producing units.

Manufacturer of Consumer Durables

Factories manufacturing consumer durables such as refrigerators, air conditioners, T.V. receivers and electrically operated kitchen gadgets and motor vehicles (chassis for buses and trucks), passenger cars, motor bicycles, scooters and mopeds are all located in the environs of metropolitan cities. Mumbai has in its environs the largest factories manufacturing consumer durables. The first two factories manufacturing passenger cars and jeeps were established in the environs of Mumbai in the late 1950's. Chennai, Bangalore, Pune and two satellite cities of Delhi, Gurgaon in Haryana and Noida in Uttar Pradesh are the current favorites for location of factories manufacturing motor vehicles. The oldest factory for manufacture of motor vehicles and another for manufacture of tyres are located in the environs of Kolkata.

The principal attraction for location of these industries in the environs of the metropolitan cities are the large markets of the cities themselves as well as availability of a well established network of distributors of their products within the region.

Faridabad, a satellite city of Delhi, in Haryana, has one of the largest factories manufacturing tractors and other mechanically operated farm equipment. This location was chosen for facility in distribution of the machines in Punjab, Haryana and western U.P. in which there is a large demand for them by farmers who use these machines as a substitute for agricultural laborers and bullocks.

Location of Refineries

The first three oil refineries established in the 1950s by the companies that had been distributing petroleum products in India for decades were located in a suburb of Mumbai. The problem of pollution of air that their location would create for the residents of the city was completely ignored in choosing the location. The companies chose the location for facility in distribution of products in the country. After large deposits of crude oil were discovered off the coast of Mumbai and Gujarat, the installations of the Oil and Natural Gas Commission and the petroleum refineries of public sector Indian Oil Company were established also in the environs of Mumbai and Vadodara in Gujarat. The latest and most modern oil refinery and plant for manufacture of petrochemicals is located in Jamnagar along the coast of Saurashtra to take advantage of proximity to petroleum deposits. Since most of the crude oil imported by India from the oil providing countries of the Arabian Gulf is imported through Mumbai or ports in Gujarat, the refinery is well located also for using imported crude oil.

Thus, the metropolitan cities are both nurseries of small industries, as well as the most favored locations for some large, highly capital-intensive industries such as manufacture of motor vehicles and petroleum refineries.

Cities as Cultural Centres and Vehicles for Modernization

Metropolitan cities are the cultural centres of the states in which they are located. Concentrated in them are the literateurs, musicians, painters, sculptors and other exponents of the fine arts of the state. Resident in them are people who set the fashions in clothing and changes in life-style which the urban affluent to middle income groups people of the state adopt in course of time. Located in them are publishers of newspapers and magazines and owners of television broadcasting stations that inform and entertain the people and mould public opinion on various issues.

Mumbai is the largest producer of films and television serials in the country. Chennai, Kolkata and Bangalore are less important centres in which films and television serials are produced in regional languages. Although no data is available on employment and value added in the entertainment industries, there can be no doubt about the large volume of both.

Metropolitan cities are vehicles of modernisation specially with reference to inculcation of modern ideas and patterns of thought and behaviour among the young. The caste system breaks down first in the large cities; no one in a metropolitan city asks the caste of a messenger or a vendor of fruit and vegetables or the other such workers. In fact, the employer of a messenger or other worker is concerned only with whether he/she is punctual, regular and efficient in his/her job. For the rest, he/she may be a *chamar* (leather workers) *kumhar* (potter) or *bhangi* (scavenger). Similarly, nobody asks the caste of a vendor of fruits and vegetables. His customers are concerned only with whether what he sells is of good quality and his prices are competitive.

The movement for independence had, since its inception in the last quarter of 19th century, its centres in metropolitan cities — Mumbai, Kolkata, Pune, Allahabad, and Delhi and, after the arrival of Gandhiji on the scene, in Ahmedabad. Ideas for social reform originated and matured in the large cities. In Maharashtra, reforms such as education of men and women began in Pune and matured in Pune and Mumbai. Religious reform movements aimed at abolition of various superstitions and barbarous customs of the Hindus such as practice of *Sati* or keeping daughters unmarried or ill treatment of child widows began among the high caste Bengali Hindus because the parents could not afford to marry them, originated and flowered in Kolkata. The Brahmo Samaj was one such reform movement that vigorously opposed these customs with considerable success. The Arya Samaj, another religious reform movement which advocated abolition of untouchability, remarriage of widows, education of men and women and a return to the ancient monotheistic faith of the Aryans in place of the prevailing Hindu faith full of superstitions and various esoteric practices, was founded in Mumbai although its adherents in Punjab and Haryana with cities like Lahore and Delhi as its principal centres. Ram Krishna Mission, which, like the Arya Samaj preached a resurgent Hinduism with a special appeal to the western educated Hindus originated and flowered in Kolkata. The reform movement among the Moslems, although it originated in Aligarh in Uttar Pradesh, had its adherents in Lucknow, Delhi and Lahore in Punjab.

Further, some metropolitan cities are serving as vehicles of modernisation in the sense of adoption of western dress, shoes, and cosmetics and of songs and dances by the young. Mumbai followed by Delhi and Bangalore are, at present, the principal vehicles of modernisation in this sense. The large Christian, Parsee and Sindhi residents of Mumbai take pride in adoption of these facets of modern culture. The film and T.V. serials industry located in Mumbai as well as the print media of the city are powerful instruments for spread of western dress, songs and dance-forms among the young. However, the Maharashtrian and Gujarati populations in its hinterland are quite conservative so that its westernizing influence is limited.

Delhi is the second most important center, of westernisation. The young among its large Punjabi population eagerly adopt and take pride in adoption of some western clothes, and other accessories. The very large student population means thousands of young men and women of the middle income group also adopt some western garments such as jeans, and other low cost undergarments for practical reasons. Large numbers of Punjabis settled in U.S.A. and the U.K. encourage adoption of these when they return home to see their parents and relatives of their children in the summer vacation. Some items of western attire such as jackets and jeans are practical in the winter of Punjab and traditional Punjabi folk songs and dances have been adapted to western music and dance. Thus, the Punjabis are the only community in Delhi's hinterland which have adopted some items of dress, songs and dance-forms in their lives.

Bangalore is the third most important city for spread of modern western dress and pattern of behaviour. It has a large Christian population that adopts them readily. It has a large number of foreigners (mainly Americans) working in its information technology industries. The Indian professionals working with them adopt some items of dress such as jeans, which are low cost and practical. However the Kannadiga population in its hinterland is also conservative and has not adopted any mode of dress, amusement or thought. Thus, Delhi is the only metropolitan city, the westernizing influence of which has had a significant effect among a large group in its hinterland.

Cities as Shelters for the Rural Poor: Economics Linkages of Migration

In every large city, there are a large number of poor people who live in slums. The slum clusters may be located in well-designated slum clusters or in unsuitable locations such as along roads. Dharavi, located near the Mumbai airport, has long been reputed to be the largest slum in Asia. In Kolkata, most of the slums, called *bustees*, are located just behind the principal markets of the city. In Delhi, the largest slum clusters are located to the east of the city, just above or on the flood plain of the Yamuna. In addition, in all these cities there are slum clusters in unsuitable locations such as along several roads. Attempts to relocate the slums to secure more efficient circulation of passenger traffic are generally met with stiff resistance by the slum dwellers and by local activists who claim to be interested in their welfare.

SOCIAL PROFILE OF SLUM RESIDENTS

The poor flock to the city, to escape poverty due to lack of opportunities for productive employment in their villages. In Mumbai most of the slum dwellers are from:

1. Ratnagiri and neighboring districts of Konkan where there is much unemployment in the dry season;
2. Dry districts of western Maharashtra;
3. Tribal areas of Maharashtra;
4. Backward underdeveloped districts of eastern U.P. and Bihar which are located at distances of upto 1500 km. from the city.

There are few slum dwellers from the districts having irrigated valleys which produce sugar cane and have sugar factories or districts producing fruit and vegetables (onions and others) for consumption within the state and for export because there are ample opportunities for employment for the rural people in production of these crops and in packing them for sale in the cities.

In Delhi, the slum dwellers can be divided into the following groups:

1. Construction workers: They are mostly from poor districts of northern Rajasthan in which there is little agricultural employment in the 8-month long dry season;
2. Migrants from backward and under-developed districts of central and eastern U.P., Bihar and Orissa;
3. Migrants from distant states particularly Tamil Nadu in the south and Darjeeling and Nepal in the north east;
4. Migrants from Bangaladesh.

The migrants work mainly in various low-paid jobs in the cities such as cycle rickshaw pullers, unskilled and semi-skilled workers in industrial units and as domestic servants. Those from Darjeeling and Nepal are almost all watchmen or domestic servants.

In Kolkata, the slum dwellers have traditionally been from eastern U.P., Bihar and Orissa and some districts of West Bengal. In all these cities there has been in recent years, a large influx of migrants from Bangaladesh. They live in existing slum clusters and work in a variety of low wage jobs. Although they are illegal immigrants, repatriating them has proved very difficult.

There are few, if any slum dwellers in Delhi from agriculturally developed states of Punjab or Haryana or the agriculturally productive districts of western Uttar Pradesh. There are adequate opportunities for employment in both agricultural and non-agricultural activities in these two states and districts. The migrants from Punjab to Delhi are artisans like carpenters, smiths, electricians, repairmen of electric and electronic appliances, mechanics of motor vehicles or white-collar workers. Most of the migrants from Haryana are either drivers of motor vehicles or watchmen or white-collar workers. They live in brick and mortar houses in 'unauthorised' colonies where they have electric supply and municipal water but no facilities for drainage or disposal of solid waste. The largest concentration of these colonies is in southwest and north Delhi.

The best example of the relation between growth of employment in the home region and decline in migration from it to cities in search of the lowest paid jobs is provided by the sharp decline in the number of domestic servants from Pauri and Tehri Garhwal districts of western U.P. During the 1950s and 1960s most of the domestic servants in Delhi were from these two districts. No longer. Employment opportunities in the districts increased considerably with stationing of a contingent of the Indian army along the Indo-Tibetan border from the late 1950s. Large numbers of men were employed in building and repair of roads and other construction works and catering to the needs of the army. Value of agricultural output increased because more land was devoted to producing vegetables and fruit for the armed forces. Many young men joined the armed forces; others became white-collar workers after getting educated. The average Garhwali young man in Delhi today is a junior official or clerk or a messenger in an office but not a domestic servant.

SOCIAL SPECTRUM OF METROPOLITAN POPULATION

The population of a typical metropolitan city has four classes of residents:

1. The affluent: their number is small. They include owners or top executives of large industrial units, rich merchants, executives of banks or multinational companies and the traditionally rich such as old property owners;
2. People of the upper middle-income group: Much larger in number than the affluent, they include professionals – physicians, lawyers, chartered accountants, journalists, high-level officials of the government, managers or professionals employed by large industrial or commercial businesses and, finally, owners and financiers of shops in high-value goods such as silk textiles and jewellery. The rich and the upper middle-income people live in the best residential neighbourhoods in the cities. Thus, in Mumbai they would be living in flats in high-rise buildings which have a good view of the sea and a good sea breeze. In Delhi, they would be living in neighbourhoods which are well served with essential urban amenities. The same is true of other metropolitan cities.
3. The lower middle-income group: Most of them are white-collar workers, shopkeepers and artisans. They live in well-built houses in the old parts of the city where there are facilities for supply of electricity and water but no sewerage or facilities for disposal of solid waste. White-collar workers and small businessmen also live in small houses or flats which have all these facilities as well as satisfactory facilities for education of children and medical care in newly developed neighbourhoods. The artisans live in unauthorized colonies located in various parts of New Delhi as well as in Shahjahanabad (Old Delhi). They have access to adequate supplies of electricity and water but no facilities for sewerage or disposal of solid waste. Insanitary conditions are a major problem in them. In most of the cities, the majority of the workers in traditional industries live in small congested houses; the *chawls* of Mumbai are a good example.

4. The poor: They include petty traders, hawkers, domestic servants, watchmen, gardeners, etc. besides beggars and those engaged in a variety of illegal or extra-legal activities. In Kolkata, Mumbai and Delhi, large proportions of the slum dwellers come from poor underdeveloped areas of eastern U.P. and Bihar. The economies of some districts in this region have been called remittance economies, because remittances from men working in large cities are the principal source of income for the families of the migrants. The traditional stereotype is that the migrant returns home to live in poverty, after a lifetime of work in the lowest paid job in the city and living in most unsanitary conditions in its slums.

BACKWARD LINKAGES OF URBAN POVERTY

The stereotype of return-migration does not, however, appear to be true in the author's personal experience. After several interviews with watchmen and gardeners in an upper middle income colony in which he has lived for many years, he has learnt that most of them remit their savings home to improve the family farm, such as by installation of an electric motor on the irrigation well, renovation of the family home, education of their younger brothers and sons so that they can become white collar workers and for marriages of their sisters and daughters preferably to white collar workers. Furthermore, many of them would after living in Delhi for several years go back to their villages and become progressive farmers. In other words, they would have used their savings from work in the city to improve the economic status of their families. It would be worthwhile conducting studies in various districts of eastern Uttar Pradesh and Bihar from which large numbers have been migrating for decades to Kolkata, coal mining areas of eastern India and in recent decades to Mumbai and Delhi or as agricultural workers in Punjab and Haryana during the busy agricultural season when there is a labor shortage in these states. Whether migration is assisting in improving the economic and social status of their families or whether they still return home to live in poverty is an important issue open to rigorous investigation.

ECONOMICS OF SLUM IMPROVEMENT

Since the affluent and the people of upper middle income group need domestic servants and construction contractors and owners of industrial enterprises need unskilled workers, they would have to pay higher wages than they do at present if economic condition of the slum dwellers has to improve. With higher wages, these workers will not live in slum clusters but in brick and mortar houses in unauthorised colonies where they would have facilities of electricity and filtered water supply but no arrangements for disposal of solid and liquid waste. And if their wages were not high enough for living in such colonies, they would build better huts in the slum clusters and keep them cleaner and send their children to school so that they can move up the economic ladder.

Metropolitan cities in most countries including the U.S.A. and Britain have their slums, but the abject poverty and squalor of the slums of Indian cities have few if any parallels in the world. Conditions in the slums can improve through welfare work by public-spirited individuals or non-government organisations and by municipal corporations. However, a much more effective way to improve conditions of the slum dwellers is to improve economic conditions and employment opportunities in their home regions and to educate children of the slum dwellers and train them for skilled labor jobs for which there are adequate employment opportunities in the cities.

INVESTMENT NEEDS FOR METROPOLITAN DEVELOPMENT

Recognizing that metropolitan cities are essential infrastructures of economic growth and national integration, it is important to make adequate investments in expansion and improvement of infrastructures in them so that they can continue to perform their roles efficiently. The central and state governments should be prepared to make such investments themselves and also to mobilize private capital for them. Improvement of living conditions in them could also make a significant impact in improving productivity of the residents.

For efficient functioning of a large and growing metropolitan city very large investment is required in:

1. Land development and construction of housing,
2. Expansion of facilities for supplies of water and electricity,
3. Construction/expansion of a sewerage system; putting in place adequate arrangements for disposal of solid waste,

4. Steady improvement in intra-city transport and expansion and improvement of in-city roads, and
5. Expansion of facilities for education, health care and recreation.

Of all these activities, only land development for housing for people of middle and high income groups can be self-financing and can generate a profit for both private developers and the development authority of the city; construction of housing for the people of middle and high-income groups can also be self-financing. However, construction of low-income group housing and expansion of all other infrastructures require large investments that must be financed through grants and loans from the national and state governments.

ECONOMIC PRIORITIES OF URBAN INFRASTRUCTURE

Private capital can be mobilized for expansion of the infrastructures if adequate returns can be guaranteed through keeping rates for usage of water and electricity such as to provide an adequate return on the investment. It is essential also to minimise theft of electricity and water and other losses in distribution. The central and state governments should be prepared to make the necessary investments themselves or mobilize funds from the private sector in order that the metropolitan cities can continue to perform efficiently their role as the political, commercial, industrial and cultural centres of the regions in which they are located and the growth points in the regional and national economies. Since manufacturing industries and service activities in which productivity per worker is much higher than in agriculture, the contribution of metropolitan cities to GDP is much higher than their share of the population. Furthermore, since the influences that lead to national economic growth originate mainly in the metropolitan cities, they can be regarded as an essential infrastructure of economic growth. The businessmen, industrialists and professionals who travel by air and the white-collar workers who travel by railways, are the principal bearers of knowledge of one region among people of other regions, live mainly in metropolitan cities. Such knowledge is essential for national integration because it is only through it that people of one region can understand and appreciate the values and life style of people of other regions. Thus, they can also be regarded as our essential infrastructure of national integration.

MUNICIPAL FINANCE AND PERSONAL MANAGEMENT IN METROPOLITAN CITIES

The number of metropolitan cities will increase progressively with more rapid economic growth. One way to ensure their efficient functioning is to have efficient well-staffed municipal corporations who have enough resources to undertake the needed expansion of infrastructures. Most of the direct and indirect taxes collected by the central and state governments are collected from residents, industrial units, companies and shops located in the metropolitan cities. A proportion of the taxes collected in them should be refunded to the corporations of the metropolitan cities for expansion of infrastructures in them with the stipulation that they be used for specific purposes. Thus, a proportion of the excise duty on petrol, diesel and other petroleum products collected in a metropolitan city and its satellite cities should be returned to their municipal corporations with the stipulation that the money be used for improvement of intra-city roads and efficient management of traffic. A proportion of the sales tax could be returned to be used to meet the investments for financing expansion of water supplies. If transmission and distribution of electric supply to a metropolitan city is handed over to a private power supply company, as was the practice before independence, instead of being run by state electricity boards as at present, the company will itself ensure that it makes a profit on its investment. It would make adequate arrangements to reduce losses in transmission and distribution by reducing theft of electricity and defective equipment and have the funds for financing part of the estimated cost of expansion of transmission and distribution facilities.

CREATION OF A CADRE OF EXECUTIVES OF MUNICIPAL CORPORATIONS

Cadre Management

The Commissioner of the corporations of most of the metropolitan cities is already a member of the Indian Administrative Service. Similarly, the Commissioners and senior deputy commissioners of Police also belong to the Indian Police Service. The top engineers in the electricity, water supply and sewerage departments should be drawn from all India Engineering Services. A separate cadre of water supply and sanitary engineers should be constituted to manage and expand water supply and sewerage systems.

Political Dividends; City's Improvements

One of the reasons that the municipal bodies are kept weak is that the state governments see them as rival centres of political power. However this is a self-defeating view: The national and state level political parties make every effort to ensure that they form the governments in the metropolitan cities. Their chances of re-election to form the state government will improve considerably, if the governments of the metropolitan cities formed by them are efficient, because, as mentioned earlier, the electronic and print media located in metropolitan cities have an important influence on public opinion in the state.

One example from Kolkata and Delhi illustrate the point. Militancy of trade unions led to closure of several large industrial units in Kolkata metropolitan district in the 1960s and flight of capital from it to western and southern India. The flight has been arrested by the present government led by the Communist Party of India, which has kept militancy of the trade unions in check. Living conditions in Kolkata have improved also through improvement of water supply, sewerage and transport systems by implementing the needed investment projects with financial assistance from the central government and the World Bank and technical assistance by the WHO. As a result, flight of capital from the CMD has been arrested and many of the units closed during the 1960s have re-opened.

In Delhi, the poor performance and in-fighting within the BJP government in the Municipal Corporation of Delhi that had been in power for nearly two decades led to its ouster in the election to the state assembly in 1998. However, since the performance of the government of the Congress party has not been any better, the BJP has won all the seats for Delhi 9th Lok Sabha elections held in 1999. However, if the government in a metropolitan city is of a party different from that in power in the state government, there should be no discrimination in allocation of funds for projects in it. The discrimination will only mean that the party in power in the state reduces its chances of capturing power in the municipal body in the near future.

ANNEXTURE

Table 8.1: India-Trends in Total and Urban Population and Population of Million-Plus Cities, 1951 – 2001 (In millions)

	1951	*1961*	*1971*	*1981*	*1991 (Provisional)*	*2001 (Projected)*
Total population (millions)	361.0	439.2	548.2	683.3	846	1029.0
Urban Population (millions)	62.4	78.9	109.1	159.5	218	294.0 (285)
Urban/total population (per cent)	17.3	18.0	19.9	23.3	25.7	28.6 (33.4)
Annual exponential growth rate of the urban population	3.47	2.34	3.21	3.83	3.09	3.09
Population of cities (millions)	27.5	39.9	61.2	94.5	138.8	N.A.
Urban population living in cities (per cent)	44.6	51.4	56.1	60.4	65.2	73.7
Number of million-plus cities	5	9	9	12	23	36 to 40
Population of million-plus cities (millions)	11.7	17.9	27.4	42.1	70.6	N.A.
Proportion of population of million-plus cities to:						
(a) Urban population	17.8	22.6	25.1	26.4	29.6	N.A.
(b) Total population	3.2	4.1	5.0	6.2	8.1	N.A.

Sources:

1. For figures from 1951 to 1991 Census of India 1991 Series 1 India. Paper 2 of 1991 Provisional Population totals: Rural – Urban distribution. Statements Nos 5 p.13; 16 p. 31; 20 p. 35 and 23 p. 39. Percent-ages have been calculated.
2. Projections for 2001: V. Nath: 1991 Population Census: Some facts and Policy Issues – II Economic and Political Weekly, Mumbai, December 21, 1991, Table 2 p. 2938

Table 8.2: Trends in Economic Growth in India, China and Selected Countries of South and South East Aisa, 1965-90

Country	*GDP Rate of Growth*		*GNP Per Capita Rate of Growth*		*Adult Literacy*		*Life Expectancy at Birth Years*
	1965-80	*1980-90*	*(U.S.$) 1990*	*(% p.a.) 1965-90*	*Male*	*Total*	
India	3.6	5.3	350	1.9	66	52	59
China	6.8	9.5	370	5.8	38	27	70
Pakistan	5.2	6.3	380	2.5	79	65	56
Sri Lanka	4.0	4.0	470	2.9	17	12	71
Philippines	5.7	0.9	710	1.3	11	10	64
Thailand	7.3	7.6	1420	4.4	10	7	66
Indonesia	7.0	5.5	570	4.5	32	33	62
Malaysia	7.4	5.2	2320	4.0	30	32	70
Singapore	10.0	6.4	11160	6.5	N.A	N.A	74

Source: World Bank: World Development Report, 1992.

Note: *Type of Economy*	*GNP per capita in 1990*
Low-income	Less than $ 610
Middle income	$ 611 – 7619
High income	$ 7620 – or more

9

Problems of Metropolitan Cities in India[1]

Metropolitan cities are defined by the Census Commissioner of India as cities with a population of a million or more. There were 23 such cities in 1991, the number having increased progressively from 5 in 1951. They can be expected to increase significantly during the 1991-2001 census period. The number will keep on increasing through the first two decades of the next century as cities with populations between 500,000 and 1 million graduate to metropolitan status as a result of natural increase and in-migration. The object of this chapter is to describe the principal problems of these cities, their causes and to suggest possible approaches to mitigate them.

THE ROLE OF METROPOLITAN CITIES

The metropolitan cities have a very important role in political, commercial, industrial and cultural life of the country, and of the region in which they are located. Besides Delhi, the national capital, 10 other metropolitan cities are capitals of large states. Several are also the commercial centers of the regions in which they are located. Furthermore, Mumbai (Bombay) is the financial capital of the country.

Kolkata (Calcutta), Mumbai, Ahmedabad, Delhi, Chennai (formerly Madras) and Bangalore are major industrial centers. Kolkata and its sister city of Howrah are home to an enormous variety of industries ranging from fabrication of steel into large structures such as bridges, heavy and light machine tools, to the manufacture of consumer goods of all descriptions. Both cities have located within them a very large number of medium and small-scale industrial units. Mumbai and Ahmedabad are the centers of the cotton textile industry, one of the oldest and largest industries in India.

Since a number of textile mills have closed in Mumbai for a variety of reasons such as, high cost of labor, militancy of labor unions, worn out machines, and indifferent management, their facilities have been taken over by a number of medium and small-scale industrial units. Furthermore, there has been a trend in the post-war years to locate a large number of industrial units along the highways radiating from the city. These units manufacture a wide range of goods like consumer goods, clothing, pharmaceuticals, toiletries, processed food, consumer durables such as refrigerators, air conditioners, electric and electronic appliances, and office and hospital furniture. Chennai and Bangalore have an increasing number of industrial units located in their environs and the number of such units is continuously increasing. Bangalore, once called the garden city of India, is now crowded and densely populated because of the industrial units located in and around it. Delhi similarly is a major industrial center with almost 30 percent of its population engaged in industrial activities.

The principal reasons for location of industrial units in large cities are the availability of pools of skilled and white collar workers, entrepreneurs, financiers, and top quality managers. Furthermore, the cities are themselves large markets for manufactured goods. The environs of these cities are alternative locations of industrial units due to low cost of land, and escape from the pollution of air and water of the inner-cities.

Metropolitan cities are also the cultural capitals of the regions in which they are located. The best painters, sculptors, and writers in regional languages live in them. The residents of these cities set the life style which residents of smaller cities adopt in the course of time. Mumbai is the principal center of India's film and television industry. Chennai in the south and Kolkata in the east similarly are the principal centers for the making of films and television serials in regional languages.

TYPES OF MIGRANTS

The migrants to the metropolitan cities can be divided into three groups:

1. Farmers with tiny, uneconomic land holdings and landless agricultural laborers from the villages, who flock to the cities to escape the grinding poverty of their rural homes. Most

are from villages in districts near the cities, but a significant number also come from distant places. Mumbai has a large community of poor farmers and landless laborers from eastern Uttar Pradesh and Bihar. Delhi has large communities of domestic servants from Nepal, the western Himalayan districts of Garhwal and Kumaon and Tamil Nadu. Besides, most of the construction laborers in Delhi are from Rajasthan.

2. Artisans, particularly carpenters, masons and electricians, come mainly from neighboring districts. They come in search of higher incomes, to learn new and more remunerative skills such as repair of motor vehicles, electrical and electronic appliances.
3. Educated youth who do not have enough employment opportunities in their rural and small town homes and are bored with life in them, the motivation in their migration is both economic and psychological. Most are from neighboring states, but a significant number are from distant places. Both Mumbai and Delhi had for several decades large communities of white collar workers from South India, particularly the states of Tamil Nadu and Kerala.

LIVING CONDITIONS OF THE MIGRANTS

The landless agricultural laborers live in the slums of the metropolitan cities. Their dwellings have mud floors, walls of mud bricks and roofs of corrugated iron sheets. The slums spring up in large areas of vacant land and often along roadsides. Dharavi in Mumbai is frequently cited as the largest slum in Asia with a population estimated at several hundred thousand. One estimate in the 1960s even put it at about one million. Slum-like conditions prevail in large parts of Mumbai, Old Delhi and several other metropolitan cities due to extreme crowding, high levels of pollution of air and water, the latter due to lack of satisfactory arrangements for disposal of solid and liquid waste, and the dilapidated condition of a majority of houses.

Slums spring up on available vacant land due to the negligence of municipal authorities or in collusion with them or local politicians. The former connive in the proliferation of slums on payment of bribes. The local politicians allow slums to spring up because they feel that slum dwellers are a reliable vote bank for them in elections to municipal bodies, or the legislatures of the states, or the Parliament. Malaria and diseases of the digestive and respiratory tracts such as diarrhea, dysentery, bronchitis, and even tuberculosis, are endemic in the slums due to poor sanitation. They take epidemic form during and after the summer monsoon when there are flooded drains and pools of stagnant water everywhere. As a result of the prevalence of these diseases, mortality and morbidity are very high, particularly among women and children. Public health officials take measures to control epidemics and improve sanitation when these diseases take epidemic form, but, after these are controlled, they neglect the slums. No continuous and sustained efforts are made to improve sanitation in the slums.

The skilled workers generally live in "unauthorized" colonies in Delhi and crowded parts of Mumbai and Kolkata. "Unauthorized" colonies are designated as such because the Municipal Corporation had not approved their location, but had allowed them to be built nevertheless. Residents live in brick and mortar houses which are electrified and have municipal drinking water, but no satisfactory arrangement for disposal of solid or liquid waste. Mortality and morbidity here is much lower than among the slum dwellers because they are educated, have higher incomes, know the basics of prevention of disease and have the money to afford the services of a doctor in case of sickness.

The educated youth live in small flats or rooms in houses rented from landlords. Environmental conditions in their living places are much better and mortality or morbidity are far lower than among the other two groups because of sanitary living environments and better education.

PLANNING FOR METROPOLITAN CITIES

Most metropolitan cities have prepared long term plans for expansion in a systematic manner and to alleviate their most urgent problems. In some cities the plans have been prepared by the municipal bodies themselves; in others, however, they have been prepared by organizations established especially for this purpose. The oldest special organization is the Kolkata Metropolitan Planning Organization (CMPO) which was established in the early 1960s to prepare a master plan (1966-86) for alleviating the multiple problems of Kolkata, India's second largest city. By the 1960s it was considered to be a dying city because of its multiple problems – abominable sanitation because of lack of satisfactory arrangements for disposal of solid or liquid waste, inability of the authorities to supply adequate or clean drinking water to the residents, the fact that a large proportion of the residents lived in slums, totally inadequate transport, and large and increasing unemployment among the educated youth. The Kolkata Corporation, corrupt and inefficient, was totally unfit to alleviate these problems or to take measures to check their growth.

The Kolkata Metropolitan Planning Organization (CMPO) was established by the joint efforts of the Central and State Governments and with technical assistance provided by the Ford Foundation. Promises from foreign aid agencies, particularly the World Bank, and financial assistance from the Central Government, alleviating the problems, and technical assistance from the World Health Organization (WHO) were forthcoming. The World Bank promised to partially finance development of a long-term programme of improvement of water supply and also the plan for improvement of intra-city transport. The WHO would provide assistance for improvement of sanitation. The Ford Foundation fielded a large team of technical experts—architects and town planners, economists, sociologists, specialist in transport, housing, and experts in finance. The Central Government made a special allocation of Rs. 100 million in its third five year plan (1961-66) for financing the plan prepared by the CMPO aimed at alleviating the problems of the city of Kolkata and 45 small adjacent townships.

Implementation of the Plan began immediately after it was accepted by the Central and State Governments in 1967. A large programme for improvement of sanitation and prevention of disease was undertaken. Water supply and sanitation were progressively improved. However, some of the projects included in the Plan such as an underground railway to improve transport in Central Kolkata and a second bridge on the Hooghly River to facilitate rail and road transport between Kolkata and other cities were completed only in the 1980s because of delays in preparing, financing and implementation of the projects. However, the problem of unemployment among educated youth could not be alleviated despite the efforts of the relatively efficient state government belonging to the Communist Party to encourage inflow of Indian and foreign capital by controlling the trade unions, whose activities in the 1960s had started the outflow of capital and closure of manufacturing units owned mainly by non-Bengalis (mainly Gujaratis and Marwaris).

Furthermore, new slums have sprung up to house the migrants from Bangladesh. As a result, conditions of poor sanitation, shortage of drinking water, pollution of air and water, shortage of intra-city transport and unemployment among educated youth are as bad as before. The Kolkata Corporation remains corrupt and inefficient and the CMPO has not prepared a second master plan and the Central Government and foreign aid agencies have not given any indication of special assistance for Kolkata. A Second Plan has to be formulated and special efforts made, and financial allocations and foreign assistance are required to reverse the trend towards the deteriorating conditions.

PLANNING FOR MUMBAI

Mumbai is India's largest city. Its population which was over 12 million in 1991 is projected to reach over 16 million by 2001. It has a very large number of industrial units of all sizes. The cotton textile mills form the great majority of the large enterprises. Medium and small-scale enterprises range from metallurgical units, foundries and enterprises producing an immense range of consumer goods, to consumer durables, and office furniture. Mumbai is also the commercial and financial capital of India. However, due to congestion there has been a trend during the post-war years to locate industrial units along the highways radiating from Mumbai or in its sister city of Thane and in green field locations at varying distances from the city.

The first master plan for the city was prepared by the Mumbai Municipal Corporation in the mid-1960s. Its principal object was to decongest Mumbai and Mumbai Port. The planners displayed an extraordinary degree of innovative thinking. They envisaged building of a new residential-cum-industrial city located on the mainland opposite Mumbai which is located on an island. The two cities, separated by water would be connected by a number of bridges. In order to relieve congestion in the port of Mumbai a new port would be built at Uran to handle a part of the growing port traffic, and especially to handle bulk goods, notably petroleum products. The plan envisaged that some of the industrial units located in Mumbai would shift to the new city as well as some of the population.

The plan has met with partial success. New Mumbai was built as a large residential-cum-industrial city. It had a population of more than 1 million by 1991. The new port of Uran was also built and is handling bulk traffic such as petroleum products. However, congestion in Mumbai city or Mumbai port has not been relieved. The industrial units located in and around the new city are those which would have been otherwise located along the highways radiating from the old city or in more distant locations. However, none of the industrial units located within Mumbai has shifted to New Mumbai to take advantages of lower cost of land and labor and opportunities for expansion in size. Similarly, there has been no shift of population. On the contrary, migrations to Mumbai and further congestion within the city have continued unabated. The Plan had envisaged that the Maharashtra Secretariat and Maharashtra Legislature would shift to the mainland, but there has been no such shift to New Mumbai. Thus, despite the large scale of development on the mainland, the central object of the Plan has not been achieved.

PLANNING FOR DELHI

The first long term (1961-81) master plan for Delhi was prepared in 1961 by a team of Indian and American architects and town planners. It was accepted by the Central Government and a new organization, the Delhi Development Authority (DDA) was established to oversee its implementation and to prepare a second master plan at the expiration of the first in 1981. The plan was essentially a land use plan which specified areas for location of housing, small and medium scale industries, and wholesale markets within the Delhi Metropolitan Area. The Plan anticipated the rapid growth of population and economic activities in Delhi and included besides expansion of housing, programmes for increasing supplies of electricity and water and sanitation in the old parts of Delhi including Shahajahanabad (Old Delhi) built by the Moghul Emperor Shah Jahan, the builder of Taj Mahal in the first part of the 18th century. The Plan envisaged a Green Belt around the city consisting of an extension into the city of the Aravali hills, which had thin forest cover, and the agricultural lands around Delhi. No construction was to be allowed within this zone.

Implementation of the Plan, slow at first, picked up gradually. In the areas earmarked for housing the Delhi Development Authority built a very large number of houses for low, medium and high income groups. In the housing colonies built by the DDA adequate space was provided for location of markets, inter-colony circulation and green areas.

Indeed, the DDA became the largest land development and house construction organization in India. The housing built by the DDA, land development and house building cooperative societies and individuals resulted in more than doubling the housing stock of Delhi and led to a large expansion of the city. However, because of its preoccupation with construction of housing, the primary objective of the DDA of overseeing implementation of the plan receded to the background. At the same time, the increase in population, expansion of industries and commercial activities, and of employment in the Central Government were faster than had been envisaged in the plan. As a result, the problems of shortages of suitable housing leading to proliferation of slums and unauthorized housing colonies, pollution of air and water, shortages of electricity and clean drinking water and intra-city transport remain. To alleviate the latter the government allowed thousands of private buses to be added to the bus fleet of the official agency, the Delhi Transport Corporation. However, the plan for construction of an underground railway through the most crowded areas of Delhi which would have greatly reduced pollution of air caused by the exhausts of motor vehicles, including tens of thousands of highly polluting two or three wheelers, was not accepted by the central government due to its high cost, but has been implemented after much delay in 1998.

The second master plan for Delhi relating to the period 1985-2001 was prepared by the Delhi Development Authority in 1985, four years after the end of the First Plan. It was not accepted by the Central Government until 1989 because the Central Government had established the National Capital Region Planning Board (NCRPB) in 1985 and was preparing a plan for integrated development of the region, which included besides Delhi state, large areas in the neighboring states of Haryana, western Uttar Pradesh in the east and a small area of northwest Rajasthan. The Central Government desired that there should be no conflict between the objectives and strategies of the two plans.

In the intervening 8 years, 1981-89, rapid growth of population and of economic activities within Delhi continued to result in proliferation of slums and unauthorized colonies, increasing levels of pollution of air and water, and shortage of electricity and drinking water. It is estimated in both plans that the population of the Delhi metropolitan area would increase from 8.4 million in 1991 to about 13 million by 2001, an increase of more than 50 percent.

An important object of both the second master plan of Delhi and the National Capital Region Plan was to decentralize and relocate highly polluting and hazardous industries which discharge poisonous liquid and solid waste including chemicals, nickel and mercury into the Yamuna river. These practices have made its water unsafe for drinking for long distances for communities located downstream of Delhi.

Some of the potential residential and industrial growth of Delhi has shifted to four locations, Gurgaon and Faridabad in Haryana, and Ghaziabad and NOIDA (New Okhla Industrial Development Area) in Uttar Pradesh. The last, located across the Yamuna from Delhi, has become a residential-cum-industrial suburb of Delhi. Three bridges across the river connect Delhi and NOIDA. The roads on the bridges are being constantly improved to facilitate the flow of traffic. Faridabad is a residential-cum-industrial suburb. Thousands of retired persons who wish to live near Delhi live in Faridabad because of lower rents and freedom from noise, air and water pollution. The road connecting the two cities is lined with factories supplying goods for Delhi or export to other cities and workshops and warehouses of companies located in Delhi. Ghaziabad in Uttar Pradesh is an industrial satellite town. Most of its industries produce consumer goods for the market of Delhi and the region.

Gurgaon, located about 30 kilometres from Delhi has similarly become a large residential-cum-industrial suburb. Hundreds of small industries and the factory manufacturing India's most popular car are located along the highway connecting the two cities. A number of other medium sized industrial units are located on this highway. Dharuheda in Haryana and Bhiwadi in Rajasthan are industrial townships located about 100 kilometres from Delhi. Both produce a variety of goods for the markets of Delhi, the region and the nation. Many of the entrepreneurs, managers and to some degree even the skilled workers in all the above six urban places live in Delhi and commute daily.

Despite a Supreme Court directive for shifting hazardous and highly polluting industries out of Delhi, the shift has just begun. The principal reasons for not shifting are:

1. The influence of the owners or managers of these factories with local political leaders has protected them from costly relocation. Until recently the state government of Delhi was in favour of further location of industries in Delhi.
2. The resistance of the workers' unions. This is best illustrated by the case of Delhi's largest textile mill, which was located in one of the most crowded areas of Delhi. The owners wanted to shift it outside Delhi and develop the land for residential purposes. They had assured employment for all workers employed in the mill. However, the workers' union resisted the move for two reasons. Many of the older workers had their own houses and had sons/daughters working in Delhi or attending schools/colleges there. If they shift, they would have to incur the additional expense of commuting and if they moved near the mill, the family pattern would be disrupted.
3. Jealousy because the workers felt that the owners would make a large profit by sale of land for housing. The mill was eventually shifted and the land was developed by its owners for residential purposes. However, the obstructive attitude of the workers not only caused a long delay in implementation of an eminently desirable project, but provided a disincentive for other industrial units to move out of Delhi.

This review brings out the achievements and limitations of long-term planning for large metropolitan cities. The plans for the three cities outlined the problems of each city in a systematic manner and indicated the directions along which action must be taken to alleviate them. The projects included in the Plan for Kolkata made a major contribution to alleviating the principal problems of the city as seen by the planners in the 1960s. However, due to developments since the 1960s the problems have returned. Shortages of housing, safe or clean drinking water for all citizens, plus intra-city transport, poor sanitation and large unemployment among educated youth remain as great as before. This has occurred despite the fact that West Bengal has had a relatively efficient and clean government for more than two decades which has made a determined effort to alleviate the problems of the city. Two of the large capital-intensive projects, an under-ground railway in central Kolkata and a second bridge on the

Hooghly included in the Plan, were completed only in the 1980s after long delays.

The Plan for Mumbai was marked by a vision which is unusual in most plans. However, despite implementation of exceptionally large projects such as building of New Mumbai, a residential-cum-industrial satellite town on the mainland opposite Mumbai, and building of a new port to handle bulk of traffic, the primary objectives of the Plan to reduce over-crowding in the city and congestion in Mumbai port have not been achieved.

The second Plan for Delhi (1985-2001) was prepared in 1985. It indicated the urgent need to reduce growth of population and economic activities in Delhi and shift particularly hazardous and highly polluting industries out of Delhi. It encouraged growth of six Delhi Metropolitan Area (DMA) towns partly to shift population and economic activities from Delhi. Four DMA towns located within 30 kilometres of Delhi have grown rapidly as residential-cum-industrial satellite cities. Some of the population resident in these cities would have otherwise crowded into Delhi. Most of the industries located in these cities have Delhi as their principal market. However, shifting of highly polluting and hazardous industries which was an important objective of the Plan has not been achieved. The shifting of such industries has just begun, due primarily to the need to comply with the directive of the Supreme Court. The shift is bound to gather momentum in future because of this directive. However, despite the growth of the satellite cities, the population of Delhi is projected to increas by more than 50 percent from 8.4 million in 1991 to about 13 million by 2001. Congestion in Delhi and problems such as high levels of pollution of water and air, shortage of safe and clean drinking water and extremely poor sanitation in older parts of the city and in the slums and unauthorized colonies, will persist in the near future.

Long-term 10-20 year plans must be made to indicate the perspective of growth of population and economic activities and to recommend implementation of major projects to alleviate present and emerging problems. However, in the highly changing economic environment of the 1990s, 15-20 years is too long a period to foresee emerging problems and envisage projects to alleviate them. Therefore, within the long-term prospective indicated by the master plans, short-term plans must be formulated to mitigate emerging problems. These must be continually revised.

FINANCIAL RESOURCES OF MUNICIPAL BODIES

Most municipal bodies do not have the income and manpower to provide the essential services needed to create conditions of healthy living for their residents. There are two main reasons:

1. Since the abolition of octroi (tax on goods entering a city) in most states, the tax on properties located in the cities is the principal source of income for the municipal bodies. However, receipts from it are much lower than they should be because of collusion between the house owners and corrupt tax assessment officers of the municipal bodies. The owners bribe the tax collection officers to assess the value of their property at a much lower rate than it should be. While the owners of the buildings and tax collection officials benefit, the municipal bodies do not get the revenue that they should get.
2. The effect of the Rent Control Act: Control on rents was introduced at the beginning of Second World War in order to ensure that in the context of near stoppage of construction of new buildings because of shortage of building materials, the owners of the buildings did not fleece the mostly poor tenants, by raising the rents of their properties. However, it has been continued without major changes, because of the influence of the strong lobby of the tenants who constitute the majority of the population. Thus, the municipal bodies do not get the tax which they would get in the absence of rent control. Furthermore, the owners of the old buildings have no incentive to keep buildings in good repair. They allow them to deteriorate steadily with the result that the buildings get dilapidated. Many of them collapse during the summer monsoon in Mumbai, killing or seriously injuring their residents. If the Rent Control Act were abolished, the owners would have an incentive to repair and renovate their buildings thus adding to the livable housing stock of the cities. The tenants would certainly have to pay higher rents, but it would be the true market rent of buildings.

The financial resources of the municipal corporations should be increased by their own efforts and by grants of transfer from the central and state governments. Licensing of industrial and commercial enterprises is one way of increasing their resources. The fees should be adequate to compensate the corporations for reducing the pollution caused by the industries and commercial establishments. Transfer to the corporations of a part of the proceeds of taxes collected within the cities by the central or state government is another way of increasing their financial resources. For example, most of the tax on petroleum products by the central government is collected in the large cities. Statutory transfers of specified proportions of these taxes are a more efficient way of augmenting the finances of these bodies than grants to them. Such transfers will make the corporations more self-reliant than grants which depend on the unpredictable decisions of the state legislatures. The co operations would feel that they are getting back what is due to them. Two additional ways to increase municipal revenue are:

1. Every corporation should devise its own innovative ways to augment its resources. Suggestions for possible measures would emerge from annual meetings of mayors and executives of the corporations.
2. Expansion of infrastructure such as electric and water supply and construction or expansion of sewerage systems, or intra-city roads should be financed by the state governments. Since the latter do not have enough funds for the enormous expenditures required, participation of private capital is essential. The governments should ensure that there is an incentive for private sector investment through adequate returns on the investments. Thus, the most congested parts of national highways could be converted into toll roads. The toll should be adequate for satisfactory maintenance of the roads. The principal users of the roads: trucks carrying goods, buses and individual motorists would gladly pay the tolls because of the saving of time in travelling on the toll highways.

IMPROVING MANAGEMENT OF CORPORATIONS

There is an urgent need to improve the quality of the top executives of municipal corporations. One possible way is to institute an All-

India cadre of corporation managers on the lines of the Indian Administrative Service. Able young men and women would be attracted to the cadre if the emoluments and other conditions of the service are attractive. The executives should be suitably trained and should be transferred among different corporations or municipal bodies of cities with populations of 500,000-1,000,000 within a state. Availability of high quality managers and technical personnel will make a significant contribution both to better collection of taxes by the municipal bodies due to reduction in leakages caused by lower paid, inefficient and corrupt staff and speedier and better implementation of projects undertaken by the municipal corporations. Finally, it should be recognized by the central and state governments that the large cities are the nerve centers of the political, economic and cultural life of the country and every effort should be made for improving their environmental conditions.

OUTLOOK FOR THE FUTURE AND RECOMMENDATIONS

As mentioned earlier, the number of metropolitan cities will continue to increase as cities with population between 500,000 to 1,000,000 achieve metropolitan status as a result of growth of the population. The increase will be faster if economic growth is rapid because the large cities have the pools of financiers, entrepreneurs, managers and skilled workers needed for starting new industrial units or increased commercial activity.

The majority of the population of the cities will continue to consist of poor migrants from rural areas who now live in slums of the large cities. They will convert the cities into shanty towns. Measures should be taken to prevent this. The municipal corporations should designate areas for housing migrants. These areas should have adequate arrangements for supply of clean drinking water and disposal of solid and liquid waste and prevention of disease. Migrants should be charged a nominal ground rent for their huts, in order to compensate the municipal corporation for its investment.

Arrangements should be made for training of youth from the slums for marketable skills ranging from those of carpenters, masons, mechanics or repairmen of various electric and electronic appliances, motor vehicles and industrial machinery to clerks in commercial establishments or government offices. The consequent increase in the number of skilled workers will contribute to faster economic growth. Furthermore, the trained youth with their higher income will move their families to colonies with brick and mortar houses, adequate drainage, clean drinking water and electricity. The municipal corporations and authorities such as the electricity boards should make every effort to maintain satisfactory environmental conditions. Furthermore, the electricity boards should also check the widespread theft of electricity by the residents of the slums and unauthorized colonies.

Control on rents of old buildings should be ended. It has long outlived its need. Its abolition will provide the owners of these buildings the incentive to repair, renovate and add to the size of their buildings thus increasing the housing stock at much lower cost than by new construction alone. There would be fierce opposition to its abolition by the tenants as witnessed recently in Delhi, when the Act abolishing rent control was sought to be enforced. However, the Central and State governments should be prepared to resist the pressure of the tenants. New large and medium sized industrial units should also be encouraged to locate in industrial estates developed on the outskirts of cities. Wholesale markets should also be encouraged to locate to the outskirts of cities.

A preparation of long and medium term plans is essential for orderly expansion of large cities. The governments of large states in which there is more than one existing or prospective metropolitan city should establish a strong metropolitan planning department to prepare and oversee implementation of plans for all the metropolitan and near metropolitan cities in the state. Establishing such departments would involve lower cost than establishing a planning organization for every metropolitan city.

The Housing Boards of the State governments should be strengthened to be able to undertake land development for expansion of every metropolitan city. As the experience of Haryana shows, such land development is not only self-financing, but profit generating. Middle income prospective house builders are prepared to pay for land provided with paved roads for intra-colony circulation and connection with state highways, adequate surface drainage, adequate and reliable electricity and water supplies in order to live in a clean and healthy environment.

Metropolitan cities are the nerve centers of the political economic and cultural life of a state. Their orderly expansion is essential for rapid economic growth and social progress. The measures suggested in the previous section would greatly assist in ensuring that the government of these cities have adequate financial resources for providing essential services to their residents so that their living environments is healthy and conducive to productive activities.

NOTE

1. Published in Geographic and Planning Research Themes for the New Millennium, Eds. Noble Allen G., Thakur Baleshwar, Mukherjee A.B., Costa Frank J., 2000

REFERENCES

Ashish Bose. (1994) "*Trends and implications of Urbanization in India During the 20th Century*", in Ashok K. Dutt et al (eds.) *The Asian City: Processes of Development, Characteristics and Planning*, Kluwer Academic Publishers, Dordrecht.

Kolkata Metropolitan Planning Organization. (1966) *Basic Development Plan for the Kolkata Metropolitan District, 1966-86.* Kolkata.

Nath, V. (1993) "*Planning for Delhi*", *Geo Journal* 29:2: pp. 171-180.

Rame Gowda, K.S. (1972) *Urban and Regional Planning*. Mysore Pragaranga, University of Mysore.

Roy, B.K. (1994) "*Indian Urbanization: Proliferation of Mega Cities and Urban Corridors*", in Dutt, A.K. *et. al.* (eds.) *The Asian City: Processes of Development, Characteristics and Planning*, Kluwer Academic Publishers,

10

Poverty in the Metropolitan Cities of India[1]

This study focuses on poverty in India's large metropolitan cities – its incidence, causes, and its ugly face which is evident in the deprivation, filth, squalor and disease in the slums of these cities in which the great majority of the poor live. Rapid growth of economic activities and of population in the cities in the post-war period has been paralleled by proliferation of slums, located on the outskirts of the cities, on any available vacant land within them and even along the pavements of roads. The extremes of metropolitan poverty and human degradation are represented, however, not by the slum dwellers but by the pavement dwellers, whose numbers are in the tens of thousands in Mumbai, Delhi and Kolkata and who live, reproduce and die without ever having a roof over their heads.

Poverty of a large proportion of their residents is the biggest problem of the metropolitan cities. The problems of shortages of housing and basic services such as water supply, sanitation, electricity, intra-urban transport, education and health care, are closely related to it. The principal causes of the shortages are two. First, fiscal policies of the central and state governments, resulting in inadequate allocation of funds for urban development in the five year plans, and second, grossly inadequate funds and management capacities of the municipal corporations of the cities, and other local bodies included within their metropolitan areas to undertake the programmes of slum improvement and expansion of housing and physical and social infrastructures needed to keep pace with the rapid growth of their population.

DEFINITION AND INCIDENCE OF POVERTY

The most widely used definition of poverty in India is based on the income required to purchase the food (primarily food-grains) which will ensure a minimum level of calorie intake per capita. The pioneering work in this area was a study entitled 'Poverty in India' by Dandeker and Rath (1971). They formulated the definition mentioned above, and calculated the proportions of population below the poverty line for India, 15 major states and the Union territories and for rural and urban areas for every year from 1961/62 to 1968/69. Their calculations were based on data of the National Sample Survey of India. They concluded their analysis with the following statement: "It seems that in 1960/61, between 175 million to 180 million people (or 41.5% of the total population of 433.9 million) in the country lived on diets inadequate even in respect of calories. This briefly is the measure of poverty prevailing in the country at the beginning of the last decade" (Dandekar and Rath, 1971).

Their work aroused much interest among economists and other social scientists, planners, administrators and other policy makers in India and among foreign scholars working on India. The interest was due in large part to their startling conclusion relating to the high incidence of poverty, and its persistence over time. The above quotation indicates that a large proportion of India's population, both rural and urban, is chronically undernourished; malnutrition is another deficiency altogether.

Furthermore, the state-wise figure for the rural and urban areas shows that that the percentages of both rural and urban populations below the poverty line were significantly higher than the national averages in several large states such as Bihar, West Bengal, Orissa, Maharashtra, Andhra Pradesh and Tamil Nadu, and the proportion of population below the poverty line was significantly higher in most states in the urban areas than in the rural areas; the national averages for the rural and urban areas were 30.9 percent and 46.5 percent, respectively (Table 10.1).

In other words, whereas less than a third of the rural population suffered from calorie deficiency, almost half of the urban population was affected by it. Dandekar and Rath cautioned, however, against using their figures of around 90 percent for the rural and urban population below the poverty line in Kerala. They explained that the high figures were due to non-inclusion of estimates of consumption of tapioca, which is an important article of food in the state.

Table 10.1: Percentage of Urban and Rural Population with Inadequate Intake of Calories in 1961-62

State	*Monthly Per Capita Expenditure (Rs.)*		*Per Capita Total Annual Consumption Expenditure (Rs.)*		*Total Calorie Equivalent of Daily Diet required*		*Percentage of Population Below this Level*	
	Urban	*Rural*	*Urban*	*Rural*	*Urban*	*Rural*	*Urban*	*Rural*
Rajasthan	15-18	8-11	202	120	2343	2495	21.84	13.29
Uttar Pradesh	15-18	11-13	202	146	2294	2237	37.60	18.13
Bihar	18-21	13-15	238	169	2365	2198	41.28	37.38
Jammu & Kashmir	18-21	13-15	239	165	2250	2380	42.30	13.69
Assam	21-24	18-21	271	233	2213	2260	23.37	47.67
Madhya Pradesh	21-24	11-13	271	147	2568	2475	51.62	25.79
Punjab & Haryana	21-24	13-15	271	165	2128	2402	52.09	13.98
Mysore	21-24	13-15	275	172	2273	2238	57.39	26.92
Andhra Pradesh	21-24	18-21	273	236	2436	2355	58.11	16.14
Gujarat	24-28	13-15	315	164	2187	2222	50.50	19.09
Orissa	24-28	13-15	310	167	2293	2342	55.57	23.88
West Bengal	28-34	15-18	374	299	2313	2233	48.53	44.09
Maharashtra	28-34	18-21	370	238	2226	2303	58.18	61.04
Tamil Nadu	28-34	18-21	374	235	2196	2321	70.78	55.19
Kerala	43-55	34-43	617	464	2672	3007	88.89	90.75
Union Territories	28-34	21-24	380	276	2292	2388	48.90	43.70
All India	21-24	13-15	274	170	2359	2394	46.50	30.92

Source: Dandekar and Rath, 1971:13.

This definition of poverty was accepted by official agencies of the Government of India and the state governments and by large number of economists and other social scientists in both India and abroad. The acceptance and keen interest in the subject resulted in a large amount of work on measurement of poverty by states, regions and economic groups and on trends in poverty over time. Notable among the work are studies by Baradhan (1974), Ahluwalia (1978), Sundaram (1986) and others.

There are significant differences, however, in the estimates of different studies on the incidence of poverty and its trends over time. The latest official estimates from 1977-78 to 1984-85 and projections to the end of the plan period 1989/90, and to the end of the century, contained in the Seventh Five Year Plan 1985-90, are reproduced in (Table 10.2).

Table 10.2: Percentages of Rural and Urban Population Below the Poverty Level 1977-78 to 2001-2002

	1977-78	*1984-85*	*1989-90*	*2001-2002**
Rural	51.2	39.9	28.2	18.6
Urban	38.2	27.7	19.3	16.6
Total	48.3	36.9	25.9	18.0

* Based on Planning Commission's Projections (Statistical Outline of India, 2000-2001, Table 249).

Source: Seventh Five Year Plan, 1985-90. Vol. I, Tables 3.6 and 2.11.

The estimates and projections indicated a significant reduction in the incidence of poverty during the 7-year period, 1977-78 to 1984-85 and continuation of the declining trend during the Seventh Plan period and beyond it to the end of the century. It may be noticed that the percentage of rural population below the poverty line would be reduced by almost 12 percentage points and of urban population by more than 8 percentage points during the Seventh Plan period. The average proportion would be reduced to 5 percent by the end of the century, indicating virtual disappearance of poverty.

The World Bank (1990) also projected a progressive decline in the incidence of poverty in India and other low income developing regions, except Sub-Saharan Africa, between 1985 and the end of the century. The Bank estimated that the number of the poor in India would go down during the period from 420 million to 255 million (Table 10.3).

The Bank's estimate and projection of the proportion of population below the poverty line, 55 percent in 1985 and 25 percent by the end of the century, were both much higher than those of the Planning Commission. The differences appear to be due to significantly different definitions of poverty adopted by the two agencies. Whereas the Planning Commission's definition was based on calorie deficiency alone, the Bank's definition included other indicators, such as life expectancy at birth, mortality under five years and enrolment in primary schools (World Bank 1990: 29). The Bank's estimate of the proportion of the poor in 1985, given above, is corroborated by the Operation Research Group (1990), which estimated on the basis of a survey during 1989/90, that almost half of India's population was below the poverty line.

Table 10.3: Poverty in Developing Regions of the World by 2000

Region	*Incidence of Poverty % of Total Pop.*		*Number of Poor (in millions)*	
	1985	*2000*	*1985*	*2000*
Sub-Saharan Africa	46.8	43.1	180	265
East Asia	20.4	4.0	280	70
China	20.0	2.9	210	35
South Asia	50.9	26.0	525	365
India	55.0	25.4	420	255
Eastern Europe	7.8	7.9	5	5
Middle East North Africa	31.0	22.6	60	60
Latin America and the Caribbean	19.1	11.4	75	60
Total	32.7	18.0	1,125	825

Source: World Bank 1990: 29 and 139.

Note: The poverty line is set at $370 annual income per capita in 1985 purchasing power parity dollars (PPP). A lower income level of $275 per capita is used to designate the extremely poor. Their numbers are not given separately.

The conclusion of progressive decline in the incidence of poverty is also disputed by a number of analysts. Some of them have failed to find a significant trend, upward or downward, over time. A balanced statement on the subject is by Sundaram who concluded his analysis of trends in rural and urban poverty from 1956-57 to 1983-84 in the following words:

"The problem is not simply that we do not have enough number of observations to meaningfully speak of time-trends; it is more basic. An analysis of rural poverty between 1956/57 and 1973/74 has shown that the sizeable fluctuations in the incidence of poverty observed over this period, a feature that underlies the absence of a statistically significant time trend, were significantly related negatively to agricultural GDP per head of rural population...In the case of urban India, there is a slight increase in the incidence of poverty between 1973/74 and 1983/84. Also, unlike in rural India, the absolute number of the urban poor was higher in 1983/84 than in 1973/74".

ALLEVIATION OF POVERTY AND REDUCING DISPARITIES IN INCOME AND CONSUMPTION

Reducing the incidence of poverty and disparities in income and consumption had been stated as an important objective of the five year plans from their beginning in 1951. Eradication of poverty was added as a primary objective of planning in the Fifth Five Year Plan, 1975-80. The two objectives have been reiterated in the sixth and the seventh five year plans and also in the Approach Paper to the Eighth Five Year Plan, 1990-95, prepared by the National Front Government in May 1990. The Paper stated:

The kind of development we have had has led to growing disparities and inequities, a felt sense of injustice and oppression...There is urgent need to remove the sources of discontent and unrest by attending to unemployment, illiteracy, ill-health and decline in living conditions of the poor and vulnerable sections...The new mandate rightly stresses the need to correct these distortions and to reorient development policy in such a way that it gives primacy to the immediate and urgent needs of the poor, namely, employment opportunities to all at minimum wages and access to adequate means of livelihood and skills, as also supplies of food, education, health and child-care services, and other basic necessities, such as housing. The guarantee of right to work, reserving at least half the public outlays for the benefit of rural areas, and emphasis on goods and services for mass consumption, using labour-intensive techniques, reflect these concerns (Planning Commission, 1990).

SOCIAL AND SPATIAL DIMENSIONS OF POVERTY

The Rural Poor

The rural poor belong mainly to the scheduled castes, the scheduled tribes and other traditionally underprivileged groups. They have sub-marginal agricultural holdings, or are landless and depend upon agricultural and non-agricultural labour as their principal or secondary means of livelihood. They live in small dwellings with unpaved floors, walls made of bamboo or sun-baked bricks, roofs made of thatch, corrugated iron sheets or tiles. Their dwellings are located either in their quarters which form part of villages or in small hamlets located near the villages. They form part, however, of the village community and although they suffer from many social disabilities and exploitation by the rural elite, especially large farmers, they have the support system of their own caste and the sympathy of the rest of the village. They have two principal problems: (i) chronic under-employment or unemployment and the threat of starvation in years of crop failure, caused by drought, floods and other natural calamities, and (ii) inadequate access to basic services – adequate and safe water supply, education, medical care etc., despite large expansion of the service facilities during the post-Independence period.

The severity of their poverty, their social disabilities, and economic exploitation have been reduced significantly in the post-Independence period as a result of social and political changes, legislative reforms, such as statutory prohibition of "untouchability", and various programmes for the welfare of the rural poor, undertaken by the central and state governments and by non-governmental organizations (NGOs). The political process, particularly elections to the village *panchayat,* and other institutions of local government, the state legislatures and the national parliament, has made a major contribution to focussing attention on their poverty and other problems and improving policies and expanding programmes for alleviation of these. The elections to the parliament and the state legislatures, held in 1989 and 1991, provide an excellent illustration of this phenomenon. In both elections, major political parties vied with one another in proclaiming their commitment to increasing welfare of the scheduled castes, the scheduled tribes and other disadvantaged groups and promising to improve policies and undertake large, country-wide programmes that would increase their employment and income raise their level of living and reduce their social disabilities.

The Metropolitan Poor: Slum and Pavement Dwellers

The great majority of the poor residents of metropolitan cities live in hovels forming part of slums, which are located, as mentioned earlier, on the fringes of the cities, in vacant lands within them and even on pavements of roads. Their number has increased rapidly during the last four decades, along with rapid growth of population of these cities. The principal reason for the increase is that migration into the cities has been much greater than expansion of employment opportunities, affordable housing and basic services in them. The figures given in Table 10.4 indicate that in 1981, almost one-third of the total population of Kolkata, Mumbai, Delhi, Chennai and Nagpur was estimated to be living in slums. The proportions in most of the smaller cities were lower; Kanpur with 37.5 percent was a conspicuous exception. The proportions were much higher in 1991 in all the cities except Lucknow where they were somewhat lower.

Table 10.4: Total Population and Population of Slum Dwellers in Metropolitan Cities (in million)

City	*Total 1981*	*Estimated Slum 1981*	*Slum/Total (Percent) 1981*	*Total 1991*	*Estimated Slum 1990*	*Slum/Total 1991 (Percent)*
Kolkata	9.2	3.0	30.4	11.0	4.4	39.8
Mumbai	8.2	2.8	29.1	12.6	4.1	32.1
Delhi	5.7	1.8	31.8	8.4	3.2	38.1
Chennai	4.3	1.4	31.5	5.4	2.1	38.9
Bangalore	2.9	0.3	10.4	4.1	1.0	25.0
Hyderabad	2.5	0.5	19.6	4.3	1.1	25.6
Ahmedabad	2.5	0.5	20.3	3.3	1.1	29.2
Kanpur	1.6	0.6	37.5	2.0	0.8	40.0
Pune	1.7	0.3	16.3	2.5	0.5	20.7
Nagpur	1.3	0.4	31.9	1.7	0.6	33.8
Lucknow	1.0	0.3	28.3	1.7	0.4	23.5
Jaipur	1.0	0.3	29.1	1.5	0.5	32.5

Source: TCPO, A Compendium on Indian Slums, 1985: 16; Registrar General and Census Commissioner, India, 1991: 39.

Note: Percentage have been calculated and rounded off to 0.1 point by the author.

The great majority of the recent migrants to the cities are being accommodated in existing slums through increased concentration or their expansion, or establishment of new slums. Increasing congestion in the older slums and proliferation of slums, that are so very evident in most metropolitan cities, indicate that both processes are at work.

The slum dwellers live in squalor and misery, are exploited by unscrupulous slumlords and are harassed by the police and other lower level officials. The poorest among the metropolitan poor, however, spend their lives, as mentioned earlier, on roadside pavements. Shelter is a far greater problem for them than for the rural poor. A roof over the head, a norm for the rural poor, becomes a privilege for the metropolitan poor. Insecurity of employment and income and even life and property are other problems.

The great majority of the slum and pavement dwellers find work as casual, unskilled labourers in the urban informal sector, which consists of a medley of activities ranging from micro-industries and handicrafts to peddling and begging. Wages or earnings are low, there is no job security and there are periods of voluntary or involuntary unemployment and loss of income. Chronic sickness often leads to destitution (Mazumdar, 1978). Insecurity of life and property is due to the fact that organised or petty crime is greater in the slums than in other parts of the metropolitan cities.

Finally, contrary to popular belief, entry into many activities in the informal sector is not open, but is tightly controlled by those engaged in them already. In a study of slum dwellers in the city of Vijayawada in Andhra Pradesh, Tataji (1986) has given a detailed account of how entry into some informal sector activities, such as loading and unloading of goods on trucks and railway wagons, and loading of passengers and goods on buses, is tightly controlled by guild-like organizations, called *muthas*. Entry into them is either inherited or has to be purchased for considerable sums of up to Rs. 8,000 to 10,000. Preference is given to relatives and friends of the existing members or those coming from their caste or region. He concludes:

The entry into many occupational categories is not easy as the conceptual scheme of the informal sector assumes. Entry into mutha labour depends on the ability of the aspirant to purchase work and the influence his caste and kinship networks have with the existing members of the mutha...The opportunities available in such occupations are not abundant and this scarcity of opportunities and competition will lead to some form of selectivity (Tataji, 1986).

Since disparities in income and consumption and differences in life styles between the rich and the poor of the metropolitan cities are sharp and evident to the point of being dramatic, the feelings of deprivation, frustration and anger are much greater than among the rural poor. Adherence to traditional values and beliefs, which assists in acceptance of poverty and deprivation by the rural poor, is also much weaker among them.

Programmes of development and welfare, undertaken by the central, state or local governments or by the non-governmental organizations, are few, limited in scope and size and have had much less impact in ameliorating their poverty and other handicaps than have programmes for the rural poor. Investment in low-cost public housing has also been small on account of financial constraints. It is only during the 1980s that official attitudes have changed towards recognition of the large and rapidly increasing number of the metropolitan poor, the prospect of continuing rapid increase in it in the foreseeable future and the urgent need for appropriate policies and programmes to alleviate their poverty and other disabilities. One result of the recognition was change from slum eradication to slum improvement as a policy objective of the Government of India. This was stated in the Sixth Five Year Plan 1980-85 in 1980, as follows:

> "It is proposed that the strategy of attempting massive relocation of slums in urban areas should be given up in the future. Such relocation not only involves substantial hardship to those affected, in terms of loss of easy access to employment centres and other amenities, but results in unnecessary destruction of existing housing capital, however sub-standard it may be. It is, therefore, important that substantially increased investments be made in the environmental improvement of slum areas. Low cost sanitation and drainage are key areas of much needed investment in the slums of our cities" (Sixth Five Year Plan: 392).

However, an indication of the size of the slum improvement programme became available only in the Seventh Five Year Plan, formulated in 1985, which stated:

> "The Environmental Improvement of Slums (EIS) programme has to be continued with greater vigour and steps should be taken to provide security of tenure to the slum dwellers so that they may develop a stake in maintaining and improving their habitat. Of the total urban population, nearly a fifth is estimated to constitute the slum population. The Sixth Plan had estimated that in 1985 the magnitude of such population needing attention would be about 33.1 million. Of this, up to March 1985, about 15.6 million slum dwellers would have been benefited, leaving a balance of 17.5 million people yet to be provided relief. Per capita assistance which was only Rs. 120 in 1972 has been stepped up from time to time and the present rate of Rs. 250 was fixed in 1984. Since many state governments considered this quantum inadequate, it has been decided to step up the per capita expenditure to Rs. 300. This order of total outlay would benefit about 9 million slum dwellers during the Seventh Plan" (Seventh Five Year Plan: 298)

The recognition was not accompanied, however, by significant increase in the allocation of funds for the slum improvement programme. The allocation of Rs. 2695.5 million in the Seventh Plan was 78 percent higher than the estimated outlay of Rs. 1514.5 million in the Sixth Plan. But after taking into account the increase in prices of about 33 percent during the intervening five years, the net increase works out to only about 34 percent. Furthermore, only about half of the slum dwellers would be benefited by it.

THE EIGHTH FIVE YEAR PLAN: 1992-97

The Eighth Five Year Plan reflects a significant change in policies from earlier plans. The change is due to recognition of widespread incidence of rural and urban poverty and the prospect of its continuation in the foreseeable future. According to the Plan, there were in 1987-88, 200 million people below the poverty line in the rural areas and 41.8 million in the urban areas and they constituted about 30 percent of the rural and 20 percent of the urban population (Planning Commission, 1990).

The Plan includes a variety of programmes for relief of poverty, but it does not contain any projection relating to reduction of poverty during the plan period or its eradication by a particular year. In the programmes for both the rural and the urban poor there is emphasis on the one hand on employment generation and on the other on raising productivity of workers. This emphasis is based on recognition of widespread incidence of under-employment, unemployment and low productivity. Furthermore, the Plan recommends making a concerted effort to integrate various programmes. Some of the latter are quite old, dating to the 1970s, while others such as the Jawahar Rozgar Yojana which was begun in 1991 and is named after the first Prime Minister of India, Jawaharlal Nehru, are recent.

In addition to programmes aimed specifically at relief of poverty, there are sectoral, special development programmes and these are for welfare of particular groups: the Scheduled Castes, the Scheduled Tribes, women and children which would alleviate poverty among the target areas or groups.

The thrust of the programmes for the urban poor is on slum improvement and providing basic services including housing, water supply and sanitation to them. Finally, in both urban and rural poverty alleviation programmes, there are allocations for training and skill formation and for providing subsidies and/or loans for self-employment in micro enterprises.

DEFICIENCY OF DATA

A major difficulty in analysis of metropolitan poverty relates to paucity of data. Except for Delhi, which is a city-state and for which data on per capita income and consumption expenditure are published by the Central Statistical Organization as part of its national and state-wise series, very little data are available on these subjects. The available data are therefore based on economic or social surveys, which have been conducted in some metropolitan cities among the slum and pavement dwellers, who are considered synonymous with the poor. The surveys have been conducted by institutes such as the Tata Institute of Social Sciences in Mumbai, planning agencies such as the Town and Country Planning Organization (TCPO) of the central government or by individual scholars. Examples of the latter are a sample survey conducted by Acharya of the Tata Institute in 1978 among the slum and pavement dwellers of Mumbai and an in-depth study, conducted in the late 1980s, by Rao in a slum of stone cutters in Pune (Acharya, 1988; Rao, 1990).

Acharya concentrated on bringing out the differences between the slum and the pavement dwellers (the housed and the houseless), in caste, place of origin, reasons for migration to Mumbai, literacy, nature of employment, levels of income and expenditure and distribution of income among food and non-food items. He found that:

1. Almost half of his respondents had come from Maharashtra;
2. A much larger percent-age of the pavement dwellers than of the slum dwellers belonged to the scheduled castes, the scheduled tribes and other backward castes, and
3. The pavement dwellers were significantly lower than the slum dwellers in the various indicators of social and economic development, mentioned above. Furthermore, he concluded that the migration of both slum and pavement dwellers was due to the 'push factor' of poverty and periodic starvation in the villages.

Rao traced the growth of a slum of stone cutters in Pune from its origin at the beginning of this century, the reasons for migration of its residents from their villages in a semi-arid area of Karnataka, their social organization, religious beliefs, patterns of political participation and the influence of outsiders on their welfare. She found that chronic under-employment or threat of starvation in years of drought in their native villages and the prospect of steady employment in their traditional occupation of stone cutting on construction sites in the rapidly growing city were the main reasons for their steady migration. Thus she brings out that both 'push' and 'pull' factors operated in their migration.

The results of the surveys and studies have been summarized in several books. Two such books are by Singh and De Souza (1980) and Alam and Ali Khan (1987). Singh and De Souza have presented data on housing, social organization, health, nutrition, education, employment and income for the slum and pavement dwellers of a number of metropolitan cities. The source materials used by them are surveys, conducted during the 1970s or earlier, by the TCPO, planning agencies of various metropolitan cities, institutes such as the Tata Institute or individual scholars.

Alam and Ali Khan have brought together studies on slum or pavement dwellers in five metropolitan cities: Mumbai, Kolkata, Delhi, Hyderabad and Chennai and the programmes undertaken or proposed for improving conditions in the slums through extension of basic services and providing affordable housing to the residents. The study of experience in slum improvement and providing tenements to the slum dwellers in Chennai, reviewed in the book is particularly valuable. It brings out that slum improvement programmes involve much smaller expenditure per family and can also be implemented more rapidly than provision of tenements. The former appears, therefore, to be the most viable solution for alleviating the problems of the slum dwellers whose numbers are increasing so rapidly.

PROSPECT AND RECOMMENDATIONS

The prospect for the 1990s and the first decade of the next century have to be assessed keeping in view the demographic and economic trends of the past four decades and the projections for the future. The most important demographic trends during 1951-91 have been the following: (i) rapid increase in total population and urban population, and (ii) increasing concentration of the urban population in the cities and the large cities among them.

The rapid increase in urban population and its concentration in large cities are caused by migration—rural to urban, and from small towns and cities to large cities. It has been estimated that almost half of the increase in population of Delhi during 1961-81 was due to migration (NCRPB 1988: 137). The migration can be controlled, easing the pressures on the cities in an authoritarian society, such as

China's, but not in other societies. It is occurring in most of the less developed countries (LDCs) of Asia, Africa and other regions and also in the newly industrialized countries (NICs) of East and Southeast Asia. It is a global phenomenon (World Bank 1992: 278–9).

The principal cause of the migration in India is large differences in productivity and income between the rural and urban workers. The latter is caused, in turn, by concentration of the rural work force in low productivity agriculture and related activities (livestock husbandry, forestry, and fishing), in which productivity and income per worker are low, and of urban workers in manufacturing industries and services, in which they are much higher. Mohan has estimated that the ratio of rural: urban net domestic product per capita, which had gone up from 1.83 in 1950–51 to 2.87 in 1980–81 would go up to 3.34 by 1994–95 (Mohan 1985).

The policies, aimed at promoting decentralization of manufacturing industries and modern service sector activities from the large metropolitan cities to medium-sized and small urban places, followed by the central and state governments since the mid-1950s, have not been too successful so far. They are not expected to be more successful in the 1990s, in the context of virtual abolition of licensing of industrial enterprises, which had been accompanied by various fiscal incentives and administrative sanctions in order to induce entrepreneurs to locate industries away from large cities and in backward regions. As a result, concentration of industries and service sector activities in large cities could increase and growth of their populations could be even higher than in the recent past.

Because of their illiteracy and lack of marketable skills, the large majority of migrants to the large cities will continue to work in the 'informal sector', or as unskilled labourers on construction works or in small trading or industrial establishments. Their wages or earnings will remain very low; there are varying periods of unemployment or under-employment. But the prospect of securing remunerative and secure employment, although achieved by only a minority of migrants, will remain the driving force behind migration. Furthermore, large numbers will migrate to the cities in order to escape starvation in the villages in years of scarcity or famine, caused by crop failure on account of drought, floods etc., or for other reasons such as a personal tragedy (Mazumdar, 1978). The great majority of the migrants will continue to be poor and to live in slums because they cannot afford better housing.

There is need for a multi-pronged programme for the welfare of the slum and pavement dwellers. The programme should concentrate on achieving the following objectives:

1. Eradication of illiteracy and imparting skills which are in great demand in the cities. These will reduce their ignorance and enable them to do skilled work at much higher wages or earnings than in unskilled labour. A percentage among them will get jobs in industrial or service enterprises; others, who are more enterprising, can, establish their own shops or tiny workshops. Most of the latter will need to be assisted by small, low interest loans, particularly for contributing to the seed capital of the enterprises, and extension-type training in the basics of management. The programmes, aimed at propagation of literacy and diffusion of marketable skills, being undertaken at present by a large number of official or non-official agencies, should be expanded and improved in the light of experience with them. Furthermore, they should not be confined to men, but should be extended to women, with appropriate modifications to suit their aptitudes and needs. The benefit/cost ratios of the programmes would be found to be comparable or higher than those of most other development programmes.
2. Encouraging workers in the metropolitan cities to live in villages and satellite towns located on the periphery of the cities. This will reduce the pressure of migration into the cities; but it will require major improvements in transport facilities between the cities and the peripheral villages and satellite towns.
3. Improvement of sanitation and provision of basic services in the slums. The services should range from provision of adequate and safe drinking water and electricity to education, medical care and social welfare. The beneficiaries should be encouraged to participate actively in both establishing the service facilities and their operation and maintenance. They should also be required to pay small, highly subsidized user charges for most of the services. The charges would not reduce the cost of providing the services significantly; their main effect would be that the beneficiaries would consider

> the services to be their own. They will use them more effectively and take an active interest in their operation and maintenance. The programmes will contribute greatly to improving the slums and raising employment, income and levels of living of the slum dwellers.

The next set of programmes should aim at progressive upgrading of the shelter provided by the slums. These would consist generally in replacement of slum dwellings with more permanent, more spacious and better-built houses. They should also be undertaken with the agreement of the slum dwellers and with their maximum participation. Grant of secure tenure in all suitable sites on which their dwellings are located, will provide to the slum dwellers a powerful incentive to contribute to improving them. Such tenure should be granted to them on payment of nominal charges. However, those living in slums, located on unsuitable sites, such as along pavement of roads or on sites earmarked for establishing or expanding facilities, which provide essential services to the community, must be relocated. Their new locations should, however, be as close to their places of work as possible in order to save them the need for expensive and time-consuming journeys from home to work and back. Careful selection of the relocation sites and notification of the proposed relocation well in advance of it will greatly reduce the disturbance in the lives of those being relocated and will also greatly reduce their resistance to the relocation. The stiff resistance to relocation by slum or pavement dwellers is generally due to the fear (or fact) of such disturbance, which is generally ignored or underrated by officials having responsibility for slum clearance and relocation (Bapat, 1992).

NOTE

1 A.K. Dutt *et al.* (eds.), The Asian City: Processes of Development, Characteristics and Planning, 295-308.

REFERENCES

Acharya, S. (1998) "*Mumbai's Weaker Sections – A Survey of their levels of living*", *The Indian Journal of Social Work*. Vol. XLIX, No. 2. pp. 99-125.

Ahluwalia, M.S. (1978) "*Rural Poverty in India, 1956-57 to 1973-74*", Occasional Papers; World Bank Staff Working Paper 279.

Ahluwalia, M.S. (1978) "*Rural Poverty and Agricultural Performance in India*", *Journal of Development Studies*, London. Vol. 14. No. 3 pp. 298-323.

Alam, S.M. and Ali Khan, F. (eds). (1987) *Poverty in Metropolitan Cities*, Concept Publishing Co., New Delhi.

Bapat, M. (1992). "*Mumbai's Pavement Dwellers' Continuing Torment*", *Economic and Political Weekly*, October 10, pp. 2217-19.

Baradhan, P.K. (1974) "*On the Incidence of Poverty in Rural India in the Sixties*", in Srinivasan, T.N. and Baradhan, P.K. (eds). *Rural Poverty in South Asia*, Oxford University Press, New York.

Dandekar M. and Rath, N. (1971) *Poverty in India Mumbai*, Indian School of Political Economy.

Government of India, Ministry of Urban Development. (1988) *Report of the National Commission on Urbanization*. New Delhi, Vol. 2, p. 38.

Mazumdar, P.S. and I. (1978) *Rural Migrants in an Urban Setting*, Hindustan Publishing Corp. Delhi.

Mohan, R. (1985) "*Urbanization in India's Future*", *Population and Development Review*, New York, No. 4. pp. 619-45.

National Capital Region Planning Board, (1988). *Regional Plan 2001*, National Capital Region. Ministry of Urban Development, New Delhi.

Government of India, Sixth Five Year Plan 1980-85.

Government of India, Seventh Five Year Plan 1985-90. Vol. I

Government of India "Towards Social Transformation – Approach to the Eighth Five Year Plan", Planning Commission, New Delhi.

Rao, Ratna N. (1990) *Social Organization in an Indian Slum*, Mittal Publications, New Delhi.

Registrar General and Census Commissioner, (1991), *Census of India*, Series-1, Paper 2, New Delhi, p.39.

Singh, A.M. and De Souza, A. (1980), *The Urban Poor – Slum and Pavement Dwellers in the Major Cities of India*, Manohar Publications, New Delhi.

Sundaram. K. (1986) *Growth Inequality and Poverty, The Indian Experience*, Centre for Policy Research, New Delhi.

Tataji, U. (1986) "*Rural-Urban Migration and Work Organization and Slums*" in Rao, M.S.A. (ed): *Studies in Migration*, Manohar Publications, Delhi, pp. 183-201.

Town and Country Planning Organization (1985), Ministry of Works, Housing and Supply, New Delhi.

World Bank. (1990), *World Development Report*: Washington D.C.

World Bank. (1992), *World Development Report*. Washington D.C.

11

A Strategy for Reducing Poverty in India's Large Metropolitan Cities

INTRODUCTION

Poverty in rural and urban areas is the most serious problem in India. While most of the poor live in rural areas, among the remainder, a considerable percentage live in slums of large metropolitan cities i.e. cities with a population of 1 million or more. This paper, outlines a strategy for reducing poverty in the large metropolitan cities. There are 3 such cities – Mumbai, Kolkata and Delhi, which had altogether a total population of 42 million in 2001; 15 percent of the total urban population. The slums of Delhi and Mumbai are selected for detailed description because the economic activities of the slum dwellers, the civic amenities that are provided to them and the hardships that they suffer in living from day to day are brought out in sharp detail in them.

The number of poor migrants to these and other cities will be reduced greatly in the next two decades as a result of increase in agricultural output and agro-industrial development in the areas from which they come. The number of illiterates who are in poor health would be reduced greatly in the home areas of the migrants as a result of greatly increased facilities for education of children and preventive health and medical care for all. Furthermore, the demand for unskilled and illiterate migrants would be much less than at present in metropolitan cities or their peri-urban areas during the next 15 or 20 years because there would be much less work for them than it is now. This would be the result of trends in the manufacturing and modern service sectors in which most of the workers have to be educated and have to possess basic mechanical and computing skills. Furthermore, they should be in good health because absenteeism or lethargy at work involves very high cost to their employers. All enlightened employers ensure that their workers are paid enough to live in brick and mortar houses, provided with all basic amenities and have a level of living by which they can remain healthy and efficient in their work. They pay for the cost of their medical treatment if they are sick.

There is a long-term trend towards concentration of the urban population in metropolitan cities. In 1951 there were 5 such cities; their population formed 17.8 percent of the urban population and 3.2 percent of the total population of the country. By 1991, the number of such cities had gone up to 23; their population constituted 32 percent of the urban population and 8.4 percent of the total population. By 2001, the number had gone upto 35 and their population, 108 million. It constituted 38 percent of the urban and 10.5 percent of the total population of the country. Almost 40 percent of the population of metropolitan cities like Mumbai and Delhi is of poor who live in slums and are migrants from rural areas surrounding the cities.

THE URBAN POOR

The urban poor are concentrated in the slums of metropolitan cities. The great majority of them are landless agricultural laborers or marginal farmers who cannot get enough remunerative work in their home villages or neighboring towns.

However, while their numbers has been reduced in several southern cities by increase in employment in their home areas, or in industries and service occupations located in the peri-urban areas of the cities, there has been no reduction in Mumbai, Delhi, Kolkata or other northern cities.

It should be mentioned however that many residents of so called slums in Kolkata and Delhi have access to facilities for education of children, preventive and health care, electricity and community hand pumps for drinking water. These facilities are provided by the municipal Corporation in Delhi and Mumbai and in Kolkata by city civic authority or by charitable organizations. A proportion of the houses in the older slum clusters are made of brick and mortar. However satisfactory arrangement for disposal of solid or liquid waste are lacking in most of the slums. Furthermore, large proportions of the huts in many slum clusters need *pucca* floors, hard brick walls, corrugated iron sheets over their roof. Otherwise they are liable to collapse during rains or being burnt in the hot summer nights of the northern summers; there are no slums in Chennai or other southern towns.

DEFINITIONS: POVERTY AND SLUMS

Two definitions of Poverty are in use at present:

The poor are people who do not get enough calories from cereals, pulses, sugar, oil and milk to keep themselves in good health. This definition has been used by the Central Statistical Organization of the Government of India since the 1970s.

The second definition, favoured by UNDP, the World Bank and other international agencies includes in addition to the above, people who do not have adequate or easy access to:

1. Clean drinking water;
2. Facilities for educating the children to secondary school level; and
3. Facilities for preventive health and medical care to maintain themselves in health.

The second definition is used in this paper.

A slum is a collection of huts or houses of the poor located in an area of the city, which has been designated for their living by the Municipal Corporation of the city. Then there are several clusters of slums located in areas which have been occupied by the slum dwellers without permission or against the wishes of the Municipal Corporation. There are large number of slum clusters of both kinds in Delhi and Mumbai.

There are two kinds of houses in a slum:

1. First, 1-3 bedroom *pucca* house with walls and floor made of baked bricks and mortar and having roof either of baked bricks and mortar, or of baked tiles. Most of the houses in a designated slum cluster are of this kind.
2. A second kind is a 1-2 room *kucha* hut with a floor of unbaked bricks, walls of similar bricks or of straw held together by a miscellany of materials. The roof is of corrugated iron sheets, overlain by straw. Most of the huts in slums in unauthorized

locations are of this kind. Such huts could collapse during a heavy downpour in the rainy season and are also vulnerable to fire.

The residents of slums located in designated areas are provided drinking water by the Municipal Corporation of the city, generally through community standpipes. Electricity is provided by the authority or company that supplies electricity in the city on payment of a nominal charge by every householder. The Corporation also makes arrangements (generally inadequate) for disposal of solid and liquid waste. Schools for education of children to primary or secondary school level are maintained by the Corporation or voluntary organizations. The Corporation also maintains dispensaries for treatment of common diseases. Hospitals maintained by the state government or by charitable trusts provide facilities for long-term treatment. These facilities are generally not adequate to serve efficiently all the poor patients who come to the hospitals.

The Corporation has no responsibility for residents of slums located in areas which are not considered suitable for them. However, their residents do get electricity and often drinking water also through connivance with the concerned junior officials of the Corporation or the electricity authority or with the help of the municipal councilor of the area who considers them to be his 'vote bank'.

Estimates of the people living in slums and unauthorized resident colonies with dependable supplies of electricity and water but with inadequate facilities for disposal of waste in the contiguously built area of Delhi located within Delhi state i.e. excluding urbanized villages is as high as 40 percent. The percentage would not be significantly low in Mumbai or Kolkata.

Proliferation of Slums

Proliferation of slums, unavoidable in the present and foreseeable future situation of extreme shortage of housing for the urban poor presents, however, very difficult problems; political, legal, economic, social and moral. The official policies (or rather non policies) towards the slums reflect an ambivalence which is partly inherent in the situation but derives also from the ambivalent attitude of the urban affluent and middle income groups towards the slum dwellers. The policies have four major components:

1. To prevent establishment of slums in the central areas of the cities and on public (or private) lands which are designated for other essential uses;
2. To clear these areas of slums, generally by moving their residents to housing colonies located in the peripheral regions of the cities. The removal generally requires use of force by the police or other authorities, although it is often accompanied by providing house sites and financial assistance for resettlement in these colonies to a proportion of the residents;
3. To tolerate existence and expansion of existing slums in other locations; and
4. Sporadically to undertake slum improvement programmes, such as improvement of approach roads, extension of bus routes and electricity and water lines, improvement of sanitation within the slums particularly by construction of drains and improvement of arrangements for disposal of solid waste, providing public water taps and street lights, and opening of schools, training centres, health centres, community centres, etc.

These programmes are undertaken most frequently before elections to the municipal bodies or to the state legislatures, and have the political motive of winning the support of the slum dwellers for the party in power. Besides improving the environmental conditions of the slums and reducing the hardships of their residents, the programmes mean recognition by the authorities, first *de facto* but later also *de jure*, of the rights of the slum dwellers to continue to live in them undisturbed.

Slum clearance is a traumatic process which causes great hardship and generally also enormous financial loss to its victims. They are left shelterless and the demolition of their homes means that their savings of many years are wiped out. As a result, it encounters fierce resistance from the slum dwellers and leads frequently to litigation which may be bitter and prolonged. The trauma and the bitterness are mitigated only partially by the provision of alternative house sites in the peripheral regions and financial assistance for rehabilitation and resettlement in them. Delays in providing the sites or the financial assistance, or in extending the basic services to the new locations due to bureaucratic inefficiency, indifference or corruption, represent one set of causes of the resentment and opposition. A second set relates to the hardship, loss of income and increase in expenditure suffered by the slum dwellers, on account of separation by long distances between their places of living and of working. The long journeys to work in the city centres are time-consuming and expensive; frequently public transport needed for the journeys is just not available. Many workers, especially those working in the informal sector, lose their jobs and become destitute. Further loss is caused by the womenfolk and other members of the households losing their jobs as domestics, etc., in the households of affluent and middle-income groups.

Recognizing these difficulties and problems of eviction and relocation of slum dwellers, the Sixth Five-Year Plan placed emphasis on environmental improvement of slums, mainly through improvement of drainage, sewerage and sanitation, which were considered to be the principal causes of an area becoming a slum. The plan proposed an investment of Rs 1500 million to benefit 10 million out of the estimated 33.1 million slum dwellers by 1985. Nearly one-fifth of the total urban population was estimated to be living in slums.

The Seventh Plan continued the emphasis on environmental improvement, and increased the total allocation for it to Rs. 2696 million, to benefit about 9 million slum dwellers; just over half of the 17.5 million estimated not to have been covered by the Sixth Plan programme by 1985. Allocation *per capita* was raised to Rs. 300 from Rs. 100 in the Sixth Plan. The plan also recommended providing security of tenure to the slum dwellers so that, 'they may develop a stake in maintaining and improving their habitat' (Planning Commission, 1985: 290, 299).

It is evident from the above that the programmes of slum improvement included in the Plans are neither comprehensive nor adequate in coverage. Environmental improvement is undoubtedly important, but so are expansion and improvement of other essential services, notably medical care, education (including education for citizenship and in improved hygiene) and training to equip for productive employment the large numbers of unemployed, most of who turn to crime to survive. It is noteworthy that the need for providing security of tenure was recognized only in the Seventh Plan. Furthermore, allotment of alternative house sites in colonies located at long distances from the city centres is made only to small proportions of the slum dwellers. The planning of the new colonies is poor, and there are long delays in providing essential services to them. Often the colonies are virtually forgotten after the evicted slum dwellers are moved to them.

These deficiencies reflect an ambivalence among the planners and other policy-makers towards the slum dwellers, which is, in our view, a reflection of the attitude of the urban affluent and middle-income groups towards them. The services of the slum dwellers, who constitute the great majority of workers in almost all sectors of the urban economy, are needed and wanted. But the affluent and the middle-income groups do not care where and how they live, except that they should not live in the central areas of the cities, where most of them work. This attitude is similar in many ways to that of the South African whites towards the blacks: the whites also want the blacks to work in the cities, but not to live in them. The ambivalence must end and give place to clear policies, backed by appropriate programmes which are comprehensive and adequate in coverage.

In Delhi, there are sprawling slum clusters along the Yamuna on land just above the flood plain of the river. These were developed and provided with all essential services – electricity, water, surface drainage, bus services to the places of work of the slum dwellers during 1974-77 when they were evicted from unsuitable locations, e.g. along or behind the roads in New and old Delhi. Here the residents were provided partially finished brick and mortar 1-3 bedroom houses with space to enlarge them with increase in the size of their families. They were provided adequate and clean drinking water by the Municipal Corporation and electricity by the Delhi Vidyut Board. Arrangements for removal of solid and liquid waste were also adequate. The area had motorable roads so that the residents could go to their jobs by bicycles. Bus services were provided also to make commuting easier.

These clusters have increased greatly in size due to increase in numbers of migrant to the city. Then there are slum clusters adjacent to every residential neighborhood, which has been developed by commercial land developers, cooperative housing societies or even by the Delhi Development Authority during the last 4-5 decades.

The great majority of the slum dwellers in Delhi apart from the construction workers work either as domestic servants, watchmen, gardeners etc. or are unskilled workers in industries, markets, porters in railway stations or bus station etc. They are from distant places such as Andhra Pradesh and Tamil Nadu in the south and Bihar, Orissa and Bangladesh. A large number of domestic servants are from Nepal settled in Daryaganj. All of them aspire to live in modest comfort in their village homes or small towns after two or more decades of work in Delhi.

LOCATION OF SLUMS IN DELHI

Location I

The largest number of houses or huts of slum dwellers are located east of the Yamuna just above the flood plain of the river. This location was selected for them during 1975-77 and the slum dwellers were forced to move to it in order to reduce congestion in 'Old Delhi' (Shahjahanabad) and to have a clean living environment in it and New Delhi.

The initial settlers in the slums were from Delhi or its satellite cities in U.P. such as Shahdara, Ghaziabad, Hapur or Meerut. However, in course of time, new settlers came illegally, mainly from Bangladesh. They squatted on the flood plain of the river itself with connivance of junior officials of the Corporation and some politicians who consider them to be their 'vote bank'. The flood plain gets flooded during the monsoon and all efforts of officials of the Corporation are directed towards preventing outbreak of communicable diseases such as cholera, typhoid, dysentery and bronchitis. Despite their efforts, there is often an outbreak of such diseases in which thousands, mostly women, children and the elderly are taken ill.

Facilities for education of children upto secondary school level were provided by the Corporation within or at the outskirts of the clusters. There were also two dispensaries within easy reach. A multi-facility hospital has also come up in course of time.

Location II

Then, there are slum clusters outside or within various residential colonies, built by the Government of India during the 1950s to the 1970s to house its employees. Ramakrishnapuram, the largest such colony, built by the Government during the 1960s and the 1970s in order to house several offices of the government or public sector undertakings, and about 10,000 employees varying in rank from messengers and clerks to Deputy Secretaries has several such clusters within it. The residents of the slums are provided clean running water by the Corporation through tankers. They are provided or steal electricity from the Delhi Vidyut Board. Since there are no arrangements for disposal of solid and liquid waste, the residents have built their huts by the side of the municipal sewage drain and throw their garbage in the drain. As a result, the stench in houses of the slum dwellers is unbearable.

Most of the residents of the slums work as domestic servants in houses located near their huts. Others work in shops in various markets located in Ramakrishnapuram. The occupation of still others range from selling newspapers to skilled work (carpenters, plumbers, masons, or repairmen of electrical or electronic gadgets). However, there are also many beggars and thieves among them. They are responsible for most of the thefts in the houses of the residents. The Corporation maintains several primary schools for children of the slum dwellers.

Location III

Vasant Vihar, the residential nieghbourhood built by a cooperative society of retired officials of the Government of India in order to have a healthy living environment in their old age has two such clusters. The larger one is located to the south west of Vasant Vihar. The second one located within a wood (forest) is towards the northwest of Vasant Vihar. The former is known as *Kusum Pahari;* the latter has several subsections each known by the predominant race inhabiting it, e.g. there is Bengali *Jughis* and Nepali *Jughis* etc. The houses of the older residents in it are of brick and mortar while the huts of the later arrivals have floors and walls of unbaked bricks and roof of corrugated iron sheets held together by straw.

Some of the residents of Kusum Pahari are domestic servants in houses in Vasant Vihar. Others work as unskilled labourers in a market located within 1 km. from their houses. The occupations of the residents of the smaller cluster located within a wood (forest) are similar to those of the residents of the larger cluster, except that more of the residents do unskilled labour in the numerous stores in the market. The Corporation has provided clean water through community stand pipes each of which serves a certain number of families. They get electricity from the electric supply company on payment of a nominal monthly charge. The Corporation also maintains a higher secondary school and a small playground for school children. Two voluntary organizations located near the slum provide medical aid. The cluster has several wards each with its own ward leader, who ensures sanitation within it. Thus, the slum has an organisation similar to that of a village. The older residents claim that the cluster is built on a village of the same name viz., *Kusum Pahari*. The word "pahari" means that the slum is located in a stony area. The residents of Vasant Vihar claim that most of the thefts in their colony are committed by people living in this slum.

Construction workers who come from districts neighbouring Delhi in Rajasthan live in both clusters. Their number is much lower now than it was in the 1970s because there is much less construction activity in Vasant Vihar than in the 1970s and the 1980s. Their stay in Delhi is seasonal. They return to their home villages during April to September, i.e. just before the monsoon season and stay there till the end of it. During their stay, in their villages they participate in harvesting the cool season crop and in planting the monsoon crop. They get grain for their families from the cool season crop and get an assurance of supply of adequate grain from the monsoon crop. Most of them come without their families. A number of landless slum dwellers migrate with their families and the entire families engage in begging when the unskilled construction work is not available.

LOCATION OF SLUMS IN MUMBAI

Location I

The largest slum cluster in Mumbai is "Dharavi" on way to the Santa Cruz airport; it claims proudly to be the largest slum in Asia. Some of the residents work as domestic servants in flats of people of the middle income or affluent groups located near them; others are clerks or professionals such as lawyers. They commute to their jobs in the central business district of Mumbai in crowded commuter trains. The professionals are not poor; but they are not rich enough to own or rent a flat even in the suburbs which extend for 40 odd kilometres from the central business district. Then there are slums in every suburb of the middle income people. The residents are domestic servants, barbers and others who render personal services to the residents of the suburb.

The Corporation provides drinking water through community stand pipes and removes solid and liquid waste. They get electricity from the electric supply company on nominal payment. The Corporation and/or voluntary organisations have opened primary schools for small children and higher secondary schools for older children. The Corporation or voluntary organisations also maintain dispensaries for treatment of communicable diseases. Voluntary organisations also maintain play grounds for children and libraries and group exercise classes for school children and young men. Thus, the basic needs of the slum dwellers are fulfilled. Cases of serious sickness are treated in a hospitals maintained by the Government and/or by charitable trust in the suburbs.

Location II

Then there is a slum just outside and partly within the port. It was built by contractors working for the port with the permission of the Port Trust. The residents work on loading and unloading cargo ships and do other work in the port. The Port Trust maintains schools for their children and dispensaries for treatment of common diseases. It pays also for their treatment in hospitals. There is also an unauthorised slum next to the port. The residents do the same work in the port as the residents of the authorised slum do, with permission of junior officials of the port. They are responsible for most of the thefts in the port.

Location III

Finally, there is a slum on the roads just below the gleaming towers of the central business district (CBD) of Mumbai. The CBD houses the Maharashtra secretariat, a luxury hotel, the best in Mumbai and offices of the national and international corporations that make Mumbai the largest centre of business and finance in India. The residents work as domestic servants in flats of affluent people located near the CBD or as messengers in offices in the CBD.

All attempts to remove the slum dwellers are resisted by them and by self styled spokesmen of the ‘poor’ including film stars.

The Corporation provides, drinking water, through community stand pipes, electricity is provided by the electric company; but arrangements for disposal of solid or liquid waste are inadequate so that the filth on the roads has to be removed by the sanitation workers of the Corporation during the night.

HOME AREAS OF THE SLUM DWELLERS

A large proportion of the slum dwellers in Mumbai come from Ratnagiri and adjoining districts of the west coast and Thane. Smaller numbers come from distant places such as the drought prone areas of south western Maharashtra, eastern U.P. and Bihar. The number of the latter has increased in recent years with rapid growth of business, industries and population in Mumbai and Nhavi Mumbai, which is a satellite city, located on the mainland opposite the main city.

The large percentage of the slum dwellers in Delhi come from Rajasthan, Uttar Pradesh, Bihar and as far as Bangladesh. A large percentage of the residents of Kusum Pahari in Delhi come from within Delhi itself. They complain that they were evicted from their small land holdings by force in building Vasant Kunj, a block of flats for people of middle-income groups (and built by the Delhi Development Authority), and several blocks built by a number of public sector undertaking for their middle income employees. The compensation given to them was small and was much delayed so that they had no alternative but to squat on or near their fields and do such work as was available. Later arrivals came from districts nieghbouring Delhi in western U.P.; others are from eastern U.P. The latest arrivals are from Bangladesh as mentioned earlier. A large percentage of the domestic servants are from Darjeeling and are of Indo-Nepalese stock or from distant areas such as Tamil Nadu.

It is significant that there are no drivers of motor vehicles, petty traders or electricians or repairmen of electrical or electronic appliances living in slums. Their income is so high that they can afford to live in brick and mortar houses provided with running water and electricity, although arrangements for disposal of solid and liquid waste may not be adequate. Such "unauthorised colonies" are located in various places in south, south west, west and northwest Delhi. Most of the residents come from Punjab and Haryana. They have been attracted to Delhi because they get much higher income in Delhi than in their home town. They and skilled workers from Delhi are employed in various industrial units located in Gurgaon and Faridabad, satellite cities of Delhi in Haryana. A percentage of the residents in the slum clusters, east of the Yamuna are also skilled workers in industrial units located in Ghaziabad and NOIDA which is now a residential-cum-industrial city located east of the Yamuna.

STRATEGY FOR REDUCING THE NUMBER OF SLUM DWELLERS

The developments that have been in progress in the home areas of the slum dwellers during the last two decades would lead to significant decline in the number of slum dwellers. The number of slum dwellers from Ratnagiri and other coastal districts has been reduced after the building, in the 1990s, of the Konkan railway along the coast. The area gets abundant rainfall, grows rice and alphonso mango which is highly prized for its taste and flavour. It used to be carried by road to Mumbai and was sent from there or directly by road to various cities in India. It is now carried much faster to Mumbai by rail for consumption within it and directly to various cities of India. It is airlifted from Mumbai to the Gulf countries for consumption by Indians in these countries and to Britain and other European countries. Since the mango has excellent keeping quality, it is highly prized. Production of mangoes has been increased by farmers because of high returns on growing it. The fishermen have increased their catch by having motorized boats. The catch is brought to Mumbai by train or road from cold storages which have been constructed by loans and subsidies from the Maharashtra government.

As a result of these developments, the farmers or agricultural labourers have much less incentive to go to Mumbai than they had earlier because they have enough work and income in their home villages. The fishermen need not go to Mumbai except in the monsoon season for work when they cannot fish because of storms in the ocean.

Increase in agricultural production and agro-industrial development especially large production of good high yield sugarcane with high sucrose content in valleys of streams which flow from the Ghats to the sea has led to growth of a large number of sugar and rice mills and industrial units which produce parts for the mills and other machine tools. The area between Mumbai and Pune is, despite the handicap of the Western Ghats, one of the most industrialized areas of the country. There is large employment in industrial units located in towns in the rail-cum-road strip.

The drought prone areas of Gujarat are Saurashtra and Kutch. There is large migration from them to Mumbai, Ahmedabad and other cities. The number of migrants could be reduced greatly after building of the Sardar Sarovar dam on Narmada River in Madhya Pradesh. The Saurashtra and Kutch coast has a large number of towns, which have fishermen who are engaged in fishing and packing them for sale to various cities and towns in India.

The number of migrants from eastern U.P. and Bihar should be much less in future since there have been major increases in agricultural output and significant agro-industrial development in their home areas. There was great potential for such development by control of floods of the Kosi, Gandak and other rivers in Bihar which caused much damage during the rainy season and Gomati and other streams that flow down Himalayan slopes in U.P. The inherent fertility of such lands has been restored by:

1. Construction of small check dams or larger dams across the streams and afforestation in the hills. The sand and silt is removed by farmers from their small holdings. They have been given loans and subsidies for this work and for buying seed of improved high yielding varieties of wheat and rice and chemical fertilizers and pesticides (as needed). As a result there is much larger production of cereals, pulses, oil seeds and potatoes, which are important cash crops even for small farmers. Most of the small farmers who cannot own tractors, hire them at fixed rates from tractor owners, most of whom are former *zamindars*.
2. The former *zamindars* whose right to get tribute from farmers has been extinguished have been given loans to buy tractors to clear the land left to them for self cultivation and pump sets driven by diesel oil or electricity on their wells for irrigation of the irrigable areas. They too grow high yield rice, wheat, oil seeds etc. They grow also high quality mangoes for which there is a high demand in Kolkata and other cities. They have constructed cold storages to store mangoes and potatoes until they are ready for the market

It should be mentioned that until the 1870s Utter Pradesh, Bihar and West Bengal were the most productive and densely populated areas of the country. Their fertility was greatly reduced by indigo planters who made large profits in growing indigo until invention of synthetic dyes by Germany during 1870s. The Scots, who owned tea gardens in Assam and the British who owned sugar plantations in Natal, South Africa, Jamaica, Trinidad and British Guyana in the Caribbean and Fiji in the South Pacific also needed labourers to work in the plantations. They recruited them from this area because local workers in these lands were unable or unwilling to do the exhausting work on the plantations. The recruited workers developed colonies in these distant lands but left eastern U.P. and Bihar without its most productive man-power.

When migration to these lands was stopped in the 1930s young men from U.P. and Bihar took to migration to Kolkata to work in the jute mills that are located along the Hooghly river for about 60 km up the river from Kolkata, and as labourers or skilled workers in various industrial units located in Kolkata or Howrah. Many of them worked as unskilled labour in jobs in the city such as, rickshaw pullers and porters at the Howrah railway station or in shops that sell food grains and other provisions in the central business district (CBD). They lived in slums called '*bastees*' in a number of streets located to the rear of the central business district.

Later in the 1960s and 1970s when there was shortage of farm workers from November to April in Punjab and Haryana, the gap was filled by migrants from eastern U.P. and Bihar. They worked for six months, November to April, on harvesting the monsoon crop and planting and harvesting the cool season crop. Most of them are landless agricultural laborers who do not find enough remunerative work in their home areas, despite agricultural and agro-industrial development. All of them look forward to leading a retired life in their home villages when they cannot do the work that they used to do.

The present Government of West Bengal has virtually ended emigration of workers from villages of the state to Kolkata and other cities by following actions:

1. It has carried out effective land reforms which have extinguished the rights of the *zamindars*, conferred full and heritable rights in land on actual cultivators, given them loans and guided them to buy, seeds, chemical fertilizers, ploughs and other agricultural implements. The former *zamindars* have been given loans to buy tractors for cultivation and pumps for irrigation of their land, which had been left to

them. Production of rice of which two crops are produced in the year and of jute has increased so much that the state which had a deficit of food from time to time is now self sufficient in food; besides production of jute has increased greatly to supply fibre that produce jute bags and other goods for the Indian and foreign markets. Similar measures would contribute to an increase in agricultural output in eastern U.P. and Bihar, which would increase also by replacement of the large numbers of irrigation wells, which are driven by bullocks by those operated by diesel oil or electricity. Significant increase in agricultural output and agro-industrial development in areas from which youngmen migrate for work in the metropolitan cities will reduce the number of migrants to these cities.

2. Expediting construction of a dam on Teesta river, the monsoon floods of which used to cover large areas with sand and silt. These areas have been reclaimed by the farmers with manual methods. The Government gave them loans and subsidies to buy seed of high yield varieties of rice, chemical fertilizers and pesticides as needed to plant rice and jute. The former *zamindars* who have lost their right to get tribute from their tenants have been given medium term loans to buy tractors to reclaim and cultivate the land left to them for self cultivation. They have been given loans also to buy pumps operated by electricity on wells to irrigate the land that can be irrigated. As a result, output of rice has nearly doubled and the state which had a deficit of rice in some years now has a surplus. Besides most of the jute required by the jute mills is produced internally and the need for import of jute from Bangladesh has been reduced. Most important, there has been a major reduction in the number of poor farmers and agricultural labourers. The economic condition of the farmers who were tenants of the *Zamindars* has improved greatly.

Similar measures have been taken by the governments of Bihar and U.P., which are determined to encourage agricultural and agro-industrial development in their states. The government of Bihar will have to first end the class war between the former *zamindars* and their former tenants. Then it must confer full and heritable rights in the land that they had been cultivating on the actual cultivators by extinguishing the rights of the *zamindars*. The latter should be given loans to buy tractors for reclamation of the lands left to them for self-cultivation and to install electric or diesel oil operated pumps for irrigation of the irrigable areas. The former tenants have also been given loans and subsidies to buy agricultural implements, livestock, seeds of high yielding varieties of rice and wheat, chemical fertilizers and pesticides, as needed. As a result, production of foodgrains (rice, wheat and pulses) and oil seeds has increased greatly. Installation of wheat and rice flour and oil mills would be the logical next step. A large proportion of the farmers who used to emigrate are now busy working on their own lands. Some of the former *zamindars* grow mangoes in north Bihar for consumption in Kolkata, Patna and other cities where there is a large demand for the fruit. They could together with traders build cold storages to preserve mangoes and potatoes which are also grown in large quantities in Bihar.

Production of grains and potatoes has increased greatly in south Bihar by increasing the irrigated area by installation of pumps operated by electricity or diesel oil on the thousands of irrigation wells that used to be worked earlier by bullocks. The total result would be major increase in agricultural production and greater employment for small farmers and agricultural laborers in agriculture and in packaging for sale of cash crops (mangoes and potatoes), increase productivity of the land and reduction of former migrants to the slums of metropolitan cities. The state has enough electricity from the high capacity power station that supply Kolkata and various industrial units in Jharkhand. The capacity of these plants could be increased. Similar measures would increase greatly output of grains (wheat, rice, chick peas) and cash crops (mangos, oil seeds and potatoes) in central and eastern U.P.

The government of U.P. did not have to contend with conflict between the former *zamindars* and their tenants. The land reform of abolition of *zamindari* had been effectively implemented during the 1950s and the former *zamindars* had either settled down to cultivation of the lands left to them for self-cultivation or had sold them to former *zamindars* or their former tenants who cultivate them. Most of the former *zamindars* have bought tractors to cultivate their lands. They drive the tractors themselves or have them driven by hired laborers. They hire the tractors at fixed rates to small farmers who cannot afford to buy their own tractors but find ploughing of land by tractors more economic than ploughing it by bullocks. Most of the former *zamindars* have installed pump sets driven by diesel oil or electricity on lands that could be irrigated. Many former tenents have also installed pumpsets on their irrigation wells. Loans for buying tractors and pump sets have been given to them by the land mortgage banks or nationalized banks. Short-term loans for buying improved seeds, chemical fertilizers and pesticides, etc. are given by cooperative societies. As a result, there has been major increase in output of food grains (high yield wheat or rice), maize, chick peas, pulses and oil seeds (mainly mustard) and vegetables.

High quality mangoes which are much in demand in cities all over north India are grown in the vicinity of Lucknow and Varanasi. Most of the orchardists are former *zamindars*; they have built cold storages in cooperation with traders to store mangoes and potatoes (another cash crop) until they are ready for markets. Small cultivators also grow potatoes and rent spaces in the cold storages. Potatoes have become an important cash crop for both small cultivators and those with larger holdings.

With increase in agricultural output and agro-industrial development in U.P. and Bihar much fewer farmers and agricultural labourers need to go to metropolitan cities in search of employment. Many of the migrants from these areas now are graduates from colleges or higher secondary schools with enough knowledge of stenography to get such jobs in various offices in Kolkata, Delhi and other cities. Another group consists of healthy and well built youngmen who work as watchmen in offices, in houses or apartment houses of the affluent or in hotels. They have enough education and presence of mind to use the firearms provided to them for their safety in case of attack by robbers. They do not live in slums but expect to live in brick and mortar houses, provided by the employers or rented by themselves. The combined numbers of migrants of both will be much smaller than that of slum dwellers who migrate from these two states now.

Demand for unskilled industrial labour will also be much less so that most of the labour force will be literate and skilled. This will reduce the cost of production and make products like cars competitive with those produced in foreign countries. Take Maruti Udyog, the car factory located just outside Gurgaon about 30 kilometres from Delhi. Most of the workers live in the colony developed for them by the company. Others who live outside the factory are paid enough to live in brick and mortar houses in Gurgaon. They are literate and the employers provide them facilities for education of their children and medical facilities so that there is minimum loss of production.

The skilled workers in small, medium or large industrial units located in and around metropolitan cities are mainly from neighbouring areas, who can be quickly trained in the specific skills required for the particular industry by their employers; and those who have skills such as those of carpenters, electricians and masons. The carpenters and electricians can be trained quickly to become skilled workers in industrial units. The masons have plenty of work in making and repair of buildings of the industrial units and of houses in colonies of workers. The electricians also have more than enough work doing electrical work in buildings of the factories. Most of these workers are from districts neighbouring the metropolitan cities. In Mumbai most of them are at present and are likely to remain from western Maharashtra from districts located between Mumbai and Pune. In Delhi, they are from Delhi state, Punjab, Haryana and western U.P. All earlier skilled migrant workers do not live in slums but in 'unauthorized colonies' where *pucca* houses can be rented/owned at reasonable price.

A SERVANT-LESS SOCIETY

It is not possible at present to visualise households of affluent or middle income people without full or part time domestic servants in either Mumbai or Delhi. In Mumbai domestic services, such as cleaning the house or flat and washing clothes are performed by women who perform a specific service and leave the house after it. The housewives have such confidence in their honesty that they can do this work even when the housewives are away at work. For housewives who work there are persons who come and cook lunch. In the morning they carry cooked meals for the men or women who work in offices. They are so efficient that the lunch is warm enough to be eaten in the lunch interval in the offices.

In Delhi, there is a large number of domestic servants in various neighbourhoods of the middle or high income people. They live in 1-2 room quarters built within the houses of their employers. They must keep their quarters, themselves and their 1-2 children clean so that they do not bring any communicable diseases in the houses of their employers. Those who cannot afford such full-time workers have part-time servants who clean the house and wash clothes and the housewives cook the meals themselves.

A large percentage of domestic servants in Delhi come from Darjeeling district of West Bengal and are Nepali nationals or are Indian nationals of Nepali origin. They may live in a slum for a short period, but expect that they would move into the employers house as soon as they get a job. Others come from distant places such as Andhra Pradesh or Tamil Nadu. They too live in quarters located within the houses of their employers.

Others live in brick and mortar houses in the suburbs and work in houses of middle-income people who are located closest to them. In the evenings the housewives who work as stenographers or receptionists in offices cook the meals themselves, with husbands doing the dishes. The noon lunch is given to children in schools and hot lunch brought for the men from homes by the *Dibbawallah*. Young children are fed by the ladies who run the creches.

The booming sales of refrigerators, washing machines and vacuum cleaners in both Mumbai and Delhi show that housewives or their husbands do most of the household jobs themselves, but cannot afford to employ even part time servants and do unpleasant house keeping jobs as cleaning the flat and doing the dishes after lunch or dinner themselves. As more and more housewives work as stenographers, receptionists or officers in offices, this trend would intensify and there would be increasing sale of these machines. The refrigerators are used to store cooked or uncooked food so that they would not spoil; air conditioners are used to keep the flat cool, dry and comfortable in Mumbai's sweltering heat.

THE FUTURE

In both cities, the number of slum dwellers should decrease in the next two decades because there would be much less demand for them in industries and various service activities. The number of illiterate men and women would decrease sharply even in the rural areas during the next 20 years. In 2001, the literacy rate 65.4 percent was almost 13 percentage points higher than the rate 52.2 percent in 1991 and almost 22 percentage points higher than in 1981 (45.6%). This increase is likely to continue and there may be a nearly literate population by 2021. The number of skilled workers would increase also because the majority of farmers in the most productive areas of the country who use tractors for ploughing their land and pump sets for irrigation of the irrigable areas have to have enough skills to be able to repair small defects in them themselves; otherwise the use of the machines would be too expensive. They have to be educated to 8-grade or secondary school level so that they can read the instructions on use of improved high yield dwarf varieties of wheat or rice along with chemical fertilizers and pesticides, as needed. They have to be educated also to understand the terms on which they have been given short term loans by cooperative societies for current cultivation and medium term (3-5 years) loans by the land mortgage or nationalised banks for buying tractors for land reclamation and pump sets for irrigation etc. They have to be educated enough also to ensure that they are not cheated by the merchants who market their crops or who supply them various inputs, consumer goods, fuel and spare parts for the machines or building materials to build brick and mortar houses.

Sons of such small farmers or agricultural labourers who go to metropolitan cities for more remunerative employment would be literate and/or have basic mechanical skills. They would get white collar jobs in offices of the Central or State Governments or of various companies. Those who are skilled, would expect to be trained by their employers in the specific skills required for work in their industrial units. Both groups would need to be in good health so that they are regular, punctual and active in the job. Their employers would expect this because absenteeism or lethargy on the job involves high cost for the employers. Most enlightened employers will pay them enough so that they can educate their children and reimburse their expenses on medical treatment. They will either provide housing with all basic amenities in them or ensure that they can afford to rent such houses.

Given this trend, it is possible to visualise a scenario in which there are much smaller slums in most of the metropolitan cities and the number of slum dwellers will be very small. This is entirely possible because during the 1990s while growth rate of GDP has been 5-7 percent p.a. and per capita income has been increasing by 3-5 percent p.a. The number of poor has fallen sharply from 54.3 percent in 1973–74 to 29.2 percent in 1996–97 and is projected to decline (by Planning Commission) to 18.0 percent in 2001–2002. UNDP, New York, has estimated the proportion of under-nourished people at 23 percent in 1991–2002 and those not having access to improved drinking water services at only 12 percent. Thus, we can expect that by 2015 there would be much fewer people in most of the states who are poor, illiterate and in poor health and who need to migrate to metropolitan cities in search of employment and live in slums.

Reduction in the number of slum dwellers in metropolitan cities will mean an enormous saving to their Corporations or companies which provide various services to the slum dwellers much below cost. They can deliver the same services to the middle income people and offices slightly above their cost to have some return on the investment. Supply of tradable amenities – electricity, safe drinking water and even disposal of solid and liquid water could provide a small profit to the Municipal Corporations or the companies that provide these.

The Central Government after years of indecision did entrust in July 2002 distribution of electricity in Delhi to two companies which have managed electricity supplies to Mumbai for more than a century efficiently and at a profit to themselves. The companies have already (August 2002) greatly reduced theft of electricity by industrial users and other large users and reduced the frequency of power cuts in Delhi's long hot summer.

With no messengers to make tea or coffee for the officers and clerks working in offices the clerks will do this job themselves. With no messengers to carry files from one desk to another, the decision-making officers will take most of the decisions themselves instead of pushing the file to a colleague for his opinion.

This development will take place first in headquarters and regional offices of companies that make goods in which there is stiff competition between different manufacturers. The list includes trendy clothes, shoes, and other leather goods; furniture for homes and offices and consumer durables, refrigerators, air conditioners, washing machines and motor vehicles from motor bicycles to passenger cars. The manufacturers of these goods must minimise cost per unit of output in order to be competitive. They achieve this by having fewer but more efficient workers and their supervisors. Certain public sector banks and manufacturing units have reduced their losses and become profitable by giving generous voluntary retirement packages to their surplus staff. Among the latter, those who are efficient, generally join other offices or start their own businesses and are often better off than they were while in service.

Others will retire and live with interest on their investments to sustain them in their old age.

CONCLUDING REMARKS

The developments outlined in the previous sections are entirely possible in the next 20 years. Two examples are given in support of this argument:

Example 1

In the 1950s and the 1960s, most of the domestic servants in Delhi were from either Tehri or Pauri Garhwal districts of Uttaranchal or from Kangra district of Himachal Pradesh. No longer. The youngmen who used to go to Delhi to work as domestic servants are so busy producing food and doing various services for the officers and men of the armed forces that guard India's border with Tibet and Nepal that they have much less need to go to Delhi or other cities.

In both states, Himachal Pradesh and Uttaranchal, tens of thousands find remunerative employment in looking after the thousands of tourists that flock to hill stations – such as Shimla, Kullu and Manali in Himachal Pradesh and Mussoorie, Naini Tal and Ranikhet in Uttaranchal—in the summer. Large numbers find seasonal or year-round employment also in looking after the Hindu pilgrims that visit the temples of Badrinath and Kedarnath, Hardwar and Rishikesh in Uttaranchal in the summer and the holy places of the Hindus and Sikhs located in Himachal Pradesh.

Those who go to Delhi now are all graduates from higher secondary schools or colleges, who aspire to work as clerks or junior officers in offices of companies or the central government. Their object is to move up the economic ladder and to ensure that their sons will become officers or clerks and that their daughters would be married to such workers. They live in brick and mortar houses provided by the government or other employers or are given house rent allowances so that they can live in such houses. Their employers pay their expenses for medical care also because, as mentioned earlier absenteeism or lethargy at work of even one employee means a high cost for his or her employer.

Example 2

More than 200,000 Tamil labourers who used to work in tea plantations in Sri Lanka were repatriated to Tamil Nadu during the 1950s, under pressure from the Government of Sri Lanka on the Government of India. It was feared that the repatriated workers would be reduced to penury because of lack of remunerative work that they used to do. This has not happened. On the contrary, the repatriated workers have acquired enough skills to work as industrial workers in the thousands of medium scale and large industrial units that make Tamil Nadu a highly industrialised state. Others work as labourers on farms in which most of the land is irrigated by canals or electrically operated pumps and which produce large crops of rice, sugar cane and oil seeds. The state is self-sufficient in rice and is besides a large producer of sugar and oil seeds.

Conditions in the slums of Delhi and Mumbai have been described in some detail in this paper and those in the slums of Kolkata have been referred to briefly. It is of interest to note that in contrast to these three cities, there are hardly any slums in Chennai. The skilled and semi-skilled workers in the thousands of industrial units located around Chennai live in brick and mortar houses provided with all basic amenities and built by the Corporation or by the employers and rented by the workers at highly subsidised low rents. These well housed and healthy workers are so disciplined and efficient that large numbers of industrial units that were located in Kolkata moved to Chennai in the 1960s in order to escape the militancy of trade unions in Kolkata.

The former slum dwellers in Chennai now live in 1-4 story flats built by the Housing Board and located both in the city or in its outskirts. They are assisted by the Municipal Corporation and the Housing Board to obtain employment in various service sector units located in Chennai or in industrial units located on the outskirts. They have to pay very low rents, the remainder is paid by the employers or by the Housing Board. The former consider the subsidy a rent, while the latter consider it a worth while expense for keeping Chennai free of slums.

As agricultural output and income of farmers increased as a result of expansion of irrigation and production of improved high yield rice and coarse grains on irrigated lands, large numbers of enterprises came up in the state to meet the needs of the middle income farmers and agricultural labourers for consumer goods and various consumer durables. As a result, Tamil Nadu has become about the most developed State in India.

There is no reason why with determined action by the Corporations and the state governments, the number of slum dwellers should not decline markedly in both Delhi and Mumbai. This development would be facilitated by ongoing exodus of industrial and service sector units from the cities to their satellite towns/cities.

The Municipal Corporation of Hyderabad and the state government of Andhra Pradesh took effective measures during the 1960s to the 1990s to provide all basic amenities to the former slum dwellers. They were assisted to build brick and mortar houses and all basic amenities in the city center. Large numbers were shifted to the suburbs or satellite cities to work in the numerous industrial units that came up in the latter in this period. Living condition in the slums were greatly improved by providing electricity and running drinking water to the residents and education of children and preventing health and medical care to all. As a result the city center of Hyderabad has improved so much that people of middle-income group have improved their homes. Large numbers have moved to the suburbs such as Banjara Hills. Hyderabad today is after Bangalore and Chennai the third most important center of the information technology industry. It has remained clean despite experiencing rapid growth in population and economic activities during the last three to four decades.

There is a definite policy in the development of metropolitan cities to shift the slums from unauthorized areas to resettlement colonies where the inhabitants will be given pucca houses with facilities for water, electricity and removal of solid wastes. A number of these colonies have been developed and at times Supreme Court had to give direction to the Delhi state government to clear the areas occupied by slums. Now because of plans of the government of India for developing Delhi, e.g. like building of metro rail and beautification of Yamuna water front, the removal of such slum settlements required for development works is being expedited. In case of the latter recently (22nd January, 2004) the government has passed orders to clear the Yamuna Pushta slum along the river and resettle almost 1.5 lakhs inhabitant by allotting them 5200 plots developed by it in Narela and Madanpur Khadar. The government has promised all assistance to the slum dwellers in shifting their belongings, and loans for construction of houses and providing other services.

12

Spatial and Socio-Economic Dynamics of Delhi's Emergence from A Medium Sized City to Megalopolis: 1947-2000

Between 1947 and 2000, a period of little more than half a century, Delhi has been transformed from a medium sized city, located within the Union Territory of Delhi to a megalopolis in which the contiguously urbanised area extends far beyond the boundaries of Delhi state to two adjoining districts each of Haryana and Uttar Pradesh. The population of the city within the Delhi state increased 12-fold from about 700,000 in 1951 to 8.4 million in 1991 and 12.8 millions as per 2001 census. The city has experienced* during the previous 3 out of 4 decades, a growth rate of more than 50 percent per decade (Table 12.1).

Table 12.1: Controlled Population Projection of Delhi UT 1981-2001

Year	*Population in Lakhs*	*Net Increase in Lakhs*	*Decadal Growth Rate(%)*	*Addition by Natural Growth(%)*	*Increase by Immigration in Lakhs(%)*
			Actual		
1961	26.59				
1971	40.66	14.07	52.91	8.82 (33.17)	5.25 (19.74)
1981	62.20	21.54	52.98	9.24 (22.74)	12.30 (30.24)
			Projected		
1991	92.55	30.35	48.79	12.44 (20.00)	17.91 (28.79)
2001	112.00	19.45	21.01	11.11 (12.00)	8.34 (9.01)

Note: Figures in brackets indicate components of decadal growth rate.

The number would be much higher if the populations of the four satellited towns – Gurgaon and Faridabad in Haryana and Gautam Buddh Nagar and Ghaziabad are added. The contiguously urbanised area extends along the highways from Delhi to these cities. Thus there is a megalopolis on both sides of the Yamuna River, with steadily increasing areas occupied by housing colonies and industrial units (Fig. 12.1).

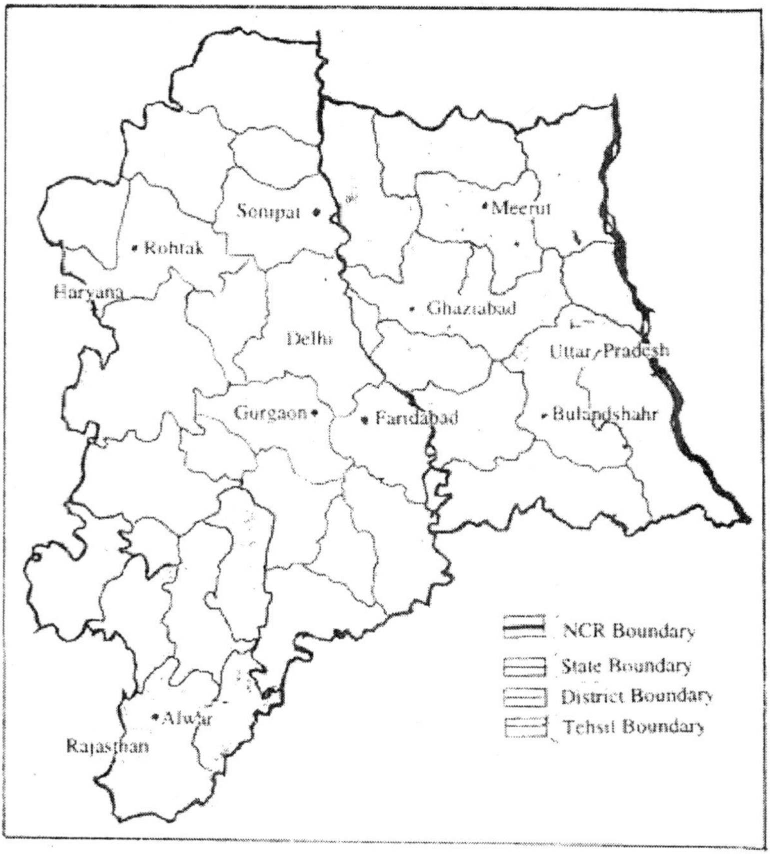

Fig. 12.1: NCR Constituent Areas.

This paper traces the evolution of the megalopolis through various stages during this period. It refers to pressures to undertake land development and house building on a large scale; the role of different agencies including those of the Government of India, cooperative group housing societies, development authorities of Delhi, Haryana and of the two cities in U.P., and of commercial land development and house building companies. The changes in the oldest (pre-1947) as well as the post-1947 parts of Delhi as well as growth of the satellite cities are traced. The last three sections discuss (i) projections of population and probable changes in economic activities during the next decade, 2000-2010; (ii) problems of expansion of infrastructures – electricity and supply of water, facilities for disposal of solid and liquid waste and (iii) measures for minimizing pollution of air and water so as to provide a healthy environment to the residents.

It should be emphasized that Delhi is different from other metropolitan cities in many ways. Being the national capital, it receives more attention and funds for running the city and expansion of infrastructures from the central government than does any other metropolitan city. It is a large industrial center with industries ranging from its traditional handicrafts to manufacture in its satellite cities of passenger cars, and a large variety of consumer goods and consumer durables. It is the principal distributing center for consumer goods and consumer durables in north western India which comprises Punjab, Haryana, western U.P., Himachal Pradesh and Jammu and Kashmir. Most parts of the region have the highest levels of per capita income and consumption of both farm products and manufactured goods. Distributive trade and industries provide more employment to workers in Delhi than does public administration (Table 12.2).

Finally, as a result of location of an Institute of Technology and two of the best multi-faculty universities in the country and the efforts of the governments of Delhi state, Haryana and Uttar Pradesh to build information technology parks it could become an important center of the information technology industries.

Since it is located on a well drained plain, Delhi does not suffer from the limits to spatial expansion that Mumbai and Kolkata suffer from. Second, because of its dry climate – hot and dry in the long summer and cold and dry in the cool season–diseases of the digestive tract are less common than in the other two metropolitan cities. Finally, it has for its size an exceptionally large number of innovative entrepreneurs and skilled workers.

Table 12.2: Distribution of Main Workers by Industrial Categories 1991, Delhi

	Agriculture and Allied Industries	*Mining and Quarrying*	*Manufacturing and Processing*	*Construction*	*Trade and Commerce*	*Transport and Communications*	*Other Services*	*Total*
	(I-III)	*(IV)*	*(V a+b)*	*(VI)*	*(VII)*	*(VIII)*	*(IX)*	*(I to IX)*
				(Numbers in 000's)				
Total	77	7	731	232	710	246	965	2968
Rural	46	4	62	24	37	25	74	273
Urban	31	3	667	208	673	221	891	2676
				Per cent-ages				
Total	3.39	0.42	28.64	6.23	21.16	9.0	31.16	100
Rural	32.83	2.79	20.53	3.88	5.35	8.04	26.58	100
Urban	1.35	0.26	28.20	6.39	22.26	9.07	31.47	100

Source: Registrar General and Census Commissioner (1991Ib: 146-47)

This paper surveys growth of and/or changes in character of principal constituents of the megalopolis viz.

1. Shahjahanabad and its older extensions that date from the building of the city by the Mughal Emperor, Shahjahan in the 18th century;
2. New Delhi built during the 1920s to house the capital of British India;
3. In-filling in New Delhi during world war II;
4. Post-1947 extensions to house displaced persons from Pakistan and the greatly expanded offices and employees of the Government of India;
5. Building of Chanakyapuri, the Diplomatic Enclave.
6. The large building activity of the Central Public Works Department, Delhi Development Authority, cooperative group housing societies and private land development and construction companies to provide housing to the rapidly increasing population, primarily of people of middle and high income groups;
7. Development east of the Yamuna to house slum dwellers and people of middle and high income groups;
8. Growth of 'Unauthorised colonies';
9. Growth of population and economic activities in the four satellite cities located in the adjoining states of Uttar Pradesh and Haryana which form an integral part of the megalopolis.
10. Delhi as a tourist center;
11. Delhi as a center for the information technology industries;
12. The twin city model of Indian city and the Megalopolis;
13. Climate and types of urban settlement
14. Prospects for the decade 2000-2010
15. Problems of expansion of infrastructures – electricity, water supply, sewerage, drainage and facilities for disposal of solid waste; evolving an efficient system of intra-urban transport and control of traffic; and
16. Efficient administration to provide security of life and property and a healthy living environment to the residents.

DELHI BEFORE 1947

Shajahanabad and its older extensions: Paharganj, Subzi Mandi, parts of Karol Bagh and The Civil Lines.

These are the oldest and except for the civil lines, the most densely populated parts of Delhi. Since the areas are extremely crowded and lack sewerage and satisfactory arrangements for disposal of solid waste, the First Master Plan of Delhi 1962-81, classified all of them as slums. It ignored the facts that: Shahjahanabad contains the principal wholesale markets of the city for provisions, textiles, sundry goods, electrical goods and bicycles; the distinctive handicrafts of Delhi, ivory work, making of jewellery and embroidery on silk to produce garments for weddings and other festive occasions are concentrated in it, and the history of Delhi from the Mughal period is embedded in its historic buildings – palaces of nobles of the Mughal period and residences of famous Urdu poets such as Mirza Ghalib and Zauk.

Shahjahanabad houses a sizeable number of rich merchants. However most of the residents are poor shopkeepers, artisans and workers in the hundreds of small and tiny industrial establishments located in it. A significant proportion of them are Moslems, the rest are Hindus and Jains.

Paharganj had the principal markets of the city for building materials—cement, timber, steel and others. Since these markets have been shifted to other locations, within the city, the whole neighbourhood is now a congested residential area for people of middle and low income groups. It has also a large number of cheap hotels in which Indian visitors and foreign tourists stay.

Sabzi Mandi, as its name indicates, had been the principal market of the city for fruit and vegetables. Besides two textile mills and a mill for producing cooking oil were located in it. The fruit and vegetable market has been shifted to two locations on the northern and southern outskirts of Delhi. One of the textile mills is closed; the other has shifted to a new location on the outskirts of Delhi.

A number of planned neighbourhoods were built between 1950 and 1990 to the north and west of Sabzi Mandi for housing both local residents and displaced persons from Pakistan. Although planned, the neighborhoods have high population density and high levels of air pollution. The gardens of the Mughal period, adjacent to Sabzi Mandi have been encroached upon by builders so that their effect on reducing pollution of air and providing facilities for recreation to the residents of Sabzi Mandi has been greatly reduced.

The great majority of the residents of Sabzi Mandi are petty traders, artisans or white collar workers. Most of the residents of the new neighbourhoods are middle income displaced persons from Pakistan. The great majority of the original residents are Hindus and Jains. Moslems, a small minority, are mainly artisans and industrial workers. The displaced persons, all Hindus and Sikhs, are mainly white collar workers and traders.

Karolbagh, located further south west of Paharganj was before Independence, a sparsely populated area of small workshops. It had a large population of Moslems. Besides there were two colonies of sweepers and leather workers in it. However the original area has been completely transformed through emigration of Moslems to Pakistan and by building of houses and shops by the displaced persons from Pakistan to the north, west and south of Karolbagh.

One of the busiest markets of Delhi, named after Khan Abdul Ghaffar Khan, a Pathan disciple of Gandhiji, is located in the western extension area of Karolbagh. It has been built by displaced persons from Pakistan most of whom are shopkeepers and white collar workers. The latter work in offices of the Government of India besides banks, insurance companies and commercial establishments located in and around Connaught Place and other areas housing office buildings. The great majority of them are of the middle income group. There are hardly any poor among them.

The Civil Lines located to the north west of Shahjahanabad and Sabzi Mandi is a large area of green with tree-lined roads. It housed the Secretariat of the Government of India between 1912 when the capital of British India was shifted from Kolkata to Delhi and before New Delhi was built in the late 1920's. It now houses the Secretariat of Delhi State, residences of its ministers and senior officers and the main (North) campus of Delhi University. The buildings of various colleges of the university are located within the campus. A large proportion of the faculty and staff of the University live in a well planned colony surrounding the colleges; other live in various locations in Sabzi Mandi and its extensions. Despite the in-filling during the last half a century, the Civil Lines remains a sparsely populated area, full of gardens and large lawns.

Shahjahanabad, although congested had large areas of green all round it. They were used for walks by the elderly, sports by the young and for holding festivals of both Hindus and Moslems. It was the greens round it that made living in the congestion of Shahjahanabad tolerable. The green between Shahjahanabad and New Delhi has been greatly reduced in size because of building of multi-storey office buildings during the 1960s. However, there has been little building to the north in the Civil Lines area.

NEW DELHI

New Delhi was built principally during the 1920s to house the Secretariat of the Government of India, the palace of the Viceroy, the Parliament House (now called Sansad Bhawan), residences of officers and houses of clerks of the Government of India. It was built according to a plan drawn up by two British architect-town planners, E. Lutyens and Howard Baker. It was and still is in parts a city of wide tree-lined roads along which the single storey bungalows of senior officers and ministers of the Government of India are built amidst large areas of green. The houses of clerks were single storey houses in which 3-4 rooms were built round a paved court yard. Most of them have since been demolished and replaced by 4-storey apartment buildings.

Connaught Place, the principal market of New Delhi, consists of several blocks of 3-4 storey buildings, built round a large area of green. Following the pattern of Sahjahanabad, a large proportion of the owners and managers of the shops lived above their shops, located on the ground floor. Others lived in a residential neighbourhood called Bengali Market, located about 2 kilometres. from it, or in other parts of Delhi. Located to the south of Connaught Place are offices of two English language daily newspapers and show rooms of automobiles.

The city had two well equipped hospitals, one for the officers and other for clerks and the general public and four higher secondary schools besides places of worship for Hindus, Moslems, Sikhs and Christians.

Altogether it is a sparsely populated city with large area of green surrounding the residences of officers located south of the central secretariat. To the east of the central secretariat there is a 3 kilometres long central vista at the end of which there is the old fort built by a Pathan ruler of Delhi. Located about 2 kilometres from the secretariat is the War Memorial, built to commemorate the memory of the dead in world war I. Like the buildings of the secretariat and the Parliament it is a rust and light brown sandstone structure, built very much like the Arc d' Triumphe in Paris. Palaces of princes of some of the largest Indian states are built around the war memorial.

The lawns of Central vista are very popular with the residents of New Delhi for picnics on Sundays and other holidays. On summer mornings and evenings they are crowded with walkers and families entertaining their children with balloons and ice cream and holding picnics during the day in the winter. Two shallow canals with little row boats in the northern part of the central vista are another reminder of Paris.

The central vista is used for holding the Republic Day parade on 26th January, the only officially sponsored event of this kind. The Independence Day celebrations on 15th August begin with a speech by the Prime Minister from the ramparts of the Red Fort. The choice of the location symbolises the fact that Delhi has been the traditional capital of India.

The Viceroy's residence which houses now the President and his staff has a very large area of green to the back of it. Located in it are bungalows of officers and houses of clerks working in the President's office. Immediately behind the residence is a formal garden, appropriately called the Mughal Garden, in which there is a pool of water with fountains playing in it and large areas of flower beds. Thus, the President's residence and its compound constitute a self-contained office-cum-residential complex.

IN-FILLING OF DELHI DURING WORLD WAR II AND POST – 1947

There was enormous building of barracks in New Delhi to house soldiers and airmen fighting in South East and East Asia during World War II and offices of the Government of India. The work force within the Government increased greatly in order to supervise the dispatch of soldiers and of food, clothes, weapons and other war materiel to them. The barracks were built mainly around the central secretariat. Most of them have been demolished but a few are still standing and house the headquarters of the Army, Navy and the Air Force. A colony containing several hundred buildings was built about 4 kilometres south of the secretariat to house junior officers and clerks of the Government of India.

Despite this infilling, New Delhi retained its original character of a sparsely populated city with tree-lined streets and large areas of green around bungalows of officers and palaces of princes. Its character began to change in the 1950s when there was an enormous amount of building in and around the city.

The first major extension of New Delhi was development of Chanakyapuri or the diplomatic enclave in the 1950s. Large areas of land were developed by the Central Public Works Department and allotted to foreign embassies for building their chanceries, residences of ambassadors, high commissioners and staff of most of the countries with which India had established diplomatic relations by then. Chanakyapuri also has large areas of green around the buildings of the diplomatic missions and a 2 kilometres long central vista, flanked by lawns. Furthermore a large park, called Nehru Park, was laid out for recreation of staff of the diplomatic missions. Earlier, New Delhi had only one park, laid out around the tombs of the Lodhi kings who ruled Delhi during the 15th century. The CPWD developed land also for building of two markets, location of several institutions including two colleges, a convent school and schools established by some diplomatic missions for educating their children.

The second phase which began in the late 1950s and continued through the 1970s included building by the C.P.W.D. of an enormous number of houses for the clerks and officers working in various ministries and departments of the Government of India. Several new townships were laid out mainly to the south west of the central secretariat. The largest township, Ramakirshnapuram (R.K. Puram) built in the 1970s, has more than a thousand of 2 or 3 bedroom houses for clerks and junior officers, several small markets, places for schools and places of worship and a number of offices of the Government of India.

The CPWD had experimented with building a few blocks of 7-8 storey apartment buildings for senior officers of the Government of India in two locations – at the northern rim of Ramakrishnapuram and on a road near the War Memorial, but it gave up the attempt finding multi-storey buildings unsuitable for various reasons. All the townships built during this period have houses with 2-storeys, and large areas of green between buildings, which are used extensively by young and old.

The hutments near the central secretariat were replaced by multi-storey buildings which house offices of several ministries of the Government of India and flank the central vista for almost a third of its length. Sansad Marg (Parliament Street) which was a wide tree-lined avenue became a congested and highly polluted road as a result of building of several multi-storey buildings for housing offices of the Government of India, banks and insurance companies. A number of high-rise buildings were built also to the east of Connaught Place to house offices of Indian and foreign banks, branches of Indian and foreign companies, tourist agencies, airlines etc. The Government of India built two luxury hotels and three hotels for middle income tourists. Domestic and international chains of hotel managers built 12 more deluxe hotels. The only hotel in New Delhi earlier had been the Imperial, located near Connaught Place.

Multi-storey buildings housing offices of English language, Hindi and Urdu newspapers, the Income Tax Office, companies and public sector industrial units were built in this period at several locations in New Delhi. Thus with the much enlarged central business district and several other roads lined with multi-storey office buildings New Delhi began to have serious problems of pollution of air and control of traffic.

However, despite all this building there are still parts of New Delhi with wide tree lined roads and large areas of green. A proposal to build high-rise buildings in them, sponsored by the government in 1998 and the Delhi Development Authority has evoked fierce opposition by architects and town planners. They have argued that building of high-rise buildings in this area will destroy the green lung which helps ameliorate to some extent the pollution of air in a busy and polluted metropolis. Delhi has the highest number per capita of passenger cars, taxis, buses, trucks, two wheeler motor cycles and scooters and is the most polluted metropolitan city in the country and one of the most polluted cities in the world.

SOUTH, WEST AND NORTH DELHI: LAND AND BUILDING DEVELOPMENT

Most of this period has witnessed hectic building activity by the Central Public Works Department, the Delhi Development Authority

(DDA), cooperative house building societies, private land developers and last but most important by individuals.

In the first phase, between 1948 and 1955 the CPWD built hundreds of 1-storey barrack type hutments and 2-storey apartment buildings to house displaced persons from Pakistan. The Land Development Office developed large areas of land in south and west Delhi in which building lots were sold to displaced persons of middle income group for building their own houses. Whole new neighbourhoods with their own markets, parks, cinemas, schools, colleges, nursing homes and places of worship were laid out in various locations mainly in south and west Delhi. Private land development companies and cooperative societies undertook land development for building houses by individuals in south, west and north Delhi. The colonies developed by them also had markets, parks, spaces for schools, cinemas and places of worship. However, the roads in them are narrower and the areas of green are much smaller than in the colonies developed by the Land Development Office. Most of the houses and shops in the markets had 2 storeys, but, as the displaced persons grew richer, they added an additional storey to their houses and the shops allotted to them in various markets. Three large multi-facility hospitals and two medical colleges were built by the Government; earlier Delhi had only one medical college for women. Private charitable institutions (including a missionary society) built four large multi-facility hospitals. The capacity of the two hospitals, built in New Delhi before Independence was greatly increased by adding large new wards to them. Several private medical practitioners added a large number of nursing homes, the best among them are well equipped mini-hospitals. A large number of higher secondary schools, some managed by reputed non-profit organisations but others managed by profit-making institutions, were also built during the 1960's to the 1980's. The central government and the Municipal Corporation of Delhi also built a number of higher secondary and primary schools.

Delhi University built a second campus in south Delhi. Half a dozen colleges were located in the campus; others were located in New Delhi and in south and west Delhi. The Delhi Development Authority built two high-rise building complexes – one in south Delhi and the other in west Delhi to house offices of companies. It developed also a large area for location of institutions. Finally, a second university, Jawahar Lal Nehru University, was built in south Delhi for post-graduate studies and research in several subjects which are not taught in Delhi University. It specialises, for instance in teaching and research in foreign languages. A Moslem foundation has built a multi-faculty university and a drug manufacturing company has built a college for training practitioners of the *Unani* system of medicine which is popular particularly among the Moslems. Thus, Delhi now has four universities.

In the next phase, which began in the 1970s and has continued into the 1990s, the principal public (and indeed the biggest) building agency has been the DDA. It had been established in the late 1950s to oversee implementation of the first master plan of Delhi 1962-81, modify it from time to time keeping in view changing economic and other conditions and to prepare the second and subsequent master plans. However, its plan formulation and overseeing implementation activities took a back seat and it took upon itself the responsibility of adding to the housing stock of Delhi in a big way by its building activity.

The DDA began by buildings blocks of 4-storey apartment buildings, primarily for people of the middle income group and 1-2 storey houses for people of low income groups in various localities in Delhi. While the majority of the houses built by the DDA have adequate areas of green between buildings for recreation and location of markets, parks, etc. others are concrete ghettoes in which there is little space between buildings.

DDA's building activity has culminated in its building during the 1980s and the 1990s, 4 large townships – Vasant Kunj in south west Delhi; Rohini in north Delhi, Pitam Pura (Patparganj) in east Delhi and Dwarka in northwest Delhi which is a few kilometres from a terminal of the international airport. Each township contains several hundred houses, besides markets, parks, places for schools, health centers and places of worship. Most of the buildings have two or three storeys. However there are in Rohini a few high-rise buildings also. Almost all the residents are people of middle income group – professionals, white collar workers employed in private firms or offices of the Government of India, or retired persons.

UNAUTHORIZED COLONIES

These have been built in various locations in south and west Delhi by artisans, workers in factories located in the designated industrial areas and elsewhere and petty traders. The colonies although not approved by the Municipal Corporation or the DDA have been provided electricity and water by the concerned authorities. But since they lack sewerage and have no satisfactory arrangement for disposal of solid waste, sanitation is a serious problem in them. Furthermore, a large number of small industrial units some of which process inflammable and hazardous materials are located in these colonies as well as in a part of Shahjahanabad. These units create a problem of occasional fires in the summer which cause much damage to life and property.

DELHI – EAST OF THE YAMUNA

There are two very different kinds of development in this area:

First, Slum clusters on or just above the flood plain of the Yamuna. A very large planned slum cluster was built by the DDA in the mid – 1970's just above the flood plain of the river. The area had good roads, adequate surface drainage and the huts were provided with electricity and water by the concerned authorities. The slum dwellers were those who were removed from roadsides and other unsuitable locations in New Delhi and its post-independence extensions. The principal problem of the slum dwellers was the cost and time taken in travel from their homes to places of work located in New Delhi or in the industrial areas located in north and west Delhi.

However, due to subsequent completely unplanned extensions by poor migrants, many of whom have built their huts on the flood plain itself, the whole area has become a mass of narrow roads and insanitary clogged drains. Conditions are so bad that diseases of the respiratory and digestive tracts are endemic and often take epidemic form during and after the monsoons.

The second, development consists of a series of planned residential colonies built by retired officials of the Government of India, companies and traders. Conditions in them are very similar to those in housing colonies in south, west and north Delhi described earlier. The colonies have adequate electric and water supplies, sewerage, their own markets, parks, schools, mini-hospitals and other public facilities.

THE SATELLITE CITIES

Uttar Pradesh

Of the four satellite cities of Delhi two are located in Uttar Pradesh, viz. Ghaziabad and Gautam Buddh Nagar (formerly called NOIDA), both being large residential-cum-industrial cities. Ghaziabad, an old town, located about 10 kilometres east of the Yamuna, has in its extensions, Loni and Shahdara, a large number of planned residential neighbourhoods for middle income group residents. Land development has been undertaken by the Ghaziabad Development Authority while houses have been built by individuals. The city has also a number of small, medium and a few large sized industrial units, manufacturing a variety of consumer goods – processed foods, garments, furnishings and other textiles, pharmaceutical drugs and building materials for the markets of Delhi, Haryana and western U.P. The industrial units in it as well as in Gautam Buddh Nagar are owned mostly by Delhi based entrepreneurs who have located the units in them to avail of lower costs of land and labour than in Delhi. The city including its extensions, has serious problems of supply of adequate drinking water and drainage which limit its expansion.

Sahibabad, located a few kilometres east of Ghaziabad is fast developing into a dormitory town because it has good railway and road connections with both Delhi and New Delhi.

Gautam Buddh Nagar, a development of the 1980s and 1990s, is a very rapidly expanding dormitory and industrial satellite city of Delhi. The Regional Plan, National Capital Region (NCR), 1988-2001 had projected a population of 500,000 for it by 2001, which will probably be exceeded keeping in view its rapid growth. It has a number of well planned residential neighbourhoods, each with its own markets, parks, schools, health centers etc. developed by its Development Authority. Houses in them have been built by people of middle or high income groups.

Among the industrial units located in Gautam Buddh Nagar, there is a large number manufacturing machine tools and consumer durables. A Korean multinational has established in the 1990's about 50 kilometres from it a large factory assembling initially from imported kits, but manufacturing, progressively from domestically purchased components, passenger cars. The factory has been located here because the company reckons that Delhi and its prosperous hinterland in Punjab, Haryana and western U.P. with a large number of medium-sized cities, middle-income white collar workers and traders and prosperous farmers, provide a large enough market for its cars. The Development Authority of Gautam Buddh Nagar has also developed an information technology park so that the city could have information technology based industries.

The principal problem of Gautam Buddh Nagar is of communication with Delhi. Traffic on the three bridges on the Yamuna which connect the city with Delhi is so heavy that it often takes up to two hours to travel by car from home in Gautam Buddh Nagar to a place of work in Delhi. It would be alleviated significantly, however, with completion by May 2001 of an 8-lane toll bridge linking NOIDA and South Delhi which is under construction.

Another serious problem in all the satellite cities in U.P. is of security of life and property. Violent crime is frequent in the cities and in the rural areas and the government of Uttar Pradesh has not been able to reduce it.

Haryana

Faridabad was built during the 1950s as a residential-cum-industrial township to provide housing and employment to displaced persons from Pakistan. It has grown over the last five decades into a large dormitory city of Delhi; besides it has a few large and a large number of small and medium sized industrial units. The biggest factory manufacturing tractors and other farm equipment in Northern India is located in Faridabad. The population of the city is increasing steadily as a number of neighbourhoods in which land development has been undertaken by the Haryana Urban Development Authority (HUDA) for sale for building houses to people of middle income groups get built up. Besides, owners and professionals working in the industrial units, large numbers of retired people have chosen to live in Faridabad because of its large open spaces and low rents. The city has a well equipped multi-facility hospital, several schools, a polytechnic and a college.

The Faridabad-Delhi highway is lined for most of its length of about 30 kilometres with housing colonies, factories, workshops and service stations owned by companies selling consumer durables – cars, commercial vehicles, air conditioners, television receivers, electrically operated kitchen gadgets, etc. in Delhi and the satellite cities. It shows ribbon development at its worst.

Infrastructure facilities—electricity, water supply, sewerage and surface drainage and telecommunications—are adequate since they have been steadily expanded. The principal factor limiting growth of Faridabad is the time taken to travel between it and south Delhi which is closest to it. The road forms part of the busy Delhi-Mathura-Agra highway. If a part of the traffic along it from eastern and western India which is not meant for Delhi, but is meant for Punjab, Haryana and other parts of north west India could be diverted by building a by-pass, as had been proposed in the Regional Plan, NCR, traffic along the road would be reduced to some extent.

Gurgaon

Gurgaon is an ancient town, located about 30 kilometres south west of Delhi and connected with it by a 4-lane motorable road. It had a population of less than 50,000 before 1950. However, it has experienced such rapid growth of population and economic activities in its environs during the 1980s and 1990s, that the projection of a population of 700,000 by 2001 contained in Regional Plan, NCR 1988-2001 could be exceeded.

The Haryana Urban Development Authority (HUDA) has developed, to the east, south and west of the old town, large areas of land and sold building lots in them to people of the middle income group for building their own houses. Many of the house owners are retired persons who like to live near Delhi but do not want to pay high rents or be bothered with the pollution of Delhi.

Industrial development, slow at first, got a big boost in the 1980's by location, in the environs of Gurgaon, works of Maruti Udyog, the largest manufacturer of passenger cars in India. Most of the industrial units located in and around Gurgaon are of manufacturers of components for Maruti cars; others manufacture various consumer durables for the markets of Delhi, Punjab and Haryana. However, in contrast to the Faridabad-Delhi highway, most of the housing colonies and the industrial units are located off the Delhi-Gurgaon road, which forms part of the Delhi-Jaipur road. The traffic along the road is very heavy, principally on account of trucks and buses carrying goods and passengers in and out of Delhi. Although ribbon development along the road is avoided, an unaesthetic development is location of offices of property brokers, small shops and restaurants located in front of villages that lie along the road.

In the 1990s three private land development and house construction companies have built, to the south east of Gurgaon, self-contained residential-cum-commercial office complexes, in which, the dwelling units are either 2-3 storey row houses or form part of towers of up to 18 storeys. The latest trend is to build ultra-modern 2 storey row houses on the model of those in Britain and the U.S.A.

One private land development company has constructed ultra-modern office buildings which have been almost fully occupied by multinational companies to locate their northern region offices. Location in Gurgaon is preferred to location in the central business district of Connaught Place because of lower rents, availability of larger office space and freedom from air and noise pollution that is such a problem in Connaught Place. The company has built near its office buildings high quality residences (in row houses or multi-storey towers) for the executives of the companies, a club and a golf course and provided space for markets, schools and health centres. Uninterrupted supplies of electricity and water are ensured by captive power and water supply stations, thus creating very desirable conditions for living and work for executives and other employees of the companies. A luxury hotel is located within 5 kilometres of this development.

The Haryana government is also encouraging building of a state-of-the-art information technology park in the environs of Gurgaon. Proximity to the Indira Gandhi International Airport is a major advantage over the information technology stations located in Delhi and Gautam Buddh Nagar.

Why the environs of Gurgaon, should be selected in preference to Faridabad or Gautam Buddh Nagar for building high quality office space and houses for executives of multinational companies is a question which needs investigation. A possible explanation is that it is at a higher elevation than Faridabad or Gautam Buddh Nagar and is free from the noise and pollution of air and water that plague the other satellite cities and finally it is close to the international airport.

DELHI AS A TOURIST CENTER

Delhi is perhaps the most visited city in India by both foreign and Indian tourists. Two of its major attractions are:

1. The historic buildings dating back to the Pathan and Mughal periods. The more than 200 ft. tall Qutab tower was built early in the 12th century, by a Pathan ruler. Tughlakabad, which is now in ruins, was built to house his capital by a quixotic Pathan ruler in the 14th century. The Red Fort, the Jama Masjid (the principal mosque for Friday prayers of Shahjahanabad), Chandni Chowk, the principal shopping street of Shahjahanabad, were built in the 18th century and
2. New Delhi with buildings of the President's palace, the central secretariat, the central vista, Connaught Place and the Diplomatic Enclave.
3. Delhi is situated on the Delhi-Agra-Jaipur tourist circuit. Foreign tourists who visit the Taj Mahal at Agra and Jaipur, the Pink City, must visit Delhi. Delhi has the infrastructure for tourists – perhaps the largest number of rooms in de-luxe and medium priced hotels of any city in India, and the airline connections that the foreign tourists need. Location on the way to Kashmir is another attraction for foreign tourists. For the domestic tourists, location near the places of pilgrimage in the western Himalayas and the birth place of Lord Krishna near Mathura is a major attraction. Finally, the very fact that it is India's capital and is a busy metropolis is its biggest attraction for tourists, both Indian and foreign. The luxury hotels, the travel agencies and the taxi services are steadily getting better organised to handle an increasing number of Indian and foreign tourists.

DELHI AS AN INFORMATION TECHNOLOGY CENTER

Reference has been made to the efforts being made by the governments of Haryana and Uttar Pradesh to attract information technology industries to Gurgaon and Gautam Buddh Nagar. Delhi itself could become a center for the industry. It has a large number of graduates in science and technology because of location of an Institute of Technology and two first-rate Universities. Several privately run institutions for training in use of computers and in business management are located in and around Delhi. Furthermore, there is a large demand for the services of information technology industries from the offices of the central government, the public sector institutions, Indian and foreign banks, insurance companies and large business houses.

THE TWIN CITY MODEL AND DELHI'S TRANSFORMATION INTO A MEGALOPOLIS

A number of geographers wrote in the 1950s and the 1960s about the twin city model of large and medium-sized Indian cities. The essence of the argument was that the typical Indian city consisted of two parts: an Indian city crowded, dirty, lacking sanitation facilities, but throbbing with trading and traditional handicraft industries, and (ii) the civil station, built by the British which contained the office of the Collector and other district officers or the Secretariat if the city was the capital of a province and residences of British and Indian officers and middle level employees of the railways and the post and telegraph departments most of whom were Anglo Indians. It was a planned town with wide tree-lined streets, spacious bungalows or smaller houses each with its own garden; one or more markets which had stores selling liquor, provisions and clothes needed by the Europeans; show rooms of cars and motor bicycles, one or more English language schools, a good hospital, one or more churches and other places of worship and at least one public park.

The larger cities, usually capitals of provinces had in addition a chamber of the legislature, a high court, a university with several arts and science colleges and professional colleges, particularly of law and medicine, a big hospital one or more hotels for Europeans and offices of one or two English language and several vernacular newspapers.

If the city had a cantonment near it the latter would have a central office of the garrison, barracks for soldiers, residences of officers, parade grounds, playgrounds and other facilities for training of soldiers and messes of officers. The cantonment had its own market(s), hospital and one or more schools and places of worship so that the soldiers did not need to go out of it and intrude on the life of the civil population.

GROWING IRRELEVANCE OF THE TWIN CITY MODEL

The foregoing survey of the growth of Delhi into a megalopolis during the last half a century brings out that this model is no longer relevant for it. It could be considered to have some relevance until the 1950s if New Delhi could be considered to be a giant civil station built next to the old city of Shahjahanabad. The civil lines could be considered to be an earlier civil station. Delhi has a cantonment, located at a short distance from New Delhi, which has the usual offices, barracks, officers' residences, markets, hospitals, parade and training grounds, sports fields and messes of officers. It is spread over a large area and is a self contained township.

The twin city model had no place for satellite towns which are, however, an integral part of all large metropolitan cities. Developments similar to those in Delhi have taken place in all the large metropolitan cities.

In Hyderabad, Pune and Bangalore which had cantonments along side the Indian city, the megalopolis has grown all around and engulfed all three cities. In Mumbai, the megalopolis has spilled over from the island to the mainland and despite the physical barrier of the Western Ghats is growing between Mumbai and Pune as well as along some of the highways that connect Mumbai with other major cities. In Kolkata, the contiguously urbanised area – the Kolkata Metropolitan District – contained in the 1960s the cities of Kolkata and Howrah, about 45 small towns including the jute mill towns located along the river Hoogly and a large number of villages located south of Kolkata. Although growth of Kolkata Metropolitan District has been slower than that of the other large metropolitan cities, the contiguously urbanised area now extends almost to Kalayani 60 kilometres to the north which has been built as a retirement community and in the south to the harbour town of Haldia.

Perhaps the most suitable model for the Indian megalopolis is that of the American metropolitan cities which are located along the north east coast such as Boston, Philadelphia and Baltimore. In each of these there is a central city, decaying until the 1960s but rejuvenated later and a series of suburbs and satellite towns. While the suburbs are new, most of the satellite towns are old towns which now form part of the contiguously urban area.

METROPOLITAN PROSPECTS OF DELHI: CONSTRAINTS AND PRIORITIES

Delhi is hot for about 8 months in the year maximum temperatures during May and June are 40°C and above for weeks; cool and dry in the 4 months of the cool season. Even in the short monsoon season, hot dry days far outnumber the rainy days. High-rise buildings, including the 4-storey apartments built by the DDA, are rather unsuitable in such a climate. Carrying water and electricity lines to the top floors of these buildings is expensive and living on these floors in such buildings becomes extremely uncomfortable when electricity fails and air conditioners do not work.

UNSUITABILITY OF HIGH-RISE BUILDINGS

The planners of Shahjahanabad had no choice but to opt for low-rise, high density pattern of settlement because the city was designed for travel by foot. The planners of New Delhi paid such attention to this need that the buildings of the central secretariat, the Viceroy's palace, the Parliament House and the shops in Connaught Place did not have more than 3 or 4 floors and furthermore, there were large verandahs around the rooms to keep them cool. The CPWD experimented with high-rise buildings but gave up the experiment rapidly because it found high-rise buildings unsuitable. It is only the commercial builders and the DDA who have flouted this basic principal in order to save on high priced land. Only time can tell whether high-rise buildings are suitable despite availability of air conditioners in a city which suffers from shortages of both electricity and water in the summer when both are needed most urgently. In our view, low-rise, medium-density settlement pattern with plenty of green spaces between buildings is most suitable for Delhi which will continue to use motorised vehicles as the principal means of transport. Water, electricity and sewerage lines will undoubtedly have to be taken over long distances with this pattern. However, the length and cost of these could be reduced significantly if living in farm houses by the affluent, which is the latest fashion in Delhi, is actively discouraged. Carrying water, electricity and telecommunication lines to the farm houses is expensive and the returns as revenue generated do not justify the cost.

POLLUTION ABATEMENT FOR HEALTHY LIVING

The fact that Delhi is located on a well drained plain ensures that there is no insuperable limit to its spatial expansion so long as essential infrastructure facilities can be expanded to meet the needs of the increasing population. It is located in one of the healthiest regions in the country; the dry climate ensures that diseases of the digestive tract or even of the respiratory tract are not endemic. Its principal problems are:

1. Pollution of air and water
2. The limitations on expansion of infrastructure: electricity, water supply and social infrastructure; and
3. Ensuring safety of life and property.

It has been mentioned earlier that Delhi suffers from a serious problem of pollution of air. A principal reason for it is absence of a mass rapid transport system (MRTS) and total dependence on motor vehicles—buses, personal cars, 4 wheeler and 3-wheeler taxis, motor bicycles and scooters for personal and public transport. Work on construction of an MRTS, proposed since the 1950s, began 2 years ago, but progress on it is slow and its first part may be expected to become operational only in about 2003. Meanwhile, the Government of the Union Territory of Delhi has, under pressure from the Supreme Court, taken some steps such as taking off the roads 3 or 4 wheeler taxis which are more than 15 years old and ensuring that only motor vehicles which meet Euro I standards of pollution of air will be registered from July, 1999 and only Euro II standards will be registered from July 2000.

The Government of Delhi is also considering introduction of 350 buses using CNG (compressed natural gas), a clean fuel, in the fleet of buses operated by the Delhi Transport Corporation in a bid to reduce pollution of air. If the move is successful, there will be intense pressure on the private bus operators to change over to CNG-run buses.

The Indian Oil Corporation, a public sector unit of the Government of India, has announced that it is reducing the sulphur content in the diesel supplied by it to a fraction of what it was earlier. Since sulphur is the principal pollutant in diesel, this measure will contribute to reducing pollution of air. The mandatory use of unleaded petrol, since the last two years has reduced the danger of slow death by lead poisoning which is particularly acute among the children. Replacement of coal burning turbines by those burning natural gas, a clean fuel in the two power stations located in and near Delhi will also reduce pollution of air.

A number of measures are being taken also to reduce pollution of water. These include repair and renovation of sewerage treatment plants and forcing factories, located in the industrial areas to build their own effluent treatment plants. The Supreme Court has ordered that the polluting industrial units should either build viable effluent treatment plants by November 1, 1999 or get out of Delhi.

ADEQUATE ELECTRICITY AND WATER SUPPLIES

However, provision for obtaining adequate supplies of power and water is itself a major problem in the long, hot summer when demand for both is greatest. Delhi obtains power from the northern grid, some of the generation stations in which are located as far away as 1000 kilometres. Cuts in power supply become a normal feature in the summer when farmers, who are provided power virtually free, use more than their allotted quota of power due to delayed or deficient monsoon rains or when there is a failure of a generating unit in any of the stations.

Delhi obtains its water supply from the Yamuna. The treatment plants are located about 75 kilometres upstream of Delhi. However, a canal from the river irrigates a large area of land in Haryana. In summer, there is intense pressure on the available supply, for irrigation from the farmers and the Delhi government for obtaining adequate drinking water for the population, often intervention by the central government is required in order to persuade the government of Haryana to release enough water for the requirements of Delhi. Other sources of water including obtaining water from rivers in Punjab will need to be explored and water conservation measures will have to be made mandatory if the needs of the growing population and economic activities of the city are to be met.

The problems of shortages of both electricity and water are greatly aggravated for legitimate users, by large-scale theft of both electricity and water by slum dwellers and other users.

ENSURING SECURITY OF LIFE AND PROPERTY

The incidence of violent crime – murder, decoity, holding businessmen for ransom and/traffic accidents involving death or serious injury to those involved have been found increasing in Delhi within recent years: Violent crime is more widespread in the satellite cities in U.P. However, neither the central government, which controls the police within Delhi state, nor the U.P. government has been able to reduce violence and crimes. One reason why the environs of Gurgaon are preferred for location of offices of multi-national corporations and residence of their executives and other employees is that there is greater security of life and property in the state.

PROSPECT FOR THE DECADE 2000-2010

Economic Continuity

Rapid growth of population on account both of normal increase of the resident population and in-migration could continue. Considering everything, the population of Delhi within Delhi state would not be much less than 13 million[1] projected in the Regional Plan, NCR, 1988-2001. Adding the population of the megalopolis, the total would be between 15 and 16 million. There are few slum dwellers among the migrants from the immediate hinterland of Delhi, Punjab, Haryana and western Uttar Pradesh. Most of the migrants from these areas are artisans, skilled industrial workers, white collar workers and traders. They live in unauthorized colonies, located in south and west Delhi that have been described earlier or in well built houses.

The slum dwellers can be divided into two main categories: (i) construction workers mainly from northern districts of Rajasthan, and (ii) migrants from poor backward states – central and eastern Uttar Pradesh, Orissa, Tamil Nadu and or countries adjoining India—Nepal and Bangladesh. They work as domestic servants, watchmen, gardeners, drivers and repairmen of motor vehicles, unskilled industrial workers, hawkers and rickshaw pullers or are engaged in a variety of illegal or extra-legal activities from begging to smuggling. Their numbers could begin to decline towards the end of the next decade, with economic development in their home regions, reduced availability of jobs in the Delhi state part of the megalopolis and effective curbing of illegal activities by the state government.

There is not likely to be any significant change in the economic status of the population. Most of the population would continue to be of people of middle income-group white collar workers in offices of the Government and public sector undertakings, Indian-foreign banks, insurance companies and other companies, shop keepers, artisans, a better paid industrial workers. However the proportion of poor slum dwellers will not be less than what it is at present. Furthermore they will not be contained to the slum clusters in East Delhi but will be spread out alongside several planned colonies of middle and high income residents. The political executive of a populist government considers slum dwellers as reliable vote banks, useful for winning elections. Furthermore, funds are available from domestic and international development agencies for undertaking welfare work in them.

As a megalopolis, Delhi will be a large industrial center for a variety of reasons. The environs of large metropolitan cities are preferred, for location of industries ranging from food processing, manufacture of shoes, to machine tools and an innumerable consumer durables. The location of plants manufacturing passenger cars, buses and trucks in the environs of Mumbai, Chennai, Pune and Delhi illustrates this tendency which is likely to characterize the growth of Delhi as a megalopolis.

Satellite Towns as Counter Magnets

Land Development and housing will be more in three satellite towns – Faridabad, Gurgaon and Gautam Buddh Nagar. Land development by the Urban Development authorities of the government of Haryana and cooperative housing building societies and companies. Housing, by individuals and the land development companies. However, the pattern of economic activities could change with the greater emphasis on information technology, construction and diverse services and much less on manufacturing and distribution activities. Information technology parks in Gurgaon and Gautam Buddh Nagar.

As Delhi advances towards megalopolis status, the need for high quality infrastructure – hospitals, universities (colleges) secondary schools run by reputed institutions in satellite towns – will have to be expanded. Otherwise residents of the satellite towns will be at a disadvantage *vis-a-vis* residents of Delhi.

Judicial Activism in Delhi

The Supreme Court and the Govt. of National Capital Territory of Delhi may be expected to continue to play an active role in efforts to reduce pollution of air and water.

It has been left to the Supreme Court, which has responsibility for upholding the Constitution of India, to ensure that the levels of pollution of air and water are reduced so that Delhi does not become the most polluted and filthiest capital in the world.

Abatement of Automobile Pollution

In two judgements delivered almost two years ago, in response to public interest petitions, the court ordered that: (i) all 3–wheeler and 4-wheeler taxis which were more than 15 years old should go off Delhi's roads; and (ii) only 1500 new vehicles, which meet Euro I standards, should be registered up to June 2000 and those that meet Euro II standards should only be registered after this date.

The foreign (Korean, Japanese and American) manufacturers of passenger cars claimed that their cars already met the standards laid down by the court. However, Maruti Udyog, the biggest supplier of passenger cars in India, petitioned the court that it needed more time in order to manufacture cars which met the standards laid down by the court. The court granted its request but observed that Suzuki Motors, which owns 50 percent of the equity in Maruti Udyog – the balance is owned by the Government of India – has been making cars meeting Euro II standard in Japan for several years but has transferred an obsolete technology to India, a practice which is common among multinational corporations investing in developing countries. Now in order to save its market share, Maruti Udyog has also brought out new models, which meet Euro II standards. The state government implemented the orders despite strikes by owners of 3-wheeler and 4-wheeler taxis. The old vehicles have gone off the roads.

The beneficial effect of the court's order is already apparent. There is significantly less solid particular matter and other pollutants in Delhi's air, although the number of motor vehicles has increased.

Reduction of Industrial Pollution

Delhi has a large number of industrial units that discharge pollutants including poisons such as chemicals containing mercury and nickel into the water of the Yamuna turning the river into a virtual sewer and making its water unfit for drinking for long distances downstream of Delhi. The court had ordered some time back that these units be closed. The state government has belatedly begun to seal these units but has allowed some units to reopen under pressure from the owners.

The case of Delhi illustrates that the Supreme Court has to intervene to effect improvements in essential civil services. Apparently despite or because of the multiplicity of various authorities to provide essential services the level of efficiency of the services remains low despite the claims to the contrary. Political pressure by various groups – polluting industries, the Delhi Jal Board (DJB) or the Sewerage Board deter implementation of policies and plans as well as delay execution of Supreme Court directives. Also too rapid growth of economic activities and population's lack of pride of belonging to a city are major problems.

NOTE

* Actual population of Delhi as per 2001 Population Census figures is 12.791 millions

13

Planning for Delhi Before and After 1947: The Emerging Pressures and Priorities

This paper reviews the planning and city building processes in Delhi in three periods—the imperial Mughal, the imperial British and the post-Independence. In the two earlier periods, the plans followed the ideals and tastes of the ruling elites and the cities were built to meet their needs, but the cities were well adapted to the technologies of the times and patterns of social interactions among the residents. Consequently, they provided, to most of their residents a living environment which was efficient, healthy and satisfying. One reason for this was that Delhi was a relatively small city and increase in population was slow. The half-century since 1941 has witnessed an unprecedented increase in population, it has gone up from less than 700,000 in 1941 to 8.4 million in 1991. The increase has been due partly in response to expansion of employment in public administration, trade, finance and manufacturing industries, and partly to large in-migration of displaced persons from Pakistan during 1947-48, and from other states of India throughout the period.

Delhi being the national capital is the center of the political life of the nation. It has also become during the last four decades a major commercial and industrial center and is fast developing into a financial center. From an essentially provincial city just over 50 years ago, it has become a metropolis with rapidly expanding industries, notably making of garments and leather goods, and manufacture or assembly of consumer durables such as refrigerators, air conditioners and television sets.

Its population of 8.4 million in 1991 has increased twelve-fold during the last 50 years; it was only 700,000 in 1941. The most rapid increase occurred during 1941-51 when the population more than doubled, from less than 700,000 to 1.4 million, as a result of a large influx, during 1947-48, of displaced persons from Pakistan. The growth rate of population in the subsequent four decades has also been more rapid than that of any other metropolitan city. The rapid growth rate has been due to large migration mainly from Uttar Pradesh, Haryana and Punjab. Delhi's present population includes, however, besides predominantly Hindi and Punjabi speaking elements, large numbers of speakers of other Indian languages and an international community of considerable size.

The efforts of the public agencies - the Central Government and the Delhi Development Authority - to expand housing have been matched by those of individuals and cooperative societies. But the efforts have been focused on providing housing to people of medium and high-income groups; the housing needs of the poor have been met by rapid growth of slums and unauthorized colonies. Expansion of physical and social infrastructure has also proved inadequate to meet the demands on it. The reliance in the absence of a mass transit facility, on a miscellany of motor vehicles for movement within the city, has resulted in very high levels of air and noise pollution.

THE PLANNING FOR URBAN GROWTH

The hopeful beginning with long-term planning, made with successful implementation of the first master plan 1961-81, has suffered a set back as a result of the failure of the Central Government to approve the second master plan 1981-2001. The Regional Plan 2001 for the National Capital Region, approved in 1988 by all the governments concerned, is also not being implemented. In the resulting, impasse there is unplanned growth of a giant conurbation adding to its various problems. The paper recommends revival of metropolitan and regional planning for direction of growth of the conurbation to 2010.

THE THREE PHASES OF EVOLUTION OF DELHI

Delhi has a long history of planning. Let us begin with the building of Shahjahanabad (present old Delhi) by the Mughal emperor Shahjahan between 1638 and 1648 when he decided to shift his capital from Agra to Delhi.

Shahjahanabad-The Mughal Capital

The principal features of the city, primarily based on Dutt (1983), were the following:

1. The Red Fort Complex, which served as the residence of the emperor and his wives and concubines, and his court (Annex. Fig. 13.1). It had within it extensive lawns and artificial canals with fountains. Its ramparts provided residential quarters for the garrison defending it. The complex was located on the western bank of the river Yamuna, at the East end of the city, from which it was separated by a large green. The river and the extensive, poorly drained lands to the East of it provided natural defence against invading armies.
2. The Jama Masjid, the mosque for Friday prayers of the nobles and the citizens was located opposite the Red Fort, overlooking a large green which separated it from the Fort. Built of pink sandstone and marble, like the palaces in the Red Fort, it is an extremely beautiful building which Aldous Huxley is reported to have considered superior even to the Taj Mahal.
3. A massive boundary wall, built of granite and other stones, had within it a garrison for the defence of the city. It was pierced at various locations by gates from which roads led to different parts of the empire. The city was surrounded by extensive greens on all sides, which had a salutary effect on its environment and also provided spaces for fairs, festivals and recreation of the residents.
4. Chandni Chowk, *the main street,* is a broad street which runs West to East for about one mile (Fig 13.1). It was designed for processions and parades, besides movement of the residents. It too had a shallow artificial canal with fountains. Covered shopping arcades on both sides of the street provided protection from heat and cold to shoppers and other pedestrians. Within the arcades, shops and workshops of luxury handicrafts, such as jewellery, silk brocades, fine wood work and ivory work, were at the street level, and residential quarters of prosperous merchants and nobles were on the first and second floors.
5. Other *Bazaars* (streets), markets and *Katras* (cul-d-sacs), housed shops and workshops of handicrafts. The *katras* opened into Chandni Chowk or the other *bazaars*. The

pattern of shops and workshops at the street level and residences of the merchants and handicraft workers on the upper floors was repeated in the bazaars and katras. An important feature was specialization of every bazaar and katras in a particular trade or handicraft. Thus there were bazaars and katras of merchants of silk and other fine textiles, jewellery, ivory work and other luxury goods. The artisans who met the daily consumption needs of the residents — coppersmiths, tailors, dyers, weavers, leather workers, potters etc. and beggars and other poor residents of the city lived in its Western half, in which was located also the *Sadar Bazaar,* the principal mart for general merchandize. As in other medieval cities, the bazaars, besides being shopping centers, were also places of social intercourse and recreation of the residents.

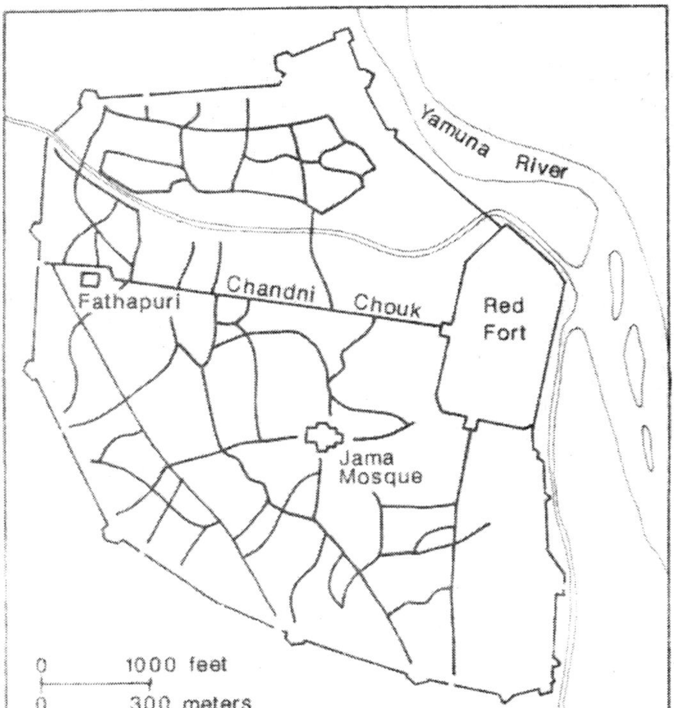

Fig. 13.1: Layout of Shahjahanabad (Old Delhi)

Source: Ashok K. Dutt; Cities of South Asia, p. 330, editor Stanley D. Brunn and Jack F. Williams, Harper and Row Publishers, New York 1983.

Shahjahanbad was a beautiful city for its age, and was renowned for its beauty and grandeur throughout India and central Asia. Its wholesale markets received goods from all parts of the empire and from lands beyond it in central Asia. It exported in return the products of its fine handicrafts, food, spices and other consumption goods. Some of its markets still remain the principal wholesale and retail markets of Delhi. Thus the Saddar Bazaar remains the principal market for general merchandise and Fatehpuri is the principal market for foodstuffs and spices.

The city has become very congested as a result of rapid growth of population during the post Independence period. The process began with influx of displaced persons from Pakistan but it has continued. It is so congested and has such insanitary conditions that it was designated as a slum in the first master plan of Delhi. But it had a human scale, and was well adapted to movement by foot and face-to-face social interaction. There is urgent need for urban renewal in the city, which should focus on preservation of its historic landmarks, such as the better preserved *havelis* (palaces) of the nobles, and residences of famous Urdu poets like Mirza Ghalib, Zauk and Haali.

New Delhi: The British Capital

The description of New Delhi in this section is primarily based on Sealey (1988). It was built to the West and South West of Shahjahanbad and was separated from it by an extensive green called the Ramleela Ground. It covers an area of 1300 ha (3200 acres), and was designed for a population of 65,000. It too is a planned city, built, between 1915 and 1930 to house the Imperial capital, after the proclamation to shift the capital from Kolkata to Delhi was made in 1912 by King George V at the Royal Darbar held in Delhi in that year. The city was planned and its construction was supervised by a team of architects and town planners headed by Edwin Lutyens and Herbert Baker, two of the most distinguished architects of their time. Lutyens[1] is regarded as a great architect and town planner of this century. The former British Cantonment and the Civil Lines, both located to the North West of Shahjahanbad, served as the temporary site for the capital from 1912 to 1931 (Fig. 13.2).

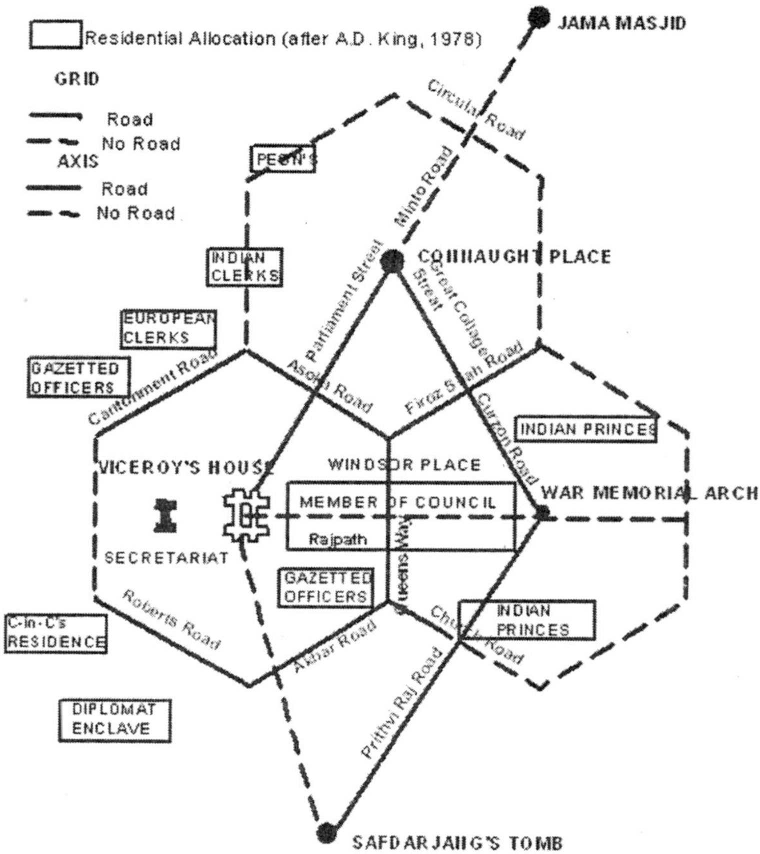

Fig. 13.2: Lutyen and Baker's New Delhi Plan, large part of which was complete between 1912-31.

Source: N. Sealy, "Planned cities of India: A study of jaipur, New Delhi and Chandigarh" in: Costa, F.; Dutt, A.K.; Ma, L.; Noble, A. (eds.), Asian Urbanization Problems and Processes, Gebrüder Borntraeger, Berlin 1988.

Principal Features of the City

The following may be considered to be the principal features of the city:

1. The Imperial Complex consisting of the Viceregal Lodge, the residence of the Viceroy of India, the Imperial Secretariat

and the building of the Central Legislative Assembly. They are all built in red and ochre sandstones, brought mainly from the vicinity of Agra and Dholpur, 160-200 kilometers from the city. The Viceregal Lodge, now the residence of the President of India and called the Rashtrapati Bhawan, is at the South end of the complex. It has behind it a formal garden called the Mughal Garden and extensive greens and woods beyond it to the South, South West and North West. It and the two buildings of the Secretariat - North Block and South Block - are built on a low eminence and overlook a large square and the central vista beyond it. The building of the Central Legislative Assembly, now called Parliament House, is at the North end of the square. It is a circular structure which faces the square at its South end. Streets lead from it to the North half of the city and to Connaught Circus, its principal shopping plaza.

2. The Central Vista: It is about 3 kilometers long. It is flanked on both sides by lawns and artificial canals, reminiscent of Shahjahanabad. It has near its East end the War Memorial, which commemorates the dead of World War I but continues beyond it to end at Purana Qila (lit. the old fort) which was built by an Afghan ruler, Sher Shah Suri, in the 16th century.
3. Bungalows: These are residential quarters of officials, clerks and messengers. The principle of segregation by rank was followed in location, size and design of the residential buildings. The great majority of the bungalows of senior officials were located to the South of the central vista. They are large, single storey houses situated amidst extensive lawns. The bungalows of junior officers and residential quarters of clerks and messengers were all located to the North of the Central Vista. The sizes of the bungalows and of the lawns attached to them decreased progressively with the rank of the occupant. The houses of clerks and messengers were built in the Indian style, in which the rooms faced a courtyard which formed part of the house. Most of them were demolished during the 1970s and 1980s to be replaced by 4-storey structures containing flats. The bungalows of the senior-most officers were located closest

to the Secretariat: those of junior officers and the houses of clerks and messengers were more distant.

4. Churches, Schools and Hospitals: The city had two important churches. The Anglican Cathedral, in which the Viceroy and senior British officers worshipped, was located at a short distance to the North of the Viceregal Lodge and the Secretariat. The Catholic Church, built by Jesuit missionaries, was about 2 kilometers to the North of the Secretariat. It had attached to it high schools for boys and girls and residences of priests and nuns. The two hospitals and other schools were also located to the North and East of the city within or near the residential areas.
5. Connaught Circus and other markets: The Connaught Circus complex, the principal shopping plaza of the city, is located about 3 kilometers from Parliament House. The street connecting the two, now called *Sansad Marg*, has multi-storey office buildings on both sides of it but, until the early 1950s, it was flanked mainly by bungalows of officers. The few office buildings along it were those of All India Radio, the State Bank of India and the New Delhi Municipal Committee.

The Connaught Circus complex consists of two concentric rings of 3-storey buildings, which surround a central green. The outer ring, which faces the city, is called Connaught Circus and the inner ring is called Connaught Place. The buildings in both rings have shops on the ground floor, and offices and residential quarters of the shop owners or managers on the first and second floors. A number of roads radiate from the complex to Shahjahanabad and to various parts of New Delhi.

A large number of multi-storey office buildings came up to the south of Connaught Circus complex during the 1970s and 1980s. With them, the Connaught Circus area has become the central business district of the city in the western sense of the term. But the development has also created severe problems of traffic congestion and pollution of air and water in it.

Broad tree-lined streets and green roundabouts: These are another important feature of New Delhi where the streets and avenues meet - on the pattern of Washington and Paris. The city was built for vehicular traffic — cars, bicycles and horse drawn carriages. A bus service was introduced only during World War II. It was a green and uncongested city. The greenery helped to reduce the severity of Delhi's hot summers and cold winters, and also helped to keep pollution of air and water low.

POPULATION GROWTH, 1939-45 (SECOND WORLD WAR)

During Second World War there was enormous expansion of the Central Government for several reasons:

1. Recruitment of several hundred thousand soldiers and officers for the Indian armies which were heavily involved in the fighting in all theatres of the war-from Libya to Iraq in the Middle East and from Burma to Indonesia in South and South East Asia.
2. India had become the principal base for supplying food, clothing, ammunition and other goods to the armies. A large organization had to be set up for their procurement and transport to the various theatres of war.
3. Introduction from 1942 of price control and rationing of basic goods to ensure their equitable distribution to the entire population. Price control and rationing became unavoidable when shortages of wheat, rice, sugar, oil, cloth, kerosene and gasoline began to be experienced as a result of diversion of supplies of these to meet the demands of the armed forces. Cessation from 1942 of the annual import of about 2 million tons of rice from Burma, after its occupation by the Japanese, exacerbated the shortage of cereals. Price control was needed to counter the increase in prices, caused partly by the shortages of supplies and partly by deficit financing of the expenditure on the war by the Government of India.
4. Passing through Delhi of tens of thousands of allied soldiers — British, American and those from British dominions and colonies — on their way to various theatres of the war. The stream of passing soldiers and officers became a flood from 1942 after the USA joined the war, and the eastern front was opened against the Japanese, who had by then occupied the whole of South East Asia and were fighting on the border between Burma and Assam.

Temporary structures were built at a frenetic speed to house the offices and employees of the Government and the soldiers. Most of the structures were demolished during the 1960s, to be replaced by multi-storey buildings to house various Ministries and departments of the Government. But, some of them are still standing and provide office space, mainly for the Ministry of Defence.

The need for residential accommodation for officers and other employees of the Government has been met by construction of hundreds of bungalows or flats for senior officers and tens of thousands of flats for junior officers and clerks, and tenements for messengers. They are all located in various new colonies to the South of pre-1947 New Delhi.

THE ERA OF FRENETIC CONSTRUCTION: 1947-70

Reference has been made earlier to the influx of hundreds of thousands of displaced persons from Pakistan. To provide housing to them a large program of land development and housing was undertaken by the Central Public Works Department, at the insistence of the Ministry of Relief and Rehabilitation. The program consisted of building thousands of: (a) single or double-storey tenements or houses for displaced persons of the low-income groups, and (b) two-storey houses, or sale of developed land for building them, to those of the middle income group. Most of the single-storey houses have since been converted by their owners into two or three storey structures; lesser additions have been made to the two-storey houses.

The second main feature of this period was the building, as mentioned above, of an enormous number of dwelling units for the employees of the rapidly expanding central government. The principle of segregation by rank was again followed in their location, size and design. The bungalows and flats for senior officers were located closest to the offices; the flats for clerks, and tenements for messengers etc. were located at greater distances.

At the same time, private developers and cooperative societies developed large areas of land for sale for housing, principally to middle and high-income groups. Most of the development was to the South and South West of New Delhi. The Delhi Development Authority (DDA), to which a reference is made below, and which has land development and housing for people of the medium and low-income groups as one of its three main functions, has also made a major contribution to the development. It has built (and continues to build) large residential colonies, principally for people of the medium income groups. Its activity for the low-income group, including slum dwellers, has been rather limited consisting primarily of land development for site-and-service housing or construction of core housing on small plots of 20 to 30 sq. meters each.

Development to the East of New Delhi remained limited during this period because of existence of poorly drained lands on both sides of the river Yamuna. Development North of Shahjahanabad was also limited for the same reason. However, there has been rapid development in both areas during the 1970s and 1980s. Tens of thousands of houses have been built, mainly by private individuals, on lands developed and sold to them by developers or by cooperative societies. The colonies developed by the cooperative societies, most of which had been formed by employees of the various ministries and departments of the central government, are located mainly in East Delhi on the well drained lands beyond the poorly drained areas.

Most of the development reviewed above has been according to the first master plan for Delhi (1961) or plans drawn up by the Ghaziabad Development Authority and the New Okhla Industrial Development Authority (NOIDA) in Uttar Pradesh. But there has also been much unauthorized construction and rapid growth of slums. Some of the largest and the worst slums of Delhi are located on the poorly drained lands East of the Yamuna. The poor drainage aggravates the problems of sanitation in them because they are prone to flooding during or after the monsoon rains.

The rapid land development and housing activity continues to make Delhi a sprawling conurbation with a population, estimated as mentioned earlier, at 8.4 million in 1991 and 12.8 million in 2001.

PLANNING FOR DELHI IN INDEPENDENT INDIA

The First Master Plan, 1961-81 was formulated in the late 1950s by a group of foreign and Indian architects and town planners working with the newly established Town and Country Planning Organization (TCPO) of the Central Government. It received approval of the Central Government and the Delhi Administration in 1961 and was published and enforced in the following year. The responsibility for making needed adjustments in the plan from time to time and for overseeing its implementation was given to the DDA, which was established soon after its approval and publication. The plan related to the whole of Delhi State, which included, besides the continuously urbanized area of the city, almost 300 villages. It outlined the land-use for the area, based on projections of growth of population and economic activities during the 20-year period, 1961-81. In order to ensure effective implementation of the plan, all undeveloped land within Delhi state was frozen so that land development for housing or other purposes would follow the land-use component of the plan and could be undertaken only with the permission of the DDA. However, growth of population of Delhi has been much faster than that projected in the plan; the projected population of 5 million by 1981 was already reached by the late 1970s; the urban population of Delhi State totaled 5.6 million in 1981.

Further freezing of land sales together with rapidly rising costs of land acquisition and development have led to steep rise in land prices, which has contributed, in turn, to considerable unauthorized construction. Large unauthorized residential colonies have come up, mainly in West and South Delhi.

IMPLEMENTATION OF THE PLAN

There have been various deviations from the plan, some of them at the insistence of the Central Government or the Delhi Administration itself and many of its recommendations, relating particularly to expansion of physical and social infrastructure, have not been implemented. But its land-use component, which outlined the design of expansion of the city and indicated locations of housing colonies, markets, shopping and other community buildings, has generally been adhered to. The principal areas of non-implementation of the plan, or deviations from it, have been the following:

1. Lack of action on shifting of non-conforming (hazardous and highly polluting) industries from within the city to locations outside it. Most of the units in these industries remain in their earlier locations.
2. Failure of the principle of segregated land-use which underlies the philosophy and design of the plan. Mixed

residential and non-residential (industrial, commercial and other service) land-uses continue not only in Shahjahanabad and other older areas of the city but also in the new (post-1960) planned residential colonies. Large numbers of offices and workshops are located within the houses in the new colonies. In some of them, such as South Extension Phase I and II in South Delhi, the majority of the houses located in the streets adjacent to the markets have shops on the ground floor and offices on the first (or higher) floors.

3. Encroachments for residential or industrial uses in the areas designated in the plan as the green belt around Delhi. The woodlands on the Aravali Ridge, which were to be maintained as a nature preserve, have been considerably reduced by the encroachments. Secondly, there has been large scale ribbon development along the highways which radiate from the city through the green (agricultural) belt. The development is most advanced along the 30 kilometers stretch of the Delhi-Faridabad highway which is now completely lined by housing colonies, offices and warehouses of companies located in Delhi or small industrial establishments. Similar ribbon development is in progress along the Delhi-Gurgaon and other highways.

THE SECOND MASTER PLAN 1981-2001

The plan has been prepared in draft form by the DDA, but it has not been finalized perhaps because the draft has not been approved either by the Central Government or by the Delhi Administration. The only available document on it is a special number of *Vikas Varta*, the official organ of the DDA (Delhi Development Authority 1985). It contains projections of growth of population of the union territory of Delhi to 2001, the needs for land development and for expansion/improvement of housing and physical and social infrastructure in it to meet the demands of population growth; it also outlines the land-use plan for the territory.

One reason for not approving the plan could be the thinking within the Central Government that it should be revised within the framework of the Regional Plan 2001 for the National Capital Region (NCR). The Region includes, besides the union territory of Delhi, large areas, both urban and rural, of the adjoining states of Haryana, Uttar Pradesh and Rajasthan, the economies of which are most affected by the growth of Delhi. Included within it are: (a) six satellite towns — Gurgaon, Bahadurgarh, Faridabad, and Ballabhgarh in Haryana, and Ghaziabad and Loni in Uttar Pradesh and (b) 11 regional centers which are located at distances of 60-160 kilometers from Delhi (Fig. 13.3). It was

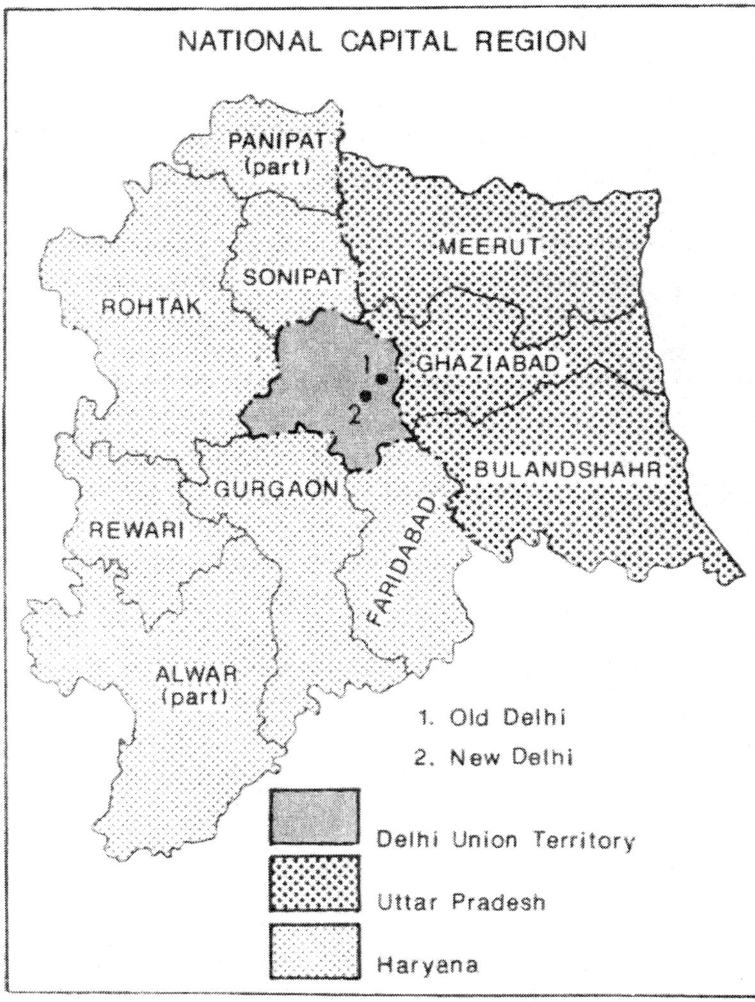

Fig. 13.3: National Capital Region. The Delhi Union Territory is at the centre.
Source: Census of India 1991. Series-I India. Paper 2 of 1991: Provisional Population Tools: Rural-Urban Distribution.

designated in 1985 and a statutory NCR Planning Board was constituted to prepare a regional plan for it. The plan was prepared and approved in 1988, but it became only partially operational after 1991. There are two main reasons for this:

1. Reservations within the Delhi Administration on the central strategy of the Regional Plan relating to dispersal of industries, markets and other economic activities from Delhi to the 11 towns located in the adjoining states, which have been designated as "regional growth centers" in order to contain the rapid growth of the population of Delhi. The Administration is not keen on reducing the status of Delhi as the principal industrial and commercial center of North West India. The non-conforming industries have not been removed despite direction for their relocation by the Supreme Court
2. The feeling within the governments of the three adjoining states that since the plan is primarily for benefiting Delhi by containing its growth, funds for its implementation should be provided mainly by the central government.

The absence of a plan for the Delhi Metropolitan Area which is most affected by the spatial expansion of Delhi is a serious lacuna in the plan. In the resulting impasse, unplanned growth of Delhi continues adding to its various problems ranging from increasing shortages of housing and mounting pressures on already overstrained physical and social infrastructures to rapidly increasing levels of water and air pollution. The threat of the latter to the health and safety of the population could become so great as to make urgent action to contain or reduce the levels unavoidable. The action would need to include effective implementation of a strategy of dispersal of industries, particularly non-conforming industries, and highly congested markets from their present locations to more suitable locations in the satellite towns, but preferably in the more distant regional growth centers.

THE REGIONAL PLAN, NATIONAL CAPITAL REGION 2001

The need for regional planning for the national capital region was recognized by the central government as far back as 1961 when the first Master Plan for Delhi was being finalized (Nath, 1988). The Plan recommended designation of a National Capital Region including the union territory of Delhi and adjoining areas of the neighboring states, and establishment of a statutory board for preparation and overseeing implementation of a regional plan for it. However, the Government of India established in 1961 an advisory board within the Ministry of Home Affairs. The Board was reconstituted in 1973 with the Minister of Works, Housing and Supplies as the Chairman, the Chief Ministers of Haryana, Uttar Pradesh and Rajasthan and the Lt. Governor of Delhi, and some senior officials of the central ministries and of these states as members.

A statutory board was not constituted due to opposition to it of the state governments of Uttar Pradesh and Haryana, which were afraid that it would interfere with their powers of planning and development in their areas included within the region. Meanwhile, rapid expansion of the metropolitan area of Delhi into adjoining areas of Uttar Pradesh and Haryana continued with profound changes in the land-use, ecology and economy of the areas. The governments of the two states encouraged and supported the expansion by providing liberal incentives for location of industries and other economic activities in them. The incentives and investments were concentrated in satellite towns like Ghaziabad, Loni and NOIDA in Uttar Pradesh and Faridabad, Ballabhgarh and Gurgaon in Haryana, which have been developed as residential-cum-industrial centers. The constitution of the statutory National Capital Region Planning Board (NCRPB) in 1985 and the impetus to planning for the NCR following it, marked recognition by the two state governments of the logical consequence of these developments.

The Board is attached to the Ministry of Urban Development of the Central Government and has the Minister as its Chairman. The other members are the Chief Ministers of Uttar Pradesh, Haryana and Rajasthan, the Lt. Governor of Delhi, and 16 other members including a full time member-secretary. In addition, the Chief Minister of Madhya Pradesh and senior officials representing the Housing and Urban Development Ministry of the Central Government and Adviser (HUD) of the Planning Commission, have been co-opted as members.

The functions of the Board relate primarily to formulation, and monitoring implementation of development plans for the NCR, which includes the union territory of Delhi, 3 districts adjoining Delhi of

Uttar Pradesh, 4 such districts and 3 tehsils of Haryana and a part of Alwar district of Rajasthan. It is a rather large region with a total area of more than 30,000 sq. km. and a total population in 1981 of more than 19 million. Less than 5 percent of its total area (about 1500 sq.km.) but almost one third of its total population (6.2 million in 1981) is within the union territory of Delhi.

The Board prepared two Interim Development Plans (IDP's) and a Draft Regional Plan (DRP) during 1986 and 1987 before preparing the Regional Plan 2001 (1988). The Plan was approved soon after its preparation. Such rapid progress was possible because the economic and other studies on which the Regional Plan is based, had been in, progress within theTown and Country Planning Organisation (TCPO) since 1971.

The development strategy of the Regional Plan focuses on shifting of manufacturing industries and service sector activities from Delhi to 11 regional growth centers. The centers are located in the three adjoining states at distances of 60 to 160 kilometres from Delhi. They range in size from Meerut, a large city which had a population of 500,000 in 1981 (and 1.17 million in 2001), to small towns such as Rewari and Palwal in Haryana with populations of less than 50,000.

The IDPs and DRP had specified the industries and service sector activities to be shifted from Delhi to the various growth centers. The lists have been omitted, however, from the Regional Plan.

The Regional Plan has two main objectives:

- To reduce growth of economic activities and of population of Delhi. A target of reducing growth of population by 2 million by 2001-from a projected 13.2 million to 11.2 million-has been indicated, and
- To promote growth of the regional centres.

Slower growth of population would reduce aggravation of the serious shortages of housing, proliferation of slums, pollution of air and water and pressures on the physical and social infrastructure of Delhi. The Draft Regional Plan had included projections of the needed increases in land development and housing and expansion of transport, water supply, waste disposal and other services, along with estimates of investment in them. They have been omitted, however, in the (final) Regional Plan, emphasis in which is on outlining the objectives, strategies and policies of the Plan over a broad area, extending from land development and expansion of housing to reducing the draft on natural resources and deterioration of the environment of the NCR and areas adjoining it.

The Regional Plan has outlined within the National Capital Region, a smaller area unit, the Delhi Metropolitan Area, which includes besides Delhi, the six satellite towns mentioned earlier. It did not recommend, however, shifting of industries or service activities from Delhi to the satellite towns on the ground that the shift would not only not reduce the problems of traffic congestion and pollution of air and water in Delhi, but would accelerate linking of the towns with Delhi and growth of a giant conurbation. A long-term plan was also not prepared for the area. This has proved to be a mistake, however, because in the absence of a plan, ribbon development along the highways connecting Delhi with the satellite towns has continued and the growth of a conurbation, which the Regional Plan had sought to prevent, has proceeded unchecked.

REDEVELOPMENT OF SHAHJAHANABAD AND NEW DELHI

Redevelopment is an important issue in case of both Shahjahanabad and New Delhi. In case of Shahjahanabad the object is to relieve the present congestion, insanitary conditions, high levels of pollution of air, and pressure on or absence of essential services in order to provide to its residents a healthier living environment. In case of New Delhi, however, the object of redevelopment is to achieve higher density land-use by building multi-storey structures to provide housing for high income earners, space for the expanding ministries and departments of the central government, offices of public and private enterprises, luxury (5-star) hotels etc.

The views and pressures for and against redevelopment for both cities are summarized below; the summary for Shahjahanabad is based on a study by Mehra (1991: Chapters IV and V) who conducted personal interviews with a large number of merchants, owners/managers of small industrial establishments, political leaders (municipal councilors and others) and residents of various neighbourhoods.

Shahjahanabad

The residents of Shahjahanabad had mixed and, indeed, conflicting, views on redevelopment of the city. They would greatly appreciate its benefits viz. relief from the present congestion and overcrowding within the neighbourhoods and most of the homes; insanitary conditions, high levels of atmospheric pollution, and inadequacy or absence of basic services such as a sewerage system, as a result of which night soil and other solid waste have to be removed through the insanitary and highly obnoxious practice of carrying them by head loads. Redevelopment could also provide partial relief from the present endemic shortages of water and electricity, and traffic jams.

On the other hand, they are afraid that they would have to pay higher rents: rents of their present homes, shops, workshops, warehouses etc., are very low because of the operation of the Rent Control Act. Another fear is of the inconvenience and expense involved in commuting long distances from their new homes to their work places (shops, workshops and offices) which are located in Shahjahanabad close to their present homes. Strong social and community ties among the residents of various neighbourhoods, which provide security of life and property, are another great advantage in a city in which violence has become endemic. Finally, there is the memory of the traumatic experience of forcible eviction from, and demolition of, their old homes and relocation in new distant homes of residents of some neighbourhoods by a development-oriented but over-enthusiastic Lt. Governor of Delhi during 1975/76.

Despite these fears and inhibitions the younger members of a large number of Shahjahanbad families have moved to new houses located in new residential neighbourhoods which have come up since 1947 while the older members stay behind in the old homes. The trend is particularly strong in affluent families, but is by no means confined to them. The movement among the families of affluent merchants and industrialists is generally accompanied by opening of shops, workshops, offices etc., in new markets or industrial estates such as those located in the New Okhla Industrial Development Area (NOIDA). Frequently, the need to expand or diversify their businesses is the principal reason for moving to new homes.

The majority of the political leaders are in favor of preserving the present settlement pattern in which they have strong political bases. Leading merchants and owners/managers of small industrial establishments also have a strong vested interest in continuing in their present locations. There is brisk business in the wholesale and retail markets of Shahjahanabad and the small size and unostentatious appearance of their establishments located in old buildings helps them in reporting low turnover and profits and save on payment of income-tax and other taxes.

New Delhi

As in case of Shahjahanabad, there are strong views in favour of and against preserving the present very low-density settlement and land-use pattern of New Delhi—with extensive lawns surrounding large, single storey bungalows of ministers and senior officials, wide shady roads and two large parks—the Lodhi Garden and the Nehru Park. As a result, New Delhi is a green oasis within a rapidly growing and increasingly congested metropolis in most parts of which levels of water and air pollution are several times higher than internationally prescribed maxima for maintenance of health and safety.

The views of those who favour the present land-use pattern have prevailed so far. But there is no doubt that in course of time the proponents of higher density land-use through construction of high-rise buildings will be dominant and New Delhi's remaining green area and sprawling single-storey bungalows will be pale shadows of their former selves.

The pressure for higher density land-use, by building multi-storey flats on lands taken from lawns is being exerted by developers and owners of bungalows with large lawns. Both see in the development an opportunity to make a killing. Even with the present dominance of the view for maintaining the low-density land-use, the density is increasing slowly. Multi-storey structures which have luxury hotels or flats for the affluent have come up in several locations. The Government initiated the process in the late 1950s by building multi-storey structures for location of offices of its various Ministries and Departments on both sides of the Central Vista and still continues to build new buildings for its offices or institutions of national importance like the National Museum.

REVIEW AND PROSPECT

This paper has presented a brief review, a thumb-nail sketch, of planning and city building in Delhi during three periods — the imperial Mughal, the imperial British and post-Independence. It has brought out that in the first two periods the concept of imperial grandeur was paramount, and that both Shahjahanabad and New Delhi were built to meet the needs and satisfy the aesthetic tastes of the ruling elites. They reflected also their preferences and ideals about building of capital cities. However, the detailed design of both cities reflected also the need for adaptation to the technologies and social structure of their times. Shahjahanabad was built for a society in which most of the residents moved within the city by foot or on horses, and traveled outside it by animal drawn vehicles. Social interaction was primarily face-to-face. In New Delhi, the private car was the principal mode of personal travel and movement within the city of the elite. But it was recognized that most residents of the city, including most employees of the Government, would depend for movement within the city on bicycles or on horse-drawn vehicles. The design and layout of the sprawling bungalows of high officials reflected the need for privacy of the British, and while the smaller bungalows of junior officials made only a grudging concession to the needs of their Indian occupants for greater social interaction with their neighbours, ample opportunities were provided for it within the neighbourhoods in which the living quarters of the clerks and messengers were located.

The principal shopping centers of the city — all except Connaught Place — schools, hospitals and smaller health centres were also located within or near these neighbourhoods. The Delhi University and its constituent colleges were located, however, at various places North of Shahjahanabad. The locations were convenient for students living in Shahjahanabad and its extensions such as *Sabzi Mandi* and *Paharganj*, but it was most inconvenient for students living in New Delhi who had to travel long distances to attend their colleges. This difficulty has been overcome, however, after the 1960s, by opening of a number of new colleges in South and West Delhi, and particularly by building of the South Delhi campus of the Delhi University on the Aravali ridge between South and West Delhi.

The two post-Independence plans — three, if the Regional Plan 2001, National Capital Region is included — have been formulated to meet the needs of a political democracy which swears by the ideal of building a socialistic society. But it is a sad commentary on its present stage of evolution that the ruling elites — ministers, other influential political leaders and the senior-most officials — continue to live in the bungalows that were formerly occupied by the British and that the principle of segregation by official status has continued to be followed in the location, size and design of the houses built by the Government. In the colonies developed by the private developers and cooperative societies, its place has been taken by income and is affected through differences in rent or cost of construction.

Another irony is that it is only in this democratic age that those who provide essential services for the city and its other residents are condemned to live in "slums" or in small overcrowded "servant quarters" attached to the bungalows of their employers. This is not because the post-Independence planners provided less adequately for their need for housing, than did the planners of Shahjahanabad or New Delhi; the principal reason is that the plans have been subverted by economic or other pressures or by personal greed.

Despite the slight slowing of the growth of its population during the 1980s, the prospect is for the total population of the Delhi urban agglomeration to double within the next 20 or 25 years. The population of the National Capital Region, 19 million in 1981, is projected to reach 33 million by the year 2000 and would approach or exceed 40 million by 2010. The challenge for the urban and regional planners is to provide to the residents of this extended metropolis a living and working environment which is healthy, satisfying and efficient. They have to achieve this objective within a national policy framework of economic liberalization which includes, at least for the present, virtual abolition of the control over location of industrial enterprises that had been exercised through the system of licensing of industries. As a result, there is an even stronger incentive, than earlier, for medium-sized or large industrial enterprises to locate in the Delhi Metropolitan Area in which they can obtain both level, well drained land at low prices, as well as access to the capital, skilled workers, entrepreneurs, trained and experienced managers and other professionals and the giant market of the Delhi Metropolitan Area.

GOALS FOR PLANNED GROWTH

There are three principal requirements for achievement of the planners' objectives:

1. Spatial Planning: Formulation of plans for the Delhi Urban Agglomeration, the Delhi Metropolitan Area and the National Capital Region within the same temporal, conceptual and spatial frameworks. All the three plans should be for the 20 year period, 2000-2020: within this period shorter, more flexible 5-year plans should be formulated and revised from

time to time in response to changing socio-economic conditions and availability of financial and other resources. Concurrence in time of the plans with the national 5-year plans will facilitate their financing and implementation. The plan for the National Capital Region should provide the spatial and conceptual envelope within which the plans for the two smaller areal units are prepared.

2. Environmental Parameters: The plans should be in harmony with the physical environment of the NCR and recognize both its high potential for land development and housing at much lower cost, than in the metropolitan areas of Mumbai or Kolkata, and its constraints, particularly prevalence of hot dry winds through much of the long summer and low annual rainfall. Because of these constraints, it is essential that the houses are airy and cool, and water supply is adequate. These conditions are best met through high density, low-rise land-use, not unlike that of Shahjahanabad. It is unfortunate that this basic consideration is being increasingly ignored and high rise flats are being built in the new colonies being developed by the DDA at long distances from Shahjahanabad or New Delhi.
3. Priority for Mass Transit System (MTS): An essential requirement for the success of the plans is construction at the earliest of a mass transit system, which will provide the facility of rapid, low cost commuting between home and work. It is unfortunate that construction of the system has been repeatedly postponed on grounds of high cost. The present reliance, in its absence, on an inefficient and unreliable bus service and multiplicity of motor vehicles (cars, taxis and two or three wheelers), results in very high costs (in time and money) in travel within the metropolis and very high levels of air and noise pollution which can only increase with growth of economic activity and population in the next 20 years.

The construction on MRTS began in 1998 is progressing very slowly. The pace will remain slow because of difficulties in land acquisition in the areas in which the Metro Rail will be at ground level.[2]

NOTES

Post Scripts

1. Lutyens' Bungalow Zone (LBZ) "is one of the finer cities to have been built in the inter-war years. It is the only complete British city in India that makes for the best urban form of the 20th Century anywhere in the world" (Ritish Nanda). However, the zone has been brutalized after being declared the most endangered heritage site". Prathna Gehlot, Times of India, April 17, 2003
2. The targets for the MRTS are being achieved in time, however, because of complete commitment of the state and central governments in supporting the efforts needed for its completion. Even the local population is supporting the MRTS by voluntarily allowing it to break certain portions of their buildings needed by the MRTS as per reports from Patel Nagar area recently (2004).

REFERENCES

Delhi Development Authority, (1985) *Delhi 2001*, *Vikas Varta* 2, 2. Special Issue.

Dutt, A.K. (1983) "*Cities of South Asia*" in Brunn, S. and Williams, J. (eds.), *Cities of the World*, Harper and Row Publishers, New York.

Mehra, A.K. (1991), *The Politics of Urban Development: A Study of Old Delhi*, Sage Publications India Private Ltd., New Delhi.

Nath, V. (1988), "*Regional Planning for Large Metropolitan Cities: A Case Study of the National Capital Region*", *Economic and Political Weekly*. 23, 5, pp. 201-214.

National Capital Region Planning Board, (1988), *Regional Plan 2001 National Capital Region*, Ministry of Urban Development, Government of India, Delhi.

Sealy, N. (1988) "*Planned Cities of India: A Study of Jaipur, New Delhi and Chandigarh*" in Costa, F. Dutt, A.; Ma, L.; Noble, A. (eds.), *Asian Urbanization Problems and Process*, Gebrüder Borntraeger, Berlin.

14

The Changing Face of a South Delhi Residential Colony[1]

This paper on urban process explains how the living environment of a very well planned neighborhood of civil servants in South Delhi has deteriorated over the course of nearly 30 years of its existence. Some of the reasons for environmental deterioration have been explained. It is further pointed out that unless there is a major change in the attitude of the residents and the officials of the Municipal Corporation, the processes, such as those listed in the paper would make even the best planned neighbourhoods in Delhi or in other metropolitan cities polluted and filthy in three to four decades.

THE PROCESS OF URBAN DETERIORATION IN DELHI

The process of environmental degradation has overtaken all neighbourhoods in South Delhi that were planned as neighbourhoods of the relatively affluent during the 1950s to the 1970s. The green area, tree-lined avenues within the colonies and houses having lawns and bougainvilleas or other flowering bushes covering their walls are still there. But their role in controlling air pollution is reduced by the large increase in the number of cars of the house-owners and tenants. Increase in pollution of air in Delhi is due to increase in emission of solid particulate matter (spm) from motor vehicles (motor cycles, scooters, taxis, buses, trucks and passenger cars) hurtling through the city's roads.

This paper in urban process explains with the example of a well-planned residential neighbourhood of relatively affluent civil servants, how there has been steady deterioration in its environment during the period of nearly 30 years of its existence. The reasons for this deterioration, to which the house-owners and commercial builders have contributed in no small way, have been explained.

The process of environmental degradation is in a large part on account of the desire for affluence of the original owners and in part due to invasion by affluent businessmen and slum dwellers in the vicinity of the colony. The Delhi Development Authority (DDA), the Municipal Corporation of Delhi and the Delhi Vidyut (Electricity) Board have not used their extensive powers to evict the slum dwellers or check environmental pollution. This process has also been operative in most of our large metropolitan cities resulting in conversion of large parts of their areas into unliveable slums.

The process affects economic growth adversely because economic activities—commerce, finance, manufacturing—which generate more than three-fourths of the national GDP and which are located in the central or peripheral areas of the cities are not as efficient as they would be in a cleaner environment. Effective measures to check the process of environmental deterioration have yet to be evolved.

A WELL PLANNED COLONY IN SOUTHWEST DELHI

The colony under discussion is located about 13 kilometres south-west of Connaught Circus, the central business district of New Delhi and the point from which distances of various colonies in New Delhi are measured. It was developed in the 1970s by a cooperative group house building society most of the members of which were middle level officers in various ministries of the Government of India or in the public sector undertakings. The DDA allotted a large piece (140 hectares) of government land to the society in the late 1960s. The office bearers of the society then approached the Central Public Works Department (CPWD) to plan the internal layout of the colony. The town planners and architects of the CPWD displayed a concern for providing a healthy living environment and love for greenery, in addition to providing essential amenities to the residents. This is virtually absent among their successors. Thus, besides providing 1,350 building lots ranging in size from 220 sq. metres to 1800 sq. metres they provided for the location of the following:

1. A large central market which has over 150 shops besides a post office, and branches of some nationalised banks and the Life Insurance Corporation of India.

2. Much smaller markets housing 30-40 shops within various neighbourhoods from where the residents can buy provisions, fresh fruits and vegetables and drugs. Thus to meet their day-to-day requirements of food and drugs the residents of the neighbourhoods can walk to the shops in these markets.
3. Wide main roads and fairly wide side streets, all lined with flowering trees, for circulation within the colony.
4. A large park, extending over 16 hectares which is crowded with walkers and joggers in the mornings during 10 months in the year, excepting the two months of Delhi's severe winter.
5. Small parks within the various neighborhoods that provide a touch of refreshing greenery to the residents. Youngsters and children play here in the afternoons and early evenings and groups of elderly women assemble here to chat for a couple of hours in the winter afternoons and summers evenings.
6. Space for the location of seven higher secondary schools. The schools include branches of three of the most prestigious schools in New Delhi. Since most of the members of the society were Hindus and Sikhs, they provided for the location of one large temple, two smaller temples and a *Gurudwara.* A Catholic mission has built a large church and a hostel for its priests and nuns and a higher secondary school.
7. Although the colony has a number of physicians, there is no hospital located here. However, two multi-facility hospitals have come up immediately to the east of it. One of these was established by a Catholic mission. The Arya Samaj runs a charitable dispensary and a small hospital here.
8. In order to limit fast moving traffic within the colony, the planners provided only three access roads.
9. Space for location of a club, with such facilities as squash and tennis courts, a swimming pool, a restaurant, rooms for playing bridge and rummy, several rooms for holding private parties, a small library and a few rooms to accommodate guests of the members.
10. The office of the society has an auditorium and facilities for holding wedding receptions. Furthermore, its office bearers advise the members on payment of property tax and other matters.

Thus, the essential needs of the original members who wanted to live in a healthy environment after retirement from service were adequately taken care of by the planner of the CPWD.

HOUSE DESIGN AND LOCATIONAL ADVANTAGES: A HOUSE TO LIVE IN AND A HOUSE TO LIVE ON

Most of the members of the society built 1-2 storey houses for their own living, with provision for extension of the house to accommodate the family of a married son or a daughter, in case they wanted to live with them. The higher level, wealthier officials built larger houses, with two wings, one of which was for rent. Some of them have been rented for location of chanceries or are the residences of ambassadors of diplomatic missions or their officials; others are occupied by officials of foreign companies or correspondents of foreign newspapers.

The colony is popular with diplomats because it is located about 6 kilometres south of Chanakyapuri, New Delhi's diplomatic enclave developed in the 1950s and 1960s. The Government of India allotted large plots for location of chanceries, residences of ambassadors or high commissioners and senior officials of the diplomatic missions of the countries with which India had established diplomatic relations by then. But since the number of such countries has increased steadily during the past four decades, a number of diplomatic missions are now located within this colony.

High Rents and Foreign Tenants

Rents in the colony are high – Rs. 100,000 to 200,000 for a 3-5 bedroom house. Thus, even a highly paid executive of a large Indian business house can only afford to live in the colony only if his employers pay the rent.

Those who desire to rent out a part of their house or a flat, prefer foreigners, especially residents of western European countries, Americans, Japanese and Koreans, as tenants. This is because they pay well and take good care of the house so that the owner does not have to spend much on repairs or renovation after they vacate the house. Diplomats of SAARC countries are not preferred because they do not take equally good care of the house. Excepting executives of large business or industrial houses, Indian tenants are lowest in the priority of those desiring to rent out their premises. The principal reason for this is that while the foreigners leave at the end of their assignment of 1 to 5 years, the Indian tenant may never leave and the house owner may be stuck with a tenant who rented the house at a much lower rent several years ago and who continues to occupy the house at a rent which is below the current market rent.

Invasion by Builders and Businessmen

The original members of the society are now old, in their late 60s to 80s. Many live in their houses with the families of a married son or daughter. However, there are others whose children are settled abroad, mainly in U.S.A. or Britain. They visit their parents for a few weeks in the summer when their children's schools close for vacation. However, they have no intention of returning to live in Delhi to start a new career. Thus, after the death of one or both the parents, the house is sold, usually to a professional builder. This change of ownership has had major effects on the environment of the colony.

The original house would have had, besides the built-up area, a small garden and adequate space for parking of one or two cars. However, since the sole object of the builder is to maximize the return on his investment, he replaces the original structure with a four-storey structure with 6 to 8 flats for the purpose of sale. In order to maximize the price of the flats, he uses expensive materials, including Italian marble, and fittings and fixtures in the bedrooms, bathrooms and kitchen. But he fails to provide adequate or any space for parking of cars of those who purchase these flats, with the result an increasing number of cars are now parked on the road. A few businessmen have bought houses in the colony through power of attorney sales. Though such sales are technically not legal they are widespread in Delhi.

On account of all these factors the number of cars in the colony is more than the heads of households. Every diplomatic mission too has a number of cars. For the rich businessmen residing in the area having a number of cars is a status symbol. Even their underage children, often possessing a driving license obtained through agents (perhaps by bribing the concerned officials), are known to drive cars. As a result of the increase in population, the number of cars and the traffic, the quite, uncrowded, large open spaces and green areas of the 1970s are steadily being eroded and replaced with dust and grime. Though the residents of the houses located away from the main roads are better off, it will not be long before they too face the same problems.

Lack of Civic Sense

Another problem that inflicts the area is lack of civic sense among the occupants and also lack of a cooperative spirit to keep the area environmentally clean. While the main roads are still quite clean and kept in good repair by the MCD, the back lanes are full of building waste—broken bricks, sand or earth and domestic waste thrown by servants, and man-holes without covers on them in which an unwary pedestrian could fall during the night and get seriously hurt. The builders and the owners who extend their houses do not care to remove the building waste, despite the small cost of doing it. Most of the shopkeepers in the markets are quite well off, many own cars, but they lack the cooperative spirit to get together in order to keep the markets clean. Those in the main market, which has a motorable road within it, make no attempt to ensure that the road is well maintained by the Corporation and that the traffic on it is regulated. Until the early 1990s the Welfare Association of the society used to launch campaigns from time to time for clearing the debris from the back lanes, but seeing that the campaigns had no long lasting effect finally gave up.

Affluence and Poverty Co-exist

Immediately to the north of the colony there are:

1. Two small colonies of rich people.
2. A large residential complex consisting of several thousand houses built by the Government of India in the 1960's for its clerks and junior officials and to house some of its offices. Within the residential complex itself there are large slums built by illegal encroachment on municipal land. Economic activities of the slum dwellers range from working as domestic servants, gardeners and watchmen in houses in the colony and the market complex to rag picking, petty thefts and smuggling.
3. Two over-grown villages. One, originally small village of Muslim artisans and farmers, now a small town. The main

road passing by it has shops selling everything from building materials to drugs, besides housing small restaurants and sweetmeat shops. The DDA has built two large blocks of four-storey flats for housing middle-income residents. However, the interior of the village is quite dirty with unpaved streets and pools of stagnant water especially during the rainy season. Sanitary conditions in the other over-grown village, which is much smaller, are much better. Most of the houses are built of brick and mortar and roads within the village are well maintained.

4. A large shopping-cum-office complex that has offices of more than 100 companies, a cinema hall, several restaurants including branches of two American restaurant chains. The restaurants are very popular with the young residents of the colony and students and faculty of the Jawaharlal Nehru University, which is located about 2 kilometres to the south of the complex. The shops in the complex sell trendy imported clothes and shoes and jewellery, high quality furniture and consumer durables such as refrigerators, air conditioners and electrically operated kitchen gadgets. Interestingly, it also has a very well stocked book-shop and a mini-super market which sells everything from meat, fish, fruits, vegetables to imported processed foods, drugs and paper backs. A deluxe hotel, with about 200 rooms, which is popular with foreign tourists, is located next to this complex.
5. In the immediate neighbourhood of the hotel there is a large slum. Thus the tourists can see within a quarter mile of the hotel, two middle-class colonies, a middle-class shopping complex as well as the poverty, filth and squalor of a slum.

WHY DECAY OCCURRED SO SOON IN DELHI?

This essay in urban process has attempted to bring out some of the reasons for the environmental degradation of a well planned neighborhood of middle class civil servants in South Delhi within a span of 30 years of its existence. The reasons are mainly invasion by slum dwellers on the fringes of the colony on the one hand, and of businessmen and diplomats within it on the other. The latter is due mainly to the desire for affluence of the original owners or the fact that the house was purchased by builders or businessmen after the original owner passed away. The invasion of slum dwellers is largely to meet the needs of the house owners and diplomats for domestic servants, gardeners, watchmen, etc., disregarding the need to provide proper housing for them. Finally, there is lack of civic sense and a strong commitment to community action to keep the living environment clean and healthy.

These are some of the reasons that have contributed to making not only the above locality but also large parts of our metropolitan cities, the nerve centers of our economy and polity: "filthy," as Queen Elizabeth II was constrained to remark during her February 1998 visit to India. The remark caused much anguish to the civic leaders of Delhi but they did nothing either to make the city clean or to reduce pollution of air and water in the city for two years. They have finally been forced to take action to reduce pollution of air and water in order to comply with the orders of the Supreme Court. However, it must be pointed out that it is their duty to ensure a clean and healthy environment for their constituents without waiting for the Court to direct them to do so. Furthermore, the constituents themselves must take cooperative action at the neighbourhoods' level to keep their environment clean and healthy and also pressurize the members of the Municipal Corporation to keep the area clean.

NOTE

1. *Urban India*, Vol. XX No. 1 (2000).

15

Need for a New Model of Indian Metropolitan City

More and more people will live in metropolitan cities. They will live, work, be educated, treated and entertained in the cities. This will be a crucible in which the rich, the super rich and the poor live side by side. They come here because they find work and patterns of living are more interesting than in village homes. The pulls of capital, entrepreneurship and skilled labour for development of factory industries are available only in the cities. They are also the main centers for distribution of products in their areas. The highly educated professionals in science and technology needed for the growth of sunrise industries – IT, Telecommunication, entertainment and broadcasting are available here. Here are located world-class harbours, airports, universities, and institutes of science and technology that are essential for rapid growth of the sunrise industries.

At present there are two slightly different patterns of growth of metropolitan cities: Southern cities – Bangalore, Chennai, Hyderabad and Coimbatore in which the State governments provide infrastructures central for efficient functioning of the cities and the more congested cities of India – Delhi, Kolkata, Mumbai and Hyderabad. The growth of factory industries and modern services in the cities of western India is so high that these cities cannot but be a collection of industries, modern services and slums. The modal for the northern – western cities must include programmes to decongest their central areas in which live both the dirt poor and a large number of residents who have been living there for generations. The ongoing process of urban renewal is quite ineffective because of the operation of the Rent Control Act. Even rapid growth of satellite cities such as New Mumbai and Thane on the mainland and western style central Mumbai has not helped. The natural process of urban decay could be stopped if the Rent Control Act was effectively ended and the owners had the incentive to reconstruct their buildings with provision for services and safety for the residents. The industrial units located in them must shift to the peri-urban areas in order to become more competitive. The implementation of the courts order to shift them to the suburbs will become more effective in due time.

In order that the metropolitan cities do not become a motley collections of neighbourhoods of the affluent and middle class residents and shanties of the poor, it is essential that the architects, town planers, engineers, administrators, economists and other social scientists evolve a model for the growth of Indian metropolitan cities so that the metropolitan cities can continue to perform roles as the commercial, industrial, modern service and cultural centers, of the regions in which they are located. The model should be cost effective so that essential services can be provided to the residents of the cities at costs which can be afforded by the municipal and the state governments.

Preliminary results of the decennial census of 2001, which have just become available indicate that there are 40 cities with a population of 1 million or more. The number has nearly doubled since 1991 when there were only 23 such cities (Table 15.1).

The list includes Delhi, Mumbai, Kolkata with more than 10 million people each in their metropolitan areas (i.e. the cities, suburbs and satellite towns that are contiguous to them) to Jalandhar, Amritsar and Patiala in Punjab; Meerut and Agra in U.P. in the north; Thiruvananthapuram in Kerala and Madurai in Tamil Nadu which have a population of over 1 million.

Almost 10 percent of the population of the country and more than 1/3rd of the urban population live in these cities. The cities are the political, commercial, industrial and cultural centres of the regions or states in which they are located. The capitals of all the major states except Orissa, Punjab and Haryana are located in such cities. The best universities, professional colleges, world-class hospitals, most of the offices of the airlines and the tourist hotels are located in these cities.

Table 15.1: Population of One Lakh Above Principal Cities

Cities	*Population (000)*	*Decennial Growth (%)*	
	1991	*1981-91*	*1971-81*
Ahmedabad	3,312	30.0	45.9
Bangalore	4,130	41.3	75.6
Bhopal (M.C.)	1,063	58.4	74.4
Mumbai (Greater)	12,596	33.6	42.9
Mumbai (Greater M.C.)	9,926	20.4	38.1
Chennai	5,422	26.4	35.3
Delhi	8,419	47.0	57.1
Coimbatore	1,101	19.7	25.0
Hyderabad	4,344	70.6	42.7
Indore	1,109	33.8	47.9
Jaipur	1,518	49.6	59.4
Kalyan (M.C.)	1,015	645.4	36.7
Kanpur	2,030	23.9	23.5
Kochi	1,141	38.1	48.8
Kolkata	11,022	19.9	23.9
Lucknow	1,669	65.6	23.8
Ludhiana	1,043	71.8	51.3
Madurai	1,086	19.6	27.6
Nagpur	1,664	27.8	40.8
Patna	1,100	19.7	66.7
Pune	2,494	47.9	48.6
Surat	1,519	66.2	87.4
Vadodra	1,127	51.3	67.4
Varanasi	1,031	29.4	25.5
Vishakapatnam	1,057	75.0	66.1

Source: Statistical Outline of India 2001-2002; Tata Services Limited; Department of Economics and Statistics, Mumbai

CONTRASTS IN URBAN GROWTH

Most of the industrial units that manufacture everything from processed foods to consumer durables such as television receivers, refrigerators and air conditioners and even motor vehicles are located in peri-urban areas at metropolitan cities. Most of the small-scale industrial units are also located in them and their peri-urban areas. Such location is due both to concentration in the cities of pools of capital, skilled labour and entrepreneurship that are needed for establishment of industries. Furthermore, the cities are major centres for distribution of products in the regions or states in which they are located. These cities are themselves large markets for products of modern factory or small-scale industries.

As a result, the contribution of the cities to the gross domestic product of the country is much greater than their share of the population. Furthermore, resident in them are the writers, poets and musicians that are the best exponents of the traditional cultures of the regions on the one hand and leaders of cultural changes on the other.

Excepting some cities in the south – Chennai, Bangalore, Hyderabad and Thiruvananthapuram — physical infrastructure facilities needed for effective functioning of the cities (adequate and dependable supplies of electricity and drinking water or facilities for disposal of solid and liquid waste) are too inadequate to serve their populations efficiently. The result is that there are large slums and unauthorised residential colonies in all these cities the residents of which are provided most inadequately with the infrastructure service facilities mentioned above. Growth of slums appears to be an integral part of the process of urbanization; In fact the slums' population in a metropolitan city increases much faster than that of the city itself.

Mumbai

In Mumbai, unending slums line the highways in Nariman Point area which houses the best hotels, offices of multi-national corporations as well as those of several large Indian corporations. Efforts to relocate the slums to more suitable locations in Mumbai have evoked such fierce resistance from the slum dwellers and the film stars or politicians acting on their behalf that the corporation and the state governments have given up all efforts to relocate the slums. Dharavi, on the way to the Santa Cruz airport, has long prided itself on being the biggest slum in Asia. Besides, the *chawls* that were built in the 1880s by the mill-owners but are still lived in by more than a million of workers are no better than slums.

Delhi

There are two very different kinds of development in this area:

Slum clusters on or just above the flood plain of the Yamuna. A very large planned slum cluster was built by the DDA in the mid-1970s just above the flood plain of the river. The area had good roads, adequate surface drainage and the huts were provided with electricity and water by the concerned authorities. The slum dwellers were those who were removed from roadsides and other unsuitable locations in New Delhi and its post-Independence extensions. The principal problem of the slum dwellers was the cost and time taken in travel from their homes to places of work located in New Delhi or in the industrial areas located in north and west Delhi.

However, due to subsequent completely unplanned extensions by poor migrants, many of whom have built their huts on the flood plain itself, the whole area has become a mass of narrow roads and unsanitary clogged drains. Conditions are so bad that diseases of the respiratory and digestive tracts are endemic and often take epidemic form during and after the monsoons.

The second development consists of a series of planned residential colonies built by retired officials of the Government of India, companies and traders. Conditions in them are very similar to those in housing colonies in south, west and north Delhi described earlier. The colonies have adequate electric and water supplies, sewerage, their own markets, parks, schools, mini-hospitals and other public facilities.

Unauthorized Colonies

These have been built in various locations in south and west Delhi by artisans, workers in factories located in the designated industrial areas and elsewhere and petty traders. The colonies although not approved by the Municipal Corporation or the DDA have been provided electricity and water by the concerned authorities. But since they lack sewerage and have no satisfactory arrangement for disposal of solid waste, sanitation is a serious problem in them. Furthermore, a large number of small industrial units some of which process inflammable and hazardous materials are located in these colonies as well as in a part of the old city. These units create a problem of occasional fires in the summer that cause much damage to life and property.

KOLKATA

In Kolkata, some of the largest slums called *bustees* are located right behind the central business district. The residents are workers such as doormen and messengers in various offices in the CBD (Kolkata Business District), rickshaw pullers, porters in the markets and the railway stations. Then there are unending slums in designated slum clusters and along the roads of south and east of Kolkata. A large proportion of the slum residents are those who work in various industrial establishments in the Kolkata Metropolitan city and in the jute mill towns located along the river Hoogly. Another large group consists of refugees from Bangladesh who are too poor to find affordable living.

PRESENT TRENDS IN URBAN RENEWAL AND DECONGESTION

Abolition or major changes in the Rent Control Act could provide a powerful incentive for urban renewal. The owners of buildings in the central areas of the cities could rebuild their multi-storey flats or old decaying houses so as to make them more liveable for people of middle-income groups including workers in small industrial units. The transfer of factory industries and population now located in the cities to satellite cities – New Mumbai and Thane or the small towns along the road to Delhi or road cum rail strip to Pune in Mumbai; to Gurgaon, Faridabad, NOIDA and Ghaziabad in case of Delhi — have done nothing to decongest Delhi or Mumbai and improve living environment within the central areas of the cities.

BENIGN FEATURES OF CITIES IN SOUTH INDIA

Several southern metropolitan cities – Chennai, Bangalore, Hyderabad and even Pune — seem to be an exception to this. They have the factory industries in their peri-urban areas. While some small industrial units may be located in the residential areas, they are free from them by and large and have only homes and markets or professionals' offices. Furthermore, both the municipal and state governments have made an effort to expand essential infrastructure facilities mentioned above. Indeed, the governments of both Tamil Nadu and Andhra Pradesh are competing with the Government of Karnataka to make

Chennai and Hyderabad the most important center of the information technology industries thus challenging the primacy of Bangalore in these industries.

Slums will remain an integral part of urban life for the foreseeable future. Millions of rural poor will continue to flood into the cities in search of employment and to live in the slums until (i) India reaches a higher stage of economic development at which per capita income is much higher than it as at present, (ii) There is equitable distribution of income so that rural and urban poverty is sharply reduced and (iii) massive public housing programs are implemented to provide housing to the poor. Meanwhile, as explained in the seventh and eighth Five Year Plans, the emphasis must remains on slum improvement programmes. These can be undertaken with the participation of and self-help by the slum dwellers if they are based on an understanding of their social life.

THE TWIN CITY MODEL – AND DELHI'S TRANSFORMATION INTO A MEGALOPOLIS

A number of geographers wrote in the 1950s and the 1960s about the twin city model of large and medium-sized Indian cities. The essence of the argument was that the typical Indian city consisted of two parts: an Indian city crowded, dirty, lacking sanitation facilities, but throbbing with trading and traditional handicraft industries, and (ii) the civil station, built by the British which contained the office of the Collector and other district officers or the Secretariat if the city was the capital of a province and residences of British and Indian officers and middle level employees of the railways and the post and telegraph departments most of whom were Anglo-Indians. It was a planned town with wide tree-lined streets, spacious bungalows or smaller houses each with its own garden; one or more markets which had stores selling liquor, provisions and clothes needed by the Europeans; show rooms of cars and motor bicycles, one or more English language schools, a good hospital, one or more churches and other places of worship and at least one public park.

The larger cities, usually capitals of provinces had in addition a chamber of the legislature, a high court, a university with several arts and science colleges and professional colleges, particularly of law and medicine, a big hospital, one or more hotels for Europeans and offices of one or two English language and several vernacular newspapers.

If the city had a cantonment near it the latter would have a central office of the garrison, barracks for soldiers, residences of officers, parade grounds, playgrounds and other facilities for training of soldiers and messes of officers. The cantonment had its own market(s), hospital and one or more schools and places of worship so that the soldiers did not need to go out of it and intrude on the life of the civil population.

The model had some relevance in planning of development of cities in pre-Independent India. Most cities had a central old part of the city around which were built a civil line, and a cantonment. The latter has the usual offices, barracks, officers' residences, markets, hospitals, parade and training grounds, sports fields and messes of officers. It is spread over a large area and is a self-contained township.

The survey of growth of Delhi into a megalopolis described in another chapter brings out that the twin city model is no longer relevant for it. The model had no place for satellite towns which are however an integral part of all large metropolitan cities. Developments similar to those in Delhi have taken place in all the largest metropolitan cities.

In Hyderabad, Pune and Bangalore, which had cantonments along side the Indian city, the megalopolis has grown all around and engulfed both. In Mumbai, the megalopolis has spilled over from the island to the mainland and despite the physical barrier of the Western Ghats is growing between Mumbai and Pune as well as along some of the highways that connect Mumbai with other major cities. In Kolkata, the contiguously urbanised area–the Kolkata Metropolitan District–contained in the 1960s the cities of Kolkata and Howrah, about 45 small towns including the jute mill towns located along the river Hoogly and a large number of villages located south of Kolkata which have grown. Although growth of Kolkata Metropolitan District has been slower than that of the other large metropolitan cities, the contiguously urbanised area now extends almost to Kalyani 60 kilometres to the north that has been built as a retirement community and in the south to the harbour town of Haldia.

Perhaps the most suitable model for the Indian megalopolis is that of the American metropolitan cities which are located along the north east coast such as Boston, Philadelphia and Baltimore. In each of these, there is a central city, decaying until the 1960s but rejuvenated later and a series of suburbs and satellite towns. While the suburbs are new, most of the satellite towns are old towns that now form part of the contiguously urban area.

OCTOPUS MODEL FOR URBAN GROWTH IN INDIA

The model that comes to mind for growth of the northern or western cities in the past five decade – Delhi, Mumbai, Ahmedabad is that of an octopus. The inhabited areas of the cities have leap-frogged across the Yamuna in case of Delhi and the creek that separates the main city on the Island and the satellite cities on the mainland of New Mumbai and Thane to make two new mega cities. The Kolkata Metropolitan District similarly includes Kolkata, Howrah and the jute mill towns along the Hoogly and a large number of villages south of Kolkata. It is spreading to the south to the Salt Lake area to the southeast towards Midnapur Sealdah in the east. Examples could be multiplied.

The government of Tamil Nadu, Andhra Pradesh and Karnataka had made the investment needed for promotion of services for electric supply, drinking water, and removal of solid and liquid waste and intra-urban transport. They have the factory industries in their peri-urban areas, while small industrial units may be located in the residential areas. These industries are free from pollutant by and large. The residential areas also include homes and offices of professionals working in the non-polluting industries. Furthermore, both the municipal and state government had made an effort to expand essential infrastructure facilities mentioned above. Indeed, the government of both Tamil Nadu and Andhra Pradesh are competing with the Government of Karnataka to make Chennai and Hyderabad the most important center of the Information Technology Industries thus challenging the primacy of Bangalore in these industries.

It is necessary that the governments of Gujarat, Delhi, U.P. and Haryana create infrastructure facilities similar to those in the southern cities so that Mumbai, Ahmedabad and Delhi remain centres of IT industries and can become, along with Vadodara centres of biotechnology industry also. They have already one or more companies manufacturing drugs from formulations for which patents have expired and others based on original research or on the ancient Ayurvedic system of medicine. It may be difficult for the state and city governments to finance such investment with their existing or foreseeable future sources of revenues or to create conditions in their peri-urban areas or satellite cities for the facilities needed for rapid growth of IT or biotechnology industries. Large investment by the Central government is essential.

The investment on infrastructure for these industries would repay itself within a few years. Corporate and income tax on the companies that provide IT services, especially entertainment or manufacture of drugs or on the income of the executives, professionals and skilled workers who work in them would be so large that the grants given by the Central government for creation of infrastructure facilities would be recovered. However, the Central government has to make the initial investment. Sales taxes from soap, hair oil, other cosmetics, drugs and various consumer durables used by the people of various income groups, including residents of improved slums, would repay the investment made by the state governments. Furthermore, the facilities for these sunrise industries cannot be provided anywhere or everywhere. They have to be focused on pre-designated cyber cafes, entertainment cities and areas for location of drug industries.

OTHER INVESTMENT NEEDS FOR IDEAL FUNCTIONING OF A METROPOLITAN CITY

For efficient functioning of a large and growing metropolitan city very large investment is required in (i) land development and construction of housing (ii) expansion of facilities for supplies of water and electricity, construction of a sewerage system, and putting in place adequate arrangement for disposal of solid waste (iii) steady improvement in intra-city transport and expansion and improvement of intra-city roads and finally (iv) expansion of facilities for education, health care, recreation. Of all these activities, land development for housing for people of middle-class high income groups can be self-financing and can generate profit for the private developers or development authority of the city. Construction of housing for the people of middle and high-income groups can also be self financing. The construction of low-income group housing and expansion of all other infrastructures requires large investment which must be financed through grants and loans from the national and state governments. Private capital can be mobilized for expansion of the infrastructure if adequate returns can be guaranteed through keeping rates for usage of water and electricity such as to provide an adequate return on the investment. It is essential also to minimize theft of electricity and water and other losses in distribution. The central and state governments should be prepared to make the necessary investment themselves or mobilize funds from the private sector in order that the metropolitan cities can continue to perform efficiently their roles as the political, commercial, industrial and cultural centers of the region in which they are located and the growth points in the regional and national economies. Since manufacturing industries and service activities in which productivity per worker is much higher than in agriculture are concentrated in the metropolitan cities, the contribution of the cities to GDP is much higher than their share of population. Furthermore, since the surpluses that lead to national growth originate mainly in the metropolitan cities, they can be regarded as an essential infrastructure of economic growth. The businessmen, industrialist and professionals who travel by air, and the white-collar workers who travel by railways are the principal bearer of knowledge from one region among people of other region. Such knowledge is essential for national integration because it is only through that the people of one region can understand and appreciate the values, customs and life styles of people of other regions.

CONCLUSION

Recognizing the metropolitan cities as essential infrastructures of economic growth and national integration, it is important to make adequate investment in expansion and improvement of infrastructure in them so that they can continue to perform their roles efficiently. The central and state governments should be prepared to make such investment themselves and also to mobilize private capital for them. Improvement of living conditions in the cities could also have a spread effect in improving productivity of the rural people. The number of metropolitan cities will increase progressively with more rapid economic growth. One way to ensure their efficient functioning is to have efficient well-staffed municipal corporations who have enough resources to undertake the expansion of the infrastructures. Most of the direct and indirect taxes collected by the central and state governments are collected from residents in the metropolitan cities. A proportion of the taxes collected in them should be returned to the metropolitan cities, with the stipulation that they be used for specific purposes. Thus a proportion of the excise duty on petrol and diesel collected in a metropolitan city and its satellite cities should be returned, with the stipulation that it be used for improvement of intra-city and inter-city roads and efficient management of traffic. A proportion of the sales tax could be returned to be used to meet the investment for financing expansion of water supplies. Transmission and distribution of electric supply to a metropolitan city should be handed over to private power supply companies instead of state electricity boards. They will themselves ensure that they make a profit in transmission and distribution and have the funds for financing a part of the generation.

Once the model for a workable growth of a metropolitan city has been accepted by the municipal and state governments, medium term plans for its growth should be formulated keeping the model in view. Such plans will be far more successful than the plans that were formulated in the 1960s and the 1970s but were not successful. They were based on an earlier model under which residential, industrial and commercial uses and government residents of people of different income groups were separated. These plans failed because in most of the cities these uses were mixed by the residents and could not be separated.

REFERENCE

Department of Economics and Statistics, Statistical Outline of India 2001-2002; Tata Services Limited; Mumbai.

16

Regional Planning for Large Metropolitan Cities: A Case Study of the National Capital Region[1]

With the sizes that our largest cities—Delhi, Bombay, Calcutta, Bangalore and Madras — have attained already[2] and their projected growth to the end of the century and beyond, regional planning with areal units much larger than the municipal areas of the cities or even their metropolitan areas, is becoming an essential part of planning for these cities.

The larger planning units are required for efficient achievement of some objectives, notably the following:

1. Dispersal of the growth potential of the city over a wider geographical area in order to avoid or mitigate on the one hand the high economic, social and environmental costs of too rapid growth of the city and to secure on the other, the benefits of accelerated economic growth and social change in the larger area;
2. Control of pollution of water and air in and around the city and preservation of ecological balance in the region, and
3. Expansion and improvement of physical infrastructures notably power, surface transport, water supply and disposal of solid and liquid wastes.

These imperatives of regional planning, which can be seen in all the cities, mentioned above, may be illustrated with Delhi as a case example.

Delhi has experienced very rapid growth during the last four decades. The population of the Delhi urban agglomeration[3] increased four-fold between 1951 and 1981—from 1.44 m to 5.74 m. The inter-censal rates of growth of 55 per cent to 64 per cent have been the highest among the five largest cities. Furthermore, the rapid growth is projected to continue. Population within the union territory of Delhi is projected to increase from 6.2 m in 1981 to 13.3 m by 2001 (Table 16.3).

The rapid growth has been due to expansion of employment in the three sectors of the economy the public sector, manufacturing industries and trade and commerce—which together provided employment to 80 per cent of the work force in urban Delhi in 1981. Besides being the national capital, Delhi has become a major industrial center, and has also acquired an enormously increased role as the principal distributive and financial center of a large region extending from Jammu and Kashmir and Rajasthan to central UP and northern Madhya Pradesh in the east.

But the city is already exhibiting symptoms of severe strain caused by too rapid growth. Thus, despite the enormous investment, both public and private, made in land development and housing and expansion/improvement of physical and economic infrastructures, there is a severe shortage of housing for the low-income groups resulting in extreme congestion and proliferation of slums. Essential urban services are severely strained because the available facilities are not adequate to meet the demands on them. Finally, the levels of water and air pollution have risen far beyond accepted international standards for maintaining health and efficiency.

Curbing too rapid growth of Delhi, through dispersal of the growth to the satellite towns and rural regions of the neighboring states, is a central objective of planning for Delhi.

The growth and physical expansion of the city has affected profoundly the land use, the ecology and the economic and social life of the surrounding areas. The metropolitan area of Delhi extends already far beyond the union territory of Delhi into Haryana and UP. Vast tracts of land (formerly agricultural, pasture, forest or waste) have been converted to non-agricultural uses—for location of housing colonies, industrial estates, markets, offices of central, state or local governments, or of various physical or social infrastructures. The process continues with further large areas being similarly converted or awaiting conversion.

The economic and social effects of the rapid growth on the residents of the villages and small towns located within the region (and beyond it) are felt through changes in their employment, income, consumption patterns, life style, social attitudes and values. Increases in income result from sale of land by the landowners for conversion to non-agricultural uses, from reorientation of agriculture to meet the increasing demands of the expanding metropolis for food, particularly high value perishable foods such as milk, vegetables, meat and poultry products, and from employment in the metropolitan area. Large numbers of people commute daily from their homes in villages or small towns to the metropolitan area—for work, for sale of agricultural produce, for purchase of consumer goods or inputs of agriculture or small industries, or for various other reasons including recreation. The results of the greatly increased urban-rural interaction are seen in major changes in the life styles, social attitudes and values of the people; their traditional patterns and norms are progressively replaced or modified to conform to those of the big city.

Finally, for expansion and improvement of some physical infrastructures for meeting the increasing demands of the city, it is necessary to tap sources of supplies located at long distances or to take measures which have effects over long distances. The city's demand for water is being met by bringing it from as far away as the Ganga river in UP and more distant sources may have to be tapped in future. Discharge of its treated or untreated sewerage into the Yamuna has led to serious pollution of the river over a long stretch, and it is necessary to take measures to reduce pollution urgently to ensure access to water supplies of acceptable quality to the cities and towns located downstream of Delhi. Delhi's demand for power is being met by drawing large blocks of it from the Bhakra, UP and Rajasthan power grids. Some of the power needs will be met in future by the nuclear power station which is being constructed at Narora in UP. Linking of Delhi's power system with the systems of the adjoining states facilitates adjustment of supplies to diurnal and seasonal variations in demand for power.

Enormous investments have been made in expansion/improvement of surface transport (road and rail) to handle the vastly increased passenger and goods traffic to-and-from Delhi, and to improve the city's links with its satellite and other towns in the neighboring states, and with the rest of the country. Some of the projects have aimed at construction of bypasses around Delhi to reduce traffic to-and-from the city.

The response of the central and/or the state governments to the need for regional planning for the largest cities is to designate planning regions, which extend far beyond their metropolitan areas and include large rural areas, besides numerous smaller cities or towns, and to constitute regional planning boards or authorities for them. The National Capital Region includes besides the union territory of Delhi, three districts of UP and the districts and tehsils of Haryana and parts of Alwar district of Rajasthan as indicated below.

1. Union territory of Delhi (1,483 square kilometers).
2. Haryana sub-region (13,413 square kilometers) comprising Faridabad, Gurgaon, Rohtak and Sonepat districts; Rewari and Bawal tehsils of Mahendragarh district and Panipat tehsil of Karnal district.
3. Uttar Pradesh sub-region (10,853 square kilometers) comprising 3 districts—Meerut, Ghaziabad and Bulandshahr.
4. Rajasthan sub-region (4,493 square kilometers) comprising six tehsils of Alwar district namely, Alwar, Ramgarh, Behroor, Mandawar, Kishangarh and Tijara.

It has within it, almost 6,700 villages and 94 cities and towns. Of its total area of more than 30,000 sq. kms, only 1,483 sq. kms or less than 5 per cent, is included within the union territory of Delhi, although the latter had in 1981 almost one-third of its total population—6.2 m out of 19.2 m (Table 16.1).

Table 16.1: Area and Population of the NCR (1961-81)

Sub-Region	*Area in 1981 (in sq kms)*	*Population (in millions)*		
		1961	*1971*	*1981*
Union territory of Delhi	1483 (4.90)	2.66 (25.11)	4.06 (28.91)	6.22 (32.41)
Haryana	13413 (44.36)	2.89 (27.33)	3.80 (27.01)	4.93 (25.73)
Rajasthan	4493 (14.86)	0.58 (5.52)	0.76 (5.39)	1.07 (5.55)
Uttar Pradesh	10853 (35.88)	4.45 (42.04)	5.44 (38.69)	6.97 (36.31)
NCR	30242 (100.00)	10.58 (100.00)	14.06 (100.00)	19.19 (100.00)

Sources: IDP '87 Table 2.5 p 13.
Note: Figures in brackets indicate proportions of respective totals for the NCR.

The National Capital Region Planning Board (NCRPB) has been constituted to prepare and oversee implementation of a long-term regional development plan. The Bombay Metropolitan Region, for which the Bombay Metropolitan Regional Development Authority (BMRDA) has been constituted, includes besides the area of the Bombay Municipal Corporation, the whole of Thane district and parts of Raigarh and Ratnagiri districts of Maharashtra.

The difficult problem of delineating the planning regions has been mitigated by making the regions coterminous with existing administrative units—districts, talukas or tehsils. This solution, although not entirely satisfactory from the methodological standpoint (e g, of the regional geographer), or for some operational purposes of planning, such as expansion of power or water supplies, has the advantage of administrative convenience. It is much easier to prepare and oversee implementation of a development plan for a region, the constituent parts of which already have administrative structures established for them. A whole range of problems, from collection of the data needed for planning to creating administrative structures for implementation of the regional plan, for a region, and its constituent parts can be solved with this solution.

The nature, scope and objectives of regional plans and the functions of regional planning bodies, such as the NCRPB and the BMRDA, have to be clearly distinguished from the objectives and scope of city or metropolitan plans, and the functions and responsibilities of the city or metropolitan planning authorities. The regional plan provides the conceptual and operational frameworks for preparation of:

a. A land use plan for the region;
b. Sectoral plans for expansion/improvement of housing and of various physical and social infrastructures;
c. Local development plans for both the metropolitan city and the other cities or towns located within the region, and
d. Plans for control of environmental pollution and preservation of ecological balance in the region.

The focus of the regional plan is on policies and strategies, and the principal function of the regional planning body is to prepare and oversee implementation of the regional plan. It must ensure that the framework provided by the regional plan is adhered to in formulation of various policy measures, and in preparation of sectoral and local development plans.

Development plans for the municipal or metropolitan areas of the cities are concerned primarily with detailed planning of land use and indicating in broad outline the Sectoral development programmes/ projects, needed for supporting the land use plan, and for providing minimum standards of housing and essential services to the existing and projected future population of the city. In many plans, the focus is on detailed land use planning i.e., designation of areas for residential, industrial, commercial and various other uses, and elaboration of policies and programmes for implementation of the land-use plan. The needs for expansion/improvement of physical and social infrastructures and the proposed sectoral development programmes/ projects are outlined; but preparation of the latter is left to specialized functional agencies. Control or reduction of environmental pollution is a relatively recent concern of city or metropolitan planning, and few plans outline policies or programmes to achieve it.

Development plans for many cities are prepared by the municipal bodies themselves. But the practice of constituting development authorities, separate from and independent of the municipal bodies, has grown during the last 3 decades and such authorities have been constituted for many cities including several cities which are not very large. These bodies frequently have, besides their functions of plan formulation, some responsibilities for plan implementation. The latter relate most frequently to land development, and in some cases, to construction of houses for the low and middle-income groups. In case of some authorities, these other responsibilities are so large as to over-shadow their plan formulation function. Thus, the Delhi Development Authority (DDA), constituted in 1957 for preparation of the first Master Plan of Delhi, its revision from time to time, and overseeing its implementation, has assumed over the years, the functions of land development and construction of housing on a massive scale. Furthermore, it has acquired some purely municipal functions, such as approval of plans for houses, markets etc, in the colonies developed by it. These functions have become so large that the planning function has been relegated to the background. The Calcutta Metropolitan Development Authority (CMDA), the successor to the Calcutta Metropolitan Planning Organization (CMPO), which was constituted in the early 1960s to prepare a long-term master plan for the Calcutta Metropolitan District, is similarly pre-occupied with implementation of sectoral development programmes or projects.

This review of the "Draft Regional Plan 2001, National Capital Region" (DRP), published by the NCRPB in July 1987, is intended to be a case study of regional planning for a large metropolitan city. The study is of particular interest because of the distinctive problems and opportunities for regional planning that arise from the status of Delhi as the national capital, and from its location on the borders of UP and Haryana, and not far from the border of Rajasthan. The most important among these are the following:

1. Unlike the planning regions of the other metropolitan cities, mentioned above, which are all located within single states, the NCR extends over the territories of 4 state-level entities—the union territory of Delhi and the states of UP, Haryana and Rajasthan. This composition delayed the establishment of a statutory planning board for the NCR by almost a quarter century because the state governments were afraid that a statutory board would infringe on their powers of planning for their areas included within the NCR.
2. Furthermore, it increases immensely the magnitude and the complexity of the tasks of co-ordination and collaboration in plan formulation and implementation. The responsibility for these tasks is not confined, as in regional planning for the other cities, to the departments and specialized functional organizations of a single state government and to the local government agencies under it, but is spread among departments, functional organizations and local government agencies under 4 state-level entities, besides various sectoral ministries of the central government and functional organizations under it.
3. The association and interest of the central government in planning for the NCR is more direct and also greater than in planning for the other cities. This is both an opportunity and a problem. The central government is expected to, and has assumed thus far, the leadership role in planning for the NCR. The NCRPB has been created by an act of Parliament, is

attached to the Ministry of Urban Development of the central government and has the Minister of Urban Development as its Chairman. The prospects of financing and implementing the NCR Plan will be determined primarily by the interest in the plan of the central government; the state governments and the financial institutions (both domestic and international) will follow the lead given by the central government. Delhi has received very large grants and loans for its development from the central government in the past. But, as discussed later, continuation into the future of this favored status and allocation of the funds needed to finance the enormous investment envisaged in the DRP, is open to serious question. Furthermore, the interest of the central government in the NCR plan breeds within the state governments an attitude of "leaving it to the center".

This review, although based on the DRP, draws materials also from the second Interim Development Plan (IDP '87), published by the NCRPB in February 1987. Reference to this document became necessary because important details of policy measures, needed for achievement of the objectives of the DRP, and estimates of investment for the sectoral development programmes, or projects, envisaged in it, which had been given in the IDP, have been omitted from the DRP. The latter explains that the details of the policy measures, and the costs of programmes/projects will be worked out by the concerned central ministries/departments of the state governments, and other agencies, as and when the programmes/projects are prepared. But details of the policy measures and estimates of investment are of great interest, because they indicate the nature of the measures that are under consideration of the NCRPB or of the concerned governments, and the order of magnitude of the investment envisaged in the Plan. An evaluation of the Plan would be greatly handicapped in the absence of these.

THE REGION AND THE INSTITUTIONAL STRUCTURES OF PLANNING

Details of the Composition of the National Capital Region (NCR), and areas and populations of its constituent units, have been given above. Within the NCR, a smaller areal unit, the Delhi Metropolitan Area (DMA) has been distinguished in the DRP. The DMA includes the union territory of Delhi and six towns—Faridabad-Ballabhgarh, Gurgaon, Bahadurgarh, and Kundli in Haryana, and Ghaziabad-Loni and NOIDA in UP—which are contiguous with the union territory and which form with it a predominantly urban area. Faridabad-Ballabhgarh and Ghaziabad-Loni are the largest among the towns (Table 16.2).

Table 16.2: Population and Growth Characteristics of Dam Towns

Constituent Units of NCR	*Population (1981) in lakhs*	*Decadal Growth (Per Cent)*		
		1951-61	*1961-71*	*1971-81*
Delhi UT	62.20	52.43	52.92	52.98
Bahadurgarh	0.37	34.43	72.28	45.23
Faridabad-Ballabhgarh	3.31	57.88	103.42	169.39
Ghaziabad including Loni	2.97	61.01	68.71	141.65
Gurgaon	1.01	103.42	50.94	76.50
Kundli	–	—Did not exist till 1981—		
NOIDA	0.42			

Source: DRP, Table 2.9, p 20.

Four of the six towns had existed before 1981; Noida is a new town developed since 1981, and Kundli has yet to come into existence. Three towns—Faridabad-Ballabhgarh, Ghaziabad-Loni and Gurgaon—have grown much faster than the union territory of Delhi during the three decades 1951-81.

NCR PLANNING BOARD

The need for a regional approach to planning for the national capital was recognized by the central government as far back as 1961 when the first draft Master Plan for Delhi was being finalized. The plan recommended designation of a National Capital Region including the union territory of Delhi and adjoining areas of the neighboring states, and establishment of a statutory board for preparation and overseeing implementation of a regional plan. However, the government of India established in 1961 an advisory board within the ministry of home affairs. The board was reconstituted in 1973 with the minister of works, housing and supplies as the chairman, and the chief ministers of Haryana, UP and Rajasthan and the Lt. Governor of Delhi, and some senior officials from the central ministries and these states as members.

A statutory board was not constituted due, as mentioned above, to the opposition to it of the state governments of UP and Haryana. Meanwhile, rapid expansion of the metropolitan area of Delhi into adjoining areas of UP and Haryana continued with profound changes in land use, ecology and economy of the areas. The governments of the two states encouraged and supported the expansion by providing liberal incentives for location of industries and other economic activities, and by making large investments in land development and housing, and expansion/improvement of physical and social infrastructures. These incentives and investments were concentrated in towns like Ghaziabad and NOIDA in UP and Faridabad-Ballabhgarh and Gurgaon in Haryana, which have been developed as residential-cum-industrial centers. The constitution of the statutory NCRPB and the impetus to planning for the NCR following it, mark recognition by the two state governments of the logical sequence of these developments.

The board is attached, as mentioned earlier, to the ministry of urban development of the central government, and has the minister of urban development as its chairman. The other members are the chief ministers of UP, Haryana and Rajasthan, the Lt. Governor of Delhi, and 16 other members including a full-time member-secretary. In addition the chief minister of Madhya Pradesh and 4 senior officials representing ministries of the central government, not represented earlier, and adviser (HUD) Planning Commission, have been co-opted as members.

The functions of the board relate primarily to formulation, and monitoring implementation of development plans for the NCR. It is assisted by a planning committee which consists of senior officials from ministries/departments of the central government and the governments of the 3 states and the union territory, and of functional organizations, notably the Town and Country Planning Organization (TCPO) and the DDA, and a convener-member from the NCRPB. The planning staff of the NCRPB consists at present of about 20 professionals—architects, town planners, engineers, economists and other specialists.

The staff has been assisted in formulation of the DRP and the two interim development plans (IDPs) published in August 1986 and February 1987, by study groups consisting of senior officials of the ministries of central government, departments of the staff governments and the union territory of Delhi, and various functional organizations. Sectoral development programmes have been formulated by these groups, 8 of which had been constituted for preparation of the DRP. In addition, 8 studies on subjects of special interest, such as migration and identification of counter-magnet areas, have been undertaken by specialized institutions, such as the National Institute of Urban Affairs, New Delhi.

OTHER STRUCTURES FOR URBAN PLANNING

Among the other structures for formulation and implementation of urban development plans in the region, the most important are the TCPO, the DDA, the town planning departments of the state governments, the Haryana Urban Development Authority and the Meerut Development Authority.

THE DRAFT REGIONAL PLAN 2001

Planning for the NCR can be considered to have begun in the 1970s under the NCR advisory board. A large volume of data was collected and a number of studies were done under the Board which have been utilized for preparation of the two IDPs and the DRP. This work done in various sectoral ministries of the central government, departments of the state governments and functional organizations, particularly the TCPO and the DDA, made possible publication of the first IDP in 1986 within a year of establishment of the statutory NCRPB.

The Draft Regional Plan (DRP) represents revision and elaboration of the two IDPs. Reference has been made above to omission in the DRP of the details of policy measures and of estimates of investment which had been given in the IDPs. On the other hand, the DRP is a more comprehensive document than either IDP. It contains chapters on education, health, counter-magnet areas, land use, environment and eco-development, management structures for the NCR, and strategies and 'priority' areas for development, which had not been included in the IDPs. Furthermore, the chapter on transport has been completely revised.

There is no change, however, between the DRP and the IDPs in the objectives and strategy of development of the NCR, viz., (i) to reduce the rapid growth of economic activities and of population in the union territory by encouraging dispersal of growth to other parts of the NCR or to the counter magnet cities located outside it; (ii) to provide minimum standards of essential services to the urban and rural populations of the NCR, through expansion/improvement of various physical and social infrastructures.

But, the recommendations on policy measures, to achieve the 'dispersal of growth' objective, contained in the IDPs, have been modified in the DRP to meet objections or to make them more effective. Secondly, while the details of sectoral programmes/projects have been omitted, the coverage of the sectors and listing of the targets of accomplishment by the year 2001 in the various sectors is more comprehensive.

The DRP will be finalized, after considering objections to it; the final NCR plan is expected to become available by the end of 1987, or shortly thereafter.

Meanwhile, preparation of the sectoral programmes/projects envisaged in the DRP, by the concerned sectoral ministries/departments of the central or state governments or by other agencies, under the general direction of the NCRPB, is in progress. The programmes/projects will be phased appropriately for financing during the remaining two years of the Seventh Plan, but principally under the Eighth or the Ninth Plan. Overseeing and expediting preparation of the programmes/projects and ensuring appropriate inter-project and inter-sectoral linkages among them will be an important task of the NCRPB, after approval of the NCR plan.

Sub-regional plans for their respective areas have also begun to be prepared by the governments of the three states and the union territory. Local development plans will be prepared by the municipal bodies, or agencies such as the development authorities of various cities, with assistance and direction provided by the town planning departments of the state governments. The plans are already being prepared for three towns—Meerut (UP), Panipat (Haryana) and Alwar (Rajasthan) which have been selected for priority development from 1988/89.

The sectoral, sub-regional and local plans will be implemented by the various agencies within their respective sectoral or areal jurisdictions. The NCR plan will thus provide the overall framework within which the various plans are prepared and implemented.

PERSPECTIVE PLAN 2001 FOR DELHI

The Perspective Plan for Delhi (PPD) was approved by the ministry of urban development in July 1987 and is reported to be awaiting approval of the cabinet. The first draft of the perspective plan prepared by the DDA in April 1985[4], was not approved by the central government because of numerous objections to it, and the government requested the Delhi Urban Arts Commission to review and, if necessary, to revise the plan. The commission published in 1986 a Conceptual Plan: Delhi 2001[5]. The PPD represents a further revision of the two documents. It may be mentioned that the PPD, which is the second master plan for Delhi, will be published 25 years after publication of the first master plan in 1962.

Objectives and Strategy of Planning for NCR

Planning for the NCR has two principal objectives:

1. To reduce the rapid growth of economic activities and of population in the union territory of Delhi by directing the growth outside it—to the six DMA towns and particularly to other towns of the NCR, and
2. To ensure provision of minimum standards of essential services to the urban and rural populations of the NCR through expansion/improvement of various physical and social infrastructures.

The DRP and the two IDPs have outlined policy measures and development programmes/projects to achieve these objectives. These include administrative sanctions, fiscal incentives (or disincentives), and programmes of land development and expansion/ improvement of physical and social infrastructures in the union territory, in the DMA towns and selected other towns of the NCR, and improvement of transport and communication links between the towns and the union territory. The programmes are designed also to assist in providing the minimum standards of essential services to the population of the NCR projected for 2001. The IDP '87 had designated 11 towns located within the NCR, outside the DMA as towns to be selected for 'priority development'. These towns are located at distances of 50 to 130 kilometers from Delhi and had in 1981 populations ranging from 47,000 (Palwal in Haryana) to 5,36,000 (Meerut in UP).

Projected and 'Assigned' Populations For 2001

The DRP and the IDPs have used the projections of growth of the urban and rural populations of the NCR and its constituent units to the year 2001, made by the Registrar General of India, using the method of urban-rural growth differentials, recommended by the Population Division of the United Nations for projecting population of urban areas.

The total population of the NCR is projected to increase from 19.2 m in 1981 to 25.4 m by 1991 and 32.5 m by 2001, the average annual rates of increase being 2.8 per cent for 1981-91, and 2.5 per cent for 1991-2001 (Table 16.3).

Table 16.3: Population Projections for the NCR

(Population in lakhs)

Sub-Region		*Population*	*Projected*	*Population*
		1981	*1991*	*2001*
Delhi UT*	Total	62.2	92.5	132.6
	Rural	4.5	4.4	3.6
	Urban	57.7	88.1	129.0
Haryana	Total	49.4	62.7	72.1
	Rural	37.3	40.3	34.4
	Urban	12.1	22.4	37.7
Rajasthan	Total	10.6	11.3	11.9
	Rural	8.9	8.7	8.5
	Urban	1.7	2.6	3.4
Uttar Pradesh	Total	69.7	87.6	108.6
	Rural	50.2	51.8	45.0
	Urban	19.5	35.8	63.6
NCR	Total	191.9	254.1	325.2
	Rural	100.9	105.2	91.5
	Urban	91.0	148.9	233.7

Source: DRP, Table 2.10, p 20.
Note: *Projection for Delhi UT is based on the draft recommendations of the Expert Committee on population appointed by the planning Commission.

Much faster growth rates of 5 per cent for 1981-91 and 4.5 per cent for 1991-2001, are projected for the urban population. The rural population, on the other hand, is projected to decline from 10.1 m in 1981 to 9.15 m by 2001.

The population of the union territory of Delhi, 6.22 m in 1981, is projected to more than double, to 13.3 m by 2001. However, having in view the need to curb the rapid growth of Delhi, a smaller, 'more manageable' population of 11.2 m by 2001, has been 'assigned' to the union territory (Table 16.4). The corresponding reduction in the population of the DMA is from 17.0 m (projected) to 15.0 m (assigned). Ninety seven per cent of the population of the DMA would be urban by 2001.

Table 16.4: Population Assignment by 2001 for Delhi, DMA AND NCR

(*In lakhs*)

	Population 2001					
Area	*Projected*			*Assigned*		
	Total	*Urban*	*Rural*	*Total*	*Urban*	*Rural*
Region	325	234	91	325	234	91
Delhi sub–region	132	129	3	112	110	2
Haryana sub Region	72	38	34	78	43.5	34.5
Rajasthan Sub Region	12	3.5	8.5	14	5	9
Uttar Pradesh Sub Region	109	63.5	45.5	121	75.5	45.5
	Delhi Metropolitan Area					
(a) Total	170	166	4	150	147	3
(b) Delhi				112	110	2
(c) Haryana				21	20.5	0.5
(d) UP				17	16.5	0.5
DMA Towns				37	37	–
(a) Ghaziabad including Loni		NA		11	11	–
(b) NOIDA				5.5	5.5	
(c) Faridabad				10	10	
(d) Gurgaon				7	7	
(e) Bahadurgarh				2	2	
(f) Kundli				1.5	1.5	
Other areas outside DMA				175	87	88
(a) Haryana				57	23	34
(b) Rajasthan				14	5	9
(c) UP				104	59	45

Source: DRP, Table 2.13, p. 23.

The reduction in growth of population is to be achieved through reduction in migration into the union territory, during the decade 1991-2001 to a minimum of 50 per cent of the rate for 1981-91; migration during 1981-91 would continue, as it would have in the absence of the measures aimed at reducing it (Table 16.5).

Table 16.5: Controlled Population Projection of Delhi UT, 1981-2001

Year	*Population Lakhs*	*Net Increase Lakhs*	*Decadal Growth Rate (Per Cent)*	*Decadal Growth by*	
				Natural Increase (Lakhs)	*Immigration (Lakhs)*
			Actual		
1961	26.59				
1971	40.66	14.07	52.91	8.82 (33.17)	5.25 (19.74)
1981	62.20	21.54	52.98	9.24 (22.74)	12.30 (30.24)
			Projected		
1991	92.55	30.35	48.79	12.44 (20.00)	17.91 (28.79)
2001	112.00	19.45	21.01	11.11 (12.00)	8.34 (9.12)

Source: DRP, Table 2.11, p. 21.

* Figures in brackets indicate components of decadal growth rate in per cent-age terms.

The reduction in migration is sought to be achieved, through restricting growth in the three major sectors of the economy of the union territory—the public sector, manufacturing industries and the distributive trades—which, as mentioned earlier, together provided employment to 80 per cent of the workforce in urban Delhi in 1981 (Table 16.6).

Growth of employment in the public sector, in which 29 per cent of the work force was engaged in 1981, and which had experienced very rapid growth rates during the two previous decades, 1961-71 (161 per cent) and 1971-81 (30 per cent), is to be curbed through a range of measures, to be taken by the central government and the public enterprises under it. Growth in manufacturing industries and in the distributive trades is to be reduced primarily by severely restricting growth of these activities within the union territory, and to

Table 16.6: Distribution of Work Force in Urban Delhi: 1951 to 1981

Categories	*1951*		*1961*		*1971*		*1981*	
	Workers	*%*	*Workers*	*%*	*Workers*	*%*	*Workers*	*%*
Primary sector	5588	1.1	11866	1.6	17870	1.6	16744	0.9
Manufacturing, processing Household industry	6632	1.3	12682	1.7	25107	2.2	31349	1.69
Other then household	80639	15.7	155099	20.7	242733	21.7	510748	27.49
`Construction	44948	8.7	32540	4.4	61517	5.5	118699	6.39
Trade and commerce	117338	22.8	143809	19.3	239719	21.6	413430	22.25
Transport and communications	34455	6.7	47387	6.3	107324	9.6	168457	9.07
Other services	224426	43.7	343430	46.0	422667	37.8	584664*	31.47*
Total workers	514026	100.0	746815	100.0	1116937	100.0	1857545	100.0
Population	1437134	–	2359408	–	3647023	–	5768200	–
Participation ratio	27.96	–	31.65	–	30.62	–	32.20	–

Source: Adapted from IDP '87, Table 4.1, p. 29.

a lesser extent in the other DMA towns, and promoting the growth in the other cities and towns of the NCR, especially the 'priority' towns. The more important measures are listed below.

Growth of employment in the public sector in the union territory of Delhi is to be severely curtailed by restricting location of new offices or expansion of existing offices—of the central government, of the public sector enterprises, of the Delhi administration or of other local authorities. This is to be achieved through strict enforcement of the accepted policies and criteria for location of offices in Delhi, viz.

(a) "That they perform ministerial functions, protocol functions or liaison functions which, by their nature, cannot be performed anywhere else except in the National Capital. The existing offices which do not perform any of the above functions should be identified and shifted from Delhi. In the case of public sector offices, there is an urgent need to scrutinize the list of existing offices and allow them to retain only very small establishments to cater for corporate and liaison functions. The rest of the establishments should be shifted out of Delhi..."
(b) "...A similar control on the opening of new central government and public sector offices in the DMA towns should be exercised" (p. 8)[6].
(c) "The offices of public sector undertakings which deal with the northern region and are functioning in Delhi... should be located in the other towns of NCR."
(d) In order to provide incentives for shifting of existing offices and against location of new offices, facilities, such as house rent and city compensation allowances, available to employees in Delhi or the other DMA towns, should continue to be available for some years also in the NCR towns to which the offices are shifted/located.

Dispersal of manufacturing industries is to be achieved by:

1. Continuing the present policy of not promoting location of medium and large scale industries within Delhi, and restricting location of even small scale industries to those employing 20 or less persons, and required either for providing or servicing the consumer needs of Delhi's population.

2. Control outside Delhi but within the DMA: No large scale or medium scale industries should be permitted to be set up also in the DMA. Only small scale units should be permitted in it.
3. Incentives for industries outside the DMA but within the national capital region: The towns selected for priority development should have a strong industrial content, and incentives should be given for location of large, medium and small scale industries in them by developing industrial estates in these towns. In addition to these towns, there should be no restrictions on the growth of industries in the region except in the areas reserved for conservation (p. 9).

The recommendation in IDP '87 relating to discouraging, amounting to practical prohibition of location of polluting, and other non-conforming industries in the DMA towns, and shifting of the existing units in such industries out of the union territory of Delhi has been dropped in the DRP, which emphasizes instead, strict enforcement of pollution control measures. It recommends also a number of other measures including establishment of a joint board for prevention and control of pollution of water and air (p. 12). But considering the past record, and the present situation of indifferent enforcement (or non-enforcement) of most of these measures and the probable delay in establishing the board and making it effective, this policy change can only slow down efforts to reduce water and air pollution in the UT and the other DMA towns.

The recommendations relating to the distributive trades are the following:

1. Disincentive within Delhi: An approach of disincentives to the wholesale trades which are not directly consumed in Delhi should be adopted. Only those wholesale trades which are directly used and consumed in Delhi and are not hazardous in nature and do not require extensive space, should be allowed to continue in Delhi.
2. Controlled development outside Delhi within DMA: The policy of checks and disincentives is also to be followed in case of the DMA towns, but with some relaxations. Only those wholesale trades which are directly used and consumed

in Delhi and the DMA towns should be allowed. There are certain wholesale trades in Delhi which are hazardous because of their location in congested areas and due to bulk handling activities such as plastic and PVC goods, chemical, timber, foodgrains, iron and steel and building materials. These wholesale trades should be encouraged to develop in DMA towns.

3. Outside DMA within NCR: Incentives, concessions and infrastructures should be made available in the regional towns to encourage and accelerate the growth of trade (p. 8).

The dispersal of distributive trades will reduce the extreme congestion in the old city caused by their concentration in it, and the hazards to life and property caused by the location of trade in hazardous goods. Furthermore, it will reduce greatly movement of goods in-and-out of the union territory, and will also strengthen the economic base of the 'priority' towns. Reference is made to a survey conducted by the DDA in 1981 which revealed that excepting goods like building materials, which have low value per unit of weight or volume, 50 to 95 per cent of the goods coming into the union territory were sent out of it (p. 46). This movement would be greatly reduced by shifting the distributive trades to the 'priority' towns. A large proportion of the movement of passengers through Delhi, caused at present by lack of transfer facilities at other railway stations within the region, could also be avoided through development of these facilities (IDP '87 p. 54).

The thrust of the policy measures is on encouraging the shifts through a system of administrative checks and fiscal incentives/ disincentives. The DRP gives particular emphasis to the latter for promoting dispersal of manufacturing industries and the distributive trades outside the union territory. Thus, it recommends elimination of the present lower rates of sales tax for most commodities, and also of many other taxes in the union territory than in the three states, and that "fiscal policies within the region should be so harmonized that the region comes to have the character of a unified whole and the growth of the different constituents of the region takes place on the basis of their comparative advantages" (p. 55).

The two IDPs had made specific proposals for shifting of particular trades to particular towns, mainly the 'priority' towns

(Table 16.7). This recommendation has been dropped, however, in the DRP as mentioned below.

Table 16.7: Proposed Shifting Of Distributive Trades from Delhi to Other Towns

Trade Items	*Towns*
Cloth	Modinagar, Meerut, Rohtak, Alwar
Bicycles	Sonepat, Rewari
Fruits and vegetables	Meerut, Alwar, Sonepat
Motor parts and machinery	Meerut, Alwar
Dry fruits, spices and Herbs	Khurja, Rohtak, Alwar
Hosiery	Panipat, Meerut
Iron and Steel	Alwar
Fuel Oil	Meerut, Alwar
Foodgrains	Hapur, Meerut, Rewari, Alwar, Khairthal
Timber	Alwar, Baraut
Furs and Skins	Alwar, Panipat
Fodder	Rohtak, Khurja
Pulses	Khurja, Rewari, Hapur, Khairthal

Source: IDP '87, p 40.

The policy measures will be supported by the sectoral development programmes. It is necessary to mention, in particular, the programme for the transport sector which is focused on diversion of passenger and freight traffic from the union territory to the other DMA towns and particularly to the 'priority' towns. This will be achieved through:

(a) Upgrading the national and state highways connecting Delhi with the other DMA towns and the 'priority' towns;
(b) Constructing road and rail by-passes around Delhi; and
(c) Developing the facilities for handling greatly increased freight and passenger traffic within the DMA the 'priority' towns.

SECTORAL DEVELOPMENT PROGRAMMES

The DRP gives, after evaluation of the existing facilities in all the important sectors, general or specific indications of the needs for expansion/improvement of physical or social infrastructures for achievement of its central objectives of dispersal of economic activities from the union territory, and for attaining minimum standards of basic services for the urban and rural populations of the NCR projected for 2001. Specific projects have been identified, however, for a few sectors only, notably power, roads and railways, and telecommunications. For all other sectors, only targets to be reached by the year 2001 have been listed.

Achievement of the targets for physical and social infrastructures will involve major expansion/improvement of facilities in most sectors. Figures for six infrastructure sectors for the union territory of Delhi alone, given in Table 16.8 indicate needs for expansion of facilities by 228 to 535 per cent.

The other major omission in the DRP is, as noted earlier, of estimates of costs of projects/programmes. The omissions of details of projects/programmes and of cost estimates can be justified on the ground that these will undergo major changes during detailed formulation of projects/programmes. On the other hand, in the absence of estimates of costs, there is no indication of the financial commitment that approval of the NCR plan will involve for the central government or the state governments.

Table 16.8: Infrastructures Growth And Requirements In Delhi: 1961-2001

Service (Units)	*Augmentation Achieved 1961-81*			*Augmentation Required by 2001*	
	1961	*1981*	*Per Cent Increase 1981/1961*	*2001*	*Per Cent Increase 2001/1981*
Water (MGD)	78	335	429	1024	306
Sewerage (MGD)	36	118	328	902	275
Electricity (MW)	80	650	813	2568	395
Telephone lines ('000)	27	224	830	1200	536
Hospital beds ('000)	7	14	200	61	436
Student seats in schools	400	1450	322	3300	228

Source: IDP '87, Table 2.12, p. 17.

COST AND FINANCE

In order to give some idea of the magnitude of the public investment required for implementation of the NCR Plan, the estimates, albeit partial and very rough, of the investment, given in the two IDPs, have been used here. Both of them had envisaged an investment of Rs. 3,040 crore by the year 2001, presumably at 1985 prices (Table 16.9).

Table 16.9: Projected Public Investment 1985-2001—Six Selected Sectors

(*Million Rupees*)

	Sector	*Tentative Cost Estimates*
1.	Land acquisition and development	10107*
2.	Roads	2921
3.	Railways	2424
4.	Telecommunications	1380
5.	Development of Economic Activities	1000
6.	Physical infrastructure (excluding power, water, sewerage and sanitaion)	12584
	Total	30417

Note: *Required as seed capital.

Source: IDP '87, Table 10.7, p. 90.

One-third of the investment, Rs. 1,010 crore, was projected for land acquisition and development; the remainder was mainly for projects in the water supply, sewerage and sanitation, transport and telecommunications sectors. Investments in power, housing and slum improvement, or in the social service sectors—education, health, social welfare and others—or for reducing levels of water and air pollution, were not included. Furthermore, investments within the union territory of Delhi were included only in so far as they formed part of investments in NCR projects, e.g., in roads, railways and telecommunications facilities linking Delhi with the other DMA towns or the 'priority' towns. After these investments are included and the escalation in projects costs since 1985 is provided for, the estimated total public investment in the NCR would be much higher than Rs. 3,040 crore.

The DRP has indicated the principal sources of finance for implementation of the NCR plan. These include grants and loans from the central and state governments, loans from the Life Insurance

Corporation, nationalized banks and other public sector financial institutions, and market borrowings through floating debentures/bonds.

International financial institutions have not been listed as possible sources of finance. These, particularly the World Bank and the Asian Development Bank, could however be important sources of finance for well-prepared projects with high internal rates of return (IRRs). Technical assistance for project formulation and appraisal could be obtained, if required, from these institutions as also from appropriate agencies of the UN system.

Grants and loans from the central and state governments may be expected to be the largest source of finance. Their magnitude, as also the prospects of raising significant funds from the financial institutions, domestic and international, will be determined mainly by the commitment of the central government and the three state governments, to financing the NCR Plan. The commitment of the central government is of crucial importance, because all others—the state governments and the financial institutions—will follow the lead given by it.

PROSPECTS OF FINANCING

The total needs for public investment in the NCR, even for partial (but substantive) achievement of the targets indicated in the DRP will be very large—much larger per capita, or per unit of area, than the averages for the other areas of UP and Rajasthan, and probably also of Haryana. The areas of UP and Haryana, included within the NCR, are already more developed and richer than most other areas of the states, having experienced more rapid economic growth than the latter during the last 3 decades. The growth has been due partly to the spill-over effects of the rapid growth of Delhi, and partly to the Green Revolution in agriculture which these areas have experienced along with most other areas of western UP and Haryana. The growth has been supported by large public investments, made by both the central government and the state governments. The governments may not be willing to continue, however, this 'favoured treatment' for a relatively developed, 'rich' and rapidly urbanizing region. The reluctance and the political pressures against large resource allocations for their NCR areas, will be particularly strong in UP and Rajasthan, in which the NCR areas are small in relation to the total sizes of the states—the NCR area of UP has 3.7 per cent of the total area of the state and had in 1981 only 6.3 per cent of its population. The reluctance would not be reduced greatly by the fact of financing of most of the investments by the central government, because the investments would be included in the plans of the states, and it would be argued that the funds, if not invested within the NCR, would be available for investment in the other, poorer and less developed regions of the states. It will not be easy for the state governments or the central government to counter such arguments and to make the large allocations needed for implementation of the NCR plan.

The tentative allocation of Rs 65 crore for the Seventh Plan period, (just over 2 per cent of the projected total outlay of Rs. 3,040 crore of the NCR Plan) made by the Planning Commission in 1986 was not helpful; it indicated both the difficulty of financing the NCR Plan and perhaps also the low priority that the central government gave to it.

The outlook for financing of the NCR Plan has worsened further as a result of the failure of the monsoon during the current year (1987-88) and the consequent near certainty of a large drop in agricultural output and low or negative economic growth. Since the Eighth Five-Year Plan is being formulated against this background, top priority may be expected to be given in it to agriculture and manufacturing industry, and to the expansion of the physical infrastructure facilities, such as power and transport, needed for supporting recovery and growth in the two sectors, particularly by removing or mitigating present shortages. In case of social and welfare services, emphasis in the Plan will be on meeting the basic needs, particularly of the rural poor. Housing and urban development may, therefore, continue to be given low priority with the small allocations for them tied, as in the last two plans, to programmes such as housing for the rural and urban poor, slum improvement and water supply and sanitation.

The NCRPB will therefore need to convince both the central and the state governments of the following:

1. That the NCR plan provides a viable and effective strategy for preventing congestion and environmental deterioration in Delhi increasing to unacceptable levels, by dispersing the growth potential of Delhi within the NCR, with spill-over effects in more distant areas, particularly in the counter-magnet cities and the rural regions in their vicinity;

2. That it will be extremely difficult to check or reverse the damage to the ecology and economy of the Delhi metropolitan area caused by unplanned, haphazard growth, in the absence of planned development; and
3. That the sectoral development programmes/projects included in the NCR plan represent: The most cost effective solutions to achieving dispersal of growth and the other objectives of the plan, and that they have also significantly higher internal rates of return (IRRs) than do most other programmes/ projects included in the central or state plans.

Secondly, the NCRPB will have to develop a strategy for aggressive and innovative financing of the sectoral programmes. The strategy should have as its objective attracting significant proportions of the needed finance from domestic and international financial institutions, and for certain programmes e.g., low income housing, slum improvement and sanitation) through resource mobilization at the household and local community levels.

NEED FOR A FINANCIAL PLAN

The strategy should be at the core of a financial plan for implementation of the final NCR Plan, which must indicate the resources expected from various sources, principally during the periods of the Eighth and the Ninth five-year plans. The financial plan should be formulated by a working group on finance and should be completed in time for consideration for the Eighth Five-Year Plan. Preparation of the financial plan will require, however, a basic change in the approach to plan formulation within the NCRPB and the concerned associated sectoral agencies of the central and the state governments.

The targets for accomplishment by 2001 in various infrastructure sectors and the development programmes/projects included in the DRP, as also in the two IDPs, have all been formulated keeping in view the needs to provide housing and public services at specified, minimum standards to the projected urban and rural populations of 2001. This "need-based" approach to plan (and programme/project) formulation will need to be replaced by a "need-cum-resource based" approach. The targets of accomplishment in various sectors and the programmes/ projects must be formulated keeping in view not only the needs of the population, but also the likely availability of finance. The change would require lowering of standards for certain types of housing and for some public services, or other modifications to reduce costs.

Thus construction of the expressways and M-I or M-II motorways, envisaged in the DRP to facilitate movement of high volume traffic between Delhi and several DMA or priority towns may need to be deferred, and more modest improvements in existing highways may only be provided. Similarly, in case of waste disposal, only the most densely populated parts of the cities could be sewered, and less expensive modes of sanitation adopted in the others. The need for adoption of low cost modes of sanitation in the outlying areas of the cities and in villages is recognized in the DRP. The recognition has to be made effective however by restricting construction of sewerage facilities to the central areas of the cities and encouraging adoption of the low cost modes elsewhere.

COST-BENEFIT STUDIES OF MAJOR PROJECTS AND REGIONAL GROWTH STUDIES

The NCRPB will be greatly assisted in its efforts for financing the final NCR plan if it can demonstrate:

1. Through cost-benefit studies of major projects included in the plan, that the internal rates of returns (IRRs) on them are higher than those on most other projects in the same or other sectors, and
2. Through regional growth studies, that rapid urban growth in the NCR will benefit its rural areas, and also through its spill-over effects other areas of UP, Haryana, Rajasthan, Punjab, Himachal Pradesh and Madhya Pradesh, particularly the counter-magnet cities and the rural areas in their vicinity.

Demonstrating both these should not be difficult. The IRRs for most projects included in the NCR plan should be significantly higher than those for most other projects in the same sectors, because of high spatial concentration of demands for public goods and services in the NCR, and consequent high social returns (in terms of increments to income and/or consumption of the population) of investment in expansion of facilities, for meeting the demands. Financial returns should also be high on projects in several sectors. Comparatively high per capita income in most parts of the area should facilitate pricing of public goods and services at or above the costs of delivering them. Prices of electricity, and of telecommunications services, for instance, can be set high enough to enable the concerned public enterprises to meet most of their capital investment needs from internal sources. The political pressures or welfare considerations, that require fixing of low user charges involving large subsidies, for some goods such as electricity for rural/agricultural users, would not be so strong in the NCR.

Comparatively high IRRs for the projects and fixing of high user charges for their outputs will take the edge off the criticism that the NCR is being favored in allocation of resources.

It will also greatly assist financing of NCR projects by institutions, particularly international institutions like the World Bank and the ADB.

Finally, the cost-benefit studies will facilitate transferring to enterprises in the polluting or hazardous industries and trades, significant proportions of the costs incurred by the public authorities in reducing pollution levels of air and water (e.g., by treating the effluents discharged by the polluting industries) or for providing services such as fire protection.

The regional growth studies should demonstrate the economic-growth-and-social-change-including effects of rapid urban growth and planned urban development in the NCR on the rural areas located within the NCR, adjoining it, or in the proximate hinterlands of the counter-magnet cities, several of which are at long distances from Delhi. The development strategy of the NCR, focusing on diversion of growth from Delhi (and the DMA) to the 'priority' towns and counter-magnet cities is oriented towards maximizing these effects, which should be felt through increased opportunities for remunerative employment in non-agricultural activities for rural workers; through increased demands for food including high value perishable foods like vegetables, milk, meat and poultry, and through more rapid spread of improved production techniques, of literacy and education, and of modern medical and health care practices. The studies will assist also in developing policy measures for optimizing the growth-and-social-change-inducing effects.

MANAGEMENT STRUCTURES FOR THE NCR

The DRP includes in Chapter 13:

1. A brief survey of the structures for formulation and implementation of sub-regional, sectoral and local plans and for maintenance and operation of the service facilities, and
2. Recommendations for strengthening or adding to the structures, for increased, more effective co-operation/ collaboration among the various agencies, or between the latter and other agencies, such as the PWDs of the state governments. An organogram at the end of the Chapter (p 132) outline the existing and proposed structures and their inter-relationships.

Among the suggestions for strengthening management structures, two are noteworthy:

1. Constituting in each of the 3 states, a high level steering committee under the chairmanship of the chief secretary, for overall co-ordination and overseeing implementation of sub-regional plans and sectoral and local development programmes, and
2. Creation of a planning cell in each state for preparing and overseeing implementation of sub-regional plans. The cell will also guide and assist local authorities—municipalities and city development authorities, where the latter exist—in elaboration of local development plans.

Since the cells are to be constituted apparently in the town planning departments they would prepare (or oversee preparation by the local authorities) only physical plans. But since economic plans also need to be prepared for each of the sub-regions of the NCR, constituting similar cells is essential also in the planning departments of the state governments. These cells should have responsibilities for preparation, assuring adequate financing (through the state plan and from other sources), and overseeing implementation of the sub-regional plans. These essential functions are unlikely to be performed satisfactorily in the absence of NCR planning cells in the planning departments, especially in UP and Rajasthan in which the NCR areas account only for small proportions of the total areas and populations of the states.

Recommendations for strengthening of/or additions to management structures have also been made in some sectoral chapters of the DRP. The most interesting among them is that for constituting a unified metropolitan authority (MTA) for co-ordinated development and operation of surface transport in the NCR. It is stated that "a task force has been set up in the ministry of urban development for studying the proposal and to make recommendations on the functions, structure, staffing pattern, etc., of the authority" (p. 69). Defining the functions, which would overlap those being performed at present by the Railway Board, the road transport authorities of the 3 states, and the Delhi Transport Corporation, is of the utmost importance, in order to minimize conflicts of jurisdiction and ensure smooth working of the new authority. It will be useful also for the task force to study the organization, functions and working of one or more successful metropolitan transport authorities abroad, such as London Transport in the UK, to understand the problems involved in development and operation of an integrated transport system for a large metropolitan area, and the most appropriate patterns of relationships between the metropolitan transport authority and other national, regional or local transport agencies. It may be useful also to obtain later, technical assistance from one of the successful foreign authorities for advice and assistance in establishing the proposed MTA and its initial operation.

AN EVALUATION OF THE DRP
TWO NOTEWORTHY OMISSIONS

Programmes of Assistance to the Urban Poor

The DRP, or the IDPs, do not contain any programmes focused specifically on assisting the urban poor—the residents of the sprawling urban slums of Delhi and of the larger DMA and 'priority' towns, and the workers in the 'informal' sector. This omission is difficult to understand in face of the rapid proliferation of slums and expansion of the informal sector during the last three decades.

Among the sectoral development programmes of the plans, the only one relating to housing is 'Land Acquisition and Development'. But the entire provision of Rs. 1,010 crore for it, mentioned in the two IDPs, is earmarked for development of land for residential, commercial, industrial and other uses. The residential use will need to be primarily of upper and middle income groups, so that proceeds from sale of developed land are high enough to make operation of the revolving fund envisaged for this programme viable. There is no mention in the IDPs or the DRP of site-and-service housing or of any other programme aimed at providing housing to the urban poor. Slum improvement is also conspicuous by its absence, although it could be argued that the large programmes of expansion/improvement of water supply and sanitation, education and health care facilities will have effects similar to those achieved through slum improvement programmes.

Similarly, there is no programme in the plans which has as its objectives: (a) expansion of employment opportunities for the unskilled workers, who form the great majority of the in-migrants to Delhi, the DMA towns or the other towns of the NCR, and (b) assisting the workers in the urban informal sector to acquire or upgrade their skills, to improve their productivity and income. Programmes of training and skill formation, and of assistance to the self-employed and the small entrepreneurs in the informal sector, are not included. The entire provision of Rs. 100 crore in the programme, "development of economic activities" outlined in the IDPs, is for establishment of industrial, commercial or office complexes, i.e., for providing developed land and the physical infrastructures, needed to assist location of industrial, commercial and other service enterprises in the DMA and 'priority' towns.

The argument that expansion of employment in these sectors will benefit the urban poor is not sustainable. The limitations of such 'trickle down' effects are too well known to be discussed here. Furthermore, the principal beneficiaries of the increase in employment will be those who possess already the skills, the education and the experience needed for the new jobs, and not the unskilled and the inexperienced. The latter will have to remain content with providing miscellaneous, poorly paid services.

The argument that programmes of assistance to the urban poor have to be included in the Perspective Plan of Delhi is also not tenable, because proliferation of slums and rapid growth of the informal sector, are as evident in the DMA towns and the other towns of the NCR, as in Delhi. Indeed, the proportions of slum dwellers and workers in the informal sector could be higher in these towns than in Delhi because of the generally lower levels of housing and development of infrastructures, and the smaller size of the formal, organized sector in them.

The omission of programmes, focused on meeting the needs of the urban poor, should be corrected by including in the final draft of the NCR plan suitable programmes of adequate size. In their absence the plan will remain oriented towards the middle and high-income groups and the urban poor will continue to be ignored in it. This could adversely affect the prospects of its approval and financing.

The Draft Regional Plan and the Perspective Plan of Delhi

The second significant omission in the DRP is of a detailed examination of the relationship between it and the perspective plan of Delhi (PPD) which, as mentioned earlier, was also approved by the ministry of urban development in July 1987. The omission could be due mainly to the operational constraint of non-availability, during most of the period of preparation of the DRP, of the final draft of the PPD, because there are numerous references in the DRP and the IDPs to the (first) master plan of Delhi, and much of their data on trends and projections—demographic, economic and on requirements for expansion of physical infrastructures in the union territory have been taken from the two predecessors of the PPD, mentioned above.

This omission will also have to be removed in the final NCR plan, which must contain an adequate analysis of the PPD, and indicate the inter-relationships between the two plans. Their strategies, policies and programmes should be harmonized by eliminating inconsistencies, conflicts or other differences. In case of the development programmes/projects, the complementarity or other linkages between the programmes/projects in the union territory and those in the rest of the NCR, should be clearly indicated. Finally, global estimates of investment, covering both the union territory and the other areas of the NCR, should be included in the NCR plan for all major sectors. The complementaries or linkages among the sectoral programmes/projects of the two plans should not be left to be inferred. This would be unavoidable; however, if the PPD describes the programmes/projects for the union territory and the NCR plan excludes these and presents details only for those in the other DMA towns and the 'priority' towns.

THE STRATEGY OF DISPERSAL OF GROWTH

There would be general agreement with the central objective of the IDP, namely, to reduce growth of population and economic activities within the union territory of Delhi by diverting some of the growth outside it to the other DMA towns and particularly to the 'priority' towns. The diversion will provide relief from increasing congestion and environmental deterioration within the union territory, and stimulate economic growth, in the towns to which the activities are diverted and also in the rural areas of the NCR.

Employment in the Public Sector

The public sector provided in 1981 employment to 5,33,000 workers, 29 per cent of the total workforce in urban Delhi. Rapid growth of public sector employment from 1,06,000 in 1951 to 5,33,000 in 1981 has been a principal factor in the rapid growth of Delhi (Table 16.10).

By 1981, however, only 42 per cent of the public sector employment was in the central government, the remainder was in offices of the local governments—Delhi Administration and the local bodies (31 per cent), and in public sector enterprises (26.5 per cent). Employment in the central government has, after very rapid growth up to 1971, grown little thereafter. Increase in local government employment has also been slow after 1971. Most of the increase in public sector employment after this year has been due to explosive growth in employment—from 56,000 in 1971 to 1,40,000 in 1981 and 1,83,000 in 1985 in public sector enterprises. The growth continued in the 1980s with the number of employees in them increasing by 30 per cent between 1981 and 1985. The DRP takes critical note of the growing practice among public sector enterprises, whose operations are spread all over India or are concentrated in locations far from Delhi, to have their head offices or large 'liaison offices' in Delhi.

Table 16.10: Growth of Employment in the Public Sector in Delhi (1951-85)

(*Figures in lakhs*)

Sector	*1951*	*1961*	*1971*	*1981*	*1985*
Central government	0.85	0.94	2.11	2.25	2.30
Delhi administration	0.07	0.25	0.53	0.58	0.65
Local bodies	0.14	0.34	0.90	1.09	0.84
Quasi-government	N.A.	0.06	0.56	1.41	1.83
Total	1.06	1.59	4.10	5.33	5.62

Source: DRP, Table 4.12, p. 42. Data are from Delhi Statistical Handbook, 1986.

The measures for curbing growth of public sector employment must concentrate on:

(a) Severely restricting growth of employment in public enterprises, and
(b) countering any trend towards resumption of rapid growth of employment in the central government or the local governments.

The policy measures outlined in the DRP, and summarized in Section III above, should be adequate for countering the latter. Some of the measures have been adopted since the 1950s, and need only to be enforced more vigorously. But in order to curb, and to reverse as far as possible, growth of employment in public sector enterprises, it will be necessary to identify the reasons why the managements of the enterprises find it necessary or expedient to locate their head offices or large liaison offices in Delhi. If, as one suspects, the practice is due to concentration of decision-making in the central ministries in Delhi, the situation can be corrected only by effective decentralization—from the ministries to the chairmen or managing directors of the enterprises, and from them to the managers of the principal operating units. The need to contain growth of population of Delhi is another reason for undertaking this reform, which is needed urgently also for improving efficiency in the public sector.

Dispersal of Manufacturing Industries

Manufacturing industry which provided employment in 1981 to 5,41,000 workers, 29 per cent of the total workforce, was the largest sector, in terms of employment, in the union territory (Table 16.6). The DRP, as also the two IDPs earlier, refer to the progressive increase in the proportion of work force engaged in manufacturing—it was only 17 per cent in 1951—and the urgent need to counter the trend through restricting industrial growth in the union territory of Delhi and, to a lesser extent, in the other DMA towns, and promoting it in the 'priority' towns. The policy measures recommended in the DRP to achieve these objectives have been summarized above. But despite these measures, industrial employment, both in the union territory and in the other DMA towns, is projected to continue to increase rapidly. Total industrial employment in the union territory is projected to increase to 1.14 million by 2001, with the proportion of industrial workers in the workforce remaining unchanged at 29 per cent (Table 16.11).

Table 16.11: Proposed Employment Structure in the DMA Towns-2001

Town	*Population 2001 (million)*	*Proposed work-participation Rate (Per Cent)*	*Total workers ('000s)*	*Proportion of Workers (Per Cent)*					
				Primary sector	*Industry*	*Construction*	*Trade and Commerce*	*Transport Storage and Communication*	*Services*
Delhi UT	11.2	35	3920	1.5	29.0	5.0	22.0	11.0	31.5
Ghaziabad	1.1	30	330	0.5	38.0	6.0	15.0	10.0	30.0
NOIDA	0.55	35	192	2.0	45.0	6.0	20.0	12.0	20.0
Faridabad Ballabhgarh	1.0	35	350	2.0	45.0	6.0	16.0	7.0	23.0
Gurgaon	0.7	35	245	2.0	40.0	10.0	16.0	10.0	22.0
Bahadurgarh	0.2	35	70	6.0	30.0	4.0	25.0	10.0	25.0
Kundli	0.15	35	50	2.0	40.0	10.0	16.0	10.0	22.0

Source: DRP Table 4.8, p. 39.

Industrial employment in the other DMA towns will also increase so rapidly that in 5 out of the 6 towns, 38 to 45 per cent of the workforce will be employed in industries.

Industrial growth in the 'priority' towns will be promoted principally through location of new industrial units. Transfer of existing units from within the union territory to the other DMA towns or to the 'priority' towns will remain limited. For units in the handicrafts and small scale sub-sectors, the existing locations offer major advantages. Location within a large market, proximity to sources of labour (including especially workers possessing the needed skills and experience), of capital and of raw materials and intermediates, and ease of supervision of the units by the proprietors/managers are the most important among the advantages. Besides, the costs of shifting would be much too high for such small units. Medium scale and large enterprises are better equipped to cope with the costs, to take advantage of cheaper land and other facilities offered by the new locations. But, the strong opposition of labour unions to the closure of the Delhi Cloth Mills, located in an extremely congested area in central Delhi, and redevelopment of the area for housing and related uses, illustrates the difficulties of shifting even large units from their present locations.

Two further facts must be recognized while considering the prospects of dispersal of industries from the union territory to the other DMA towns, or to the 'priority' towns. First, many of the towns suffer from serious infrastructural deficiencies, and their transport-and-communications links with Delhi are poor. Faridabad-Ballabhgarh, for instance, has suffered from an acute shortage of power for several years, and the telephone service between it and Delhi is very unsatisfactory. Furthermore, facilities for higher education, medical care and recreation in most of these towns are limited, or are of poor quality. These deficiencies have retarded growth of industries in these towns, and have also resulted in large numbers of proprietors, managers or other professionals working in the factories located in the DMA towns, living in Delhi and commuting between their homes and factories. A major objective of the sectoral development programmes, outlined in the DRP (and at greater length in the two IDPs), is to mitigate or remove these constraints of the DMA and 'priority' towns, and to make them more attractive locations for industries, and other economic activities. Second, Delhi and the DMA towns like NOIDA located closest to it, are the most suitable locations for establishment of small or medium scale units in new industries with potential for rapid growth. Examples of these industries are the new high technology or information or research-based industries, and those catering to specialized demands, e.g., of domestic middle and high-income groups or of the export market. These industries have experienced rapid growth in the 1980s and similar growth can be projected for the foreseeable future. The principal reasons favouring growth of these industries are: concentration of highly trained professionals and young entrepreneurs looking for opportunities for establishing new manufacturing or service-based enterprises; relatively developed infrastructures including among the best facilities in the country for air transport and external telecommunications, and easy access to sources of finance and of vital information about policies of the central government. As a result, there will be a progressive change in the mix of industries in Delhi––from older, polluting, stagnant or declining industries, to new, rapidly growing industries. This change in the industrial mix, and the related changes in the trade and commerce sector, mentioned in the following sub-section, should be noted in the NCR plan, and facilitated because they are in both regional and national interests.

DISPERSAL OF DISTRIBUTIVE TRADES

Trade and commerce, with 22.3 per cent of the workforce engaged in it in 1981 is the third largest sector in the economy of urban Delhi (Table 16.6). It includes both retail trade, to meet the consumption needs of the population of Delhi, and wholesale trade. As mentioned earlier, Delhi is the principal distribution center for a large hinterland in north-west and north-central India. The wholesale markets are all located in the old city, having grown up there for historical reasons including location of the old Delhi railway station.

The strategy and policy measures included in the DRP aim at shifting most of the wholesale trades out of this congested area in order to relieve the congestion in it and the hazards to life and property, caused by the presence of trades in hazardous commodities. The relocation would also eliminate the large flows in-and-out of Delhi of goods, that are not used locally but are re-exported.

The two IDPs had proposed relocation of particular trades to particular towns, most of them 'priority' towns, located at distances of 50 kilometers or more from Delhi. Thus, the cloth trade was proposed to be shifted to Modinagar, Meerut, Rohtak and Alwar; the trade in motor parts and machinery was to be shifted to Meerut and Alwar, and that in iron and steel to Alwar (Table 16.7). The DRP omits these specific proposals for shifts, and concentrates instead on removing the fiscal and other advantages of the union territory of Delhi, such as lower rates of sales-tax and most other taxes than in the neighboring states, which contribute to concentration of the wholesale trades in the union territory. Thus, emphasis has shifted in the DRP from directing relocation through administrative measures to encouraging relocation over a period of time through economic and fiscal measures.

One reason for this change could be that the IDPs' proposals for relocation had evoked strong opposition of Delhi Merchants Chamber, which had charged that they reflected lack of understanding of the structure of Delhi's economy. The opposition was due partly to the proposals being at variance with those of the draft Perspective Plan of Delhi. The latter involves relocations over much shorter distances, generally in the suburbs of Delhi or in the rural areas of the union territory; similar relocations had been accomplished successfully earlier in case of trades in fruits and vegetables and in various building materials. Such relocations over short distances have much lower costs and involve much less dislocation than do the relocations to distant towns proposed in the IDPs. The latter would involve, besides relocations of the operating units (shops and warehouses), changes in residence by the proprietors, managers and other workers, and establishment of new links—with banks and other financial institutions, with regulatory agencies of the government, with the railways or road transport agencies, and with agencies providing other essential services.

Since relocation of most wholesale trades is essential, if the extreme congestion in the old city and the hazards to life and property caused by concentration in it of trade in hazardous goods are to be eliminated, concrete proposals for relocation, which are effective in achieving these objectives, are acceptable to the mercantile community, and harmonize with the proposals in the PPD, need to be evolved. This should be done by working groups constituted for individual trades (or groups of trades), which have strong representation on them from the mercantile community. The working groups should also look carefully at the data of the DDA survey, mentioned above, because the interpretation put on the data in the IDPs or the DRP is suspect. It is difficult to believe, for instance, that 95 per cent of the textiles and 80 per cent of the radio-TV parts and accessories imported into Delhi, are re-exported. Delhi, besides being a large market for these goods, is also a major manufacturing center for them. 'Textile and textile products' with 46,000 workers in 1981, is the largest industry in Delhi, and 'manufacture of electrical machinery' with 15,000 workers in 1981 is another important industry. It is more than likely that large proportions of the 'exports' consist of goods, assembled in Delhi from imported components or finished from semi-finished materials.

The DRP recognizes that despite the shifting of many wholesale trades out of the old city, growth of trade and commerce in the union territory of Delhi will be rapid enough to more than double the total workforce in the sector, from 4,13,000 in 1981 to 8,62,000 in 2001. Furthermore, the proportion of workforce in the sector to the total workforce is projected to remain unchanged at 22 per cent (Table 16.11).

But, as in case of manufacturing industries, the DRP does not refer to a change in the composition of the 'trade and commerce' sector—progressive reduction in the proportions of trade in traditional goods, and increase in that of trade in new products, such as the inputs and outputs of the new, rapid growth manufacturing industries, mentioned earlier. Furthermore, it does not mention a related development–rapid growth of financial services—as a result of which Delhi has already become a major financial center, ranking third in importance after Bombay and Calcutta. Both changes have been in progress since the 1950s, have accelerated in the 1980s and may be expected to continue. These developments are also due mainly to the advantages of Delhi, mentioned earlier, for growth of new manufacturing industries. Two other factors favoring growth of the financial services industry are: (a) rapid growth in the manufacturing, trade and commerce, and construction sectors with large demands for institutional finance, and (b) relatively high income levels in the union territory, in the NCR, and over large areas of Delhi's hinterland, accompanied by significant numbers in both the urban and rural populations, of people who have investible savings and are willing to invest them in new financial instruments.

THE SETTLEMENT PATTERN—RURBAN CORRIDORS AND COUNTER-MAGNET CITIES

The most important feature of the settlement pattern, envisaged in the DRP, relates to progressive development of rurban corridors, radiating from Delhi and passing through the DMA towns and 'priority' towns. Nine such corridors had been identified in IDP '87 (Fig.16.1).

The Delhi-Faridabad-Ballabhgarh, Delhi-Ghaziabad-Meerut, and Delhi-Gurgaon portions of 3 corridors are already urbanized along the roads and railways, and if present trends continue, most parts of the other corridors will also be similarly urbanized by the year 2001. The corridors are envisaged as the principal areas within the NCR of location of nonagricultural activities including manufacturing industries, of rapid urbanization and of movement of people and goods. The sectoral development programmes, outlined in the DRP are all designed to support these developments through major expansion/improvement of the physical, economic and social infrastructures of the DMA towns and the 'priority' towns, and their transport and telecommunications links with Delhi.

But the DRP has also identified as many as 36 cities (19 in UP alone) which could serve as alternative growth foci or counter magnets to the Delhi Metropolitan Area, attracting significant proportions of the migrants, who would otherwise come to it. Promoting growth of the 'priority' towns and of the counter-magnet cities are the principal components of the strategy for reducing in-migration to and population growth in the DMA. The counter-magnet cities are located in 5 states––Punjab and Madhya Pradesh, in addition to the 3 states of UP, Haryana and Rajasthan which are represented in the NCR already. The cities are located at distances of 100-600 kilometers from Delhi, and have populations ranging from just over 1,00,000 (Sambal in Moradabad district of UP) to more than 1.5 million (Kanpur). The principal criteria for selection as counter-magnet cities were:

(i) That they should not be within commuting distance of Delhi;
(ii) That they should have their own established roots and inherent growth potential; and
(iii) That they should not be centers of, (a) religious, cultural or strategic importance, or (b) located in ecologically sensitive areas.

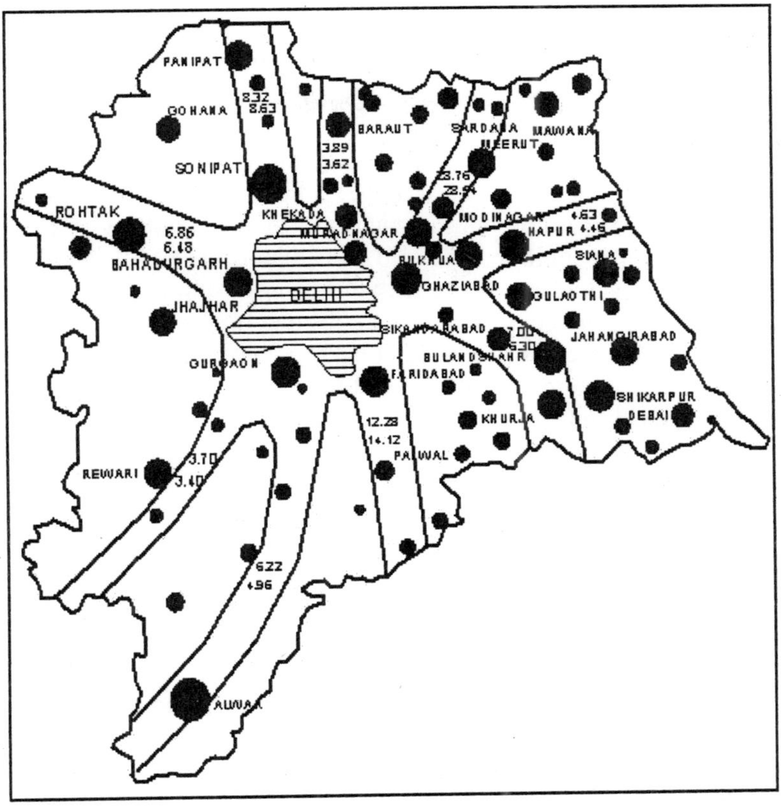

Fig 16.1: Urban Population and Workforce Concentration in Transport Corridors 1981.

Source: IDP 1987 p. 50.

Notes: 1. Top figure indicate per cent of urban population in that corridor to NCR's urban population.

2. Bottom figure indicate per cent of workforce in that corridor to NCR's total workforce.

The DRP recognizes that the preliminary list of 36 counter-magnet cities is too large, and that only a few of the most suitable cities among them, can be selected for development as strong counter-magnets.

The cities selected as counter-magnets should, in our view, be of medium size (population 5,00,000 and 15,00,000), should have a good economic base, and fairly well developed physical, economic and social infrastructures. They should also be free from serious constraints on growth—environmental, socio-economic or political. These attributes are essential to make them attractive locations for manufacturing industries and other economic activities, and also as residences of proprietors/managers of enterprises, and other professional personnel. They should, preferably, have experienced rapid growth in the recent past. Jaipur and Lucknow, with 1981 populations of about one million each, are good examples of such cities. But the list could include also cities like Kanpur, Allahabad, Gwalior and Chandigarh, whose growth has been hampered, despite their considerable growth potential, by economic or political constraints, which can be reduced at manageable costs. The efforts to stimulate growth in the latter would range from rehabilitation, if possible, of old industries, or their replacement by new ones with high growth potential (Kanpur), to removal of the political constraint on growth (Chandigarh).

Cities with population below 5,00,000 should not normally be considered for selection as counter-magnets. Growth of the smaller cities, e.g., through further industrial growth in Kota, or industrial diversification and modernization of the existing brass industry in Muradabad, should be encouraged through other sectoral or regional development programmes.

The DRP does not discuss the relative merits of the alternative settlement patterns resulting from (a) concentration on dispersal of growth in the radial corridors located within the NCR, and (b) development of counter-magnet cities. But its preference for the former is clear from its strategy, policies and programmes. The counter-magnet cities would benefit primarily from those affects of growth within the NCR, which are strong enough to induce growth in distant cities.

There are two strong reasons for the preference of the DRP for the radial corridor pattern:

(i) It is in accordance with the worldwide trend for settlement, manufacturing industries and other non-agricultural economic activities to disperse out of large cities along the principal lines of communications, particularly highways. It is particularly attractive in the developing countries where communications and management structures are much less developed than in the developed countries and proprietors/

managers of industrial and commercial enterprises (and heads of government offices), want their enterprises/offices to be located at distances at which they can exercise personal supervision and control over them, through quick and easy travel or telecommunications.

(ii) Its development within the NCR is too far-gone to be reversed now. Failure to take account of this fact and attempts to curb the development and concentrate on development of counter-magnets, will only result in substituting in place of planned development, unplanned, haphazard growth, which it would be extremely difficult to reverse later.

It is necessary to refer, however, to three of the several arguments against development of radial corridors.

First, it will further increase traffic to-and-from Delhi, and congestion in its central business-and-administrative districts. The proprietors/managers and other executives of the enterprises and offices, located in the other DMA towns and the 'priority' towns, will travel frequently to Delhi for accomplishing a wide variety of tasks—arranging supplies of raw materials, spares and other industrial inputs, marketing of outputs; processing of their applications for loans from financial institutions, licenses or various other permissions, and obtaining information on the latest changes in policies of the central government. Large numbers among them may continue to live in Delhi and commute to work, in the DMA towns and even in the 'priority' towns, for the same reasons that have kept them in Delhi so far. A proportion of the higher paid skilled or clerical workers may also do the same for personal reasons. Improvement of highways, reducing travel time between Delhi and the DMA and 'priority' towns, and of telecommunications, will only strengthen the trend. The DRP or the IDPs do not discuss these effects of dispersal of economic activities to and rapid growth of the DMA and 'priority' towns, and do not outline any measures to counter it.

The second argument focuses on the need to maintain sufficiently large green belts around expanding metropolitan cities. The green belt is essential for several reasons including the following:

(i) To provide an escape to the resident of the metropolis from the stresses and strains of living in a highly congested, polluted environment and working under conditions of keen competition, besides low incomes and financial insecurity for most. The green belts provide them opportunities for recreation, and to be close to nature, at distances to which they can afford to travel on weekends and holidays and, sometimes, also before or after work on working days.

(ii) Preservation of environmental quality and ecological balance. This is extremely important because, as mentioned earlier, the levels of water and air pollution in the DMA are already extremely high and are increasing rapidly. A green belt of adequate size along the Yamuna, narrow along the river's course through the DMA and widening considerably downstream of it, is essential to allow the river to recover from the massive pollution caused by inflow into it of pollutants (including increasingly chemical and other industrial wastes), during its passage through the DMA. Similarly, a large enough green belt to the south-west of Delhi, mainly on the Aravali ridge, is essential to provide a degree of protection against the dust laden (and extremely hot during the summer) winds from Rajasthan.

Land use within the green belt along the Yamuna could be a mix of agricultural lands, pastures and woodlands, while that to the south-west would be predominantly of woodlands. The agricultural lands and pastures would contribute to supplies to Delhi of high value perishable foods milk, vegetables, poultry products, etc while the woodlands would supply firewood, which is still the principal fuel of the urban poor.

The DRP recognizes the need for maintaining adequate green belts around Delhi, and outlines in chapters 11 and 12, proposals for achieving this objective. But the proposals have not been worked out in sufficient detail. More important, it does not outline policy measures for countering the strong trend, past and present, towards encroachment on the green belts, resulting in their practical disappearance over large areas which hand been reserved for them in the first (1962) Master Plan of Delhi.

Third, the radial corridor pattern will reinforce the trend towards ribbon development along the highways, until entire stretches of the highways linking Delhi with the other DMA towns, and progressively also the 'priority' towns are covered by industrial or service enterprises, housing colonies (planned or unplanned) and other non-agricultural developments. This development has already occurred along the Delhi-Faridabad stretch of the highway and over large stretches of the Delhi-Meerut highway, and threatens increasing stretches of the other highways. The DRP envisages maintenance of 500 meter-wide 'green wedges', along the highways. They will, if maintained (doubtful), provide aesthetic relief from the dreaded monotony of ribbon development, but will have little other environmental effect.

CONCLUSION

Constitution of the statutory NCRPB and publication of the DRP are important first steps in establishment of regional planning as an integral part of planning for Delhi. They have to be followed by a large number of other steps beginning with preparation of the final plan for the NCR, and of an action plan for its implementation. The more important steps, some of which are being taken already, are listed at the end.

Successful establishment of regional planning for Delhi is important for its establishment for the other large cities. Because of the interest of the central government in planned development of the national capital, the success of regional planning here will stimulate development of institutions, processes and patterns of central assistance which could give a big push to regional planning for the other large cities. Experience with preparation of the first 'master plan' for Delhi is instructive in this regard. It led to greatly increased awareness among the planners and other policy makers in the central and state governments of the importance of planning for urban development to meet the challenges of rapid urbanization. The TCPO was established under the central government to advise and assist the state governments in preparation of urban and regional development plans. Long-term 'master plans' were prepared for a large number of cities including the largest—Calcutta, Bombay and Madras. Planning and development authorities were established for formulation and implementation of these plans in cities where the municipal corporations were not equipped for these tasks. The quantum of central assistance for financing urban development projects was also increased, and a number of projects relating particularly to water supply and sanitation, and housing for specially designated low income groups were financed through central assistance supplemented by assistance from international institutions, particularly the World Bank/IDA.

Furthermore, since the problems and coordination and collaboration in plan formulation and plan implementation are much greater and more complex in regional planning for Delhi because of the involvement in it of a much larger number of agencies (under the central government and the state governments) than would be the case in the other large cities, successful resolution of these problems in the NCR will have valuable lessons for resolving them in other regions.

This review had the limited purpose of analyzing the objectives, strategies, policies and development programmes of the DRP. Although primarily descriptive, it includes comments and recommendations to make the plan more effective and acceptable for financing, principally under the Eighth and Ninth Five Year Plans. It is necessary to reiterate here the needs for, (i) correcting the omissions of programmes for the urban poor and of analysis of the relationships between the NCR Plan and the Perspective Plan for Delhi and (ii) avoiding a wide gap between the cost of the plan and the resources that are likely to become available for its implementation.

FURTHER STEPS IN THE PLANNING PROCESS

The most important and urgent further steps are finalization of the NCR Plan with provision for its periodic revision, at suitable intervals and development of adequate and appropriate management structures for plan formulation and overseeing implementation at the NCR, sub-regional and sectoral levels.

The final NCR Plan should be prepared through revision of the DRP:

(a) to meet objections raised by concerned organizations or individual experts, etc. and to remove inconsistencies;
(b) to harmonize it with the Perspective Plan of Delhi in projections, strategy, policies, achievement targets and sectoral development programmes;
(c) to revise the targets of accomplishment and the sectoral development programmes, keeping in view the constraints

of time, finance and capacity for programme implementation at various levels. Several of the targets and programmes will need to be scaled down to levels which are considered feasible by the planners in the central and state governments, keeping in view both implementation capacity and available finance.

(d) to include a detailed scheme for financing the Plan. The scheme should be ready in time for consideration of the NCR Plan for financing under the Eighth Five Year Plan.

A major revision of the NCR Plan should be undertaken in the early 1990s after data of the 1991 Census of Population become available, and preparation of sectoral and local development programmes has been completed or is far advanced. The revised plan should be suitable for financing under the Ninth Five Year Plan.

Related steps for plan preparation at the sectoral, sub-regional and local levels are as follows:

(i) preparation of detailed sectoral programmes/projects with phasing for implementation under the Seventh, Eighth and Ninth Five Year Plans;

(ii) preparation of sub-regional physical and economic plans, respectively by the town planning departments and the planning departments of the state governments, with similar phasing, under the three five year plans;

(iii) revision/elaboration of the existing development plans of the DMA and 'priority' towns and preparation of plans for the towns for which they do not exist;

(iv) conducting cost-benefit studies of major projects, as part of feasibility studies for them, and regional growth studies, focusing on the influence of rapid urban growth on rural economic growth and social change, within the NCR, in areas adjoining it and in the counter-magnet areas.

DEVELOPMENT OF MANAGEMENT STRUCTURES

The development should aim at creation of appropriate management structures for plan formulation and overseeing plan implementation at the NCR, sectoral, sub-regional and local levels.

The principal measures needed is strengthening of the NCR secretariat to include in it high level professionals, in disciplines, such as economics, public administration, sociology, regional planning and management, which are either not represented in it at present or are represented by junior level staff. However, in order to avoid creation of a large secretariat, the alternative of having a small nucleus of high level professionals within it and drawing upon the expertise available in various central ministries/departments of the state governments, functional organizations, public enterprises, universities and research institutions, for preparation of development projects, elaboration of strategies and policies and detailed studies of particular issues or problems. This would mean, in effect, the following:

(a) making the study groups constituted for preparing the IDPs and the DRP permanent, and
(b) greatly increasing use of specialized institutions and consultants, for specialized tasks, such as preparation of feasibility studies of major projects and study of city-region relationships.

NOTES

1. Published in *Economic and Political Weekly*, January 30 1988 pp. 201 –214.
2. The figure of cities with a million plus people is expected to go up from 23 in 1981 to 51 by 2011 – 2.3 of these will be in the south, Maharashtra and Gujarat, 22 in the north and six in the east, home in all, to about 110, million, two-fifth of the urban population. Jharkhand's capital Ranchi will be one of the new cities in this group. In 20 years' the Ahmedabad-Vadodra-Surat-Vapi corridor will have 16 million people, or 57 per cent of the state's projected urban population. the Vasi-Mumbai-Pune corridor will have 30 million people, more than half of Maharashtra's projected urban population. Sourashtra already has 87 towns and expected to be home to about six million people – despite its water problem. The Bangalore-Belgaum and Bangalore-Mysore corridors will have nearly 70 per cent of Karnataka's projected urban population of 27 million. In the north, there are the Udaipur-Kota and Delhi-Jaipur stretches. Amritsar and Jhansi is accepted to be a "great arc of urban growth" as well — this is already evident in the Amritsar-Jalandhar, Chandigarh-Delhi and Delhi-Agra, segments. Delhi Dehradoon and Delhi-Moradabad are becoming similar corridors." (Source: *Times of India,* November 26, 2000).

3. The city, its suburbs and the adjoining smaller towns which together form a continuously urbanized area. The term 'urban agglomeration' used in the Censuses of Population is a close approximation. The term 'Delhi Metropolitan Area' has been used, however, specifically for the union territory of Delhi and the six towns listed in Table 16.2.
4. Delhi Development Authority: Delhi 2001, *Delhi Vikas Varta*, Vol. 2, No. 2, Special Issue 1985.
5. Delhi Urban Arts Commission: Conceptual Plan 2001. Circulated by PHD Chamber of Commerce and Industry, New Delhi (no date).
6. Unless indicated otherwise, all page numbers relate to the "Draft Regional Plan, 2001, the National Capital Region—New Delhi", National Capital Region Planning Board, Ministry of Urban Development, 1987.

17

Master Plans for Metropolitan Growth Management: Five Case Studies in India

This paper discusses the planning process for five large cities, Kolkata, Mumbai, Chennai, Hyderabad and Pune. With the exception of Pune, the others are the largest metropolitan cities in India. Plans for expansion of the cities for residential, industrial and other uses and for expansion of supplies of electricity and water, facilities for disposal of solid and liquid waste, expansion and improvement of intra-urban transport, improvement of relocation of slums which house the poor residents have been drawn up for all the cities except Chennai. However, as the review shows the plans have achieved their objects only partially. The principal reason for this is that during the period of the plans, there have been major developments, which could not be foreseen at the time of their formulation.

BASIC ELEMENTS OF LONG-TERM PLANNING

A long-term (10-20 years) master plan for a city has five basic elements:

1. A forecast of growth of population and economic activities during the plan period;
2. Programmes for expansion of physical infrastructure and social services to meet the needs of the increasing population and economic activities;
3. A land use plan, designating the areas for residential, industrial and commercial uses and for location of education, health care and recreation facilities. Such a design is essential

if haphazard growth of the city which would create difficult problems later is to be avoided;

4. A plan for improvement and relocation, if necessary, of the slums which house the poor population of the city; and
5. A design for a real expansion of the city to house its increasing population and economic activities. In particular, it should identify the satellite towns/cities in which the industries and markets located earlier in the city are to be shifted to reduce pollution of air and water in the city and in which are to be located new industries serving the consumption needs of the city or the region and which could serve also as the dormitory towns/cities for the main city.

The municipal corporations of the cities are in no position to finance the investment. The best run among them can only operate basic municipal services such as lighting of streets and keeping them clean, construction and maintenance of intra-city roads, diversion of traffic and running the public transport system which may or may not be self-financing. The only activity which can be self-financing or generate profit is development of land for housing for people of middle or high income groups and markets. However, this is done as well by private developers as by the development authorities of the city. Nevertheless, during the last 3 decades, large investments have been made by the development authorities of many cities or as in the case of the Haryana Urban Development Authority by a state government on development of land for housing and other needs.

The 1960's were the period when preparation of long term master plans became popular and plans were drawn up for several metropolitan cities. However, the following detailed city wise review shows that second master plans have not been proposed for any of these cities, although the need for them is greater now than in the 1960's and the early 1970's when the plans for the metro cities were prepared. This is an unfortunate development because with increase in population of the cities, diversification of their economies and greatly increased pressures on the physical and social infrastructures, the need for formulation and implementation of plans is more urgent now than in the 1960's and 1970's.

APPROPRIATENESS OF MEDIUM-TERM TIME FRAME

Part of the reasons for not preparing subsequent plans to the first plan is that the first master plans were formulated for 10 to 20 years. This period is too long for meaningful planning because of rapid changes in the national economic policies and national and international economic situation, which affect the rate of growth of the cities and bring about changes in the economic activities of their population.

A more appropriate period for formulation of development plans for large cities is 10 years, which should be divided into two sub-periods of 5-years each. The 10-year plan will provide a medium-term perspective of growth of the city, i.e. of the size and economic activities of their populations and of the needs for expansion of physical and social infrastructures. The sub-periods should coincide with the periods of the national development plans because most of the funds for expansion of the infrastructure will need to be provided by the government of the state or the central government. Coincidence of the periods of the 5 year plans for the cities with the national plan will provide an indication of the funds that are likely to become available for implementation of the plans. The coincidence is essential because most of the funds for expansion of infrastructure must come from the central government.

KOLKATA METROPOLITAN DISTRICT (CMD) PLAN 1966 – 1985

Kolkata, India's second largest city with 13.2 m. population in 2001 (and its capital up to 1912), and the principal port serving a vast hinterland of Eastern India, was considered to be a dying city in the mid-1960's, because of the numerous problems that it faced.

KOLKATA'S CATALOGUE OF PROBLEMS

The problems ranged from total collapse of civic services to large-scale unemployment among educated Bengali youth. The water supply was both inadequate and polluted; the sewerage and drainage systems required urgent repairs and renovation. There was extreme congestion on the roads of the city, which began with the failure of the Howrah bridge on the river Hooghly to clear quickly the passenger and goods traffic coming to it from other parts of the country.

Almost half the population was living in slums called *bustees*. The slum dwellers included both workers who performed the lowest paid jobs in the city from rickshaw pullers to porters on the railway stations, the markets and the port and refugees from Bangladesh who had fled their homes in order to escape persecution by the Moslems to seek shelter in huts located along the main streets of the city. While the older slum clusters were located on the roads, just behind the central business district, the slums in which the refugees from Bangladesh lived lined all the main roads.

The transport system was chaotic. The buses, the principal means of intra-urban transport, were inadequate to handle the traffic. They were extremely crowded; they left behind a trail of smoke as they plied on the streets and traffic jams, which took hours to clear, were frequent. Large numbers of industrial units were closed because of militancy of trade unions and there was flight of capital from the city to southern and western India. The object of the plan was to revive the economy of the city by expansion, repair and renovation of the basic infrastructure needed for its efficient functioning and to improve environmental conditions in the slums.

The Kolkata Metropolitan District was designated to include the cities of Kolkata and Howrah and about 45 small municipalities and townships. The latter included both jute mill towns located along the Hoogly river and small towns and villages located south of Kolkata which served both as dormitories for workers in Kolkata and suppliers of fresh produce – milk, vegetables, fruit, poultry products and fish for the city.

CMPO – A NEW PLANNING INITIATIVE

Since the Kolkata Corporation, weak and ridden with corruption, was in no position to prepare a plan, a new organization – The Calcutta Metropolitan Planning Organization (CMPO)—was created for formulating the plan. The organization was established by the state government. The Ford Foundation, an American foundation assisting India's planning efforts in the 1960's, provided large technical assistance in the form of a team of about 20 experts for formulating the plan. The central government made a special provision of Rs.100 million in the Third Five Year Plan (1961-65) for development of the city. The World Bank promised and did provide large funds for financing expansion of water supplies and improvement of slums and also indicated its readiness to part-finance construction of two major transport projects – a second bridge on the river Hooghly to reduce the load on the existing Howrah bridge and an underground railway. The World Health Organisation provided technical assistance for improvement of drainage and expansion of the sewerage system. The government of West Bengal promised to provide the counterpart funds needed for financing the pan-assisted development projects.

The outline plan was formulated in May 1966. Approval and start of implementation were immediate. While the slum improvement programme and projects for improvement and expansion of water supplies and of drainage and sewerage systems were implemented by the mid 1970's, the two transport projects were completed only in the 1980's.

Implementation Woes

Implementation of the plan received a set-back in the late 1960's, when Kolkata experienced serious labor unrest caused by militant trade unions, which resulted also in flight of capital from the city on a large scale. Another result was closure of a number of industrial units. Implementation of the plan was resumed only after the present government of the Communist party came to power in the early 1970's. Meanwhile the slum population increased continuously due to migration of Hindus from Bangladesh. Intra-urban bus transport had previously been in the hands of Punjabi bus owners; they also owned most of the taxis. Both of these were run quite efficiently. However, the government of West Bengal had nationalized the transport system and adopted a policy of allotting permits for operating taxis only to Bengali young men in order to provide employment to them. The result was a sharp fall in efficiency of operation of both buses and taxis. The state run buses, inadequate in number and inefficiently maintained, were extremely crowded and left behind a cloud of smoke as they plied on the roads. Electricity was supplied earlier by an efficient private company. It was nationalized and because of inefficient functioning of the state run electricity board, long power cuts became common in the 1970's and early 1980's. Construction of the underground railway took several years with the result that heaps of debris on the main roads in central Kolkata remained a common sight for many years.

Success After Short Falls

There has been considerable improvement in the situation in recent years. Due to increase in sources of power supply and more efficient functioning of the State Electricity Board, power cuts have become a distant memory. Municipal Water supply is adequate to serve most parts of the city and drainage and sewerage systems created problems only in the monsoon season, when some streets may be flooded for days. However, the buses continue to be inadequate, poorly maintained and over-crowded. Furthermore, despite the strenuous efforts of the Chief Minister and his colleagues there has been no return of capital to the city.

The plan had envisaged building of Kalyani, located about 60 kilometre north of Kolkata, a residential township for those who may wish to move out of the city on account of its over-crowding, pollution and other problems including high cost of living. The well planned township would also provide a congenial environment for living of retired officials, business executives and other old people. Another important component of the plan related to building of a harbour at Haldia to reduce congestion in Kolkata port and particularly to handle bulky cargo such as petroleum products, steel, cement, etc. Both Kalyani and Haldia have been built and are serving the purposes intended for them. The government's plan for building a petroleum refinery and a petro-chemical complex at Haldia have also been completed although after many delays and cost over-runs.

Improvements in Housing and Transport

The addition to the city's housing stock both through construction of new buildings or repair or renovation of old houses or commercial buildings was so meager until the 1990's that even people of middle income group lived in small 1-2 bedroom flats or parts of houses, located on crowded and dusty streets. The heaps of debris that were found in the city's streets when the underground railway was being built disappeared by the late 1980's, after the underground railway became operational. The long power cuts that followed nationalization of the electric supply company are a distant memory because of expansion of power stations and improvement in distribution. The second bridge on the river Hooghly envisaged in the CMPO Plan was completed and began to handle the large traffic to southern and western India. The plan, however, did not envisage rapid growth of population of the city until the various services in it were improved; the population increased slowly upto the 1980's partly due to shortage of housing, however, there has been rapid increase in the 1990s. Land developed in the areas was done by the joint efforts of the Kolkata Metropolitan Development Authority (KMDA) and cooperatives of the house owners. But construction of housing was done by people of middle-income group in south Salt Lake.

NEEDED: THE SECOND KMDA MASTER PLAN

The transport situation has improved with completion of the first phase of underground railway, which covers about 16 kilometre of the distance between the airport and the city center. However, despite a lapse of almost 2 decades since completion of the first master plan, a second master plan has not been formulated by the KMDA. The latter is important because the KMDA staffed by able professionals, continues to do useful studies, but has not been given the mandate to provide a second master plan. This is unfortunate because implementation of various projects included in the first plan made a significant contribution to reducing deficiency in essential infrastructure and improving living conditions for the people of middle-income group and the slum dwellers.

The second plan would continue the process and would ensure that expansion of infrastructure would keep pace with needs for them. Furthermore, it would help restore Kolkata's position as the principal port for its vast hinterland that includes West Bengal, Bihar, Orissa, Assam and the 7 hill states of the north-east besides Nepal and Bhutan. Its ports Haldia and Kalkota would be the principal ports, along with Chennai, for India's trade with south East Asia linking Thailand to India and Australia and New Zealand.

MUMBAI: INITIAL MOMENTUM MUST BE REGAINED BY BOMBAY METROPOLITAN REGIONAL DEVELOPMENT AUTHORITY (BMRDA) PLAN

The Mumbai Corporation with assistance from some young visionary planners formulated in the early 1960s a plan, which provided for decongestion of the city and the port and for providing space for its expanding population and industries. The plan was outstanding in boldness of conception. It envisaged building of:

1. New Mumbai – a new industrial-cum-residential satellite city of Mumbai located on the mainland across from the old city which is located on an island;
2. A number of road and rail bridges across the creek that separate the two cities;
3. A new port at Uran or Nava Shevha to handle bulk products such as crude oil, petroleum products, food-grains and cement. The port would meet the expanding needs for port facilities and relieve congestion in the old port;
4. Shifting the Maharashtra Legislature and the Secretariat of the Maharashtra government from the old to the new city. The shift would involve movement of thousands of employees of the government to the new city. Furthermore, location of industrial units in New Mumbai and its environs would receive a powerful stimulus because the owners/ managers of the new units would have the facility of obtaining various licenses, incentives for exports of products and other facilities from the government. The plan was approved in 1966 and its implementation began immediately.

Success and Short Falls

New Mumbai has grown during the last 4 decades into a thriving residential-cum-industrial satellite city of Mumbai; it had a population of almost one million in 1991. The industrial units located in it are those which would have been otherwise located on the outskirts of Mumbai or in various locations along the road-cum-rail route between Mumbai and Pune. One eight-lane road bridge across the bay has been completed and serves as the link between the two cities. The port of Uran has been built and is handling bulk products such as crude oil and petroleum products.

These developments have involved employment of thousands of civil servants, professionals and white-collar workers in Indian and foreign companies. The result is a major addition to the work force of the city.

However, the Maharashtra Legislature and the Secretariat have not moved as had been envisaged in the plan. They are located on land reclaimed from the sea under the Back Bay Reclamation project which had been started soon after World War II to provide space for offices and housing for high and middle-income group residents. Located in the area are the legislature and offices of the Maharashtra government, offices of large Indian commercial and industrial houses, multinational corporations that make Mumbai the commercial and financial capital of India besides its largest industrial city and a luxury hotel.

Congestion in Mumbai port has not been reduced, despite the development of Uran. Thus despite implementation of major projects envisaged in the plan, its central objective of relieving congestion in Mumbai or its port have not been achieved.

Population Growth and Land Misuse

Mumbai has experienced rapid growth in both population and economic activities during the last 4 decades because it is the principal financial center, the largest commercial center and the center of production of films and television serials in the country. Most of the workers live in distant suburbs and commute from home to work on over crowded suburban trains or buses. Spending 2 to 3 hours a day in commuting from home to work is normal.

The plan had envisaged that the lands located in the center of the city, and vacated by textile mills which had closed, should be used for public purposes such as location of schools, health centres, parks and housing people of low income groups. Instead, the land has been occupied by hundreds of small industrial units, and in some cases by multi-storey apartments for people of middle and high-income groups. This has been due to the Corporation succumbing to pressure by builders of multi-storey flats who have made millions by selling 1-3 bedroom flats to their prospective residents.

Slums: Growth and Pollution

Slum dwellers continue to form an important (almost 40% of the total population) part of the population of the city. There are slums in every suburb that extend for 30 or more kilometres from the city center and in which live most of the middle-income workers in the service sector and industrial units located in the city. The slum dwellers perform various services such as cleaning the houses or flats, washing dishes or clothes for the middle-income residents.

The large slum, which claims to be the largest in Asia, is Dharavi on the way to the Santa Cruz domestic airport. The Corporation maintains primary and secondary schools for the children of the slum dwellers and dispensaries for treatment of the sick. Hospitals, maintained by charitable organizations, mainly of the Parsees and Gujaratis, provide for treatment of serious sickness. Voluntary organizations also provide recreation facilities for children and maintain libraries and organize group exercise classes for adults.

There are large slum clusters just behind the gleaming towers of the offices and apartment complexes of the Back Bay Reclamation Area as well as just outside the port. Since all attempts to shift the slum dwellers have been resisted by the slum dwellers and self-styled champions of the poor, the Corporation provides them with drinking water; electricity is provided at a nominal charge by the electric supply company. However, similar arrangements for solid and liquid waste disposal are inadequate. The central business districts of Mumbai and its port are saturated by filth of the slum dwellers.

Industrial Location: Change for the Worse

Industrial dispersal is a major policy objective of the government. However, the principal dispersal has been location of a number of large industrial units along the highways radiating from the city and particularly along the Mumbai-Pune rail-cum-road strip of 175 kilometres. The less developed regions of the state particularly Marathwada in southeast Maharashtra, which had formed part of the Nizam of Hyderabad and is drought-stricken partly because development of irrigation had been neglected, remains backward. The state government has provided no incentive, such as a waiver of taxes on earnings for the first few years or making needed expenditure for expanding electricity, water supplies, telecommunications, motorable roads in Aurangabad (the principal city in Marathwada) to induce industrialists to locate their units in it in preference to Mumbai or Pune. No incentive has been provided also for location of large or small industrial units in Vidarbha in preference to those in western Maharastra.

BMRDA Must Prepare a New Master Plan

The Maharashtra government had established the Bombay Metropolitan Regional Development Authority (BMRDA) as an organization for overseeing implementation of the first plan and formulating a new plan. However, no new plan has been formulated so far; nor is one likely to be formulated in the foreseeable future. A second plan must be formulated for achieving the unachieved objects of decongestion of Mumbai city and its port so that the city can perform efficiently its central role of the principal financial, commercial and entertainment center of a growing economy.

CHENNAI: SATISFACTORY POLICIES FOR INDUSTRIAL LOCATION WITHOUT A PLAN

Chennai is India's fourth largest city after Mumbai, Kolkata and Delhi. Besides being a major port and with 6.4m population in 2001. Capital of Tamil Nadu, it has become a large industrial center in recent years with manufacture of motor vehicles and information technology as the most important industries. In contrast to Mumbai, Kolkata and Delhi, no long-term development plan was formulated in the 1960's for guiding expansion of Chennai. Therefore, as industries began to be located in Chennai partly as a result of relocation of many industrial units from Kolkata during the late 1960's and early 1970's and since it experienced rapid increase in population, the principal concerns of the state government and the municipal corporations remained two:

1. Supply of adequate drinking water and electricity for the industries and population of the city, and
2. to preserve the beauty of its sea front – the nearly 5 kilometre long beach and the Mount Road along which are located the Secretariat, the University, several colleges and other public institutions and offices of several companies. The road runs along the beach.

Affordable Services for Industrial Workers

Estates were developed for location of industries (along with colonies for residence of workers) mainly to the north of the city. The companies which established industrial units in the estates also built, with financial and technical assistance from the State Housing Board (SHB), 1-2 bed room tenements for residence of their workers. The employees paid a part of the rent for residence in the flats. The SHB also built thousands of 1-2 bedroom tenements for residence of slum dwellers. These tenements were provided with all basic amenities – electricity, potable water, facilities for disposal of solid or liquid waste and secondary schools for education of children and health centers for treatment of the sick. The slum dwellers could get these flats on payment of nominal rent. They could own them also over a period of years by making small annual payments to the Board. They are now living in them from which they can easily reach their work place by buses, a service run by the Corporation very efficiently.

However, despite the rapid growth of industries and the limited objectives of the state government and the Corporation, Chennai has remained a clean city. The beauty of its beach has been preserved and the poor population lives in areas designated for it. The city remains attractive for location of industries because of its disciplined labour force – hard working, quick to learn new techniques and untainted by militancy of trade unions. This is due mainly to the fact that appropriate housing, having all basic amenities and facilities for education of their children and preventive health and medical care has been provided for them.

The case of Chennai illustrates that a city can do as well without a long-term master plan, if its municipal authorities or the state government take effective measures to expand essential infrastructure and provide suitable places for location of industries, residences of industrial workers and for housing the expanding population of the city.

PUNE: GOOD MANAGEMENT OF INDUSTRIAL AND URBAN GROWTH

Pune, with a population of 2.5 million in 1991, (3.7m in 2001) is the second largest city in Maharashtra and the ninth largest city in India. The city has experienced rapid growth in population and economic activities since 1931. Growth of population, which was only 140,000 in 1901, was slow during 1901-1931 because of large mortality from epidemics of bubonic plague in the first decade of the 20th century and the influenza of 1918-1919.

Pune had been the seat of the Peshwas, but after the defeat of the Peshwa rulers of Maharashtra early in the 19th century, the British government had established a cantonment in Pune. The cantonment was the headquarter of the Western command established for defence of western India. Pune was made the summer capital of Bombay

Presidency after construction of the Bombay-Pune railway line and a highway in the latter half of the 19th century. The government would shift to Pune during the monsoon season in order to escape the heat and humidity of Mumbai. This practice was, however, discontinued after India became independent in 1947.

Industrialization and Population Growth

As an ammunition factory had been established in a suburb of Pune in the 19th century; a number of ordinance factories were added during World War II. The population of both the cantonment and the city experienced major increases during the war years and immediately after Independence; the latter was due partly to influx of refugees from Sindh. The area between the old city and the cantonment (once covered with gardens, military barracks and houses of army officers) was steadily occupied by houses, markets and other facilities needed by the increasing population so that the old city and the cantonment became one large metropolitan area.

Production in the ammunition and ordinance factories had increased rapidly during World War II to meet the needs of the armed forces. Establishment of the Kirloskar Pumps factory, a bulk drug manufacturing unit owned by the Government of India and establishment of a number of industrial units owned by industrialists in Mumbai marked the beginning of rapid growth of modern industries in the city. The earlier industries in the city had consisted mainly of handicrafts – weaving of cotton and silk textiles, manufacture of jewellery, bangles, brassware and clay figurines.

City Surveys and Urban Planning

Due to the presence in the city of the Gokhale Institute of Economics and Political Science, a number of city surveys have been done periodically since 1936. These analyzed the economic activities and status of the population and problems of the city and the situation relating to supplies of water and electricity, disposal of solid and liquid waste and location of slums. Two municipal bodies – the Pune Municipality and Pimpri-Chinchwad Municipal Council had been constituted early in this century to provide municipal services in the city and in the Pimpri-Chinchwad Industrial Area. The two were merged to form the Pune Municipal Corporation in 1947. Because of allegations of widespread corruption in the municipal corporation, the affairs of the city were managed by an Administrator who during 1947-49 prepared a draft land-use plan for expansion of the city during the next 20 years. Earlier the design of expansion of the city had been provided from time to time by the Pune Improvement Trust.

Factors Favorable to Urban Growth

An Economic Survey carried out by the Gokhale Institute in 1956 revealed that the city had a large number of unemployed workers. The slum population formed almost 1/5th of the population of the city. The revised plan for the Pune Metropolitan Region prepared in 1970-71 noted following features of rapid industrial development in the Pune Metropolitan Area after 1956:

1. Restriction by the state government on location of industries in the Mumbai Metropolitan Area. Pune was favoured because of easy access by rail and road to Mumbai, availability of educated and skilled workers due partly to location of several higher secondary schools and colleges for white collar workers; adequate supplies of water and electricity and of facilities for disposal of solid and liquid waste and an adequate and reasonably efficient bus service. Furthermore, it had a large number of un-skilled workers who had migrated from neighbouring villages because of lack of work in their villages and could be employed in the industries. Exemption for payment of octroi duty on machinery and industrial raw materials by industrial units located in one large industrial estate also assisted industrial development.
2. Rapid growth of industries was, thus, favoured by the Maharashtra government in Pune which in the 1960's prohibited establishment of new industries in the Mumbai Metropolitan Area. Pune was favoured because of easy access by rail and road from Mumbai and availability of large areas of land at much lower cost than in Mumbai. Its salubrious climate, presence of a large number of educated persons and availability of large numbers of unskilled workers who could be trained to become skilled industrial

workers also favoured development of industries. The industries were located mainly in the Pimpri – Chinchwad Industrial Area along the railway and highway between Mumbai and Pune and also along other highways radiating from the city to other cities in Maharashtra and other states.

The Kirloskar Pumps factory and a central government-owned factory manufacturing drugs in bulk were for a long time the largest industrial units in Pune. The former has, because of its management and the high quality of its products, become the most respected manufacturer in India of compressors for refrigerators and air conditioners, besides being the largest manufacturer of pumps for lifting water on irrigation wells. A factory for manufacturing chasses for buses and trucks was established by the Tatas in the 1980's. Its production capacity has been increased from time to time in response to increase in demand. A unit for manufacture of passenger cars was added during 1991-2000. These units were established in the environs of Pune in preference to Jamshedpur because of easier access to the principal markets in western, northern and southern India.

The collapse of the Panshet Dam located above the city in 1971 resulted in washing away of large number of huts in squatter settlements and slums located below the dam. The Pune Housing and Urban Development Board was formed to build huts for re-housing the slum dwellers as well as houses for people of the low-income group. The Board has mobilized funds from various agencies to construct housing for people of the low-income group. However, much greater in volume than the housing activity of the Board has been that by private land developers and builders who have built multi-storey apartments for residence of middle and high income groups or sold developed land for building houses by them.

Needed – A Resurvey and a New Master Plan for Pune

Although a second master plan has not been formulated almost a decade after the end of the first Master Plan, the government of the city has with funds provided by the state government and other sources expanded progressively the infrastructure needed for the steadily increasing population and industrial activity in the city. However, there is urgent need for a re-survey of economic activities and status of the population and of the needs for expansion of infrastructure to serve the needs of its increasing population and industries; Pune is experiencing steady growth in population and industries. Furthermore, because of availability of a large number of educated persons it can become an important center for location of information technology industry. Another industry is making of films and television serials (mainly in Marathi) partly because it was one of the earlier centers of making films.

HYDERABAD: OLD PROBLEMS AND NEW CHALLENGES

Before accession of Hyderabad state to the Indian Union, Hyderabad was the capital of the Nizam's state of Hyderabad. The Hyderabad Metropolitan Area consists of the twin cities of Hyderabad and Secunderabad. The latter, the location of the British garrison for defence of Nizam's territories, had been built at a distance from the old city and was an un-crowded city until the late 1960's in contrast to the Nizam's city which was not only very crowded at the center but had also a number of suburbs including one in which was located the Osmania University.

A number of large industrial units, owned by the Government of India were located in the environs of Hyderabad during the 1960's and the 1970's, oblivious of the problems of air or water pollution that their location would create. These units are located along the roads to Mumbai or Chennai so that long stretches of these roads are occupied by them and by the residential colonies of workers in the units. Pollution of air and water is most acute in the old city. However, it is noteworthy that within the city, public gardens, shopping areas and residences of people of the middle and high-income groups exist side by side with slums of its poorest residents.

Urban Planning: Objectives and Obstacles

A new large residential suburb, Banjara Hills, was developed after the 1940's according to a plan drawn up by the Hyderabad Improvement Trust. In different parts of it are located houses of professionals, retired government officers, some offices of the Andhra Pradesh government and houses of a large number of people of middle and high-income group.

The Hyderabad Urban Development Area (HUDA) was

demarcated in 1975 and a master plan was formulated and approved in the same year. HUDA extended upto 15 kilometres from the city center although urban influence did not extend beyond 5-7 kilometres from the city center. This was done in order to ensure regulated development and planned land-use in the entire metropolitan area. The Hyderabad Urban Development Authority was constituted at the same time in order to acquire large areas of land for developing it for housing for middle and low-income groups and for other essential public purposes such as location of public institutions of training. However, despite the creation of HUDA, large areas of vacant land have been acquired by land grabbers at low prices by manipulating the land records of the Nizam's government. The development for the city had aimed at:

1. Re-development of the old city as a residential and commercial area with suitable housing of residents for people of both middle and low income groups; improvement of parks, renovation of historical buildings, museums, etc.;
2. Regulating land use along the highways which were experiencing ribbon development due to location of industrial units and residential colonies of workers along them;
3. Planning for increasing water supplies and electricity and facilities of disposal of liquid and solid waste. Most of the central areas of the city and the new residential colonies have underground sewerage although there are uncovered areas in both the city and the suburbs.

Needed: A Plan for Metropolitan Hyderabad

The plan has been implemented with modifications from time to time keeping in view ongoing developments and to accommodate powerful political interest groups. However, two major projects viz. de-congestion of the old city and re-development of Banjara hill, the most important residential suburb for residents of middle-and high-income groups have not been implemented or implemented with long delays.

Furthermore, it is noteworthy that even after lapse of a quarter of a century since the formulation and enforcement of the first plan, a second plan has not been formulated. As a result, unplanned growth in various parts of the city and ribbon development for location of industrial units, residential colonies of workers and training and research institutions continues along the major highways.

Hyderabad has a salubrious climate. The heat is not oppressive except in the rainy months of July and August. The present Chief Minister of Andhra Pradesh is keen on making the city a center of the information technology industry, banking on its salubrious climate and the presence of a large number of educated young men and women. An Information Technology city has been built in the last few years at some distance from the city, and is being rapidly occupied by computer software and other information technology units. All these would surely necessitate careful implementation of medium term and long term urban development plans for an emerging metropolis.

PLANNING FOR MEGA-CITY GROWTH: REVIEW AND CONCLUDING REMARKS

From this review of planning for five of India's largest metropolitan cities it is possible to arrive at some broad conclusions about the role and limitations of planning for metropolitan cities.

The plan for Kolkata did make a major contribution to improving the water supply and sewerage system and ameliorating living conditions in the slums. Two major transport projects – the second bridge on the Hooghly and the underground railway through a central part of Kolkata have been built and are serving the purposes intended for them. The retirees community of Kalyani located about 60 kilometres north of Kolkata has been built and is popular for residence of retired people of the middle and high income groups. The port of Haldia has been built and is serving the purpose for which it was intended. However, there has been no significant improvement in the living environment of the city. There are two reasons for it:

1. Continued influx of poor refugees from Bangladesh who live in slums that line several of the city's streets;
2. There has been no significant return of capital to Kolkata. Although some of the largest steel fabrication units have re-opened hardly any new large manufacturing unit has been established;

PROBLEMS OF URBAN RENEWAL

Hence, despite the fact that the militancy of trade unions (which was responsible for the flight of capital) has been kept in check by the Communist party government led by Mr. Jyoti Basu who has made strenuous efforts without much success to attract industries to the Kolkata Metropolitan District, many scars mar the metropolitan status of Calcutta.

Confidence about investment in the city remains so low that there has been little addition to the housing stock of the city. The corporation, corrupt and inefficient is not even able to clear the garbage off the main streets. Citizen's initiative to clean up Kolkata is totally lacking. The case of Kolkata shows two things viz. (i) that business confidence, once shaken, is very difficult to rebuild (ii) it is easy to let living conditions in a city deteriorate but extremely difficult to improve them.

The case of Mumbai is, in many ways, quite different from that of Kolkata. Vital parts of a bold plan for the city were implemented. However, mainly because of the refusal of Maharashtra government to move industries out of the city, tens of thousands of new jobs have been attracted to it, making it about the most congested city in India.

The government while formulating policies prohibiting new industrial development in the Mumbai Metropolitan Area and directing that new large industries should be located in the backward areas of the state and to cities like Aurangabad, has at the same time allotted land vacated by closed textile mills in the center of the city for location of hundreds of small industrial units and apartment buildings for people of middle-and-high-income groups instead of reserving it for public purposes such as location of schools, health centers, parks for housing for low income groups.

The review of plans for both Pune and Hyderabad show that the schemes of the housing boards set up to build housing for low and middle income groups have been exceeded by those of private land developers and builders who have built multi-storey apartments for the people of middle and high income groups or sold land to them for building houses. The competition between public purpose envisaged in the Plan and private good is starkly evident.

The review also shows that, except in Kolkata, there is no lack of private investment for commercial or industrial activity. The problem is to keep pollution of air and water in check in over-developed areas.

Despite their limitations, which are detailed below, it is essential to formulate plans for physical expansion of cities, especially large metropolitan cities.

LIMITATIONS AND NEED FOR PLANNING

A metropolitan plan is a projection of growth of population and economic activities in a city and provides a framework for location in its metropolitan area of housing colonies, industrial units, and institutions of higher learning, hospitals and facilities for recreation.

Such a design must exist if expansion of the city has to be orderly and haphazard growth is to be avoided. The areas to be kept green have to be specified in order to keep environmental pollution to the minimum. However, plans, particularly long term 20 years metropolitan plans, are of limited use because in the situation of rapid changes in economic policies of governments and factors which contribute to economic growth and growth of cities, 20 year is too long a period to forecast the nature and direction of growth of a city. A 10-year period divided into two 5-year periods each coinciding with the periods of national development plans is far more suitable for formulation of metropolitan development plans.

Further, it is essential that the plans be continuously revised in view of changes in economic and social conditions, the policies of governments and the direction in which the city has expanded, in fact. Planning for expansion of water supplies, electricity, facilities for disposal of solid and liquid waste, intra-urban public transport and other essential services – education and medical care must form an integral part of city plan. The projects for expansion of these facilities, their cost and mobilization of finance for their implementation should also form an integral part of any plan. The coincidence with the period of the national development plan will also indicate the funds available for implementation of the plans.

It must be realized that while funds for land development and housing for middle and high income group housing, construction of markets, etc. are easily forthcoming, those for expansion of water supplies, electricity and especially expansion of sewerage system and of intra-urban transport present serious problems. The resources for expansion of water supply and electric supplies could be easily mobilized if user charges are adjusted to meet the costs of generation and distribution and if thefts of electricity and water are effectively checked – the thefts are not only by slum dwellers but also by influential and commercial users. However, expansion of the sewerage system and intra-urban transport are generally not self-financing and must rely on grants from the state or central governments. Improvement and relocation of slums also require large grants from the state and central governments because the Corporations could not spend enough on these activities.

18

The Politics of Metropolitan Cities

Metropolitan cities are the political, commercial, financial and industrial centres of the regions in which they are located. The population of the 23 metropolitan cities, 74 million in 1991, was only a little more than 8 per cent of the total population of the country, but its contribution to the gross domestic product of the country was far greater.

CITIES AS INDUSTRIAL NURSERIES

Cities serve as the financial and commercial capitals of the regions in which they are located. Furthermore, excepting industries that process high weight or volume but low-value raw materials which are located near sources of raw materials, most of the others—manufacture of consumer goods, consumer durables including motor vehicles—are located in the peri-urban areas of these cities. Cities are the nurseries of small industries. Sunrise industries such as computer software for export and domestic use, which have experienced exponential growth during the last 3 decades have been born and have matured in these cities. The print and electronic media that influence public opinion in various regions and the writers, artists, poets and musicians etc., that are the exponents of the culture of different regions are all concentrated in these cities.

This paper discusses the politics of metropolitan cities in India, with brief reference to the politics in the pre-Independence period. One section is devoted to discussing the contrast between politics in India and that in the U.S.A. and Britain. The reasons for the difference and the results of the present policies on the welfare of the residents of the cities are discussed here.

POLITICS AND URBAN CENTERS BEFORE 1947

Metropolitan cities were, along with the high courts, the nurseries of the leaders of the Independence movement in the pre-Independence period. All the greatest leaders of the movement acquired their oratorical, legislative and managerial skill while working as mayors, secretaries or members of the corporations of the cities in which they lived.* Some of the largest cities – Mumbai, Calcutta and Ahmedabad were major industrial centres. There was a serious problem of pollution of air and water in these cities and the workers lived in slum-like dwellings built by mill-owners or by the workers themselves. The chawls of Mumbai, the *bustees* of Calcutta and small houses in overcrowded areas of Ahmedabad are examples. The civic leaders tried hard to keep the cities clean and provide adequate electricity and water supplies and other facilities so that they could ensure a livable environment for the affluent and middle income group people and for location of business and finance from which most of the income of the corporations was derived.

In smaller cities such as Allahabad, Chennai, and Lahore in Pakistan, which had high courts, the courts were the nurseries for acquiring political leadership training. Some of the greatest political leaders were lawyers who got their oratorical skills while serving as advocates in the high courts. The courts allowed them to acquire experience as eloquent speakers and the municipalities, experience as executives.

URBAN GROWTH AND MUNICIPAL SERVICES

As population increased, the mayors and corporators ensured that the electricity, water supplies and waste disposal systems were expanded so that the cities could function efficiently. Electricity supplies were provided usually by companies which themselves ensured adequate and uninterrupted supply; rates were kept low so as to keep the consumers pleased. However, they ensured adequate returns on their investment. Mumbai, Calcutta and Chennai had suburban trains, which brought workers living in distant suburbs to work in the city centres. The trains were owned and operated by the railways, which tried hard to ensure that their capacity was adequate to meet the needs of the commuters. The fares on these trains were kept low enough so that the commuters, most of them poor, could afford to use them.

This is in sharp contrast to the situation today when these trains are so crowded that the commuters use them at constant risk to life and limb.

ATTRACTIONS OF METROPOLITAN LIFE

Two of the attractions of living in metropolitan and other large cities for residence of the affluent and middle-income group were:

1. The cities alone had the facilities for training of professionals- – lawyers, doctors, engineers, architects, teachers and graduate and post-graduate training in the humanities and the sciences. As a result, the children of the residents could after graduation from these institutions enter these well-paid professions or enter government service as officers or senior clerks.
2. The cities had the markets, which stocked clothes and shoes in fashion and facilities for entertainment such as cinema and theatres. They had also large parks within or just outside them.

CHANGE AND CRISES AFTER WORLD WAR II 1939–45

The situation changed radically during World War II. The population of some industrial cities, Mumbai, Calcutta and Ahmedabad increased rapidly due to influx of workers in the textile mills and various other industrial units in order to meet the demands of the troops. In a way, Delhi was a major beneficiary of the World War II as its authorities got thousands of houses constructed to meet the troops' housing needs while there was no such construction in Calcutta or Mumbai. In Calcutta, the migrants from East Pakistan crowded into slums along the highways in the suburbs. The middle income ones, shared rooms with their relatives and friends. In Mumbai new houses were built mainly in the suburbs in which there was no rent control. Delhi also experienced rapid increase in population on account of influx of workers in the Government of India, however, there was little expansion of housing for them. Promulgation of the Rent Control Act in 1940 in order to prevent exploitation of poor tenants by the landlords, left them no incentive to build new houses or workers' tenements. Furthermore, the available building materials were all used to build barracks for soldiers, seamen and airmen fighting in various theatres of the war and passing through the cities on their way to the front. In Delhi, the Government of India built thousands of barracks and hundreds of one bedroom flats for residence of officers, soldiers and airmen (including British and American) who passed through the city for fighting in South East and East Asia. These buildings proved invaluable in housing the hundreds of thousands of displaced persons who flooded the city from Pakistan after the partition of India in 1947. In the next 10 years, the Central Public Works Department built in Delhi thousands of 1-bed room barracks type tenements and 2-bedroom flats for sale to the displaced persons on a no-profit no-loss basis. The CPWD built also in the next 15-20 years, thousands of 2-3 bedroom flats for officers and clerks of the Government of India.

However, despite the difficulties created by the war, the interest of the mayors and corporators remained focussed on keeping the cities clean and ensure efficient functioning of basic services.

CONTOURS OF METROPOLITAN POLITICS IN DEVELOPED AND DEVELOPING COUNTRIES

Politics of metropolitan cities in India in the pre-independence period was similar to that in the western countries, the U.S.A. and Britain, in the 20th century. However, today it is radically different from that in the developed countries. In cities in the United States, mayors and councilors were elected from the 1920's to the 1970's for what they could do to promote the interests of their constituents: the Irish and other in-migrants in the cities in the eastern United States in the 1920's to the 1970's, the blacks in several cities in the 1960's and the 1970's. In Britain, similarly, mayors of large cities are elected on basis of what they have achieved in improving conditions of the poor or encouraging commercial and industrial activities in the suburbs or preventing exodus of the employment generating activities from the inner cities.

WESTERN MAYORS KEEP THE CITIES RUNNING

Despite the flights of the middle income and the affluent residents of the cities and of industries to the industrial suburbs or satellite towns, the mayors and councilors in Britain and in USA ensure that the cities remain the principal centres of banking and finance, luxury shopping, entertainment (theatres and night clubs) and visits to places of historic interest. These facilities are provided not only to the residents of Britain but also to the millions of tourists who flock to Britain from its former colonies and dependencies but also to millions of tourists from the U.S.A., Canada and Australia in the summer. In the U.S.A., the tourists are from other cities and from foreign countries. Thus, business and the tourists provide most of the income for running the cities.

The central areas of European cities – Paris, Rome, Amsterdam, Brussels, perform similar functions as the central areas of London. Large areas are designated as "no car zones" so that the tourists from within the country or abroad can walk through these areas and savour life as it has been lived through the ages while window or serious shopping and patronizing the restaurants.

RADICAL CHANGE IN URBAN POLITICS IN INDIA

It can be said that the politics of the metropolitan cities in India in the pre-independence period was similar to that in the British, European and Anglo American cities today, but that it has changed radically in recent decades in many metropolitan cities in northern and western India but not in southern India. The reasons for this radical change in some regions of this country but not in others have to be investigated.

CITY POLITICS AS AN APPENDAGE TO STATE POLITICS

After independence, however, and especially during the last three decades, metropolitan city politics is seen as an appendage to state level politics. The parties in power in the state – the Indian National Congress for 40 years after Independence but other parties in recent years — try very hard to remain in power in the corporations of the metropolitan cities. Loss of power in the corporation is seen as a precursor to loss of control over the state legislature. As a result, use of muscle and money power in elections to the corporations of metropolitan cities is as high as elections to the state legislatures. In the last two-or three decades, however, municipal politics has been focused on encouraging development of unauthorized colonies and proliferation of slums by squatting on public land. Some of the biggest builders in Mumbai and Delhi carry on their extra-legal construction with the tacit approval of politicians. It is the politics of granting favours to rich in exchange for money and handouts to the poor in their slums in support of their re-election. In case of Mumbai an unworthy aspect of metropolitan politics is growth of gangs of criminals of Hindus and Muslims, one of whom have history of enacting communal riots and the other of destroying public and private buildings and encouraging bribe, extortion, murder etc. This tendency has increased after enactment in 1992 of the 74th Amendment to the Constitution of India which was enforced in 1993. Under this law, every state government is obliged to conduct elections to the municipal bodies in the state, every five years. These bodies cannot be suspended or dissolved at the pleasure of the governments. If it wishes to dissolve a municipal body, the government must give its reasons in writing and seek the President's assent to it. Furthermore, it must conduct fresh elections to the dissolved municipal body within six months.

POPULIST POLICIES, REVERSAL IN SOUTH INDIA

The municipal councilors in many cities today look the other way as population increases with in-migration of the poor and proliferation of slums with the slum dwellers squatting on public lands, meant for location of parks, schools, health centres, etc. The in-migration increases pressures on electricity and water supply and increases filth because there are no arrangements for disposal of solid and liquid waste from the slums.

These objectives have been reversed during the last few years in some southern cities viz. Hyderabad, Chennai and Bangalore in order to provide a pollution free environment with assured supplies of electricity and water for the information technology industries which have witnessed exponential growth during the last two decades. Further, information technology parks have been built on the outskirts of the cities to provide a pollution free environment, assured electricity and water supplies. The cities themselves are being cleaned up. The result is that many consumer durable industries including manufacture of motor vehicles have been attracted to these cities.

DELHI SCENARIO

In Delhi, the information technology industries are located in two satellite cities – Gurgaon in Haryana and NOIDA in Uttar Pradesh.

Manufacture of consumer goods and consumer durables is also located in these two cities as well as in Ghaziabad in U.P. and Faridabad in Haryana. Manufacture of motor vehicles is located in the outskirts of Gurgaon and about 70 km. out of NOIDA. In these satellite cities office space, with assured supplies of electricity and water, has been built along with residences with fitness clubs and golf courses for the executives and other employees of multinational and Indian companies. Most of it is occupied because many multinational and Indian corporations have shifted their regional offices to Gurgaon in preference to Connaught Place, the old central business district of New Delhi.

In Delhi, the Supreme Court has taken the initiative in ordering reduction of pollution of air and water. Squatting on public lands by slum dwellers has been checked; the highly polluting 2-3 or 4 wheeler motor vehicles which are more than 8 years old have been forced to go off Delhi's roads. A large number of industrial units which throw poisons such as nickel and mercury into Yamuna river are being forced out of the city. The municipal employees and the councilors who had connived in continuation of these industrial units are being forced to reverse course. However, money politics is so strong that in Delhi, Pune and Mumbai many areas reserved for public purposes have been released to the builders.

Thus, it is only in the southern states that the state governments have taken effective action to clean up their metropolitan cities. In northern and western India, the trend is mixed with clean up and crowding occurring side by side. The reasons for this difference in behaviour of the mayors and councilors of the cities need to be investigated.

CONCLUSIONS AND RECOMMENDATIONS

Large investment is needed for maintenance, creation or expansion of electric and water supplies, systems for disposal of solid and liquid waste, construction and maintenance of intra-city and inter-city roads, providing housing to the poor, etc. Such investment has to be financed primarily by loans and grants from the state and central governments. The financial resources of the richest municipal corporations, derived from taxes on residential and commercial properties, traders and professionals are barely sufficient to finance performance of the most basic municipal functions such as lighting and cleaning of streets, construction and repair of intra-city roads and management of traffic.

The central and state governments should provide this investment without hesitation in order to ensure that the cities continue to function as the political, commercial, financial and industrial centres of the regions in which they are located. The corporations should have efficient commissioners and other senior officers belonging to the Indian Administrative, Revenue and Engineering services so that local taxes are collected efficiently and also well spent in efficient running of the infrastructures. Some facilities such as supply of electricity could be entrusted to private companies instead of being left to be managed by state electricity boards. The company will reduce losses in transmission and distribution by checking theft of electricity by various users of various classes. Selective other services could also be privatized.

NOTE

* Subash Bose served as the secretary of the Calcutta Corporation. Some of the earlier presidents of Indian National Congress won their seats as executives of the corporation of their cities.

Index